Community Policing and Problem Solving

Strategies and Practices

FIFTH EDITION

KENNETH J. PEAK

University of Nevada, Reno

RONALD W. GLENSOR

Reno, Nevada, Police Department

Upper Saddle River, New Jersey 07458

Library of Congress Cataloging–in–Publication Data

Peak, Kenneth J.,
   Community policing and problem solving: strategies and practices / Kenneth J. Peak,
Ron W. Glensor —5th ed.
      p. cm.
   Includes bibliographical references and index.
   ISBN 0-13-239257-7
   1. Community policing.   2. Crime prevention—United States—Citizen participation.   3.
Police administration.   4. Police-community relations.   5. Community policing—United
States.   6. Police administration—United States.   I. Glensor, Ronald W.   II. Title.

HV7936.C83P43 2008
363.2'3—dc22   2006051017

Editor-in-Chief: Vernon R. Anthony
Senior Editor: Tim Peyton
Associate Editor: Sarah Holle
Marketing Manager: Adam Kloza
Managing Editor: Mary Carnis
Production Liaison: Ann Pulido
Production Editor: Janet Bolton
Manufacturing Manager: Ilene Sanford
Manufacturing Buyer: Cathleen Petersen
Senior Design Coordinator: Christopher Weigand
Cover Design: Rob Aleman

Cover Image: Aurora & Quanta Productions Inc.
Composition: TexTech
Printing and Binding: Hamilton Printing/Castleton
Cover Printer: Phoenix Color
Copy Editor/Proofreader: Maine Proofreading Services
Director, Image Resource Center: Melinda Patelli
Manager, Rights and Permissions: Zina Arabia
Manager, Visual Research: Beth Brenzel
**Manager, Cover Visual Research
   and Permissions:** Karen Sanatar
Image Permission Coordinator: Angelique Sharps

Pearson Prentice Hall™ is a trademark of Pearson Education, Inc.
Pearson® is a registered trademark of Pearson plc
Prentice Hall® is a registered trademark of Pearson Education, Inc.

Pearson Education LTD.
Pearson Education Australia PTY, Limited
Pearson Education Singapore, Pte. Ltd.
Pearson Education North Asia Ltd.
Pearson Education Canada, Ltd.
Pearson Educacion de Mexico, S.A. de C.V.
Pearson Education—Japan
Pearson Education Malaysia, Pte. Ltd.
Pearson Education, Upper Saddle River, New Jersey

10 9 8 7 6 5 4 3 2 1
ISBN-13: 978-0-13-239257-0
ISBN-10 0-13-239257-7

To Kathryn Ann—our family's heart, core, and cheerleader—and to our newest grandchild, Dominic William Miller.

–K.J.P.

To my wife, Kristy; my son, Ronnie; my daughter, Breanne; Derek Jones; and my beautiful granddaughter, Addison.

–R.W.G.

Brief Contents

Contents

CHAPTER
5

INFORMATION TECHNOLOGY: TOOLS FOR THE TASK   120

CHAPTER
6

FROM RECRUIT TO CHIEF: CHANGING THE AGENCY CULTURE   142

CHAPTER
7

CHAPTER
8

Preface

This book is about policing at its most important and challenging levels—in neighborhoods and in communities across the nation and abroad. It is about a new policing, one that encourages collaboration with the community and other agencies and organizations that are responsible for community safety. It is a style of policing that requires officers to obtain new knowledge and tools such as problem solving, and it is grounded in strategic thinking and planning to enable agencies to keep up with the rapid societal changes such as homeland defense. This policing style also allows agencies to make the necessary organizational and administrative adjustments to maintain a capable and motivated workforce.

The book is grounded on the assumption that the reader is most likely an undergraduate or graduate student studying criminal justice or policing, or perhaps the reader is a police practitioner with a fundamental knowledge of police history and operations or is working in a government agency outside policing and is interested in learning about community policing and problem solving. Citizens who are collaborating with police to resolve neighborhood problems in innovative ways can also be well served by reading this book.

This fifth edition also imparts some of the major underpinnings, prominent names, theories, practices (with myriad examples), and processes that are being implemented under community oriented policing and problem solving (COPPS) to control and prevent crime, disorder, and fear. A considerable number of textbooks have already been written about community policing. Most of them, however, emphasize its philosophy and provide little information about its *practical* aspects—putting the philosophy into daily practice. The application of community policing and problem solving is the primary focus of this book, as indicated in its title.

While some fundamental components of COPPS contribute to its success, no one single model exists—there is no cookie-cutter approach that can guarantee success. COPPS is an individualized, long-term process that involves fundamental institutional change, going beyond such simple tactics as foot and bicycle patrols or neighborhood police stations. It redefines the role of the officer on the street from crime fighter to problem solver. It forces a cultural transformation of the entire police agency, involving changes in recruiting, training, awards systems, evaluations, and promotions.

It has been said that problem solving is not new in policing, that police officers have always tried to solve problems in their daily work. As is demonstrated throughout this text, however, problem solving is not the same as solving problems. Problem solving in the context of COPPS is very different and considerably more complex. It requires that officers identify and examine the underlying causes of recurring incidents of crime and disorder. Such policing also seeks to make "street criminologists" of police officers, teaching them to expand their focus on offenders to include crime settings and victims. Such an approach presents great challenges for those patrol officers who are engaged in analytical work.

Given the extent to which COPPS has evolved since the publication of our fourth edition, the authors understand the challenges involved with writing this text. Like its four predecessors, this fifth edition might still be viewed as a work in progress; today's "snapshot" of what is occurring nationally with respect to COPPS may need to be drastically revised in the future.

We also emphasize that this book is not a call to ignore or discard policing's past methods, nor do we espouse an altogether new philosophy of policing in its place. Instead, we recommend that the police borrow from the wisdom of the past and adopt a holistic approach to the way police organizations are learning to address public safety more successfully.

We are quite pleased with the work that has been done by many police practitioners and academicians here and abroad who have made substantive contributions to the COPPS approach. But the traditional reactive "cops as pinballs" philosophy is still very much alive in many agencies. Merely creating a "crime prevention specialist" position, putting an officer on foot or bicycle patrol, or anticipating the receipt of federal dollars does not equate with implementing COPPS. Such activities not only misrepresent the true potential and functions of COPPS but also set unrealistically simplistic goals and expectations for its work.

This book describes how many agencies should, and are, actively going about the process of revolutionizing their philosophy and operations.

Organization and Contents of the Book

Like its four predecessors, this book is distinguished by its *applied* approach. In doing so, it showcases more than 50 exhibits and provides dozens of additional case studies and examples of problem solving in the field.

While it provides updated information about crime in the United States, with particular emphasis placed on terrorism and homeland defense, also addressed in a new chapter (Chapter 5) are the advancements and applications of information technologies (IT) in policing and the changing role of the crime analyst to support COPPS. Chapter sections on such major problems as drugs, gangs, youth, computer crime, and special populations (the mentally ill and the homeless) have also been added or updated, and chapters on engaging the community, problem solving, police culture, training, and the future have received major revisions.

To understand the methods and challenges of community policing and problem solving, we first need to look at the big picture. Thus, in the first three chapters we discuss (1) the history of policing and the major transformations over time that led to the present community policing era; (2) the need for, and means of, engaging the community in all components of the criminal justice system (included is a look at our nation's demographics and shifts in crime); and (3) a specific examination of COPPS (along with Chapters 4 and 5, Chapter 3 composes the heart and soul of the book). It is imperative that the reader have a firm grasp of these first five chapters prior to moving on to the remaining chapters. Following is a more comprehensive breakdown of the book's 15 chapters.

Chapter 1 begins with a brief discussion of Britain's and Sir Robert Peel's influence and the Metropolitan Police Act in England. Next we review the evolution of policing in America, followed by a look at police and change. Then we examine the community problem-solving era, including what its principal components are, why it emerged, and how it evolved to its current third generation. We will also examine the elevated importance and use of COPPS in homeland security.

Chapter 2 opens with an examination of what is meant by "community" and (as noted above) why the criminal justice system should partner with the public in making neighborhoods safer. Included is a review of the many rapid changes that are occurring in the United States, particularly concerning its demographics and the changing nature of crime. New to this edition and chapter are discussions of social capital, community and restorative justice, community service centers, and e-government.

As mentioned earlier, another foundational chapter of the book is Chapter 3, which includes discussions of the development and methods of community policing and problem-oriented policing. We maintain throughout the book that these are complementary core components. The problem-solving process, known as S.A.R.A., is discussed as the primary tool for understanding crime and disorder. Included are the basic principles of police problem solving, the role of the street officer within it, some difficulties with problem solving, and some ways to tailor strategies to individual neighborhoods.

Crime prevention involves much more than developing programs and distributing brochures. Chapter 4 looks at two important and contemporary components of crime prevention: crime prevention through environmental design (CPTED) and situational crime prevention. These approaches help officers to understand how opportunities for crime can be blocked and how environments can be designed or changed to lessen a person's or location's vulnerability to crime. Included are discussions of the role of designing out crime, the use of second-generation CPTED, and the obstacles to adoption of CPTED. The chapter concludes by delineating what approaches work, what approaches do not appear to be successful, and what approaches hold promise for crime prevention.

Chapter 5—Information Technology: Tools for the Task—contains information that is mostly new to this fifth edition. The chapter begins with a discussion of the methods available for a most important function: crime analysis. Included here are computer-aided dispatch (CAD), mobile computing, records management system (RMS), geomapping, CompStat, Global Positioning Systems (GPS), use of the Internet, and surveys. This chapter concludes with a discussion of counterterrorism and the changing role of the crime analyst.

In Chapter 6, we recognize that police agencies have a life and culture of their own, and we first present some basic theories and lessons learned about how police agencies go about modifying their culture, including their core values, in order to fully embrace COPPS. The separate roles and responsibilities of chief executives, middle managers, supervisors, and rank-and-file officers are included, as are some case studies of agencies that have modified their culture for adopting the COPPS approach.

Chapter 7 discusses the planning and implementation of COPPS and stresses the need for police organizations to engage in strategic thinking and management. This chapter also explains the strategic planning process and how to assess local needs and develop a planning document as a road map. Then it shifts to the implementation of COPPS per se, considering some principal components. Included are several examples, some general obstacles to implementation, and some ways to undermine COPPS.

Although COPPS has been implemented and embraced by police agencies across our nation as well as in foreign venues, a challenge that remains is determining how to assess the success of this strategy. Chapter 8 confronts the issue of evaluation, beginning with the rationale for evaluating COPPS and social interventions generally and then reviewing the different methods for evaluation and the criteria that can be employed to assess agencies' efforts. Case studies of agencies and research are presented.

Another difficult challenge for those agencies involved in COPPS is the training and education of police officers and others, which are addressed in Chapter 9. First, we consider ways adult and problem-based learning are infused into these training programs, which focus on problem solving, and the importance of developing a learning organization in police agencies for facilitating the change process more smoothly. Next, we review why police officers comprise a unique and challenging learning audience as well as some means of and approaches to training. We also examine the current research concerning the role of higher education in COPPS and some ideas for a COPPS-based curriculum.

Chapter 10 examines the history of relations between minorities and the police and some ways COPPS can enhance those relations. Included are discussions of racial profiling and bias-based policing; police responses to hate crimes; cultural differences, customs, and problems; diversity and recruiting in police organizations; and some scenarios.

Today's police struggle with an almost overwhelming array of gang-, drug-, and youth-related problems. Chapter 11 describes the application of COPPS to those problems. Topics covered in this chapter include methamphetamine use, drug labs, open-air drug markets, raves, graffiti, youth gun violence, disorderly youth, underage drinking, and school violence and bullying.

Chapter 12 then addresses other selected issues and problems confronting the police, including identity theft, special populations (the mentally ill and the homeless), domestic violence, neighborhood disorder, prostitution, traffic problems (cruising and street racing), false alarms, misuse of 911, and computer crimes. Exhibits and case studies are included throughout this chapter that demonstrate the power of collaborative partnerships and problem solving.

Chapter 13 highlights agencies' efforts to implement COPPS in the United States. Featured are brief discussions of COPPS in 21 jurisdictions: 7 large (categorized as having more than 250,000 population), 9 medium-size (between 50,000 and 250,000 population), and 5 small (less than 50,000 population). Brief descriptions of such initiatives also appear in several exhibits throughout the chapter.

COPPS has indeed gone international, and much can be learned from looking at the activities and approaches undertaken in foreign venues. So in Chapter 14 we "travel" to Canada, Japan, Australia, Great Britain, and other selected locations. Several venues are also discussed in chapter exhibits.

Chapter 15 explores the future, with a look at those forces that may influence COPPS in years to come. Highlighted are homeland defense, the role of the rank-and-file police officer, and the changing nature of crime and high technology.

Three appendices include several award-winning case studies of excellent problem solving and examples of a community survey and a strategic plan survey.

We believe that this book comprehensively lays out how COPPS is being embraced here and abroad. A major strength of this book lies in its many case studies and exhibits, which demonstrate how the concept is planned, implemented, operationalized, and evaluated. As Samuel Johnson wrote, "Example is always more efficacious than precept."

We are most grateful for the helpful suggestions made by the following reviewers of this edition: Ellen Cohn, Florida International University, Miami, Florida and Dena Martin, Criminal Justice Program Chair, Ivy Tech Community College, Terre Haute, Indiana.

Ken Peak

Ron Glensor

About the Authors

Kenneth J. Peak, Ph.D., is a professor and former chairman of the criminal justice department at the University of Nevada, Reno. Beginning his career in Reno in 1983, he has been named "Teacher of the Year" by the University of Nevada, Reno, Honor Society and served as acting director of public safety. He has authored or coauthored 18 textbooks on justice administration, general policing, community policing, women in law enforcement, and police supervision and management; he has published more than 50 journal articles and additional book chapters on a wide range of justice-related subjects. He has served as chairman of the Police Section, Academy of Criminal Justice Sciences, and is a past president of the Western and Pacific Association of Criminal Justice Educators. Dr. Peak entered municipal policing in Kansas in 1970 and subsequently held positions as criminal justice planner for southeast Kansas; director of the Four-State Technical Assistance Institute, Law Enforcement Assistance Administration; director of university police, Pittsburg State University; and assistant professor at Wichita State University. He received two gubernatorial appointments to statewide criminal justice committees while in Kansas and holds a doctorate from the University of Kansas.

Ronald W. Glensor, Ph.D., is a deputy chief of the Reno, Nevada, Police Department (RPD). He has more than 31 years of police experience and has commanded the department's patrol, administration, and detective divisions. In addition to being actively involved in RPD's implementation of community oriented policing and problem solving (COPPS) since 1987, he has provided COPPS training to thousands of officers, elected officials, and community members representing jurisdictions throughout the United States as well as Canada, Australia, and the United Kingdom. Dr. Glensor was the 1997 recipient of the prestigious Gary P. Hayes Award, conferred by the Police Executive Research Forum, recognizing his contributions and leadership in the policing field. Internationally, he is a frequent featured speaker on a variety of policing issues. He served a 6-month fellowship as problem oriented policing coordinator with the Police Executive Research Forum in Washington, D.C., and received an Atlantic Fellowship in public policy, studying repeat victimization at the Home Office in London. He is

coauthor of *Police Supervision and Management in an Era of Community Policing* (second edition), with K. Peak and L. K. Gaines, and coeditor of *Policing Communities: Understanding Crime and Solving Problems,* with M. Correia and K. Peak; he has also published in several journals and trade magazines. Dr. Glensor is an adjunct criminal justice professor at the University of Nevada, Reno, and instructs at area police academies and criminal justice programs. He holds a doctorate in political science and a master's of public administration from the University of Nevada, Reno.

Foreword

Community policing and problem oriented policing have been around for some 25 to 30 years, the concepts continuing to evolve in theory and practice. Defying some predictions that these ideas would be but passing fads in the history of police reform movements, they clearly have spoken to some fundamental and enduring aspects of the policing enterprise.

Community policing has spoken most directly to the nature of the relationship between the police and the public they serve by reestablishing two complementary foundational principles of policing in free and democratic societies: first, that the police are ultimately accountable to the public; second, that the public retains some measure of responsibility for self-policing. Problem oriented policing—or problem solving, as it has commonly been abbreviated—speaks directly to the need for the police to be more effective in promoting public safety and security.

Community policing and problem solving are not at all radical departures from traditional policing but rather paths back to the true origins of democratic policing. Unless the case can be made either that the police ought not to be accountable and responsive to the public or that the police ought not to be interested in becoming more effective, community policing and problem solving are likely to remain viable concepts well into the future. What remains to be worked out is whether the particular forms that these concepts take do in fact make the police more accountable, responsive, effective, and fair.

While community policing and problem solving have become firmly entrenched in the theory and practice of modern policing, some are still inclined to wonder whether these approaches will be supplanted by other approaches or whether they will continue to have relevance in the face of emerging challenges to public safety such as terrorism. Obviously, those questions will only be answered in time, but there is every reason to believe that the principles underlying community policing and problem solving—whatever becomes of the terminology—will prove as important and viable in the future as they have been over the past few decades. Similar questions about the viability and relevance of these ideas were asked in the face of the tremendous challenges posed by the dangerous drug markets that emerged in the 1980s. By most accounts, community policing and problem solving proved not only viable but instrumental in helping police and communities address street drug problems. Similarly, if properly applied, community policing and problem solving hold tremendous promise for helping protect societies from terrorism and preserving the very rights and freedoms that define a free and open society.

In this new edition, Ken Peak and Ron Glensor carefully link the principles and methods of community policing and problem solving to the basic issues and historical developments of policing in democratic societies, thereby helping readers understand why and how these concepts are so essential to understanding and practicing modern policing. They explain the basic principles and methods of community policing and problem solving. They also connect community policing and problem solving to other policing concepts such as hot spot policing, team policing, and CompStat; to other social and criminal justice movements such as community justice and restorative justice; and to crime prevention approaches such as situational crime prevention and crime prevention through environmental design.

Much of traditional criminology has concerned itself with exploring the broad social, cultural, and historical conditions that contribute to crime and the constitutional and developmental factors that influence criminal offenders. Interesting and important though this research has been, it hasn't had much relevance for the police because the police are seldom in a position to alter or even influence these conditions. But new branches of criminology (for example, environmental criminology) have produced criminological theories such as routine activity theory, crime pattern theory, and rational choice theory that have tremendous relevance for the police. They explore the so-called near causes of crime—causes and conditions that the police are in a position to affect—rather than the distant causes. Students of policing need also to be students of environmental criminology.

Peak and Glensor go on to explore the myriad managerial, organizational, and technological issues pertaining to the adoption of community policing and problem-solving approaches within police agencies. And perhaps most importantly, they connect readers with the emerging body of knowledge about how the police and communities can most effectively address the wide range of discrete public safety problems confronting them.

The recent emergence of an organized, well-researched, and readily accessible body of knowledge about police effectiveness in controlling specific crime and disorder problems is among the most significant developments in the long march toward the true professionalization of the police. Having such a body of professional knowledge—essential to other professions such as medicine, psychiatry and psychology, law, accounting, engineering, and the military—has too long been lacking in policing. Without such a body of knowledge from which to draw, police practitioners have relied on custom, politics, myth, improvisation, and guesswork to inform their decisions about what ought to be done by whom to address crime and disorder. In the absence of more sensible and customized responses, the police have continued to rely all too heavily on such standard practices as high-volume arrests and preventive patrol, practices that are often only partially effective and nearly always expensive.

As research and practice continue to refine our understanding of the specific social and environmental conditions that contribute to crime and disorder, the police will increasingly find themselves in the powerful position of being able to help broker the respective responsibilities of police, government, community groups, nongovernmental organizations, corporations, and individual private citizens for controlling these criminogenic conditions. Such a capacity would dramatically and fundamentally alter the police function in society from a largely reactive force that is consigned to dealing with the aftermath of crime to a more proactive and preventive force that is equipped to help communities understand and prevent crime and disorder. Not only would such a functional shift likely benefit society through reduced crime and disorder, but it would also likely better control the abuses of police authority that are endemic to institutions that are granted limited authority yet given impossible mandates.

This latest edition of *Community Policing and Problem Solving: Strategies and Practices* should, like earlier editions, prove essential reading for all students interested in working in or with the police profession. It provides a solid foundation of knowledge on which readers can build a career practicing or studying policing. More so than ever, the strength and endurance of free and open societies will depend on the existence of well-informed practitioners and observers of the police function.

Michael S. Scott

The Evolution of Policing

Past Wisdom and Future Directions

Key Terms and Concepts

Community oriented policing and problem solving (COPPS)

Community problem-solving era

Homeland security

Metropolitan Police Act

Peel's Principles

Police-community relations

Political era

Professional era

Reform of policing

Research findings

Wickersham Commission

Learning Objectives

As a result of reading this chapter, the student will:

- Understand the evolution of policing from its nonprofessional origins in England to modern-day professional policing in the United States
- Have a foundation in community oriented policing and problem solving (COPPS)
- Know how research studies of policing resulted in major changes in methods and approaches
- Be able to distinguish between the primary eras of policing
- Know the three generations of community policing and problem solving
- Understand how community policing and problem solving relate to homeland security

> Fellow citizens, we cannot escape history.
>
> *—Abraham Lincoln*

> To understand what is, we must know what has been, and what it tends to become.
>
> *—Oliver Wendell Holmes*

INTRODUCTION

It is difficult to accurately establish the beginning of community oriented policing in America. This is possibly owing to the fact that the notion of community policing is not altogether new; parts of it are as old as policing itself, emanating (as will be seen later) from concerns about policing that were indicated in the early nineteenth century.

We also must mention at the outset of this book that community oriented policing and problem solving (COPPS) is not a unitary concept but rather a collection of related ideas. Several prominent individuals, movements, studies, and experiments have brought policing to where it is today. In this chapter we examine the principal activities involving the police for more than a century and a half—activities which led to the development of community policing and problem solving.

This historical examination of policing begins with a brief discussion of Britain's and Sir Robert Peel's influence and the Metropolitan Police Act in England. Then we review the evolution of policing in America, including the emergence of the political era and attempts at reform through the professional crime fighter model. Next we look at police and change, including how "sacred cow" policing methods have been debunked by research, demonstrated the actual nature of police work, and shown the need for a new approach.

Following is an examination of the community problem solving era, including what the principles of this new model are, why it emerged, and how it evolved. In this connection we discuss how local police departments and sheriff's offices have evolved and rewritten their agency's history by adopting the COPPS strategy, how they have greatly expanded their use of the Internet to share this information with the public, and what COPPS can do to enhance the nation's defense and homeland security.

BRITISH CONTRIBUTIONS

The population of England doubled between 1700 and 1800. Parliament, however, took no measures to help solve the problems that arose from the accompanying social change.[1] London, awash in crime, had whole districts become criminal haunts and thieves became very bold. In the face of this situation, Henry Fielding began to experiment with possible solutions. Fielding, appointed in 1748 as London's chief magistrate of Bow Street, argued against the severity of the English penal code, which applied the death penalty to a large number of offenses. He felt the country should reform the criminal code in order to deal more with the origins of crime. In 1750 Fielding made the pursuit of criminals more systematic by creating a small group of "thief-takers."[2] When Fielding died in 1754, his half-brother John Fielding succeeded him as Bow Street magistrate. By 1785, his thief-takers had evolved into the Bow Street Runners—some of the most famous policemen in English history.

Later, Robert Peel, a wealthy member of Parliament, felt strongly that London's population and crime problem merited a full-time professional police force, but many English people and other politicians objected to the idea, fearing possible restraint of their liberty. They also feared a strong police organization because the criminal law was already quite harsh (by the early nineteenth century there were 223 crimes in England for which a person could be hanged). Indeed, Peel's efforts to gain support for full-time, paid police officers failed for seven years.[3]

Peel finally succeeded in 1829. His bill to Parliament, titled "An Act for Improving the Police in and Near the Metropolis," succeeded and became known as the **Metropolitan Police Act** of 1829. The *General Instructions* of the new force stressed its preventive nature, saying that "the principal object to be attained is 'the prevention of crime.' The security of persons and property will thus be better effected, than by the detection and punishment of the offender after he has succeeded in committing the crime."[4] It was decided that constables would don a uniform (blue coat, blue pants, and black top hat) and would arm themselves with a short baton (known as a truncheon) and a rattle (for raising an alarm); each constable was to wear his individual number on his collar where it could be easily seen.[5]

Peel proved very farsighted and keenly aware of the needs of a community oriented police force as well as the need of the public who would be asked to maintain it. Indeed, Peel perceived that the poor quality of policing was a contributing factor to the social disorder. Accordingly, he drafted several guidelines for the force, many of which focused on improving the relationship between the police and the public. He wrote that the power of the police to fulfill their duties depended on public approval of their actions; that as public cooperation increased, the need for physical force by the police decreased; that the officers needed to display absolutely impartial service to law; and that force should be employed by the police only when the attempt at persuasion and warning had failed and only the minimal degree of force possible should be used. Peel's statement that "The police are the public, and the public are the police" emphasized his belief that the police are first and foremost members of the larger society.[6]

Peel's attempts to appease the public were well grounded; during the first three years of his reform effort, he encountered strong opposition. Peel was denounced as a potential dictator; the *London Times* urged revolt, and *Blackwood's Magazine* referred to the bobbies as "general spies" and "finished tools of corruption." A national secret body was organized to combat the police, who were nicknamed the "Blue Devils" and the "Raw Lobsters." Also during this initial five-year period, Peel endured one of the largest police turnover rates in history. Estimates range widely, but it is probably accurate to accept the figure of 1,341 constables resigning from London's Metropolitan Police from 1829 to 1834.[7]

Peel drafted what have become known as **Peel's Principles** of policing, most (if not all) of which are still apropos to today's police community. They are presented in Box 1–1.

BOX 1–1

Peel's Principles of Policing

1. The basic mission for which the police exist is to prevent crime and disorder as an alternative to the repression of crime and disorder by military force and severity of legal punishment.

2. The ability of the police to perform their duties is dependent upon public approval of police existence, actions, behavior, and the ability of the police to secure and maintain public respect.

3. The police must secure the willing cooperation of the public in voluntary observance of the law to be able to secure and maintain public respect.

4. The degree of cooperation of the public that can be secured diminishes, proportionately, the necessity for the use of physical force and compulsion in achieving police objectives.

5. The police seek and preserve public favor, not by catering to public opinion, but by constantly demonstrating absolutely impartial service to the law, in complete independence of policy, and without regard to the justice or injustice of the substance of individual laws; by ready offering of individual service and friendship to all members of the society without regard to their race or social standing; by ready exercise of courtesy and friendly good humor; and by ready offering of individual sacrifice in protecting and preserving life.

6. The police should use physical force to the extent necessary to secure observance of the law or to restore order only when the exercise of persuasion, advice, and warning is found to be insufficient to achieve police objectives; and police should use only the minimum degree of physical force which is necessary on any particular occasion for achieving a police objective.

7. The police at all times should maintain a relationship with the public that gives reality to the historic tradition that the police are the public and that the public are the police; the police are the only members of the public who are paid to give full-time attention to duties which are incumbent on every citizen in the interest of the community welfare.

8. The police should always direct their actions toward their functions and never appear to usurp the powers of the judiciary by avenging individuals or the state, or authoritatively judging guilt or punishing the guilty.

9. The test of police efficiency is the absence of crime and disorder, not the visible evidence of police action in dealing with them.

Source: W. L. Melville Lee, *A History of Police in England* (London: Methuen, 1901), Chapter 12.

POLICING IN AMERICA: THE POLITICAL ERA

Early Beginnings

The New York Model. Americans meanwhile were observing Peel's overall successful experiment with the bobbies on the patrol beat. Industrialization and social upheaval had not reached the proportions that they had in England, however, so there was not the urgency for full-time policing that had been experienced in England. Yet by the 1840s, when industrialization began in earnest in America, U.S. officials were watching the police reform movement in England more closely.

To comprehend the blundering, inefficiency, and confusion that surrounded nineteenth-century police in what would be called the **political era** of policing; we must remember that this was an age when the best forensic techniques could not clearly distinguish the blood of a pig from

New York Police Department officers initially refused to wear uniforms because they did not want to appear as "liveried lackeys." A blue frock coat with brass buttons was adopted in 1853.

Courtesy NYPD Photo Unit.

that of a human and the art of criminal detection was little more than divination. Steamboats blew up, trains regularly mutilated and killed pedestrians, children got run over by wagons, injury very often meant death, and doctors resisted the germ theory of disease. In the midst of all this, the police would be patrolling—the police being men who at best had been trained by reading pathetic little rule books that provided them little or no guidance in the face of human distress and disorder.[8]

The movement to initiate policing in America began in New York City. (Philadelphia, with a private bequeath of $33,000, actually began a paid daytime police force in 1833; however, it was disbanded in three years.) In 1844, New York's state legislature passed a law establishing a full-time preventive police force for New York City. This new body was very different from that adopted from Europe, deliberately placed under the control of the city government and city politicians. The mayor chose the recruits from a list of names submitted by the aldermen and tax assessors of each ward; the mayor then submitted his choices to the city council for approval. Politicians were seldom concerned about selecting the best people for the job; instead, the system allowed and even encouraged political patronage and rewards for friends.[9]

The police link to neighborhoods and politicians was so tight that the police of this era have been considered virtual adjuncts to political machines.[10] The relationship was often reciprocal: political machines recruited and maintained police in office and on the beat while police helped ward leaders maintain their political offices by encouraging citizens to vote for certain candidates. Soon other cities adopted the New York model. New Orleans and Cincinnati adopted plans for a new police in 1852; Boston and Philadelphia followed in 1854, Chicago in 1855, and Baltimore and Newark in 1857.[11] By 1880, virtually every major American city had a police force based on Peel's model, pioneered in New York City.

From the East to the Wild, Wild West.   These new police were born of conflict and violence. An unprecedented wave of civil disorder swept the nation from the 1840s until the 1870s. Few cities escaped serious rioting, caused by ethnic and racial conflicts, economic disorder, and public out-rage about such things as brothels and medical school experiments. These occurrences often made for hostile interaction between citizens and the police, who were essentially a reactive force. Riots in many major cities actually led to the creation of the "new police." The use of the baton to quell riots, known as the "baton charge," was not uncommon.[12]

Furthermore, while large cities in the east were struggling to overcome social problems and establish preventive police forces, the western half of America was anything but passive. When people left the wagon trains and their relatively law-abiding ways, they attempted to live together in commu-nities. Many different ethnic groups—Anglo-Americans, Mexicans, Chinese, Indians, freed blacks, Australians, Scandinavians, and others—competed for often-scarce resources and fought one another violently, often with mob attacks. Economic conflicts were frequent between cattlemen and sheep herders, often leading to major range wars. There was constant labor strife in the mines. The bitterness of the slavery issue remained, and many men with firearms skills learned during the Civil War turned to outlawry after leaving the service (Jesse James was one such person).[13]

Despite these difficulties, westerners established peace by relying on a combination of four groups who assumed responsibility for law enforcement: private citizens, U.S. marshals, businessmen, and town police officers.[14] Pri-vate citizens usually helped to enforce the law by use of posses or through individual efforts, such as vigilante committees.[15] While it is true that they occasionally hanged outlaws, they also performed valuable work by ridding their communities of dangerous criminals.

Federal marshals were created by congressional legislation in 1789. As they began to appear on the frontier, the vigilantes tended to disappear. U.S. marshals enforced federal laws, so they only had jurisdiction over fed-eral offenses, such as theft of mail, crimes against railroad property, and murder on federal lands. Their primary responsibility was in civil matters arising from federal court decisions. Finally, when a territory became a state, the primary law enforcement functions usually fell to local sheriffs

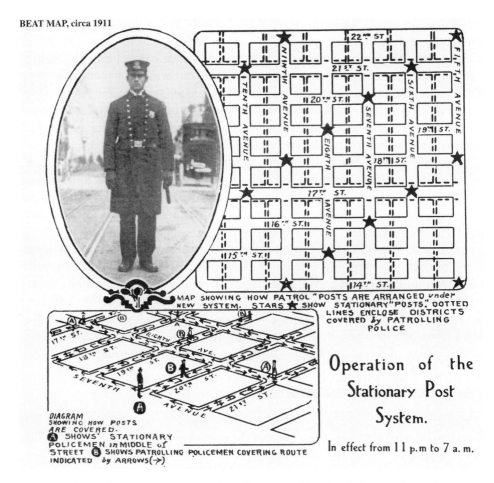

BEAT MAP, circa 1911

MAP SHOWING HOW PATROL "POSTS ARE ARRANGED *under* NEW SYSTEM. STARS ★ SHOW STATIONARY "POSTS." DOTTED LINES ENCLOSE DISTRICTS COVERED *by* PATROLLING POLICE

DIAGRAM SHOWING HOW POSTS ARE COVERED. Ⓐ SHOWS STATIONARY POLICEMEN *in* MIDDLE *of* STREET Ⓑ SHOWS PATROLLING POLICEMEN COVERING ROUTE INDICATED *by* ARROWS(→)

Operation of the Stationary Post System.

In effect from 11 p.m to 7 a. m.

Foot patrol was the primary strategy for policing neighborhoods during the early 1900s.
Courtesy NYPD Photo Unit.

and marshals. Sheriffs quickly became important officials, but they spent more time collecting taxes, inspecting cattle brands, maintaining jails, and serving civil papers than they did actually dealing with outlaws.[16]

Politics and Corruption

During the late nineteenth century, large cities gradually became more orderly. American cities absorbed millions of newcomers after 1900 without the social strains that attended the Irish immigration of the 1830s to 1850s.[17]

Partly because of their closeness to politicians, police during this era provided a wide array of services to citizens. Many police departments were involved in crime prevention and order maintenance as well as a variety of social services. In some cities they operated soup lines, helped find lost children, and found jobs and temporary lodging for newly arrived immigrants.[18] Police organizations were typically quite decentralized, with cities being divided into precincts and run like small-scale departments—hiring, firing, managing, and assigning personnel as necessary. Officers were often recruited from the same ethnic stock as the dominant groups in the neighborhoods; they lived in the beats they patrolled and were given considerable discretion in handling their individual beats. Decentralization encouraged foot patrol, even after call boxes and automobiles became available. Detectives operated from a caseload of "persons" rather than offenses, relying on their caseload to inform on other criminals.[19]

The strengths of the political era centered on the fact that police were integrated into neighborhoods. This strategy proved useful as it helped contain riots and the police assisted immigrants in establishing themselves in communities and finding jobs. There were weaknesses as well: The intimacy with the community, the closeness to politicians, and a decentralized organizational structure (and its inability to provide supervision of officers) also led to police corruption. The close identification of police with neighborhoods also resulted in discrimination against strangers, especially minority ethnic and racial groups. Police often ruled their beats with the "end of their nightsticks" and practiced "curbside justice."[20] The lack of organizational control over officers also caused some inefficiencies and disorganization; thus the image of Keystone Cops—bungling police—was widespread.

Emergence of Professionalism

In summary, the nineteenth-century police officer was essentially a political operative rather than a modern-style professional committed to public service. Because the police were essentially a political institution and perceived as such by the citizenry, they did not enjoy widespread acceptance by the public. As political appointees, officers enjoyed little job security, and salaries were determined by local political factors. Primitive communications technology of the era meant that police chiefs were unable to supervise their captains at the precinct level; thus policy was greatly influenced by the prevailing political and social mores of the neighborhoods. As a consequence, police behavior was very much influenced by the interaction between individual officers and individual citizens. The nature of that interaction, later termed the problem of **police-community relations,** was perhaps even more complex and ambiguous in the nineteenth century than in the late twentieth century.[21]

THE PROFESSIONAL ERA

Movement Toward Reform

The idea of policing as a profession, however, began to emerge slowly in the latter part of the nineteenth century. Reform ideas first appeared as a reaction to the corrupt and politicized state of the police. Reformers agreed that partisan politics was the heart of the problem. Even reformers in the

National Prison Association bemoaned the partisan politics that hindered the improvement of the police. Slowly the idea of policing as a higher calling (higher than the concerns of local politics, that is), as a profession committed to public service, began to gain ground. Two other ideas about the proper role of the police in society also appeared. One emphasized improvement in the role of police with respect to scientific techniques of crime detection. The other idea was that police could play more of a social work role; by intervening in the lives of individuals, police officers could reform society by preventing crime and keeping people out of the justice system. These reformers were closely tied to the emerging rehabilitative ideal in correctional circles in what is termed the **professional era.**[22]

New Developments and Calls for Reform

There were several important developments in the **reform of policing** during the late 1800s. Policing realized the beginning of a body of literature. Most authors were closely tied to the police and thus painted an inaccurate picture in some respects (e.g., the corruption that existed in many police departments), but their writings were also very illuminating. They provided glimpses into the informal processes that governed police departments and focused on the individual officer, a focus that would be lost in the later professionalization movement with its emphasis on impersonal bureaucratic standards. Furthermore, the late 1800s witnessed improvements in the areas of testing and training. The physical and mental qualifications of police officers concerned new police commissioners, and formal schools of instruction were developed (the best being Cincinnati's, which required a total of 72 hours of instruction). During the late 1800s, there was also the appearance of police conventions such as the National Police Chiefs Union (later named the International Association of Chiefs of Police [IACP]) and fraternal and benefit societies.[23]

August Vollmer, pioneer of police professionalism from 1905 to 1932, rallied police executives around the idea of reform during the 1920s and 1930s, emerging as the leading national spokesman for police professionalism. What is often overlooked among the abundance of Vollmer's contributions to policing was his articulate advocacy of the idea that the police should function as social workers. The belief that police officers should do more than merely arrest offenders, that they should actively seek to prevent crime by "saving" potential or actual offenders, was an important theme in police reform. It was an essential ingredient in the notion of professionalism. Indeed, in a series of addresses to the IACP, Vollmer advanced his ideas in "The Policeman as a Social Worker" (1918) and "Predelinquency" (1921). He began by arguing that the "old methods of dealing with crime must be changed, and newer ones adopted."[24]

Vollmer's views were very prescient for today, especially given the contemporary movement toward community policing. Vollmer felt that traditional institutions and practices were no longer adequate for a modern and

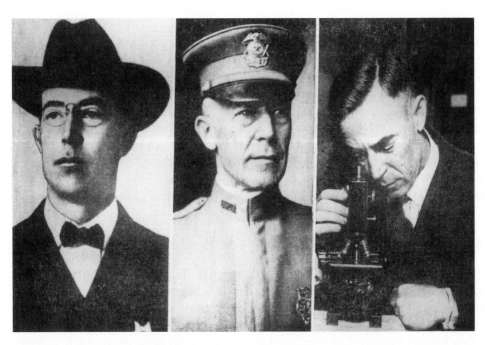

August Vollmer, a national spokesman for and early pioneer of police professionalism, established one of the first fingerprint bureaus and formal police schools while he was chief of police in Berkeley, California.

Courtesy Samuel G. Chapman.

complex industrial society. He believed that the police should intervene and be involved with people before they entered lives of crime, and he suggested that police work closely with existing social welfare agencies and become advocates of additional reform proposals. Vollmer also suggested that police inform voters about overcrowded schools and support the expansion of recreational facilities, community social centers, and antidelinquency agencies. Basically, he was suggesting that the police play an active part in the political life of the community, yet the major thrust of police professionalization had been to insulate the police from politics. This contradiction illustrated one of the fundamental ambiguities of the whole notion of professionalism.[25]

Other reformers continued to reject political involvement by police, and civil service systems were created to eliminate patronage and ward influences in hiring and firing police officers. In some cities, officers could not live in the same beat they patrolled, to isolate them as completely as possible from political influences. Police departments, needing to be removed from political influence, became one of the most autonomous agencies in urban government.[26] However, policing also became a matter viewed as best left to the discretion of police executives to address. Police organizations became law enforcement agencies, with the sole goal of controlling crime. Any noncrime activities they were required to do were "social work." The "professional model" of policing was in full bloom.

The scientific theory of administration was adopted, as advocated by Frederick Taylor during the early twentieth century. Taylor had studied the work process, breaking down jobs into their basic steps and emphasizing time and motion studies, all with an eye toward maximizing production. From this emphasis on production and unity of control flowed the notion that police officers were best managed by a hierarchical pyramid of control. Police leaders routinized and standardized police work; officers were to enforce laws and make arrests whenever possible. Discretion was limited to the extent possible. When special problems arose, special units (e.g., vice, juvenile, drugs, tactical) were created rather than assigning problems to patrol officers.

Crime Commissions and Early Police Studies

The early 1900s also became the age of the crime commission, including the **Wickersham Commission** reports in 1931. President Herbert Hoover, concerned with the lax enforcement of Prohibition and other forms of police corruption, created the National Commission on Law Observance and Enforcement—popularly known as the Wickersham Commission after its chairman, former U.S. Attorney General George W. Wickersham. This commission completed the first national study of crime and criminal justice, issuing 14 reports and recommending that the corrupting influence of politics be removed from policing, police chief executives be selected on merit, patrol officers be tested and meet minimal physical standards, police salaries and working conditions be decent, and policewomen be used in juvenile and female cases. Many of these recommendations represented what progressive police reformers had been wanting over the previous 40 years; unfortunately, President Hoover and his administration could do little more than report the Wickersham Commission's recommendations before leaving office.

The most important change in policing during this decade was the advent of the automobile and its accompanying radio. Gradually the patrol car replaced foot patrol, expanding geographic beats and further removing people from neighborhoods. There was also Prohibition (which affected the police very little in a long-term way), a bloody wave of racial violence in American cities, and the rise and defeat of police unionism and strikes. The impact of two-way radios was also felt, as supervisors were able to maintain a far closer supervision of patrol officers, and the radio and telephone made it possible for citizens to make heavier demands for police service. The result was not merely a greater burden on the police but also an important qualitative redefinition of the police role.[27]

The 1930s marked an important turning point in the history of police reform. The first genuine empirical studies of police work began to appear, and O. W. Wilson emerged as the leading authority on police administration. The major development of this decade was a redefinition of the police role and the ascendancy of the crime fighter image. Wilson, who took guidance from

J. Edgar Hoover's transformation of the Federal Bureau of Investigation (FBI) into an agency of high prestige, became the principal architect of the police reform strategy.[28] Hoover, appointed FBI director in 1924, had raised eligibility and training standards of recruits, giving FBI agents stature as upstanding moral crusaders and developing an incorruptible crime-fighting organization. He also developed impressive public relations programs that presented the bureau in the most favorable light. Municipal police found Hoover's path a compelling one. Following Wilson's writings on police administration, they began to shape an organizational strategy for urban police that was analogous to that pursued by the FBI.

Also by the 1930s the policewomen's movement, begun in the early 1900s, had begun losing ground. Professionalism came to mean a combination of managerial efficiency, technological sophistication, and an emphasis on crime fighting. The social work aspects of policing—the idea of rehabilitative work, which had been central to the policewomen's movement—were almost totally eclipsed. The result was a severe identity crisis for policewomen: They were caught between a social work orientation and a law enforcement ideology. Later, by the 1960s, women would occupy an extremely marginal place in American policing.[29]

In sum, under the reform era's professional model of policing, officers were to remain in their "rolling fortresses," going from one call to the next with all due haste. As Mark Moore and George Kelling observed, "In professionalizing crime fighting, the 'volunteers,' citizens on whom so much used to depend, [were] removed from the fight. If anything has been learned from the history of American policing, it is that, whatever the benefits of professionalization (e.g., reduced corruption, due process, serious police training), the reforms . . . ignored, even attacked, some features that once made the police powerful institutions in maintaining a sense of community security."[30]

Professional Crime Fighter

Emphasis on Efficiency and Control. The decade of the 1930s ended the first phase in the history of police professionalization. From the 1940s through the early 1960s, police reform continued along the lines that were already well established. Police professionalism was defined almost exclusively in terms of managerial efficiency, and administrators sought to further strengthen their hand in controlling rank-and-file officers; however, many of the old problems, such as racial unrest and an unclear definition of the police role, persisted. Nonetheless, by the late 1930s and early 1940s, there was a clear sense of mission for the police, a commitment to public service where one had not existed before.[31] Also, policing had begun to develop its own sense of professional autonomy. And, ironically perhaps, the most articulate groups and the most creative thinking were to be found in nonpolice groups: the National Prison Association, the social work profession, and the field of public administration. The efforts by reformers to remove political influence over police, though not entirely successful, were beginning to take hold as police boards and powerful police chiefs met their demise. Police unions reappeared, however, and the emergence of careerism among police officers significantly altered their attitudes toward the job and the public they served.

The professional model demanded an impartial law enforcer who related to citizens in professionally neutral and distant terms, personified by television's Sgt. Friday on "Dragnet": "Just the facts, ma'am." The emphasis on professionalization also shaped the role of citizens in crime control. Like physicians caring for health problems, teachers for educational problems, and social workers for social adjustment problems, the police would be responsible for crime problems. Citizens became relatively passive in crime control, mere recipients of professional crime control services. Citizens' responsibility in crime control was limited to calling police and serving as witnesses when asked to do so. Police were the "thin blue line." The community's need for rapid response to calls for service (CFS) was sold as efficacious in crime control. Foot patrol, when demanded by citizens, was rejected as an outmoded, expensive frill. Professionalism in law enforcement was often identified in terms of firearms expertise, and the popularity of firearms put the police firmly in the anti–gun control camp.[32]

Citizens were no longer encouraged to go to "their" neighborhood police officers or districts. Officers were to drive marked cars randomly through streets, to develop a feeling of police omnipresence. The "person" approach ended and was replaced by the case approach. Officers were

NYPD's Emergency Services was formed in 1926 to drive criminals, gangsters, and disorderly characters from the streets.

Courtesy NYPD Photo Unit.

judged by the numbers of arrests they made or the number of miles they drove during a shift. The crime rate became the primary indicator of police effectiveness.

Reestablishment of Communication: Police-Community Relations.   While much of the country was engaged in practicing and "selling" police reform embodied in the professional model of policing, a movement was beginning in Michigan to bring the police and community closer together. Louis Radelet served on the executive staff of the National Conference of Christians and Jews (NCCJ) from 1951 to 1963, when he became a professor in what was then the School of Police Administration and Public Safety at Michigan State University (MSU). In 1955 Radelet, having conducted many NCCJ workshops dedicated to reducing tensions between elements of the community, founded the National Institute on Police and Community Relations (NIPCR) at MSU; he served as institute director from 1955 to 1969 and was also coordinator of the university's National Center on Police and Community Relations, created to conduct a national survey on police-community relations, from 1965 to 1973.[33]

The institute held 5-day conferences each May during its 15-year existence, bringing together teams of police officers and other community leaders to discuss common problems. In peak years, more than 600 participants came from as many as 165 communities and 30 states as well as several foreign countries. As a result of the institute's work, such programs proliferated rapidly across the nation. We believe the stated purposes of the many programs initiated during this period are still applicable today and are listed here[34]:

1. To encourage police-citizen partnership in the cause of crime prevention
2. To foster and improve communications and mutual understanding between the police and the total community
3. To promote interprofessional approaches to the solution of community problems and to stress the principle that the administration of justice is a total community responsibility
4. To enhance cooperation among the police, the prosecution, the courts, and corrections
5. To assist the police and other community leaders to achieve an understanding of the nature and causes of complex problems in people-to-people relations and especially to improve police-minority relationships
6. To strengthen implementation of equal protection under the law for all persons

The NIPCR was discontinued at the end of 1969. Radelet wrote that its demise was "a commentary on the evolution of issues and social forces pertinent to the field. The purposes, assumptions, and institute design of past years may have been relevant in their time. But it became imperative now to think about police-community relations programs in different terms, with more precise purposes that could be better measured."[35]

Problems with the Professional Model

Several problems with the professional model of policing began to arise during the late 1960s.

Crime began to rise, and research suggested that conventional police methods were not effective. The 1960s was a time of explosion and turbulence. Inner-city residents rioted in several major cities, protestors denounced military involvement in Vietnam, assassins ended the lives of President John F. Kennedy, Robert F. Kennedy, and civil rights leader Rev. Martin Luther King, Jr. The country was witnessing tremendous upheaval, and such incidents as the so-called police riot at the 1968 Democratic National Convention in Chicago raised many questions about the police and their function and role. Largely as a result of this turmoil, five national studies, each with a different focus, looked into police practices during the 1960s and 1970s: the President's Commission on Law Enforcement and the Administration of Justice (termed the "President's Crime Commission," 1967); the National Advisory Commission on Civil Disorders (1968); the National Commission on the Causes and Prevention of Violence (1968); the President's Commission on Campus Unrest (1970); and the National Advisory Commission on Criminal Justice Standards and Goals (1973). Of particular note was the aforementioned President's Crime Commission of 1967, charged by President Lyndon Johnson to find solutions to America's internal crime problems. Among the commission's recommendations

During the 1960s, for the first time in history, Americans watched police on television respond to antiwar and civil rights demonstrations and were shocked at the treatment of students and minorities by the police.

A scene from the Walker Report of the 1968 Chicago Democratic National Convention.

for the police were hiring more minorities as police officers to improve police-community relations, upgrading the quality of police officers through better-educated officers, and using better applicant screening and intensive preservice training.[36]

The President's Crime Commission brought policing full circle, restating several of the same principles that were laid out by Sir Robert Peel in 1829: that the police should be close to the public, that poor quality of policing contributed to social disorder, and that the police should focus on community relations.

Police administrators became more willing to challenge traditional assumptions and beliefs and to open the door to researchers and their **research findings.** That willingness to allow researchers to examine traditional methods led to the growth and development of two important policing research organizations: the Police Foundation and the Police Executive Research Forum (PERF).

Fear rose. Citizens abandoned parks, public transportation, neighborhood shopping centers, churches, and entire neighborhoods. What puzzled police and researchers was that levels of fear and crime did not always correspond: Crime levels were low in some areas, but fear was high, and vice versa. Researchers found that fear is more closely associated with disorder than with crime. Ironically, order maintenance was one of the functions that police had been downplaying over the years.

Many minority citizens did not perceive their treatment as equitable or adequate. They protested not only police mistreatment but lack of treatment—despite attempts by most police departments to provide impartial policing to all citizens.

The antiwar and civil rights movements challenged police. The legitimacy of the police was questioned: Students resisted police, minorities rioted against them for what they represented, and the public (for the first time at this level) questioned police tactics. Moreover, minorities and women insisted that they be represented in policing if the police were to be legitimate.

Some of the myths on which the reform era was founded—that police officers use little or no discretion and that their primary duty is law enforcement—could no longer be sustained. Over and over, research underscored that the use of discretion was needed at all levels and that law enforcement comprised but a small portion of police officers' activities.[37] Other research findings shook the foundations of old assumptions about policing; for example, two-person patrol cars are neither more effective nor safer than one-person cars in reducing crime or catching criminals.[38] Other "sacred cows" of policing that were debunked by research are discussed below.

Although managers had tried to professionalize policing, line officers continued to have low status. Police work continued to be routinized; petty rules governed officer behavior. Meanwhile, line officers received little guidance in the use of discretion and had little opportunity for providing input concerning their work. As a result, many departments witnessed the rise of militant unionism.

The police lost a significant portion of their financial support. Many police departments were reduced in size, demonstrating an erosion of public confidence.

Police began to acquire competition: private security and the community crime control movement. Businesses, industries, and private citizens began to seek alternative means of protecting themselves and their property, further suggesting a declining confidence in the capability of police to provide the level of services that citizens desired. Indeed, today there are more than 1.5 million private police personnel employed in the United States—two to three times more personnel than there are in all federal, state, and municipal police agencies combined.[39] The social upheaval of the 1960s and 1970s obviously changed the face of policing in America. Not to be overlooked is the impact of the courts during this period as well. A number of major landmark Supreme Court decisions curtailed the actions of police and, concurrently, expanded the rights of the accused.

Changing Wisdom of Policing: More Recent Studies of Police Work

As a result of the problems mentioned earlier and the civil unrest that occurred during the professional era of policing, research evolved a new "common wisdom" of policing. As will be shown, much of this research shook the foundation of policing and rationalized the changes in methods we offer in later chapters. We discuss what might be termed the two primary clusters of police research that illuminated where policing has been and what officers actually do.

The first cluster of research actually began in the 1950s and would ultimately involve seven empirical studies of the police: the early work of sociologist William Westley concerning the culture of policing[40]; the ambitious studies of the American Bar Foundation[41]; the field observations of Jerome Skolnick[42]; the work of Egon Bittner analyzing the police function on skid row[43]; Raymond Parnas's study of the police response to domestic disturbances[44]; James Q. Wilson's analysis of different policing styles[45]; and the studies of police-citizen contact by Albert Reiss.[46] These studies collectively provided a "new realism" about policing[47]:

- Informal arrangements for handling incidents and behavioral problems were found to be more common than was compliance with formally established procedures.
- Workload, public pressures, and interagency pressures as well as the interests and personal predilections of functionaries in the criminal justice system were found in many instances to have more influence on how the police and the rest of the criminal justice system operated than the Constitution, state statutes, or city ordinances.
- Arrest, commonly viewed as the first step in the criminal process, had come to be used by the police to achieve a whole range of objectives in addition to that of prosecuting wrongdoers (e.g., to investigate, harass, punish, or provide safekeeping).
- A great variety of informal methods outside the criminal justice system had been adopted by the police to fulfill their formal responsibilities and to dispose

of the endless array of situations that the public—rightly or wrongly—expected
them to handle.

- Individual police officers were found to be routinely exercising a great deal
  of discretion in deciding how to handle the tremendous variety of circumstances with which they were confronted.

These findings also underscored that the police had, in the past,
depended too much on the criminal law in order to get their job done; that
they were not autonomous but rather were accountable, through the political
process, to the community; and that dealing with fear and enforcing public
order are appropriate functions for the police.[48] Other early studies indicated
that less than 50 percent of an officer's time was committed to CFS, and of
those calls handled, over 80 percent were noncriminal incidents.[49]

The five national studies of policing practices during the riots and the
Vietnam War of the 1960s and 1970s (discussed in the previous section)
began a quest for new directions. Later, a second cluster of police research
occurred that provided further knowledge about police methods. The
Kansas City Preventive Patrol Experiment of 1973 questioned the useful-
ness of random patrol in police vehicles.[50] Other studies showed that officers and detectives are limited in their abilities to successfully investigate
crimes[51] and that detectives need not follow up every reported unsolved
crime.[52] In short, most serious crimes were unaffected by the standard
police actions designed to control them.

Since the 1970s, additional studies have dispelled many assumptions
commonly held by police about their efficiency and effectiveness. For
example, preventive patrol has been shown to be costly, producing only minimal results in the reduction of crime.[53] Rapid response to calls has been
shown to be less effective at catching criminals than educating the public to
call the police sooner after a crime is committed.[54] We now know that police
response time is largely unrelated to the probability of making an arrest or
locating a witness. The time it takes to report a crime is the major determining factor of whether an on-scene arrest takes place and whether witnesses are located.[55] Despite their best efforts, police have had little impact
on preventing crime.[56] Box 1–2 shows several studies and experiments in
policing that were undertaken from 1972 to the present.

Viewing of "Sacred Cow" Police Methods with Caution

What did the studies mentioned previously mean for the police? Was the
professional model of policing (discussed earlier) completely off base? No,
in fact it still has a place in a police agency lacking organization, efficiency, and control. However, these studies do show that the police erred
in doggedly investing so much of their resources in a limited number of
practices that were based on a rather naive and simplistic concept of the
police role.[57] Furthermore, as we noted above, the police got caught up in

BOX 1–2

Police Studies and Experiments, 1972–Present

Year	Subject	Focus
2003	National Institute of Justice use of biometrics and face and iris recognition technologies in prisons and schools	Security and criminal justice
2002	National Institute of Justice study of less-lethal weapons aboard commercial aircraft	Focus on thwarting onboard attacks
2001	National Institute of Justice onsite assistance for terrorist attacks	Post 9-11 search-and-rescue tools and technology, protective gear
2000	COPS Program—National Evaluation	Federal Office of Community Oriented Policing Services (COPS) grants
2000	National Evaluation of the Problem Solving Partnerships Project for federal COPS office	Success of 447 police agencies receiving problem-solving grants
1999	National Evaluation of Project Weed and Seed (discussed in Chapter 12)	Proactive drug enforcement and prevention
1998	National Evaluation of Youth Firearms Violence	Approaches to reduce firearms-related violence
1998	Information Systems Technology Enhancement Project	Technology uses for COPPS
1997	Federal Study of Crime Prevention Programs	Broad range of programs
1995	Repeat Victimization	Prevention of revictimization
1995	Integrated Criminal Apprehension Program	Crime analysis–based deployment
1993	"Tipping Point" Studies	Examination of crime epidemics
1992	Crime Prevention Through Environmental Design	Use of designing out crime
1992	Situational Crime Prevention	Reduction of crime opportunities
1991	Quality Policing in Madison, Wisconsin	Quality management study
1990	Minneapolis "Hot Spot" Patrolling	Intensive patrol of problem areas
1988	Police Decoy Operations	Criminal targeting tactic
1987	Problem Oriented Policing, Newport News, Virginia	Crime problem solving model
1987	Houston and Newark Fear of Crime Studies	Fear reduction study
1985	Repeat Offender Programs	Focus on career criminals
1984	Minneapolis Domestic Violence Experiment	Analysis of effective police action
1983	Differential Police Response Field Test	Call priority and alternative reporting
1982	Directed Patrol National Survey	Survey of patrol strategies
1981	Newark Foot Patrol Experiment	Cost benefits of foot patrol
1977	Split Force Patrol Experiment, Wilmington, Delaware	Patrol deployment study
1977	Patrol Staffing in San Diego	One- vs. two-officer cars
1976	Kansas City Response Time Study	Police response to crimes
1975	RAND Study of Investigations	Detective and patrol effectiveness
1975	Field Interview Study, San Diego	Link between field interviews and crime
1974	Kansas City Preventive Patrol Experiment	Effectiveness of random patrol
1973	Team Policing Experiment in Seven U.S. Cities	Team vs. traditional policing
1973	Police-Community Relations	Study of organizational orientation
1972	Policewomen on Patrol	Evaluation of women on patrol

the "means over ends" syndrome, measuring their success by the numbers of arrests, quickness of responses, and so on (the means) while often neglecting the outcome of their work (the ends).

As we have seen, the "We've always done it this way" mentality, still pervading policing to a large extent, may be not only an ineffective means of organizing and administering a police agency but also a costly squandering of valuable human and financial resources. For many police agencies today operating under the traditional incident-driven style of policing, the *beat* (rather than the *neighborhood*) is, to borrow a term from research methodology, the "unit of analysis." Under this timeworn model, officers have been glued to their police radios, flitting like pinballs from one call for service to the next as rapidly as possible. Furthermore, police officers seldom leave their vehicles to address incidents except when answering a CFS. They know very little about the underlying causes of problems in the neighborhoods on their beats.

The results of employing conventional police methods have been inglorious. Problems have persisted or been allowed to go unnoticed and grow while neighborhoods deteriorated. Officers became frustrated after they repeatedly handled similar calls, with no sign of progress. Petty offenses contributed to this decline and drove stable community members away once the message went out to offenders and vandals that no one cares about the neighborhood. Yet many in the police field are unaware of or refuse to accept that the old ways are open to serious challenge.

Time for a New Approach

We believe it is clear from all we've discussed thus far that police agencies must change their daily activities, their management practices, and even their view of their work in order to confront the changes that are occurring. We maintain that given the current levels of violence and the public's fear of it, the disorder found in countless American neighborhoods, the poor police-community relations in many cities, and the rapidly changing landscape of crime and demographics in America, the police need to seriously consider whether a bureaucratic overhaul is needed to meet the demands of the future.

Police research also demonstrated the need for agencies to evaluate the effectiveness of their responses. Both quantitative and qualitative data should be used as a basis for evaluation and change. Departments need to know more about what their officers are doing. Agencies are struggling to find enough resources for performing crime trend analyses; most also do not conduct proper workload analyses to know what uncommitted time is possessed by their officers.

Research has also provided the realization that policing consists of developing the most effective means for dealing with a multitude of troublesome situations. For example, problem solving is a whole new way of thinking about policing and carries the potential to reshape the way in which police services are delivered.[58]

One of several things the police must do to accomplish their mission is to reacquaint themselves with members of the community by involving citizens in the resolution of neighborhood problems. Simply stated, police must view the public as well as other government and social services organizations as "a part of," as opposed to "apart from," their efforts. This change in conventional thinking advocates efficiency with effectiveness and quality over quantity, and it encourages collaborative problem solving and creative resolutions to crime and disorder.

THE COMMUNITY PROBLEM-SOLVING ERA

Team Policing, Foot Patrol, and Shattered Myths

In the early 1970s it was suggested that the performance of patrol officers would improve more by using job redesign based on "motivators."[59] This suggestion later evolved into a concept known as "team policing," which sought to restructure police departments, improve police-community relations, enhance police officer morale, and facilitate change within the police organization. Its primary element was a decentralized neighborhood focus to the delivery of police services. Officers were to be generalists, trained to investigate crimes and basically attend to all of the problems in their area, with a team of officers being assigned to a particular neighborhood and responsible for all police services in that area—the **community problem-solving era.**

In the end, however, team policing failed for several reasons. Most of the experiments were poorly planned and hastily implemented, resulting in street officers not understanding what they were supposed to do. Many midmanagement personnel felt threatened by team policing; as a result, some sabotaged the experiment. Furthermore, team policing did not represent a completely different view of policing. As Samuel Walker observed, "It was essentially a different *organizational approach* to traditional policing: responding to calls for service (CFS), deterring crime through patrol, and apprehending criminals" (emphasis in original).[60]

There were other developments for the police during the late 1970s and early 1980s. Foot patrol became more popular, and many jurisdictions (such as Newark, New Jersey; Boston, Massachusetts; and Flint, Michigan) even demanded it. In Newark, an evaluation found that foot patrol was readily perceived by residents and that it produced a significant increase in the level of satisfaction with police service, led to a significant reduction of perceived crime problems, and resulted in a significant increase in the perceived level of safety of the neighborhood.[61] Flint researchers reported that the crime rate in the target areas declined slightly; CFS in these areas dropped by 43 percent. Furthermore, citizens indicated satisfaction with the program, suggesting that it had improved relations with the police.[62]

These findings and others discussed below shattered several long-held myths about measures of police effectiveness. In addition, research conducted during the 1970s suggested that *information* could help police improve their ability to deal with crime. These studies, along with those of foot patrol and fear reduction, created new opportunities for the police to understand the increasing concerns of citizens' groups about disorder (e.g., gangs, prostitutes) and to work with citizens to do something about it. Police discovered that when they asked citizens about their priorities, citizens appreciated their asking and often provided useful information.

The Community Patrol Officer Program (CPOP), instituted by the New York City Police Department in 1984, was similar in many respects to the Flint foot patrol program. Officers involved in this program were responsible for getting to know the residents, merchants, and service providers in their beat area; identifying the principal crime and order maintenance problems confronting the people within their beat; and devising strategies for dealing with the identified problems.[63]

Principles of the New COPPS Model

Simultaneously, Herman Goldstein's problem-oriented approach to policing was being tested in Madison, Wisconsin; Baltimore County, Maryland; and Newport News, Virginia. These studies found that police officers enjoy operating with a holistic approach to their work, have the capacity to do problem solving successfully, and can work with citizens and other agencies to solve problems. Also, citizens seemed to appreciate working with police. Moreover, this approach was a rethinking of earlier strategies of handling CFS: Officers were given more autonomy and trained to analyze the underlying causes of problems and to find creative solutions. These findings were similar to those of the foot patrol experiments and fear reduction experiments.

Community oriented policing and problem solving (COPPS) requires not only new police strategies but a new organizational approach as well. There is a renewed emphasis on community collaboration for many police tasks. Crime control remains an important function, but equal emphasis is given to *prevention*. Police officers return to their wide use of discretion under this model and move away from routinization and standardization in addressing their tasks. This discretion pushes operational and tactical decision making to the lower levels of the organization.

Participative management is greatly increased, and fewer levels of authority are required to administer the organization; middle management layers are reduced. Concurrently, many cities have developed what are, in effect, "demarketing" programs, attempting to rescind programs (such as the area of rapid response to CFS and to 911 calls except for dire emergencies) that had been actively sold earlier.

Police storefronts and substations provide convenience and improved customer service to neighborhoods.

Courtesy Huntington Beach, California, Police Department.

Community problem solving has helped to explain what went wrong with team policing in the 1960s and 1970s. It was a strategy that innovators mistakenly approached as a tactic. Team policing also competed with traditional policing in the same departments, and they were incompatible with one another. A police department might have a small team policing unit or conduct a team policing experiment, but the traditional professional model of policing was still "business as usual."

The classical theory of police organization that continues to dominate many agencies is likewise alien to the community problem-solving strategy. The new strategy will not accommodate the classical theory of traditional policing; the latter denies too much of the real nature of police work, continues old methods of supervision and administration, and creates too much cynicism in officers attempting to do creative problem solving.

Risks come with attempting the new strategy. The risks, however, "for the community and the profession of policing, are not as great as attempting to maintain a strategy that faltered on its own terms during the 1960s and 1970s."[64]

Why the Emergence of COPPS?

Although we will discuss COPPS in greater detail in Chapters 2, 3, and 4, following is a summary of the factors that set the stage for the emergence of COPPS:

- Narrowing of the police mission to crime fighting
- Increased cultural diversity in our society and heightened concern with police violation of minority civil rights
- Detachment of patrol officers in patrol vehicles and of administration from officer and community input
- Increased violence in our society

- Downturn in the economy and, subsequently, a "do more with less" philosophy regarding the police
- Increased dependence on high-technology equipment rather than contact with the public
- Emphasis on organizational change, including decentralization and greater officer discretion
- Desire for greater personalization of government services
- Burgeoning attempts by the police to adequately reach the community through crime prevention, team policing, and police-community relations

Most of these elements contain a common theme: the isolation of the police from the public. In sum, the police got caught up in the "means over ends" syndrome, wherein they measured their success by the numbers of arrests, quickness of responses, and so on. They often neglected the outcome of their work—the ends. For many decades, this isolation often resulted in an "us versus them" mentality on the part of both the police and the citizenry. The notion of community policing therefore "rose like a phoenix from the ashes of burned cities, embattled campuses, and crime-riddled neighborhoods."[65]

Well Entrenched: Three Generations of COPPS

COPPS is the established paradigm of contemporary policing, both at home and abroad (see Chapter 14); it enjoys a large degree of public acceptance[66] and receives widespread attention by academicians who have published a growing number of journal articles and doctoral dissertations on the topic.[67] Furthermore, it has now moved through three generations, according to Willard Oliver: innovation, diffusion, and institutionalization[68]:

1. The first generation of COPPS, *innovation,* spans the period of 1979 through 1986, beginning with the seminal work of Herman Goldstein concerning needed improvement of policing,[69] coupled with the "broken windows" theory by James Wilson and George Kelling.[70] Early concepts of community policing during this generation were often called "experiments," "test sites," and "demonstration projects" and were often restricted to larger metropolitan cities. The style of policing that was employed was predominately narrow in focus (e.g., foot patrols, problem-solving methods, and community substations). These small-scale test sites provided a source of innovative ideas for others to consider.

2. The second generation, *diffusion,* spans the period from 1987 through 1994. The concepts and philosophy of community policing and problem solving spread rapidly among police agencies through a variety of communication means within the policing subculture. Adoption of the strategy was fast becoming a reality during this generation, as evidenced by the fact that in 1985 slightly more than 300 police agencies had adopted some form of community policing,[71] whereas by 1994 it had spread to more than 8,000 agencies.[72] The practice of community policing during this generation was still generally

limited to large- and medium-size cities, and the style of policing during this generation was much broader than the first, being more involved with neighborhood and quality-of-life issues. The strategies normally targeted drug use and fear of crime issues while improving police-community relationships. Much more emphasis was placed on evaluating outcomes through the use of appropriate research methodologies.

3. The third generation, *institutionalization,* goes from 1995 to the present and has seen widespread implementation of community policing and problem solving across the United States: Today nearly 7 in 10 (68 percent) of the nation's 17,000 local police agencies, *employing 90 percent of all officers,* have adopted this strategy.[73] This generation has seen COPPS become deeply entrenched within the political process and has featuring federal grant money through the Violent Crime Control and Law Enforcement Act of 1994. This act authorized $8.8 billion over six years to create the Office of Community Oriented Policing Services (COPS) in the U.S. Department of Justice, added community policing officers across the country, created 31 regional community policing institutes (RCPIs) to develop and deliver community policing training, and allowed agencies of all sizes to apply for community policing grants. (As of January 2006, the COPS office had provided $11.4 billion in funding assistance to nearly 13,000 jurisdictions through 27 different grant programs, including funding for about 118,000 community policing officers across the country. Table 1–1 shows the history of funded programs and personnel of the COPS office, from 1994 to the present.) The style of policing under this generation has extended to such programs as youth firearms violence, gangs, and domestic violence, while extending into geo-mapping software and crime prevention through environmental design (CPTED, discussed in Chapter 5).

COPPS has obviously become the culture of many police organizations, affecting and permeating their hiring processes, recruit academies, in-service training, promotional examinations, and strategic plans. COPPS is also having an impact in the form of community-oriented government and in the criminal justice system. There is little doubt that COPPS is the future of policing. In this regard, the relationship between COPPS and homeland security is discussed below, and a view of the future of community policing is presented in Chapter 15.

Table 1–2 summarizes the three eras of policing that were discussed above: political, reform, and community.

Sharing of History via the Internet

A look at the Internet's Web pages of many city police departments and county sheriff's offices reveals many such agencies presenting a history of their organization, including their conversion to the COPPS initiative. In a sense these agencies are explaining to the public—and to their own employees—how they have evolved at the local level. This approach serves a twofold purpose. First, it serves to educate those persons *outside* the

TABLE 1–1

History of the Federal Office of Community Oriented Policing Services

1994

The Violent Crime Control & Law Enforcement Act passes both the House and the Senate, authorizing an $8.8 billion expenditure over six years. The Office of Community Oriented Policing Services is created to distribute and monitor these funds.

COPS launches three new programs: Accelerated Hiring, Education and Deployment (AHEAD), Funding Accelerated for Smaller Towns (FAST), and Making Officer Redeployment Effective (MORE).

COPS awards $200 million to 392 agencies for 2,700 additional community policing professionals.

Total program funding for fiscal year 1994: $148.4 million.

1995

COPS funds 25,000 more officers.

COPS announces the Universal Hiring Program (UHP), which incorporates FAST and AHEAD.

COPS awards grants totaling $10 million through the Youth Firearms Violence Initiative.

Total program funding for fiscal year 1995: $1,225.1 million.

1996

COPS funds more than 52,000 officers through UHP.

COPS announces its Anti-Gang Initiative and Community Policing to Combat Domestic Violence Program.

COPS announces its Problem-Solving Partnership initiative.

Total program funding for fiscal year 1996: $1,209.2 million.

1997

COPS publishes and releases a report entitled *Police Integrity: Public Service with Honor*.

COPS funding establishes a nationwide network of Regional Community Policing Institutes (RCPIs).

Total program funding for fiscal year 1997: $983.9 million.

1998

COPS has now funded 75,000 new community policing professionals nationwide.

COPS introduces three new programs: Distressed Neighborhoods Pilot Project, Police Corps Program, and Small Communities Grant Program.

COPS launches the Methamphetamine Program, through which it awards $34 million throughout the fiscal year.

COPS awards a total of $38 million through its Technology Program.

Total program funding for fiscal year 1998: $1,490.7 million.

1999

COPS announces its COPS in Schools (CIS) grant program.

COPS funds its 100,000th community policing professional in May 1999.

COPS announces its Tribal Resources Grant Program (TRGP).

Total program funding for fiscal year 1999: $1,127.7 million.

2000

COPS launches its Police as Problem-Solvers and Peacemakers program, through which it awards $1 million to five law enforcement agencies.

COPS announces its Justice-Based After School (JBAS) and Value-Based Initiatives (VBI) programs.

COPS awards $12 million to 41 state law enforcement agencies for the purchase of 2,900 in-car cameras.

Total program funding for fiscal year 2000: $685.3 million.

2001

COPS launches two new series of publications: COPS Innovations and Problem-Oriented Policing Guides.

COPS awards $600,000 through JBAS to seven law enforcement agencies.

COPS supports the NYPD and Arlington County Police Department as they respond to the September 11 attacks.

Total program funding for fiscal year 2001: $558.1 million.

2002

COPS awards more than $70 million through the Methamphetamine Program.

COPS awards more than $154 million through the Technology Program.

COPS announces $128 million in UHP grants that allow 367 agencies to hire 1,750 community policing professionals.

Total program funding for fiscal year 2002: $656.9 million.

2003

COPS launches the Homeland Security Overtime Program (HSOP) and awards $59.6 million to 294 law enforcement agencies throughout the United States.

The Interoperable Communications Technology Program is created by COPS, awarding $66.5 million to 14 communities to develop integrated communications networks among emergency response agencies.

COPS awards over $41 million in CIS grants.

Total program funding for fiscal year 2003: $635 million.

2004

COPS awards $47.2 million in grants through the Universal Hiring Program to 178 law enforcement agencies to hire 905 community policing officers.

COPS allocates $4.6 million to 19 jurisdictions to combat methamphetamine use and to develop and enhance eradication strategies.

More than $82 million in grants is awarded by COPS to 23 communities in 17 states to develop interoperable communications networks.

Source: U.S. Department of Justice, Office of Community Oriented Policing Services, Washington, D.C. http://www.cops.usdoj.gov/Default.asp?Item=44 (Accessed February 21, 2006).

agency concerning the agency's history and identity, underscoring that COPPS is not to be viewed as a temporary independent "program" but as part of the agency's method of service delivery. Second, it conveys to those persons who are employed *inside* the organization a sense of who they are and what the agency's philosophy is.[74]

A search of police Web sites on a popular search engine revealed nearly 1,000 sites. Often the sites are used for public information purposes, such as to let the community report crimes; know about programs and initiatives, recruitment and employment opportunities, special events and activities; and post contact information and frequently asked questions. Some go further, posting crime statistics (including hate crimes), wanted and missing person reports, sex offender alerts, and annual reports; transmitting intelligence information to detectives in the field; and even allowing people to pay parking tickets and make anonymous tips. The Chicago Police Department's Web site consists of 1,500 pages of information, which are color-coded and

TABLE 1–2

The Three Eras of Policing			
	POLITICAL ERA (1840s TO 1930s)	REFORM ERA (1930s TO 1980s)	COMMUNITY ERA (1980s TO PRESENT)
Authorization	Politics and law	Law and professionalism	Community support (political), law, and professionalism
Function	Broad social services	Crime control	Broad provision of services
Organizational design	Decentralized	Centralized and classical	Decentralized using task forces and matrices
Relationship to community	Intimate	Professional and remote	Intimate
Tactics and technology	Foot patrol	Preventive patrol and rapid response to calls	Foot patrol, problem solving, and public relations
Outcome	Citizen and political satisfaction	Crime control	Quality of life and citizen satisfaction

Source: Adapted from George L. Kelling and Mark H. Moore, *The Evolving Strategies of Policing* (Washington, D.C.: U.S. Department of Justice, National Institute of Justice Perspectives on Policing, November 1988).

have header bars to help categorize and navigate the site.[75] Some jurisdictions even have chat rooms for citizens and allow informants to continuously provide information to police.[76]

COPPS AND HOMELAND SECURITY

New Threats and New Measures

Unquestionably, historians of the future will maintain that terrorist acts of the early twenty-first century changed forever the nature of policing efforts in the area of **homeland security** in the United States. Words are almost inadequate to describe how the events of September 11, 2001, forever modified and heightened the fears and concerns of all Americans—and the police—with regard to domestic security and the methods necessary for securing the general public.

Police have several means to address domestic terrorism. First, and perhaps the most fruitful, is military support of law enforcement. The Posse Comitatus Act of 1878 prohibits using the military to generally execute the laws; the military may be called on, however, to provide personnel and equipment for certain special support activities, such as domestic terrorism events involving weapons of mass destruction.[77]

To further combat terrorism, the U.S. Department of Homeland Security (DHS) was formed in 2002, with five directorates (Border and Transportation Security; Emergency Preparedness and Response; Chemical, Biological, Radiological, and Nuclear Countermeasures; Information

The terrorist attacks on New York's World Trade Center linked forever the concepts of community policing, problem solving, and homeland security.

AP Wide World Photos

Analysis and Infrastructure Protection; and Management) and $14 billion in new monies for safeguarding the nation.[78]

But securing our homeland remains a daunting task. Within the 50 states, there are 3,000 counties and 18,000 cities that must be protected. The job of getting law enforcement, emergency services, public health agencies, and private enterprises coordinated and working together at local, state, and federal levels is also a challenging task.[79]

Role of COPPS

What can COPPS contribute to the goal of maintaining our nation's defense? As an overarching answer to that question, 9-11 taught all Americans that we—the police and citizens—must work together to ensure our collective safety; the responsibility of responding to terrorist threats falls directly on the shoulders of state and local law enforcement and their government and community partners. Furthermore, the philosophy underlying COPPS can be directed toward trying to prevent terrorist activities before they occur. A task force report put it thusly:

> Most of the real frontlines of homeland security are outside of Washington, D.C. Likely terrorists are encountered, and the targets they might attack are protected, by local officials—a cop hearing a complaint from a landlord, an airport official who hears about a plane some pilot trainee left on the runway, an FBI agent puzzled by an odd flight school student, or an emergency room resident trying to treat patients stricken by an unusual illness.[80]

Beat officers are also a vital part of our safety. They know their neighborhoods, provide community policing, track identity theft and fraud, and develop trusted local sources. As one policy analyst put it, "They are in the best position to 'collect' the dots that federal agencies need to 'connect' to forecast the next attack."[81]

Terrorism is obviously a local issue, and homeland security and COPPS have much in common. Homeland security requires a shift in the culture of law enforcement agencies that involves the creation of external partnerships, citizen involvement, problem solving, and transformation of the organization. COPPS serves as a solid framework for the development of an effective prevention strategy for homeland security by local law enforcement agencies.[82]

Certainly crime-mapping systems, data collection and analysis protocols, and other kinds of COPPS technologies that are discussed in Chapter 5 may be used as platforms for gathering intelligence to assess terrorism vulnerability and to implement preparedness plans. As examples, agencies that use geographic information systems (GIS) to conduct crime mapping and analysis can also use GIS to conduct terrorism target mapping and analysis; agencies that use their Web site to disseminate crime prevention information can use it to disseminate homeland security information.

In sum, factors associated with the COPPS philosophy and implementation of homeland security strategies within police agencies are highly related.[83] COPPS also involves intergovernmental and interagency collaborations with state and federal agencies that are essential for the collection and exchange of intelligence and the sharing of resources in the event of an attack.[84]

▲ SUMMARY

This chapter has shown the evolution of policing in America, up through and including its contemporary emphasis on homeland defense. Problems with some of the old methods, as well as the willingness of police leaders to rethink their basic role and develop new strategies, led us to community oriented policing and problem solving (COPPS). It is much more than simply "a return to the basics" but is instead a retooling of the basics, coming full circle.

The incorporation of past wisdom and the use of new tools, methods, and strategies via COPPS offer the most promise for detecting and preventing crime, addressing crime and disorder, and improving relations with the public. These partnerships are essential for addressing the "broken windows" phenomenon[85] (an influential theory asserting that once the process of physical decay begins, its effects multiply until some corrective action is taken). The lesson, Wilson and Kelling argued, was that we should redirect our thinking toward improving police handling of "little" problems. In short, the police need to be thinking like what might be termed "street-level criminologists," examining the underlying causes of crime rather than functioning like bureaucrats. This theme will be echoed at various points throughout the book.

ITEMS FOR REVIEW

1. Describe the British contributions to American policing.
2. Explain when and where modern-day policing first came to America and what its primary challenges were.
3. Distinguish between the political and professional eras of American policing; include the primary problems associated with both.
4. Explain what is meant by the new "common wisdom" of policing, and discuss the major research findings of the latter half of the 1900s regarding policing methods.
5. Describe the community policing era in general as well as the three generations of COPPS.
6. Review the role of COPPS in homeland security.

NOTES

1. David R. Johnson, *American Law Enforcement History* (St. Louis, Mo.: Forum Press, 1981), p. 11.
2. *Ibid.,* p. 13.
3. *Ibid.,* pp. 14–15.
4. Leon Radzinowicz, *A History of English Criminal Law and Its Administration from 1750, Vol. IV: Grappling for Control* (London: Stevens & Son, 1968), p. 163.
5. Johnson, *American Law Enforcement History*, pp. 19–20.
6. A. C. Germann, Frank D. Day, and Robert R. J. Gallati, *Introduction to Law Enforcement and Criminal Justice* (Springfield, Ill.: Charles C Thomas, 1962), p. 63.

7. Clive Emsley, *Policing and Its Context, 1750–1870* (New York: Schocken Books, 1983), p. 37.

8. Eric H. Monkkonen, *Police in Urban America, 1860–1920* (Cambridge, U.K.: Cambridge University Press, 1981), pp. 1–2.

9. Johnson, *American Law Enforcement History*, pp. 26–27.

10. See K. E. Jordan, *Ideology and the Coming of Professionalism: American Urban Police in the 1920s and 1930s* (Dissertation, Rutgers University, 1972); Robert M. Fogelson, *Big-City Police* (Cambridge, Mass.: Harvard University Press, 1977).

11. Johnson, *American Law Enforcement History*, p. 27.

12. James F. Richardson, *Urban Policing in the United States* (New York: Oxford University Press, 1970), p. 51.

13. Johnson, *American Law Enforcement History*, p. 92.

14. *Ibid.*

15. *Ibid.*

16. *Ibid.,* pp. 96–98.

17. *Ibid.*

18. Monkkonen, *Police in Urban America, 1860–1920*, p. 158.

19. John E. Eck, *The Investigation of Burglary and Robbery* (Washington, D.C.: Police Executive Research Forum, 1984).

20. See George L. Kelling, "Juveniles and Police: The End of the Nightstick," in Francis X. Hartmann (ed.), *From Children to Citizens, Vol. II: The Role of the Juvenile Court* (New York: Springer-Verlag, 1987).

21. Samuel Walker, *A Critical History of Police Reform: The Emergence of Professionalism* (Lexington, Mass.: Lexington Books, 1977), pp. 8–9, 11.

22. *Ibid.,* p. 33.

23. *Ibid.,* pp. 33–34, 42, 47.

24. *Ibid.,* p. 81.

25. *Ibid.,* pp. 80–83.

26. Herman Goldstein, *Policing a Free Society* (Cambridge, Mass.: Ballinger, 1977).

27. Albert Reiss, *The Police and the Public* (New Haven, Conn.: Yale University Press, 1971).

28. See Orlando Wilson, *Police Administration* (New York: McGraw-Hill, 1950).

29. Walker, *A Critical History of Police Reform*, pp. 93–94.

30. Mark H. Moore and George L. Kelling, "'To Serve and Protect': Learning from Police History," *The Public Interest* 70 (Winter 1983):49–65.

31. Peter K. Manning, "The Police: Mandate, Strategies, and Appearances," in Jack D. Douglas (ed.), *Crime and Justice in American Society* (Indianapolis, Ind.: Bobbs-Merrill, 1971), pp. 149–163.

32. Walker, *A Critical History of Police Reform*, p. 161.

33. Louis Radelet, *The Police and the Community* (4th ed.) New York: Macmillan, 1986), p. ix.

34. *Ibid.,* p. 17.

35. *Ibid.,* p. 21.

36. William G. Doerner, *Introduction to Law Enforcement: An Insider's View* (Englewood Cliffs, N.J.: Prentice Hall, 1992), pp. 21–23.

37. Mary Ann Wycoff, *The Role of Municipal Police Research as a Prelude to Changing It* (Washington, D.C.: Police Foundation, 1982).

38. Jerome H. Skolnick and David H. Bayley, *The New Blue Line: Police Innovation in Six American Cities* (New York: Free Press, 1986), p. 4.

39. William C. Cunningham, John J. Strauchs, and Clifford W. Van Meter, *The Hallcrest Report II: Private Security Trends, 1970–2000* (McLean, Va.: Hallcrest Systems, 1990).

40. William Westley, *Violence and the Police: A Sociological Study of Law, Custom, and Morality* (Cambridge, Mass.: MIT Press), 1970.

41. American Bar Foundation, *The Urban Police Function,* approved draft (Chicago: Author, 1973).

42. Jerome Skolnick, *Justice Without Trial: Law Enforcement in Democratic Society* (New York: John Wiley & Sons, 1966).

43. Egon Bittner, "The Police on Skid Row: A Study of Peace Keeping," *American Sociological Review* 32 (1967):699–715.

44. Raymond I. Parnas, "The Police Response to the Domestic Disturbance," *Wisconsin Law Review* 4 (1967):914–955.

45. James Q. Wilson, *Varieties of Police Behavior: The Management of Law and Order in Eight Communities* (Cambridge, Mass.: Harvard University Press), 1968.

46. Albert J. Reiss, Jr., *The Police and the Public* (New Haven, Conn.: Yale University Press), 1971.

47. Goldstein, *Policing a Free Society*, pp. 22–24.

48. *Ibid.,* p. 11.

49. Elaine Cumming, Ian Cumming, and Laura Edell, "Policeman as Philosopher, Guide, and Friend," *Social Problems* 12 (1965):285; T. Bercal, "Calls for Police Assistance," *American Behavioral Scientist* 13 (1970):682; Reiss, *The Police and the Public.*

50. George Kelling, Tony Pate, Duane Dieckman, and Charles E. Brown, *The Kansas City Preventive Patrol Experiment: A Summary Report* (Washington, D.C.: Police Foundation, 1974).

51. Peter W. Greenwood, Joan Petersilia, and Jan Chaiken, *The Criminal Investigation Process* (Lexington, Mass.: D.C. Heath, 1977); John E. Eck, *Managing Case Assignments: The Burglary Investigation Decision Model Replication* (Washington, D.C.: Police Executive Research Forum, 1979).

52. Bernard Greenbert, S. Yu Oliver, and Karen Lang, *Enhancement of the Investigative Function, Vol. 1: Analysis and Conclusions, Final Report, Phase 1* (Springfield, Va.: National Technical Information Service, 1973).

53. Kelling, Pate, Dieckman, and Brown, *The Kansas City Preventive Patrol Experiment.*

54. *Ibid.*

55. Joan Petersilia, "The Influence of Research on Policing," in Roger C. Dunham and Geoffrey P. Alpert (eds.), *Critical Issues in Policing: Contemporary Readings* (Prospect Heights, Ill.: Waveland Press, 1989), pp. 230–247.

56. James Q. Wilson, *Thinking About Crime* (New York: Vintage Books, 1975).

57. Herman Goldstein, *Problem-Oriented Policing* (New York: McGraw-Hill, 1990), p. 13.

58. *Ibid.,* p. 3.

59. Thomas J. Baker, "Designing the Job to Motivate," *FBI Law Enforcement Bulletin* 45 (1976):3–7.

60. Samuel Walker, *The Police in America: An Introduction* (2nd ed.) (New York: McGraw-Hill, 1992), p. 185.

61. Police Foundation, *The Newark Foot Patrol Experiment* (Washington, D.C.: Author, 1981).

62. Robert Trojanowicz, *An Evaluation of the Neighborhood Foot Patrol Program in Flint, Michigan* (East Lansing, Mich.: School of Criminal Justice, Michigan State University, 1982).

63. Michael J. Farrell, "The Development of the Community Patrol Officer Program: Community-Oriented Policing in the New York City Police Department," in Jack R. Greene and Stephen D. Mastrofski (eds.), *Community Policing: Rhetoric or Reality* (New York: Praeger, 1988), pp. 73–88.

64. George L. Kelling and Mark H. Moore, *The Evolving Strategy of Policing* (Washington, D.C.: National Institute of Justice, November 1988), p. 14.

65. Robert Trojanowicz and Bonnie Bucqueroux, *Community Policing: A Contemporary Perspective* (Cincinnati, Ohio: Anderson, 1990), p. 67.

66. George Gallup, *Community Policing Survey* (Wilmington, N.Y.: Scholarly Resources, 1996).

67. Willard M. Oliver, "The Third Generation of Community Policing: Moving Through Innovation, Diffusion, and Institutionalization," *Police Quarterly* 3 (December 2000):367–388.

68. *Ibid.*

69. Herman Goldstein, "Improving Policing: A Problem-Oriented Approach," *Crime and Delinquency* 25 (1979):236–258.

70. James Q. Wilson and George L. Kelling, "Broken Windows: The Police and Neighborhood Safety," *Atlantic Monthly* (March 1982):29–38.

71. Samuel Walker, *The Police in America: An Introduction* (New York: McGraw-Hill, 1985).

72. T. McEwen, *National Assessment Program: 1994 Survey Results* (Washington, D.C.: National Institute of Justice, 1995).

73. U.S. Department of Justice, Bureau of Justice Statistics, *Law Enforcement Management and Administrative Statistics: Local Police Departments 2000* (Washington, D.C.: Author, January 2003), p. iii.

74. See, for example, Donna Rogers, "Online Police Resources: How Departmental Web Sites and Internet Services Are Making a Difference," *Law Enforcement Technology* (November 2001):70–74.

75. *Ibid.,* p. 71.

76. Chad Nilson and Tod W. Burke, "Policing by Internet: High Tech Community Policing," *Law and Order* (August 2002):36–39.

77. D. G. Bolgiano, "Military Support of Domestic Law Enforcement Operations: Working Within Posse Comitatus," *FBI Law Enforcement Bulletin* (December 2001):16–24.

78. White House news release, http://www.whitehouse.gov/news/releases/ 2003/10/20031001-4.html (Accessed February 25, 2006).

79. J. Meisler, "The New Frontier of Homeland Security," *Government Technology, Tech Trends 2002: Combined Effort* (August 2002):26–30.

80. Markle Foundation Task Force, *Protecting America's Freedom in the Information Age: A Report of the Markle Foundation Task Force* (New York: Author, 2002), p. 10.

81. Michael E. O'Hanlon, "Homeland Security: How Police Can Intervene," *The Washington Times*, August 18, 2004. http://www.brookings.edu/view/op-ed/ ohanlon/20040818.htm (Accessed February 22, 2006), p. 2.

82. Jose Docobo, "Community Policing as the Primary Prevention Strategy for Homeland Security at the Local Law Enforcement Level," *Homeland Security Affairs* 1(1) (Summer 2005):1.

83. *Ibid.,* 60.

84. *Ibid.,* 2.

85. Wilson and Kelling, "Broken Windows," pp. 29–38.

COPPS

Engaging a Changing Society

Key Terms and Concepts

Communitarianism

Community court

Community engagement

Community policing

Community prosecution

Community service center

Demographics

E-government

Restorative justice

"Second-generation" station house

Social capital

Volunteerism

Learning Objectives

As a result of reading this chapter, the student will:

- Have a grasp of what is meant by "community" and the roles that communitarianism, social capital, and volunteerism play in it
- Know why it is essential for government and the police to view citizens as invaluable customers
- Comprehend the meaning of community policing, and understand how it differs from traditional policing
- Understand the challenges posed to the police by our nation's shifting demographics, immigration patterns, and high technology
- Be familiar with the implications of an aging nation as well as the challenges posed by younger generations of people and the changing nature of crime
- Know what some jurisdictions are doing to make their police station houses more warm, open, and community-oriented

No problem can be solved by the same consciousness that created it. We must learn to see the world anew.

—Albert Einstein

When earth breaks up and heaven expands,
How will the change strike me and you . . . ?

—Robert Browning

INTRODUCTION

What is meant by the word "community," and how do the police go about engaging it? Furthermore, what are some of the major changes our nation is undergoing, and how must the police prepare to deal with them?

This chapter examines those questions, beginning with a look at some of the elements that compose a community. Included in this discussion, and to better understand how our nation and policing have evolved into the current community policing era, we examine one of the basic premises on which that strategy is founded: All agencies of government should view their citizens as invaluable customers and should understand the roles that communitarianism, social capital, and volunteerism play in that view.

Next is a discussion of how agencies of criminal justice are specifically partnering with citizens through community and restorative justice; included here is a look at how units of government are reaching out with community service centers and e-government activities. Then we discuss the point to which all of this has evolved: community oriented policing. This portion of the chapter, together with Chapter 3, composes the heart and soul of the book; we review community policing's basic principles and how this philosophy differs from traditional policing.

Following that is a review of some of the challenges that exist today as police agencies attempt to engage this changing nation, with its demographics, its immigration issues, its aged and its young, and its high technology, as well as deal with the overall nature and fear of crime.

The emergence of **community policing** was discussed in Chapter 1; it is demonstrated in this chapter why the police and the community must partner to engage in crime fighting. We view community policing as inextricably entwined with problem oriented policing—thus this book's theme is community oriented policing and problem solving (COPPS), and all other chapters of this book directly bear on COPPS per se. We do not examine community policing at length here except to describe its tenets and to emphasize how it differs from traditional policing.

It is also important to mention that although the concept of community policing and problem oriented policing (see Chapter 3) are commonly treated as separate and distinct entities, we maintain here and throughout the remainder of the book that they are complementary and integral components. Therefore, in later chapters we will make reference to what we term "community oriented policing and problem solving (COPPS)," which we believe is the most effective and efficient approach to policing now and into the future.

WHAT *Is* COMMUNITY?

Basic Ingredients

This chapter is essentially about community. But what is meant by the term "community," and how do the police interact with it? Those fundamental questions must be addressed before proceeding to discuss how this nation is changing.

First, it is important to note that today's notion of community, under COPPS, is quite different from the traditional view. The traditional community was homogeneous (as will be seen below); today most of us live with heterogeneity. Traditional communities experienced little change from one year to the next, commonly demanded a high degree of conformity, were often unfriendly to strangers, and could boast generations of history and continuity. In short, as much as we may value the memory of the traditional community and its creation of the interlocking networks of community life, today we are building anew. We must seek to reconstruct comparable structures of interdependency in the workplace, the neighborhood, the school, the civic organizations, and so forth.

John Gardner[1] very thoughtfully delineated what he perceived as the six characteristics of a community:

1. *Wholeness incorporating diversity.* In our system, the common good is first of all preservation of a system in which all kinds of people can lawfully pursue their various visions of that concept. A community of diverse elements has greater capacity to adapt and renew itself in a swiftly changing world. But community implies some degree of wholeness; wholeness does not characterize our cities today. They are seriously fragmented, torn by everything from momentary political battles to deep and complex ethnic rifts. But there are a good many cities and nations where markedly heterogeneous populations live and work together peaceably.

2. *Reasonable base of shared values.* There have to be some core shared values. Of all the ingredients of community, this is the most important. The values may be reflected in written laws and rules, in a shared vision of what constitutes the common good. The community teaches, and it imparts a coherent value system. It is the community and culture that hold the individual in a framework of values.

3. *Caring, trust, and teamwork.* The members of a good community deal with one another humanely, respect individual differences, and value the integrity of each person. A good community fosters an atmosphere of cooperation and connectedness, recognizes and gives thanks for hard work, and knows that its citizens need one another. There is a sense of belonging and identity.

4. *Participation.* Our society requires a dispersed network of leaders spread through its every segment. Individuals voluntarily sharing achieve a workable level of unity and motivation. The healthy community has many ways of saying to the individual, "You belong, you have a role to play, and the drama has meaning."

5. *Affirmation.* A healthy community reaffirms itself continuously. It builds its own morale and has confidence in itself. There are always young people to instruct and newcomers to welcome. Individuals are generally members of more than one community, and the communities that survive the competition are likely to be those that press their claims.

6. *Institutional arrangements for community maintenance.* In a city, the most conspicuous arrangements for community maintenance are those we call

government. In a nonprofit organization, it is the board of directors and staff, and perhaps some volunteer committees. There are a number of individuals throughout the system who share leadership tasks on their own initiative, working to maintain group motivation, to heal rifts, and to do volunteer work.

A community's quality of life is obviously determined by its citizens[2]; therefore, it is important that the public be empowered by government to engage in the identification and resolution of neighborhood concerns. It is well established that people act more responsibly when they control their own environments than when they are controlled by others. Empowerment is an American tradition.[3] Citizens should understand their community's problems, and "good citizens make strong communities."[4]

Communitarianism

A concept that has application to policing is **communitarianism.** This term, promulgated by prominent sociologist Amitai Etzioni and other academics, argues that we have gone too far toward extending rights to our citizens and not far enough in asking them to fulfill responsibilities to the community as a whole. Focusing not so much on politics as on the process of government, "it is a mindset that says the whole community needs to take responsibility for itself. People need to actively participate, not just give their opinions . . . but instead give time, energy, and money."[5]

In this view, communitarianism is an attempt to nurture an underlying structure of "civil society"—sound families, caring neighbors, the whole web of churches, Rotary clubs, block associations, and nonprofit organizations that give individuals their moral compass and communities their strength. Communitarians see our political culture as being in very bad shape, not just because elected officials have done a bad job but because citizens have not attended to what citizenship is all about.[6]

Citizen surveys provide police departments with vital information about their performance and citizens' concerns.

Courtesy Reno, Nevada, Police Department.

As a result, communitarians support processes such as problem solving, where neighborhoods have taken matters into their own hands, closing off streets and creating other physical barriers to disrupt the drug trade, working to overcome problems of homelessness and panhandling, and so on. This is where communitarians overlap with the objectives of community problem solving: the recognition that many of the answers to community problems lie not with government but in the community at large.

Social Capital

Social capital concerns those "features of social organization such as networks, norms, and trust that facilitate cooperation or coordination for mutual benefits."[7] In other words, civic participation is essential within American communities. Building partnerships between citizens and police is part of a larger community-building movement that requires high levels of trust and **community engagement.** For example, as will be seen below, making city services more accessible, increasing citizen volunteers in government agencies, and developing neighborhood-based governing organizations have helped to increase problem-solving efforts.[8]

The first and most basic form of social capital is found among members of a family and between citizens within a community. Therefore, the importance of organizing a community cannot be overemphasized; doing so is the most effective way to work against often well-organized adversaries (criminals).

The second level of social capital consists of those social networks tying the individual to broader community institutions: churches, schools, civic and voluntary organizations. These informal associations with other citizens help build familiarity and trust among individuals and keep individuals engaged in communal affairs.

If communities lack strong social cohesion, citizens are not likely to engage in collective activities, and police agencies will have difficulty implementing initiatives that require long-term citizen participation.

Volunteerism

A concept that is related to communitarianism and social capital is the need for greater support for **volunteerism.** It is estimated by Independent Sector, a group that studies and represents nonprofit organizations, that there are now 93 million volunteers in America, donating a stunning 20.3 billion hours of their time—an average of 218 hours per person. Only about 8.4 percent of those 93 million volunteers, however, work in "human services," a broad category that includes aiding the homeless, counseling families, and helping the Red Cross; only about 1.2 percent volunteer as mentors or substance-abuse prevention counselors.[9]

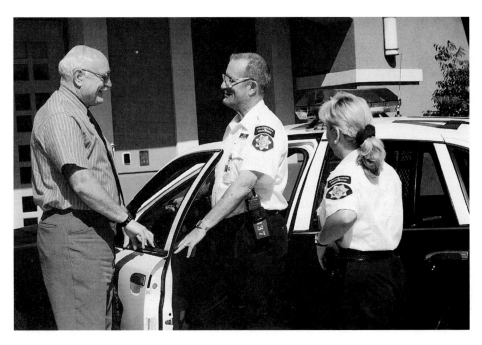

Volunteers provide a vital service to communities.

Courtesy Concord, California, Police Department.

Volunteers are viewed by some as people who do not have anything better to do with their time. Nothing could be further from the truth. Most are simply looking for a meaningful opportunity to contribute and give something back to their communities. Most prefer to have challenging assignments that combine the knowledge and skills they have developed in their professional career with new applications in policing.[10] Volunteering can build a sense of community, break down barriers between people, and raise our quality of life.

Volunteers quickly lose interest if not given meaningful work; therefore, police and other government agencies and nonprofit organizations need to ensure that their volunteers are active. Also, the attitude that "Volunteers who work for free can't be valuable" must be cast aside. Such community efforts as community policing need to be focused and powerful and involve working with other people. This is the form of volunteering that is most likely to get at society's core problems.[11]

Exhibit 2–1 provides an example of how one police agency uses, and benefits from, the public's interest in volunteerism.

The federal government did its part to foster a culture of service, citizenship, and responsibility with the creation of the USA Freedom Corps in 2002. A part of this initiative is the Volunteers in Police Service (VIPS) Program. Managed by the International Association of Chiefs of Police and the U.S. Department of Justice, VIPS has the sole objective of enhancing the capacity of state and local law enforcement agencies to utilize volunteers.[12]

EXHIBIT 2–1

Volunteering in Clearwater, Florida

Located in the extreme west-central part of Florida and having about 108,000 citizens to protect, Clearwater's police force has volunteers ranging from 18 to 82 years of age and brags that it has something for everyone: Homeland security volunteers check the city's infrastructure, government sites, and areas of importance that might be vulnerable to terrorists; administrative volunteers work in the criminal investigation, personnel/training, and records sections; park patrol volunteers are uniformed and check all parks for criminal activity, homeless people and camps, truancy, and other situations; beach and trail patrol volunteers are both uniformed as well, watching the beaches and trails for criminal activity, people in need of assistance, safety hazards, and so forth. In addition, a Quick Response Team is uniformed and available for traffic accidents requiring traffic control, crime scene protection, searches, hurricane details, and other critical situations.

Source: Volunteers in Police Service. http://www.policevolunteers.org/programs/index.cfm?fuseaction=dis_pro_detail&id=940 (Accessed March 3, 2006).

PARTNERS IN COMMUNITY JUSTICE

In today's complex and diverse society, all agencies of criminal justice—not only the police but the courts and corrections organizations as well—understand full well that community engagement is at the core of successful problem solving. Next we examine some of the activities they employ in engaging the public, beginning with a relatively new concept known as restorative justice.

Community and Restorative Justice

Recently, as the police began rethinking their mission and approach, the courts and corrections components also began to change their strategies and approaches to a concept of community justice. Community justice is a new way of thinking about the criminal justice system; it is a systemic approach to public safety, emphasizing problem solving and focusing on community concerns. Increasingly, all segments of society as well as the nation's criminal justice system are realizing that the only viable approach to mediating their problems is community-wide participation and cooperation.[13]

Closely related to the concept of community justice is **restorative justice,** the elements of which include repairing harm (first taking care of the victim who suffered the harm prior to trying to help the offender become a better citizen), reducing risk (managing the offender in such a way that he or she will not commit another crime), and building community (taking responsibility for the behavior of community members and becoming involved in the resolution process, not just turning crime over to

TABLE 2–1

Comparison of Retributive and Restorative Justice	
OLD RETRIBUTIVE JUSTICE	NEW RESTORATIVE JUSTICE
Crime defined as a violation of the state	Crime defined as a violation of one person by another
Focus on blame, guilt, and the past	Focus on problem solving, liabilities, and future obligations
Adversarial relationships	Dialogue and negotiation
Imposition of pain to punish, the goal being deterrence/prevention	Restitution as a means of restoring both parties, the goal being restoration
The community as a passive observer represented by the state	The community as facilitator
A "debt" owed to society	A "debt" to the victim recognized

Source: Adapted from Michael Phillips, "The New Paradigm of Justice," *Government Technology (Special Report: Building Digital Government) in the 21st Century* (February 1, 2001), p. 41.

government to be dealt with). Table 2–1 compares the traditional standard of retributive justice with restorative justice, which concerns active involvement of victims and the community.

Community justice services aim to identify and solve the problems that foster crime and injustice. Next, though, we present some of the means by which the police, courts, and corrections components of the justice system have worked successfully to revitalize their communities.

Police

"Four R's."   It is probably difficult for a police officer who was just kicked, bitten, scratched, and otherwise injured by a citizen to think in terms of collaboration with the public. Nonetheless, the fact remains that most of the people with whom the officer interacts do not conduct themselves in that manner. Moreover, citizens expect and deserve a public servant who is wearing the uniform to provide specific things. The "four R's" that citizens want from their police are reliability, responsiveness, reassurance, and results. Certainly the officer's providing excellent customer service, being a good listener, and using excellent communication skills will go far toward meeting those four desires.[14]

Much has been said above about the need for and the means of community building by the police; Exhibit 2–2 presents a case study of how the police and citizens work together in a true mobilization effort to solve crime and quality-of-life issues and forge an effective alliance.

Now Missing in Some Areas: "Station House Blues."   A relatively new and important way in which some police agencies are engaging in community building involves the design and amenities of their station houses. Generally,

EXHIBIT 2–2

An Example of Community Mobilization

City Heights is an area of San Diego, California, that has a very diverse population of over 60,000 and contains many drug- and youth-related crime problems. City Heights residents expressed their desire for positive changes, but few actively participated in creating those changes. There was a lack of trust between citizens and police, and a fear of retaliation reigned, reinforcing silence, submission, and acceptance of crime and decay. Language barriers, cultural clashes, and lack of knowledge concerning community resources and problem-solving techniques served to further exacerbate the situation. The City Heights Neighborhood Alliance was formed and employed door-to-door outreach and community meetings. Door-to-door outreach involved two community organizers mobilizing residents within a 12-block area; they went to every home and apartment to actively engage residents in a partnership with police to solve crime problems. This effort established connections and familiarity with former strangers and brought out quality-of-life problems. They compiled crime statistics, identified crimes and problem locations, developed flyers to educate residents on the severity and extent of crime in their area, and depicted the state of crisis in the area. Residents were also invited to attend a community meeting to address their concerns. A police officer and a community organizer facilitated the meeting. Over 200 residents received training in problem-solving and community organization skills and met community leaders and governmental officials who could help with their mobilization efforts. Residents solved several community drug problems. They held community meetings in front of the problem locations, contacted property owners, signed petitions, and brought in outside resources such as code compliance and other officials; they also threatened to picket or file lawsuits when necessary. Three community cleanups were held, and a police assistance team moved in to arrest 320 drug dealers.

Source: Rachel Stewart-Brown, "Community Mobilization: The Foundation for Community Policing," *FBI Law Enforcement Bulletin* (June 2001):9–17.

the public areas of most station houses are very stark, cold, unfriendly places. And, as with their dentist, few people go to their police station voluntarily. But some jurisdictions are hoping to change that.

In the Los Angeles Police Department's West Valley station, in Reseda, residents will find ATMs in the light-filled lobby, kitchen-equipped meeting rooms for public use, and even an inviting outdoor courtyard with barbecue facilities. Gone from such **"second-generation" station houses** are the small windows that were located high off the ground to deter drive-by shootings but that made the buildings look like bunkers and armed camps. Such police stations also typically offer more areas that are open to the public (such as cafeterias where officers and civilians can eat together), bigger lobbies where people can comfortably sit, and community rooms where people can hold meetings and training sessions.[15]

In a related vein, later in this chapter we discuss some police uses of the Internet to provide citizens with real-time information concerning officer responses to crimes and other calls for service.

The Los Angeles Police Department's West Valley "second-generation" station house.

Courtesy Los Angeles Police Department. Used with permission.

Courts

Community prosecutors can focus on criminal and civil problems in specific neighborhoods and develop a long-term proactive partnership between their office, police agencies, the community, and public and private organizations. The community prosecutor steps out of the traditional role (see Exhibit 2–3). Instead of reacting to a crime after it happens and a suspect is arrested, he or she uses such tools as nuisance abatement, drug-free and prostitute-free zones, restorative justice (discussed above), truancy abatement, and graffiti cleanup to improve neighborhood safety.[16]

Today about half of all prosecutors' offices practice **community prosecution** in some form, using tools such as those described above to address community problems. The community prosecutor works with police to identify the problems and develop the best responses, whether through administrative means or through **community courts.** As shown in Exhibit 2–3, community prosecutors attend meetings of community groups to become familiar with neighborhood issues, to familiarize residents with the program, and to become familiar with community policing, the major problems officers confront, and the results of their activities; they meet with community leaders, police, and nonprofit social services and health groups; they evaluate data from community surveys; and they create a priority

EXHIBIT 2–3

Community Prosecution in Denver, Colorado

Through community justice councils (which bring stakeholders together to set priorities and develop problem-solving strategies), accountability boards (which use community volunteers to determine restorative sanctions for offenders), and a community court, Denver's district attorney's office has encouraged the community to take an active leadership role in helping to identify crime and quality-of-life problems and to develop strategies for addressing them. One tool is a "connect the dots" exercise, where community prosecution staff meet with neighborhood residents and ask them to discuss local concerns; using large posters listing all the issues raised, citizens place green dots next to any issues they feel are neighborhood problems and place red dots next to the issues they deem the most important. This gives the group a concrete measure of which issues are of greatest collective concern. Denver prosecutors also worked to create a community court that hears youth offenses in a high-crime neighborhood, holding offenders accountable for their behavior while also providing services to them to lessen the likelihood of their reoffending. Community prosecutors also survey residents to decide where to focus their efforts; one such survey resulted in their addressing problems of family violence, drug sales, and alcohol-related crimes.

Source: Robert V. Wolf and John L. Worrall, *Lessons from the Field: Ten Community Prosecution Leadership Profiles* (Alexandria, Va.: American Prosecutors Research Institute, November 2004), pp. 9–15.

list to address the problems.[17] Constitutional issues can be explained at community meetings, and mock trials are conducted to demonstrate the difficulty of establishing proof beyond a reasonable doubt in certain crime situations. Similarly, community prosecutors can advise the police on what they can and cannot do and can provide an alternative channel of communication to citizens to access the legal system.[18]

Defense attorneys know about their clients and the communities from which they come; the staff see their communities as a series of interconnected family networks. Relatives often call the office out of concern for a person's safety as he or she entered the justice system. The program provides a deeper understanding of clients through continuity of representation and better investigation, better presentation of sentencing options through greater connection to community resources, and greater ability to represent residents' support for a less severe sentence.

Community courts can also assume a problem-solving role in the life of a community, helping to craft solutions to problems that communities face. These courts have developed individual programs that differ in important ways, experimenting with a broader range of matters, including juvenile delinquency, mental illness, and housing code violations. They focus on neighborhoods and are designed to respond to particular concerns of their community.[19]

A good example of a community court's activities is the Midtown Community Court in New York City.[20] This court targets quality-of-life offenses such as prostitution, illegal vending, graffiti, shoplifting, fare beating, and vandalism in midtown Manhattan. Residents, businesses, and social service agencies collaborate with the court by supervising projects and providing onsite services, including drug treatment, health care, and job training. Social services located in the court provide the judge with these services as well as a health education class for prostitutes and "johns," counseling for young offenders and mentally ill persons, and employment training. For offenders with lengthier records, the court offers a diversionary program. Many defendants return to court voluntarily to take advantage of these services, including English as a second language and General Educational Development (GED) classes.

Other partnerships that can involve the courts and citizens include child care during trials for victims and witnesses, law-related education, and job training and referral for offenders and victims. A community-focused court can also practice restorative justice, emphasizing the ways in which disputes and crimes adversely affect relationships among community residents, treating parties to a dispute as real individuals rather than abstract legal entities, and using community resources in the adjudication of disputes.[21]

Sentencing low-risk offenders to community work projects is one community-based corrections strategy.

Courtesy Washoe County, Nevada, Sheriff's Office.

Corrections

With the recent spate of domestic violence, stalking, and child sexual abuse crimes, today the public demands more information about offenders (e.g., where they are living and what the criminal justice system is doing with them). As a result, the corrections end of the criminal justice spectrum—probation and parole—is steadily taking on a more visible role in the community policing strategy. Collaborative efforts are being made to make communities safer. Interagency groups monitor offenders who are at risk of committing new offenses and find ways of directing them away from criminal activity while engaging the community in the process. Community corrections officers and police officers are working as teams, with the community as a partner, to provide a range of prevention, intervention, and support services to the offenders. A good example of a collaborative initiative involving corrections and other agencies is provided in Exhibit 2–4.

In other jurisdictions, such as Richmond, Virginia, where 820 probation and parole officers supervise more than 36,000 offenders, officers have frequent interaction with the police and work side by side with community policing officers. One very successful program in Bristol, Virginia, involves a probation and parole services office that opened in a housing project, where officers work closely with local police and simply walk or bicycle through the community, talking with local residents.[22]

Community Service Centers

Beginning in the mid-1980s, when community policing was becoming more widespread, police storefronts also became more popular. Today, however,

EXHIBIT 2–4

Corrections Partners with Others in Ohio

In Richland County, Ohio, a partnership exists between the county adult probation office, sheriff's office, police department (city of Mansfield), and state parole authority, with teams of community policing and community corrections officers conducting major joint operations. They engage in joint inspections of local bars, check for curfew violations, do fugitive surveillance, and perform joint visitations of probationers' and parolees' homes to seek out and question clients for possible violations. Community policing officers handle specific clients, which enhances their familiarity with supervised offenders; likewise, corrections officers supervise offenders in the police department's beat areas, which gives them greater knowledge of the neighborhoods in which their clients reside. Crime statistics reveal a much greater reduction in violent and property crimes in areas where these agencies work together.

Source: David Leitenberger, Pete Semenyna, and Jeffrey B. Spelman, "Community Corrections and Community Policing," *FBI Law Enforcement Bulletin* (November 2003):20–23.

cities are going beyond just using a storefront, instead providing a **community service center** where citizens can do "one-stop shopping" to access government services. In addition to filing police reports or obtaining information, following is a list of some other kinds of services being provided:

- Affordable housing listings
- Alarm permit applications
- Business licenses
- Bus schedules
- City job listings and applications
- Community event information
- Community maps and plans
- Crime prevention information
- Dockets of city council meetings
- Dog license applications
- Notary services
- Park and recreation class and event schedules
- Passport applications
- Permits
- Social service referrals
- Tax forms
- Water bill payments

Police neighborhood resource centers (PNRCs) are also helping to break down barriers between the police department and the community and now offer a wide range of services, such as the following[23]:

- English as a second language (ESL) classes
- School district outreach services
- Mobile public library services
- Blood pressure screenings
- Computer classes
- Purchase of vehicle stickers

E-Government

The Internet is dramatically changing the way government operates—in terms of not only a greater ability of residents or businesses to interact with public agencies but also the manner in which government delivers services: **e-government** at work. Now obtaining information is literally just a click away. Exhibit 2–5 shows some of the kinds of services and information that may be obtained online from the city government in Clearwater, Florida, a community of about 108,000 on the state's west-central coast (see http://www.myclearwater.com/services/index.asp). The Clearwater Police Department uniquely provides an "Active Calls for Service" Web site whereby citizens can, in near real-time terms, see calls

EXHIBIT 2–5

City Home | Information | Services | Activities | **Government** | Employment   Site Map | Español | Contact Us

■ Police Home Page ■ Welcome ■ Active Calls ■ Calendar ■ Contact Police ■ Police Site Map

Police Home

Clearwater Police Department
Sid Klein, Chief of Police

Monday, September 11, 2006

Employment

Administration

Districts & Neighborhoods

Criminal Investigations

Patrol Operations

Support Services

Community Policing

Neighborhood Watch/Crime Prevention

Traffic Enforcement

Records, Reports, & Permits;Crime Data and Maps

Active Calls

Active Cases

Security Alarm Ordinance and Permits

Quality of Service

Laws and Ordinances

AmeriCorps Clearwater

Volunteer

Hispanic Outreach

Hiring Off Duty Officers

Statistical Snapshot

F.A.Q.

History

Memorial

Links

Site Map

Program Highlights:

Child Development-Community Policing (CD-CP)

Published Articles from CPD

Department Awards Program

Citizen Police Academy

Clearwater Homeless Intervention Project

Police Chaplain Program

A Good ACT: Officers Rewarding Kids

CLEARWATER POLICE NEWS

Personal Trainer Charged With Two Counts of Murder
Killed couple in their home; stole cabinet safe...

Blueline CPD Online Interactive Survey
Help us serve you better! Take our new online survey and let us know how we are doing...

Child Development-Community Policing (CD-CP)
An innovative approach to addressing trauma in children exposed to violence...

An Open Letter to Clearwater Police Retirees
If you are retired from CPD, sworn or civilian, please check this important announcement...

News Release Archive...

BLUE INE C.P.D.
Clearwater Police Interactive Television
Next new broadcast Tuesday, September 26, 2006
7:00 p.m. C-VIEW Channel 15
Streaming Video

The Clearwater Police Motorcycle Unit & members of the Honor Guard at the 2006 statewide Police Memorial in Tallahassee

36% of homes have a dog...

...40% of homes have a gun

Watch: Asking Saves Kids
campaign for gun awareness in homes

Subscribe
Clearwater POLICE*Email*
Email news from CPD

BLUE INE C.P.D.
Now in Online Streaming Video

FDLE
Sexual Offender/Predator Database

NEW!

Unsolved Homicides

Missing Persons

Windows:
Broadband
Dial-Up

RealMedia:
Broadband
Dial-Up

Clearwater Police
Web Video

[Previous Page]   [Top of Page]

City Home | Information | Services | Activities | Government | Employment
Site Map | Español | Contact Us | Legal Notices
Page last updated Wednesday, August 30, 2006

Clearwater
©2006 City of Clearwater

Courtesy Clearwater Police Department.

EXHIBIT 2–6

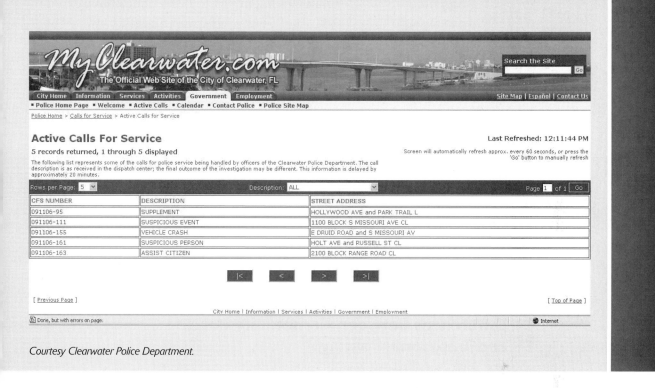

Courtesy Clearwater Police Department.

that are being dispatched to police officers. Exhibit 2–6 shows a display of that screen (it may be viewed at http://www.clearwaterpolice.org/cfs/active.asp). Other Web-based functions are discussed in Chapter 5.

With such services available to them, constituents perceive government as a responsive entity, with greater convenience and ease of use, better and faster information, and a level of service that customers had come to expect only in the private sector.

WHERE ALL THESE ROADS HAVE LED: COMMUNITY POLICING

Basic Principles

As was stated in the Introduction section to this chapter, for several reasons—primarily because all chapters bear directly on community policing, which we term COPPS—we do not examine community policing at length here except to describe its tenets and to emphasize how it differs from traditional policing.

As we noted in Chapter 1, Robert Peel emphasized the police and community working together in the 1820s when setting forth his principles of policing: "The police are the only members of the public who are paid to give full-time attention to duties which are incumbent on every citizen in the interest of the community welfare."[24]

Unfortunately, as Herman Goldstein posited, the police have erred in recent decades by pretending that they could take on, and successfully discharge, all of the responsibilities that are now theirs:

> It is simply not possible for a relatively small group of individuals, however powerful and efficient, to meet those expectations. A community must police itself. The police, at best, can only assist in that task. We are long overdue in recognizing this fact.[25]

In the early 1980s, the notion of community policing emerged as the dominant direction for thinking about policing. It was designed to reunite the police with the community. "It is a philosophy and not a specific tactic; a proactive, decentralized approach, designed to reduce crime, disorder, and fear of crime, by involving the same officer in the same community for a long-term basis."[26] But no single program describes community policing. It has been applied in various forms by police agencies in the United States and abroad and differs according to the community needs, politics, and resources available.

Differences Between Community Policing and Traditional Policing

It is important to understand where community policing departs from traditional policing; the major points of departure may be seen in Table 2–2. Note that the definition, role, priorities, and assessment of the police differ between the two models.

Many past and present practitioners have become staunch proponents of the concept. For example, former Atlanta, Houston, and New York City Chief of Police Lee P. Brown wrote:

> I believe that community policing—the building of problem solving partnerships between the police and those they serve—is the future of American law enforcement. In essence, we are bringing back a modern version of the "cop on the beat." We need to *solve* community problems rather than just *react* to them. It is time to adopt new strategies to address the dramatic increases in crime and the fear of crime. I view community policing as a better, smarter and more cost-effective way of using police resources.[27]

It should be emphasized, however, that community oriented policing can be a long-term process in some tradition-bound agencies, and it involves fundamental institutional change. One scholar warned police managers that "if you approach community oriented policing as a program, you will likely fail. Beware of the trap that seeks guaranteed, perfect, and immediate results."[28]

TABLE 2–2

Traditional Versus Community Policing: Questions and Answers

QUESTION	TRADITIONAL POLICING	COMMUNITY POLICING
Who are the police?	A government agency principally responsible for law enforcement.	Police are the public and the public are the police: The police officers are those who are paid to give full-time attention to the duties of every citizen.
What is the relationship of the police force to other public service departments?	Priorities often conflict.	The police are one department among many responsible for improving the quality of life.
What is the role of the police?	Focusing on solving crimes.	A broad problem-solving approach.
How is police efficiency measured?	By detection and arrest rates.	By the absence of crime and disorder.
What are the highest priorities?	Crimes that are high value (e.g., bank robberies) and those involving violence.	Whatever problems disturb the community most.
With what, specifically, do police deal?	Incidents.	Citizens' problems and concerns.
What determines the effectiveness of police?	Response times.	Public cooperation.
What view do police take of service calls?	Deal with them only if there is no real police work to do.	Vital function and great opportunity.
What is police professionalism?	Swift, effective response to serious crime.	Keeping close to the community.
What kind of intelligence is most important?	Crime intelligence (study of particular crimes or series of crimes).	Criminal intelligence (information about the activities of individuals or groups).
What is the essential nature of police accountability?	Highly centralized; governed by rules, regulations, and policy directives; accountable to the law.	Emphasis on local accountability to community needs.
What is the role of headquarters?	To provide the necessary rules and policy directives.	To preach organizational values.
What is the role of the press liaison department?	To keep the "heat" off operational officers so they can get on with the job.	To coordinate an essential channel of communication with the community.
How do the police regard prosecutions?	As an important goal.	As one tool among many.

Source: Malcolm K. Sparrow, *Implementing Community Policing* (Washington, D.C.: U.S. Department of Justice, National Institute of Justice: U.S. Government Printing Office, November 1988), pp. 8–9.

Community policing goes beyond simply implementing foot and bicycle patrols or neighborhood stations. It redefines the role of the officer on the street, from crime fighter to problem solver and neighborhood ombudsman. If forces a cultural transformation of the entire department, including a decentralized organizational structure and changes in recruiting, training, awards systems, evaluations, promotions, and so forth. Furthermore, this philosophy asks officers to break away from the binds of incident-driven policing and to seek proactive and creative resolution to crime and disorder. To demonstrate the point about community oriented policing and problem solving being different from traditional policing, see Figure 2–1.

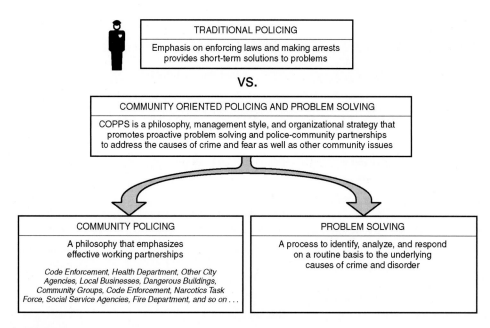

FIGURE 2–1
Traditional Policing Versus Community Oriented Policing, Problem Oriented Policing, and Neighborhood Police Officers.

UNIQUE CHALLENGES: ENGAGING A CHANGING NATION

Certainly the changing demographics and greater heterogeneity of today's America pose unique challenges for the police in terms of engaging the community (discussed above). In this section we examine specifically how America is evolving in terms of its demographics, its aging population, its generational differences, and its technology.

Demographics: Who We Are and How Immigration Influences Us

Although Chapter 10 specifically addresses how the police can engage a diverse society, here we briefly discuss how America is being transformed in terms of its **demographics.** In 2008, about 300 million people will be living in America. Today approximately 80 percent of the population of the United States is white, nearly 13 percent is black, and nearly 7 percent is Asian, Pacific Islander, American Indian, or of two or more races. About one-fourth (26.4 percent) of all households are headed by one person.[29] The mean age of Americans is estimated to be 37.5 years; about one-fourth of the population (27.5 percent) is less than 19 years of age, while about 12.8 percent are over 65.[30]

There is an increasing number of fatherless children in this nation, children who are more often prone to delinquency and other social pathologies.

Of the 72 million children under age 18 living in the United States, about a third (31.4 percent) live where there is either one parent or no parent present in the household (23 percent live with their mother only).[31] Many problems in crime control are strongly related to absence of a father: About 90 percent of all homeless and runaway youths are from fatherless homes, as are 71 percent of high school dropouts, 70 percent of youths in state institutions, 75 percent of adolescent patients in substance abuse centers, and 85 percent of rapists who were motivated by displaced anger.[32]

With the Asian and Hispanic populations being the fastest growing in the United States,[33] the face of America is indeed changing. Each year since 1990, between 600,000 and 1 million aliens have been lawfully admitted into this country for permanent residence.[34] The Hispanic population is projected to increase rapidly over the 1995 to 2025 period, accounting for 44 percent of the growth of the nation's population (32 million Hispanics out of a total of 72 million persons added to the nation's population).[35] Currently the nation's population is 14 percent Hispanic.[36]

The influence of immigration to America and the growth of minority group populations in general cannot be overstated. Certainly many challenges will be posed to our country's infrastructure—and its police organizations—now and in years to come. Exhibit 2–7 discusses the extremely diverse nature of two of the nation's largest cities, Los Angeles and Chicago, and some of the resulting challenges.

Hispanics account for approximately 54 percent of the illegal immigrant population in the United States.

Courtesy Harold Beasley.

EXHIBIT 2–7

A Tale of Two Cities: Los Angeles* And Chicago**

The city of Los Angeles is one of the most diverse cities in the Western Hemisphere. This poses a particular problem for the police in trying to gain voluntary compliance with the law as well as build community partnerships. Many people arrived there from their native lands with myriad different customs and cultural practices, some of which may even be deemed illegal in this country. There are over 112 different nationalities of people and more than 100 different languages spoken. With the Russian-, Armenian-, Korean-, Farsi-, Spanish-, and Thai-speaking communities and their cultural barriers, walls are often created and a lack of cooperation fostered between police and the community, with a distrust among the people of either reporting a crime or stepping forward as a witness.

Chicago is the third most popular destination city for new immigrants. Since the 1990s census, the city has become home to tens of thousands of newly documented immigrants from Mexico alone as well as large numbers of undocumented immigrants. Smaller numbers of immigrants also have arrived from the Middle East, the Philippines, and Poland. The city's Chinatown neighborhood is expanding in several directions, and refugees from Southeast Asia are forming new communities of their own. Members of each group arrive with established views of how to relate to the police and find themselves accommodating these views to a new environment and America's big-city problems.

*Adapted from David Kalish, "West Bureau Community Access Seminars." http://lapdonline.org/community/op_west_bureau6 .htm, p. 1 (Accessed January 29, 2003).

**Adapted from U.S. Department of Justice, National Institute of Justice, *Community Policing and "The New Immigrants": Latinos in Chicago* (Research Report) (Washington, D.C.: Author, July 2002), p. 3.

New Language Technologies. As we have seen above, non-English-speaking people are becoming more commonplace in America. Indeed, according to the National Institute of Justice, one in five U.S. residents speaks a foreign language in his or her home, and only about half of these people can speak English "very well."[37] Therefore, a very valuable tool for the police has been developed to assist with lowering the language barriers they often confront: a voice response translator (VRT). The VRT is a one-way translator that stores a computerized audio file of a complete foreign-language sentence recorded by a fluent speaker of that language. In less than a second, the VRT repeats the command in the desired language. For example, an officer who pulls over a Spanish-speaking motorist might say the trigger phrase, "Too fast." The VRT would instantly repeat the phrase in English for verification and then issue the appropriate full sentence in Spanish. Or an officer might say, "You in pain?" and the VRT will ask the query in Haitian Creole. The VRT is programmed for such common policing matters as traffic stops, domestic problems, lost children, and medical emergencies.[38]

Many police agencies also subscribe to a language bank—a 24-hour on-call service in which officers can dial emergency dispatchers, who in turn locate interpreters to help police in situations where a language barrier

A police officer works with Asian business owners to improve a shopping center that was run-down and was experiencing increased crime.

Courtesy Community Policing Consortium.

exists. For example, recently in Seattle a woman driver struck three parked cars; the officer could not speak Swahili to communicate with her but found someone via the language bank who did. The process allows officers to complete their tasks more effectively.[39]

Graying of America: Implications and Concerns

As indicated above, we live in a "graying" country as well, with 12.4 percent of the total population being at least 65 years old.[40] The golden years for baby boomers represents a graying of the population. The first boomers reached age 50, or midlife, in 1996; soon they will command the aging agenda as they prepare for retirement in 2010 through 2030. The good news is the elderly are less likely than younger people to become victims of violence and are less likely to be injured during a violent crime; only about 2.1 violent crimes per 1,000 are committed against persons over 65 years of age.[41] Elderly victims are more likely to have been killed during the commission of a felony. Furthermore, with brittle bones, when they are injured, their injuries are more severe and their victimization can be permanently disabling. Being on fixed income, they cannot receive the best medical care; most are female. They also have a high fear of crime but are less likely to take protective measures than younger people and more likely to report a crime. They can also be victimized in nursing homes and hospitals, and their relative isolation can lead to a high percentage of their victimization occurring in their homes. They are targeted more often for fraud involving finances than other people, which can lead to severe depression and other serious health problems.[42]

Certainly the police must become more adept at preventing and investigating those types of crimes that tend to target our seniors. Their susceptibility to fraudulent schemes, purse snatchings, theft of checks from the mail, and crimes in long-term care settings poses unique challenges for investigative personnel.

A Generational Divide and Its Effects on Policing

While this nation is "graying," it also has a sizeable youthful contingent that will affect the future of our social fabric and workforce as well as policing and crime. These newer generations of people who were born between 1965 and 1980 have been given their own names: Gen X and Gen Y. Generation X was born between 1965 and 1975; Generation Y was born between 1976 and 1980.[43] The Gen X-ers grew up very quickly amid rising crime rates and violence, as hostage crises and major disasters unfolded around them.[44] They have been maligned by some for being unreliable, not being willing to work long hours, thinking in terms of "job" rather than "career," and having unrealistic expectations about raises and promotions.[45] The Y Generation, or Echo-Boomers, are viewed by some as coddled, confident, and technologically savvy.[46] Gen Y-ers are primarily children of the baby boomers (born between 1946 and 1964), and Gen X cohorts (some of whom are children of what has been referred to as the Silent Generation) are mostly children of retires born between 1925 and 1942. Finally, there are those who have been termed the "New Silent Generation"—a proposed term to describe the generation whose birth years begin in 2001 and continue to an as-yet-unknown year in the future.[47] American society has thus become a playing field of competing viewpoints and values, with these two generations as well as two more—the Silent Generation and the baby boomers—attempting to navigate unknown cultural territory.[48] Clearly, a major challenge and diversity issue in the United States is age diversity. It is obviously important for us to understand the potential for clashes between seasoned and young persons over issues such as work ethic, respect for authority, dress, music, value systems, and so on.

How does this generational divide affect policing? First is the present need to understand the Gen-X and Gen-Y work ethic and workplace needs. Today's employees value time off, are willing to relocate, and want to actively participate in their work role. While the private sector offers flextime, day care, and opportunities for employee input, most police organizations do not lend themselves well to these ideas. The traditional paramilitary, chain-of-command structure can cause friction with today's employees, many of whom are quicker to challenge the status quo and higher authority than earlier generations.[49] Agencies can recruit Gen-X and Gen-Y employees if

EXHIBIT 2–8

The "Digital Divide": Haves and Have-Nots in Information Technologies

Access to the Internet is no longer a luxury; now more than 42 million people per month use the Internet to upgrade job skills, gather medical data, make major financial or investment decisions, or seek a new job. Three-quarters of this nation's households with incomes greater than $75,000 have a computer, however, compared with only one-third of households with incomes between $25,000 and $35,000. This unbalanced access worries people who are serving on a 26-member President's Information Technology Advisory Committee, who have had a lot of discussion on what is called the "digital divide." The committee wants to ensure that economic or geographic barriers do not prohibit anyone from using advanced communication technologies, especially at this point in time when more women and minorities need to be trained for information technology careers. Fortunately, the federal government is investing in information technology in a national Technology Opportunities Program that established Community Technology Centers (CTCs) so that low-income people can access digital technology and the Internet; in fiscal years 2002 and 2003, nearly $50 million in funding was awarded by Congress for this purpose.

More information about CTCs and their funding can be found at http://www.ed.gov/offices/ovae/adulted/ctc/ (Accessed April 28, 2003).

they are more willing to examine their policies and structure in light of this new work ethic.

High Technology

The world has rapidly become more technological; today more than 311 million English-speaking people as well as 500 million non-English-speaking people use the Internet.[50] The ability to produce and analyze information has become very important to our country economically in terms of a person's social standing or ability to get a job.

Yet there exists what can be termed a serious "digital divide" (see Exhibit 2–8). "Smokestack America" is largely gone; today there are fewer blue-collar jobs and more white-collar positions. The fastest-growing careers are those requiring more language, mathematics, and reasoning skills. In sum, today's economy is based on knowledge and the ability to process information; whereas employers in the past mostly wanted muscle, today more and more jobs presuppose skills, training, and education.

SHIFTS IN CRIME

As with challenges to the police that are caused by alterations in our demographics, so are the police being challenged by shifts in criminal behavior. While we will discuss in Chapters 11 and 12 how problems involving gangs, drugs, and other crimes are being addressed under COPPS, here we mention in more general terms the violent nature of our society and our fear of being victimized.

Violent Venue

The rate of serious violent crimes in the United States fell from 1993 to 2006 (in the latter year, the overall number of violent offenses rose 2.5 percent). Certainly the overall aging of the population, longer prison sentences for habitual offenders, and a relatively healthy economy contributed to that overall decline. More and more, however, experts are also pointing to community oriented policing and problem solving as prominent reasons for the decreases.

Notwithstanding that crime rates have generally been dropping in the United States, the fact remains that we reside in a violent country. It would seem that John Bunyan understood the human capacity for violence in 1686 when in his *Book for Boys and Girls* he wrote:

> Children become, while little, our delights,
>
> When they grow bigger, they begin to fright's.
>
> Their sinful Nature prompts them to rebel,
>
> And to delight in Paths that lead to Hell.[51]

One only need look at the television, read the newspapers, or (in some cases) merely look in their own neighborhoods to realize that life and the property of others are almost valueless to a large number of Americans. Following are some all-too-typical crime news accounts occurring in the nation. These incidents reflect the kinds of crimes that are reported with startling regularity across the country each year:

- A 17-year-old Illinois girl faces up to 60 years in prison for killing a classmate whose body was beaten, burned, and sawed into pieces after an argument over boys.[52]
- A 15-year-old Georgia girl decided in mid-2004 that she had enough of living with her grandparents, both in their 70s, nor did she wish to give up seeing her girlfriend, whom her grandparents had forbidden her to see. The two girls attacked and killed the grandparents, administering a total of 35 stab wounds.[53]
- Santa Ana, California, police arrested two brothers, ages 15 and 20, suspected of killing their mother and trying to escape detection by chopping off her head and hands the way they had seen it done on "The Sopranos."[54]
- In a Queens, New York, park, a gang of six homeless men dragged a woman into their squalid encampment, raping and beating her for two hours; she sued the city for $50 million, saying the city failed to "take proper action" to make the area safe.[55]

According to the National Crime Victimization Survey, there are about 5.2 million violent crimes and 18.6 million property crimes committed

While juvenile crime has been declining, concern about youth crime and violence continues.

Courtesy Washoe County, Nevada, Sheriff's Office.

annually in this country.[56] Americans now spend about $167 billion per year for federal, state, and local criminal justice activities (including law enforcement, courts, and corrections agencies). Nearly half (about $70 billion) of this amount is for police protection, while about $38 billion is for the courts and $58 billion is for corrections.[57] On any given day, there are about 2,135,900 million persons incarcerated in this nation's prisons and jails; state and federal prisons hold about 1.47 million inmates, while local jails hold about 714,000 men and women.[58]

A number of factors contribute to criminality: immediate access to firearms, alcohol and substance abuse, gangs, drug trafficking (gangs and drugs are discussed more fully in Chapter 11), poverty, racial discrimination, and cultural acceptance of violent behavior.[59]

Fear of Crime

Crime, fear, and disorder frighten Americans. More than one-third (36 percent) of all Americans fear walking alone at night within a mile of where they live.[60] The fear of crime is also the number one factor keeping business out of high-poverty neighborhoods.[61]

We know that neighborhood disorder affects a person's perception of safety as much as crime does. People express greater fear of strangers loitering near their homes than they do the threat of murder. They fear being bothered by people they view as sinister: panhandlers, drunks, addicts, rowdy teens, mental patients, and the homeless. They also fear physical disorder: litter, abandoned buildings, potholes, broken streetlights and windows, wrecked cars, and other indicators of neighborhood decline.

Thomas Hobbes wrote in 1651 that the "fundamental purpose of civil government is to establish order, protecting citizens from a fear of criminal attack that can make life nasty, brutish, and short."[62] It would appear,

Drunks, panhandlers, and the homeless add to people's perceptions of safety as much as do actual crimes.

using this Hobbesian scale, that "the current level and distribution of fear indicate an important government failure."[63] For the past 30 years, the dominant police strategy has emphasized motorized patrol, rapid response time, and retrospective investigation of crimes. Those strategies were not designed to address root community problems but instead targeted criminal detection and apprehension—the "crime fighter" cop.

▲ SUMMARY

This chapter has defined what is meant by "community," demonstrated several means by which the police and other justice organizations are partnering with the community, and shown why COPPS offers the best hope for meeting the challenges posed to justice agencies and communities. Also discussed were several means by which government entities are expanding their community building and customer service through the Internet.

We examined a number of changes that are occurring in America, particularly with respect to the nature of its people and their crimes. While violent crime has been declining of late, the years ahead certainly may not be tranquil. We cannot afford to hurtle into the future with our eyes fixed firmly on the rearview mirror. Social, political, and economic events of today will cause policing to change forever. A failure to anticipate and plan for what many people predict will be a turbulent and complex future could produce untenable consequences. "Business as usual" will probably not suffice.

ITEMS FOR REVIEW

1. Explain what is meant by "community," including its ingredients and the roles that communitarianism, social capital, and volunteerism play in it.
2. Describe why it is essential for government and the police to view citizens as invaluable customers.
3. Compare the ways in which community policing differs from traditional policing.
4. Review the challenges posed to the police by our nation's shifting demographics, immigration patterns, and use of high technology.
5. Outline the implications of an aging nation as well as the challenges posed by younger generations of people and the changing nature of crime.
6. Explain the kinds of characteristics of a "second-generation" police station house that serve to make it more warm, open, and community-oriented.

NOTES

1. John Gardner, "Building a Responsive Community," in Ronald W. Glensor, Mark E. Correia, and Kenneth J. Peak (eds.), *Policing Communities: Understanding Crime and Solving Problems* (Los Angeles: Roxbury, 2000), pp. 67–74.
2. David Couper and Sabine Lobitz, *Quality Policing: The Madison Experience* (Washington, D.C.: Police Executive Research Forum, 1991), p. 65.
3. David Osborne and Ted Gaebler, *Reinventing Government: How the Entrepreneurial Spirit Is Transforming the Public Sector* (Reading, Mass.: Addison-Wesley, 1992), p. 51.
4. Tom Dewar, quoted in David A. Lanegran, Cynthia Seelhammer, and Amy L. Walgrave (eds.), *The Saint Paul Experiment: Initiatives of the Latimer Administration* (St. Paul, Minn.: City of St. Paul, 1989), p. xxii.
5. Rob Gurwitt, "Communitarianism: You Can Try It at Home," *Governing* 6 (August 1993):33–39.
6. *Ibid.,* 39.
7. R. Putnam, "Tuning in, Tuning Out: The Strange Disappearance of Social Capital in America," *Political Science and Politics* (December 1995):664–683.
8. Mark E. Correia, "Social Capital and Sense of Community Building: Building Social Cohesion," in Ronald W. Glensor, Mark E. Correia, and Kenneth J. Peak (eds.), *Policing Communities: Understanding Crime and Solving Problems* (Los Angeles: Roxbury, 2000), pp. 75–82.
9. Michael J. Gerson, "Do Do-Gooders Do Much Good?" *U.S. News & World Report* (April 28, 1997), p. 27.
10. Karen Siemsen, "For a Full Menu of Policing Services, Partner with Volunteers," *Community Policing Exchange* (September/October 1998):8.
11. *Ibid.,* 33–34.
12. Volunteers in Police Service, "About VIPS," http://www.policevolunteers.org/about (Accessed March 4, 2006).

13. Laurie J. Wilson, "Placing Community-Oriented Policing in the Broader Realms of Community Cooperation," *The Police Chief* (April 1995):127.

14. Gerald W. Garner, "Exceptional Customer Service," *Law and Order* (June 2003):103–106.

15. Sheila Muto, "Arresting Design: Police Stations Get a Lift," *The Wall Street Journal* (January 5, 2005), p. B-1.

16. American Prosecutors Research Institute and the National District Attorneys Association, "What Is Community Prosecution?" http://www.ndaa-apri/programs/community_pros/whis_is_community_prosecution.html (Accessed March 3, 2006).

17. Karen McDonough, "Oceanside's Community Prosecution," *Law and Order* (August 2002):114–116.

18. U.S. Department of Justice, National Institute of Justice, *Community Prosecution in Washington, D.C.: The U.S. Attorney's Fifth District Pilot Project* (Washington, D.C.: Author, April 2001), pp. 14, 34.

19. U.S. Department of Justice, Office of Justice Programs, *Community Courts: An Evolving Model* (Washington, D.C.: Author, October 2000).

20. *Ibid.*

21. *Ibid.*, pp. 46–51.

22. Ray Arp, "COPPS: Crossing Over Boundary Lines," *Community Policing Exchange* (May/June 1999):5.

23. See, for example, the Des Plaines, Illinois, Web site, http://www.desplaines.org/Services/Police/PNRC.htm (Accessed March 3, 2006).

24. W. L. Melville Lee, *A History of Police in England* (London: Methuen, 1901), Chapter 12.

25. Herman Goldstein, "Toward Community-Oriented Policing: Potential, Basic Requirements, and Threshold Questions," *Crime and Delinquency* 33 (1987):17.

26. Robert Trojanowicz and Bonnie Bucqueroux, *Community Policing: A Contemporary Perspective* (Cincinnati, Ohio: Anderson, 1990), p. 154.

27. Lee P. Brown, "Community Policing: Its Time Has Come," *The Police Chief* 62 (September 1991):10.

28. Jerald R. Vaughn, *Community-Oriented Policing: You Can Make It Happen* (Clearwater, Fla.: National Law Enforcement Leadership Institute, no date), p. 8.

29. U.S. Census Bureau, "U.S. and World Population Clocks—POPClocks," http://www.census.gov//main/www/popclock.html (Accessed February 24, 2006); also see U.S. Census Bureau, "Population Projections for States by Age, Sex, Race, and Hispanic Origin: 1995–2025," http://www.census.gov/population/www/projections/pp147.html (Accessed February 22, 2006).

30. *Ibid.*; also see U.S. Census Bureau, "United States—Fact Sheet—American FactFinder." http://factfinder.census.gov/servlet/ACSSAFFFacts?_event=&geo_id=01000US&_geo (Accessed February 23, 2006).

31. U.S. Census Bureau, *Population Profile of the United States: Living Arrangements of Children in 2002* (Washington, D.C.: Author, 2003), p. 1.

32. U.S. Census Bureau, *Statistics in Brief: Population and Vital Statistics* (Washington, D.C.: Author, 2000), pp. 13–16.

33. U.S. Citizenship and Immigration Services, "Immigrants," in *2003 Yearbook of Immigration Statistics,* http://uscis.gov/graphics/shared/aboutus/statistics/IMM03yrbk/2003IMM.pdf (Accessed February 23, 2006).

34. *Ibid.,* p. 6.

35. Pearson Education, Information Please Database, "Population of the United States by Race and Hispanic/Latino Origin, Census 2000 and July 1, 2004," http://www.infoplease.com/ipa/A0762156.html (Accessed February 23, 2006).

36. U.S. Census Bureau, "Population Projections for States by Age, Sex, Race, and Hispanic Origin."

37. Mark P. Cohen, "The Voice Response Translator: A Valuable Police Tool," http://www.ojp.usdoj.gov/nij/journals/252/voice_response.html (Accessed April 11, 2006).

38. *Ibid.*

39. Margaret Taus, "Finding the Words to Increase Trust in a Diverse Community," http://seattlepi.nwsource.com/local/35942_lang21.shtml (Accessed April 11, 2006).

40. U.S. Census Bureau, "USA Statistics in Brief: Population by Sex, Age, and Region," http://www.census.gov/statab/www/pop.html (Accessed February 22, 2006).

41. U.S. Department of Justice, Bureau of Justice Statistics, "Violent Victimization Rates by Age, 1973–2004," http://www.ojp.usdoj.gov/bjs/glance/tables/vagetab.htm (Accessed February 25, 2006).

42. Andrew Karmen, *Crime Victims: An Introduction to Victimology* (6th ed.) (Belmont, Calif.: Wadsworth, 2006), p. 228.

43. "Stephen's Generation X Site," http://www.metro2000.net/-stabbott/genxintro.htm (Accessed February 3, 2005).

44. Dan King, "Defining a Generation: Tips for Uniting Our Multi-Generational Workforce," http://www.careerfirm.com/generations.htm (Accessed February 3, 2005).

45. Claire Raines, "Managing Generation X," http://www.generationsatwork.com/articles/genx.htm (Accessed February 3, 2005).

46. *Ibid.,* p. 2.

47. Wikipedia, "New Silent Generation," http://en.wikipedia.org/wiki/Generation_z (Accessed April 11, 2006).

48. King, "Defining a Generation," p. 1.

49. Troy Mineard, "Recruiting and Retaining Gen-X Officers," *Law and Order* (July 2003):94–95.

50. "Internet World Stats: Usage and Population Statistics," http://www.internetworldstats.com/stats7.htm (Accessed February 23, 2006).

51. John Bunyan, *A Book for Boys and Girls: Or, Country Rhimes for Children* (London: N. P., 1686), pp. 71–73.

52. Yahoo! News, "Teenage Girl Convicted in Ill. Killing," http://news.yahoo.com/s/ap/20060222.ap_on_re_us/teen_dismembered_trial&printer (Accessed February 27, 2006).

53. CourtTV, Crime Library: Criminal Minds and Methods, "Killer Teen Couples," http://www.crimelibrary.com/features/fea_printPage.asp?curPage=&thisFile=notorious (Accessed February 27, 2006).

54. Mid-Day Multimedia Lt., "Sopranos Inspires Teens to Kill Their Mom," http://www.mid-day.com/news/world/2003/january/42893.htm (Accessed February 27, 2006).

55. *Newsday* (March 6, 2003) "Rape Victim to Sue the City of New York, Seeking $50 Million," http://www.newsday.com/mynews/ny-nyrape053157790mar05 .story (Accessed February 27, 2006).

56. U.S. Department of Justice, Bureau of Justice Statistics, "National Crime Victimization Survey," *Criminal Victimization, 2004* (Washington, D.C.: Author, September 2005), p. 1.

57. U.S. Department of Justice, Bureau of Justice Statistics, "Expenditure and Employment Statistics," http://www.ojp.usdoj.gov/bjs/eande.htm (Accessed February 27, 2006).

58. U.S. Department of Justice, Bureau of Justice Statistics, "U.S. Prison Population Approaches 1.5 Million," http://www.ojp.usdoj.gov/bjs/pub/press/p03pr.htm (Accessed February 27, 2006).

59. Lee P. Brown, "Violent Crime and Community Involvement," *FBI Law Enforcement Bulletin* (May 1992):2–5.

60. The Gallup Organization, "The Gallup Poll," http://www.gallup.com/poll/ (Accessed February 27, 2006).

61. See James K. Stewart, "The Urban Strangler: How Crime Causes Poverty in the Inner City," *Policy Review* (Summer 1986):6.

62. Thomas Hobbes, "Leviathan," in C. B. Macpherson (ed.), *Leviathan* (Baltimore, Md.: Pelican Books), p. 5.

63. Mark H. Moore and Robert C. Trojanowicz, *Policing and the Fear of Crime* (Washington, D.C.: National Institute of Justice, 1988), p. 2.

COPPS

Problem Oriented Policing

Key Terms and Concepts

Analysis

Assessment

Controller

Guardian

Manager

Problem analysis triangle

Problem oriented policing (POP)

Problem solving

Response

Scanning

Situational policing

Learning Objectives

As a result of reading this chapter, the student will:

- Comprehend the development of problem solving for the police
- Be aware of the basic principles of problem oriented policing and how it differs from incident-driven policing
- Understand the four steps in the S.A.R.A. problem-solving process
- Be able to explain the potential difficulties with problem solving
- Recognize the three identifiable stages of neighborhoods
- Understand the four different types of neighborhoods
- Know the meaning of situational policing

It seemed that the next minute they would discover a solution. Yet it was clear to them that the end was still far, far off, and that the hardest and most complicated part was only just beginning.

–Anton Chekov

INTRODUCTION

In this chapter we analyze problem oriented policing: its origin, the broadened role of the street officer, and the four-stage problem-solving process. Included in this discussion is an overview of some possible difficulties that are involved with problem solving and how differing types of neighborhoods may require different approaches by the police in terms of problem-solving strategies.

As we noted in Chapter 2, although the concept of community policing and the subject of this chapter, problem oriented policing, are commonly treated as separate and distinct, we maintain here and throughout the remainder of the book that they are complementary core components. Therefore, as stated in Chapter 2 as well as in this and later chapters, we believe the term "community oriented policing and problem solving (COPPS)," to be the most effective and efficient approach to policing for the future.

Note that important adjuncts to this chapter's discussion of problem solving are situational crime prevention (e.g., crime prevention through environmental design, or CPTED) and technology, crime analysis, and mapping, all of which are addressed in Chapters 4 and 5.

PROBLEM SOLVING

Early Beginnings

Problem solving is not new; police officers have always tried to solve problems (we define the word "problem" below). The difference is that, in the past, officers who were dealing with problems received little guidance, support, or technology from police administrators. The routine application of problem-solving techniques is new. It is based on two facts: that problem solving can be applied by officers throughout the agency as part of their daily work and that routine problem-solving efforts can be effective in reducing or resolving problems.

Problem oriented policing (POP) was grounded in different principles than community oriented policing (COP), but they are complementary. POP is a strategy that puts the COP philosophy into practice. It advocates that police examine the underlying causes of recurring incidents of crime and disorder. The problem-solving process, discussed in later chapters, helps officers to identify problems, analyze them completely, develop response strategies, and assess the results.

Herman Goldstein is considered by many to be the principal architect of POP. His book, *Policing a Free Society* (1977),[1] is among the most frequently cited works in police literature. A later work, *Problem Oriented Policing* (1990),[2] provided a rich and complete exploration of POP. Goldstein first coined the term "problem oriented policing" in 1979 out of frustration with the dominant model for improving police operations: "More attention

[was] being focused on how quickly officers responded to a call than on what they did when they got to their destination."[3] He also bemoaned the linkage between the police and the telephone: "The telephone, more than any public or internal policy, dictates what a police agency does. And that problem has been greatly aggravated with the installation of 911."[4]

As a result, Goldstein argued for a radical change in the direction of efforts to improve policing—a new framework that should help move the police from their past preoccupation with form and process to a much more direct, thoughtful concern with substantive problems. To focus attention on the nature of police business and to improve the quality of police response in the course of their business, Goldstein argued that several steps must be taken[5]:

1. Police must be equipped to define more clearly and to understand more fully the problems they are expected to handle. They must recognize the relationships between and among incidents—for example, incidents involving the same behavior, the same address, or the same people.

2. The police must develop a commitment to analyzing problems. It requires gathering information from police files, from the minds of experienced officers, from other agencies of government, and from private sources as well. It requires conducting house-to-house surveys and talking with victims, complainants, and offenders.

3. Police must be encouraged to conduct an uninhibited search for the most effective response to each problem, looking beyond just the criminal justice system to a wide range of alternatives; they must try to design a customized response that holds the greatest potential for dealing effectively with a specific problem in a specific place under specific conditions.

Basic Principles

In earlier chapters we mentioned the limitations of traditional methods of policing in trying to deal with incidents. The first step in POP, therefore, is to move beyond just handling incidents, recognizing that incidents are often merely overt symptoms of problems. It requires that officers take a more in-depth interest in incidents by acquainting themselves with some of the conditions and factors that cause them. Everyone in the department contributes to this mission, not just a few innovative officers or a special unit or function.[6]

Figure 3–1 shows incident-driven policing as it attempts to deal with each incident. Like band-aid application, this symptomatic relief is valuable but limited. Because police leave unresolved the underlying condition that created the incidents, the incident is very likely to occur.

A problem-oriented police agency would respond as described in Figure 3–2. Officers use the information in their responses to incidents, along with information obtained from other sources, to get a clearer picture of the problem. Then they address the underlying conditions. As James Fyfe asked, "Can anyone imagine the surgeon general urging doctors to attack AIDS without giving any thought to its causes?"[7] If successful,

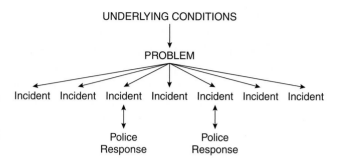

FIGURE 3–1
Incident-Driven Policing

Source: John E. Eck and William Spelman, *Problem-Solving: Problem-Oriented Policing in Newport News* (Washington, D.C.: U.S. Department of Justice, National Institute of Justice, 1987), p. 4.

fewer incidents may occur; those that do occur may be less serious. The incidents may even cease.[8]

The problem-oriented approach also addresses a major dilemma for the police: the lack of meaningful measures of their effectiveness in the area of crime and disorder. Crime rate statistics are virtually useless because they collapse all the different kinds of crime into one global category and are an imperfect measure of the actual incidence of criminal behavior.[9] Goldstein also maintained that the police should "disaggregate" the different problems they face and then attempt to develop strategies to address each one.[10] Domestic disturbances, for instance, should be separated from public intoxication; murder should be separated from sexual assault. In this respect, POP is primarily a *planning process*.

Broader Role for the Street Officer

A major departure of POP from the conventional style lies with its view of the line officer, who is given much more discretion and decision-making

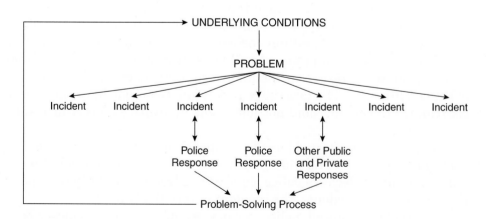

FIGURE 3–2
Problem Oriented Policing

Source: John E. Eck and William Spelman, *Problem-Solving: Problem-Oriented Policing in Newport News* (Washington, D.C.: U.S. Department of Justice, National Institute of Justice, 1987), p. 4.

ability and is trusted with a much broader array of responsibilities. POP values thinking officers, urging that they take the initiative in trying to deal more effectively with problems in the areas they serve. This concept more effectively uses the potential of college-educated officers, "who have been smothered in the atmosphere of traditional policing."[11] It also gives officers a new sense of identity and self-respect; they are more challenged and have opportunities to follow through on individual cases, to analyze and solve problems, which will give them greater job satisfaction. We ought to be recruiting as police officers people who can "serve as mediators, as dispensers of information, and as community organizers."[12]

Under POP, officers continue to handle calls, but they also do much more. They use the information gathered in their responses to incidents together with information obtained from other sources to get a clearer picture of the problem. They then address the underlying conditions.

S.A.R.A.: THE PROBLEM-SOLVING PROCESS

A four-stage problem-solving process has been developed and is known as "S.A.R.A.," for *scanning, analysis, response,* and *assessment.*[13] This process is depicted in Figure 3–3.

Scanning: Problem Identification

Scanning means problem identification. As a first step, officers should identify problems on their beats and then look for a pattern or persistent repeat incidents. At this juncture the question might well be asked, "What is a 'problem'?" A problem has been defined this way: A group of two or more incidents that are similar in one or more respects, causing harm and therefore being of concern to the police and the public.

Incidents may be similar in various ways:

- *Behaviors.* A pattern of behavior is the most frequent type of indicator and includes such activities as drug sales, robberies, thefts, and graffiti.
- *Locations.* Problems occur in hot spots, such as downtown cruising areas, housing complexes plagued by burglaries, and parks where gangs commit crimes.

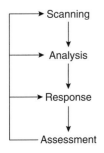

FIGURE 3–3
A Problem-Solving Process

Source: John E. Eck and William Spelman, *Problem-Solving: Problem-Oriented Policing in Newport News* (Washington, D.C.: U.S. Department of Justice, National Institute of Justice, 1987), p. 43.

- *Persons*. They can be repeat offenders or victims; both account for a high proportion of crime.
- *Times*. There may be a time pattern (e.g., seasonal, day of week, hour of day) due to traffic congestion, closing times for bars, or tourist activity.
- *Events*. Crimes may peak during such events as university spring breaks, rallies, and rock concerts.

There does not appear to be any limit to the types of problems patrol officers can work on; there are several types of problems that are appropriate for problem solving. The following list demonstrates the diversity of problems identified and addressed in several jurisdictions[14]:

- Series of burglaries from trailers at a construction site
- Drug activity, drinking, and disorderly conduct at a community park
- Suspected drug activity at a private residence
- Thefts from autos at a shopping mall
- Juvenile loitering at a shopping center and near a bar
- Vagrants panhandling downtown
- Problems with false and faulty alarms at commercial addresses
- Parking and traffic problems
- Street prostitution and related robberies in a downtown neighborhood
- High rate of burglaries at a run-down apartment complex
- Repeat domestic assault calls to certain addresses

If the incidents police are responding to do not fall within the definition of a problem, then the problem-solving model is not applicable. The police should handle the incident according to normal procedures.

There are numerous resources available to the police to identify problems, including calls for service (CFS) data, especially repeat calls from the same location or a series of similar incidents. Other ways are through citizen complaints, census data, data from other government agencies, and media coverage of community issues, officer observations, and community surveys.

The primary purpose of scanning is to conduct a preliminary inquiry to determine if a problem really exists and whether further analysis is needed. During this stage, priorities should be established if multiple problems exist and a specific officer or team of officers assigned to handle the problem. Scanning initiates the problem-solving process.

Analysis: Heart of Problem Solving

The second stage, **analysis,** is the heart of the problem-solving process. For this reason, we will dwell on it at greater length. Comprehensively analyzing a problem is critical to the success of a problem-solving effort. Effective tailor-made responses cannot be developed unless people know what is causing the problem. Thus, the purpose of analysis is to learn as much as possible about problems in order to identify their causes; officers must gather information from sources inside and outside their agency about the scope, nature, and causes of problems.

Researching a Problem.   One will greatly reduce the time spent searching for information about a problem if the problem is tightly defined. An Internet search might yield hundreds of results. The best way to begin is by visiting Web sites that are most likely to contain the kinds of information that one is seeking. Following are some that would be very useful for searches relating to COPPS:

- Center for Problem-Oriented Policing (www.popcenter.org). The center is the first place to look for information concerning how to address problems of crime and disorder; it has myriad resources to draw from, including dozens of problem-oriented guides that show means of addressing problems of crime and disorder.
- Community Policing Consortium (www.communitypolicing.org). The consortium is funded by the above-mentioned COPS Office and is a training partnership of five of the nation's leading law enforcement organizations. Its mission is to deliver COPPS training, and its Web site's electronic library contains many publications and reports.
- National Criminal Justice Reference Service (NCJRS) (http://abstractsdb .ncjrs.org). This is an information clearinghouse created by the U.S. Department of Justice for people involved in research, policy, and practice; the Web site includes an online tutorial on how to search its abstracts.
- Office of Community Oriented Policing Services (COPS Office) (www.cops .usdoj.gov). This office funds the aforementioned Center for Problem-Oriented Policing; its Web site allows you to download or order COPS publications, and it has links to regional community policing institutes (RCPIs).
- Police Executive Research Forum (PERF) (www.policeforum.org). PERF is a national membership organization of police executives from large law enforcement agencies. Its Web site may be entered by a guest or a member. It contains POPNet, a searchable database of COPPS projects.

Other sources to be sought out for information on problem solving would include the Police Foundation (www.policefoundation.org), the International Association of Chiefs of Police (IACP) (www.theiacp.org), the RAND Public Safety and Justice Center (www.rand.org/psi), and the *FBI Law Enforcement Bulletin* (www.fbi.gov/publications/leb/htm).

Determining the Nature and Extent of the Problem.   A complete analysis includes identifying the seriousness of the problem, all the persons/groups involved and affected, and all the causes of the problem and then assessing current responses and their effectiveness. Many people essentially skip the analysis phase of S.A.R.A., believing that the nature of the problem is obvious, succumbing to pressure to quickly solve the problem, or feeling that the pressure of CFS precludes their having time for detailed inquiries into the nature of the problem. Problem solvers must resist these

An abandoned residence vandalized with gang graffiti shows how quickly a neighborhood may decline.

Courtesy Sgt. Dominic Licavoli, LAPD.

temptations, or they risk addressing a problem that does not exist and/or implementing solutions that are ineffective in the long run.

For example, computer-assisted dispatch (CAD) data in one southeastern police department indicated that there was a large auto theft problem at a local shopping mall. However, after reviewing incident reports and other records, it became clear that many of the reported "thefts" actually involved shoppers misplacing their cars and then mistakenly reporting them as stolen.[15]

Identifying the Harms.   A discussion of harms is important to analyzing problems and responding to them. The problem of gangs serves as an example. We must begin by asking, Why are gangs a problem? We can find the answer to this question by focusing on harmful behaviors. Not all gang members are criminals or engage in harmful behaviors. It is therefore important that each community examine the behaviors of its gangs, determine which behaviors are harmful, and design responses appropriate to deal with those behaviors.

Common gang behaviors may include wearing "colors," spreading graffiti, being involved in drug use and sales, and having a threatening presence. For example, the wearing of colors to school creates fear among students and teachers and may result in fights between rival gang members.

These behaviors present harm to the community and should be the focus of police problem-solving efforts. By identifying harmful behaviors, gangs—a huge nondescriptive term/problem—are broken down into smaller, more manageable problems. This helps to identify the underlying causes or related conditions that contribute to illegal gang activity and is the basis for officers' responses.

Seeking "Small Wins."   Karl Weick explained that people often look at social problems on a massive scale.[16] The public, media, elected officials, and government agencies often become fixated on problems and define

Motels converted to daily and weekly rentals often result in an increase in calls for service and crimes in the area.

them by using the simplest term (gangs, homelessness, poverty, mental illness, violent crime, and so on). Viewing problems in this manner leads to defining problems on a scale so massive that they are unable to be addressed and people become overwhelmed in their attempts. For this reason, Weick introduced the "small wins" concept. One must understand that some problems are too deeply ingrained or too rooted in other complex social problems to be eliminated. Conversely, however, adopting the small wins philosophy helps people to understand the nature of an analysis and a response to problems.

As indicated above, the more appropriate response to these problems is to break them down into smaller, more controllable problems. Although an individual small win may not seem important, a series of small wins may have a substantial impact on the overall problem. Eliminating the harms (graffiti, drug sales, and so on) is a sensible and realistic strategy for reducing the impact of gang behaviors. Therefore, it makes sense to address a large problem at a level where there can be a reasonable expectation of success.

The idea of small wins is also helpful when prioritizing problems and working together in a group. We have discussed the benefits of collaborating with the community and other outside agencies to address problems. Small wins can help the group understand the problem better, select realistic objectives, and formulate more effective strategies. It also helps to build confidence and trust among group members.

Using the Problem Analysis Triangle.   Generally, three elements are needed for a problem to occur: an offender, a victim, and a location. The **problem analysis triangle** helps officers visualize the problem and understand the relationship between these three elements. Additionally, it helps officers to analyze problems, it suggests where more information is needed, and it assists with crime control and prevention.

The relationship between these three elements can be explained as follows. If there is a victim and he or she is in a place where crimes occur but there is no offender, no crime occurs. If there is an offender and he or she is in a place where crimes occur but there is nothing or no one to be victimized, then no crime will occur. If an offender and a victim are not in the same place, there will be no crime. Part of the analysis phase involves finding out as much as possible about the victims, offenders, and locations where problems exist in order to understand what is prompting the problem and what can be done about it.

The three elements must be present before a crime or harmful behaviors—problems—can occur: an *offender* (someone who is motivated to commit harmful behavior), a *victim* (a desirable and vulnerable target must be present), and a *place* (the victim and offender must both be in the same place at the same time) (see Figure 3–4). (We discuss locations more below.) If these three elements show up over and over again in patterns and recurring problems, removing one of these elements can stop the pattern and prevent future harms.[17]

As an example, let us apply the problem analysis triangle to the issue of graffiti, using Figure 3–5. The place is marked buildings and areas immediately around them. The victims are the owners and users of the buildings; the offenders are the writers of the graffiti (see the inside triangle of Figure 3–5; the outside triangle is discussed below). Removing one or more of these elements will remove the problem. Strategies for removing one of these elements are limited only by an officer's creativity, availability of resources, and ability to formulate collaborative responses.

Some jurisdictions, for example, are setting aside an area for graffiti "artists" (even having graffiti contests) to give them an outlet for their illegal tagging activities, while others are using nonadhesive paint on buildings and property (protecting locations) to discourage taggers ("offenders"). Other jurisdictions have contemplated outlawing the sale of spray paint or limiting the sale of broad-tip markers to juveniles, while still others

FIGURE 3–4
Problem Analysis Triangle

Source: U.S. Department of Justice, Bureau of Justice Assistance, *Comprehensive Gang Initiative: Operations Manual for Implementing Local Gang Prevention and Control Programs* (Draft, October 1993), p. 3.

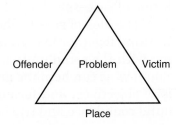

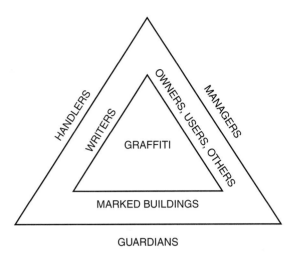

FIGURE 3–5
Graffiti Problem Triangle: The Role of Third Parties

Source: Adapted from John E. Eck, "Police Problems and Research: A Short, Furious, Concise Tour of a Complex Field." Unpublished draft 1.2, January 20, 2002, p. 4; and U.S. Department of Justice, Bureau of Justice Assistance, *Comprehensive Gang Initiative: Operations Manual for Implementing Local Gang Prevention and Control Programs* (Draft, October 2003), pp. 3–11. Used with permission.

have enacted graffiti ordinances to help business owners ("victims") to keep their locations graffiti-free.

Police engaged in problem solving need to also be aware of three types of third parties that can either help or hinder the problem-solving effort by attempting to act on behalf of one or more of the three elements discussed in the problem analysis triangle in Figure 3–4. We will again use examples and Figure 3–5 to explain the role of third parties:

1. *Controllers.* There are people who, acting in the best interests of the potential offenders, try to prevent them from committing crimes. **Controllers** of gang members might be parents, adult neighbors, peers, teachers, and employers. However, these youths may live in a poor one-parent home or not be attending school or working. Controllers can often restrict the tools used by gang members, such as putting spray cans in locked bins, restricting the wearing of colors, and passing laws obstructing the sale of semiautomatic and automatic weapons.[18]

2. *Guardians.* There are people or things that can exercise control over each side of the triangle so that crime is less likely and are called **guardians.** For instance, if the crime problem is drug dealing in a house and the offender side of the triangle includes dealers and buyers, then a list of guardians would include police, parents of dealers/buyers, probation and parole officers, landlords, city codes, health and tax departments, and neighbors. Tools used by guardians can include crime prevention techniques (discussed more later).[19]

3. *Managers.* People who oversee locations are called **managers.** For example, apartment managers can help prevent or solve problems by installing security equipment in their buildings, screening tenants carefully, and evicting troublemakers or criminals. Conversely, where managers are absent or lax, risks will be higher.[20]

Police should constantly look for ways to improve the effectiveness of third parties, as these groups of individuals have the authority to deal with the problem. There will always be the temptation on the part of society to

Seeking information from a variety of resources (e.g., business owners)
will assist officers in understanding the underlying conditions and factors
related to problems.

Courtesy Community Policing Consortium.

use the police as handlers, guardians, or managers. Although this may be
effective for a short time, there are rarely enough officers to control a
recurring problem in the long run.

Response: Formulation of Tailor-Made Strategies

After a problem has been clearly defined and analyzed, the officer confronts the ultimate challenge in problem oriented policing: the search for
the most effective way of dealing with it. This stage of the S.A.R.A. process
focuses on developing and implementing a **response** to the problem. Before
entering this stage, an agency must overcome the temptation to implement
a response prematurely and need to be certain that it has thoroughly analyzed the problem; attempts to fix problems quickly are rarely effective in
the long term.

To develop tailored responses, problem solvers should review their
findings about the three sides of the crime triangle—victim, offender, and
location—and develop creative solutions that will address at least two
sides of the triangle.[21] It is also important to remember that the key to
developing tailored responses is making sure the responses are very focused
and *directly linked* to the findings from the analysis phase of the project.

Responses may be wide-ranging and often require arrests (but apprehension may not be the most effective solution), referral to social service
agencies, or changes in ordinances. Potential solutions to problems can be
organized into five groups[22]:

1. *Totally eliminating the problem.* Effectiveness is measured by the absence of the types of incidents that this problem creates. It is unlikely that most problems can be totally eliminated, but a few can.

2. *Reducing the number of incidents the problem creates.* A reduction of incidents stemming from a problem is a major measure of effectiveness.

3. *Reducing the seriousness of the harms.* Effectiveness for this type of solution is demonstrated by showing that the incidents are less harmful.

4. *Dealing with a problem better.* Treating participants more humanely, reducing costs, and increasing the effectiveness of handling incidents are all possible choices. Improved victim satisfaction, reduced costs, and other measures can show that this type of solution is effective.

5. *Removing the problem from police consideration.* The effectiveness of this type of solution can be measured by looking at why the police were handling the problem originally and the rationale for shifting the handling to others.

Box 3–1 provides an elaboration on the possible alternative responses to problems.

Problem-solving officers will often seek the assistance of the community, other city departments, businesses, private and social service organizations, and anyone else who can help with their efforts. Box 3–2 is a guide to collaboration, to guide officers in developing networks with people and other agencies.

In recent years, the police have been increasingly pressing for a more rational distribution of responsibilities for solving problems. Depending on the situation, the police, private citizens, industry, or the government may bear some responsibility for addressing a problem. There are few firm rules that dictate who is primarily responsible for addressing a particular public safety problem. What rules, for example, dictate who is responsible for preventing or addressing retail theft? Is it the police? The retail store? The consumer? The insurance carrier? The difficulty arises because every problem stems from a variety of sources. Much depends on who possesses the skill, knowledge, authority, and resources to implement changes that will effectively reduce or control the problem.

Nevertheless, because of an increased police emphasis on crime prevention, the deployment of police officers in the most efficacious manner due to accountability and limited resources, the police are increasingly seeking to shift and/or share responsibility for addressing problems. COPPS depends heavily on strong, mutually trusting partnerships.[23]

Box 3–3 shows how the police can apply a variety of methods to get others to assume greater responsibility for public safety problems. This list is not exhaustive but is illustrative.

Assessment: Evaluation of Overall Effectiveness

Finally, in the **assessment,** officers evaluate the effectiveness of their responses. A number of measures have traditionally been used by police agencies and community members to assess effectiveness. These include

BOX 3–1

Range of Possible Response Options

1. *Concentrate attention on the individuals accounting for a disproportionate share of the problem.* A relatively small number of individuals usually account for a disproportionate share of practically any problem, by causing it (offenders), facilitating it (controllers, managers, guardians), or suffering from it (victims).

2. *Connect with other government and private services.* A thorough analysis of a problem often leads to an appreciation of the need for (a) more effective referrals to existing governmental and private services, (b) improved coordination with agencies that exert control over some of the problems or individuals involved in the incidents, and (c) initiative for pressing for correction of inadequacies in municipal services and for development of new services.

3. *Use mediation and negotiation skills.* Often the use of mediation and negotiation teams can be effective responses to conflicts.

4. *Convey information.* Relating sound and accurate information is one of the least used responses. It has the potential, however, to be one of the most effective for responding to a wide range of problems. Conveying information can help (a) reduce anxiety and fear, (b) enable citizens to solve their own problems, (c) elicit conformity with laws and regulations that are not known or understood, (d) warn potential victims about their vulnerability and advise them of ways to protect themselves, (e) demonstrate to people how they unwittingly contribute to problems, (f) develop support for addressing a problem, and (g) acquaint the community with the limitations on government agencies and define realistically what can be expected of those agencies.

5. *Mobilize the community.* Mobilizing a specific segment of the community helps implement a specific response to a specific problem for as long as it takes to deal with the problem.

6. *Make use of existing forms of social control.* Solve problems by mobilizing specific forms of social control inherent in existing relationships—for example, the influence of a parent, teacher, employer, or church.

7. *Alter the physical environment to reduce opportunities for problems to recur.* Adapt the principles of crime prevention through environmental design and situational crime prevention to the complete range of problems.

8. *Increase regulation, through statutes or ordinances, of conditions that contribute to problems.* An analysis of a specific problem may draw attention to factors contributing to the problem that can be controlled by regulation through statutes or ordinances.

9. *Develop new forms of limited authority to intervene and detain.* Examination of specific problems can lead to the conclusion that a satisfactory solution requires some limited authority (e.g., to order a person to leave) but does not require labeling the conduct criminal so that it can be dealt with through a citation or a physical arrest followed by a criminal prosecution.

10. *Make more discriminate use of the criminal justice system.* Use of the criminal justice system should be much more discreet than in the past, reserved for those problems for which the system seems especially appropriate, and used with much greater precision. This could include (a) straightforward investigation, arrest, and prosecution; (b) selective enforcement with articulated criteria; (c) enforcement of criminal laws that, by tradition, are enforced by another agency; (d) more specific definitions of behavior that should be subject to criminal justice prosecution or control through local ordinances; (e) intervention without making the arrest; (f) use of arrest without the intention to prosecute; and (g) new conditions attached to probation or parole.

11. *Use civil law to control public nuisances, offensive behavior, and conditions contributing to crime.* Because most of what the police do in the use of the law involves arrest and prosecution, people tend to forget that the police and local government can initiate a number of other legal proceedings, including those related to (a) licensing, (b) zoning, (c) property confiscation, (d) nuisance abatement, and (e) injunctive relief.

Source: Adapted from Herman Goldstein, *Problem-Oriented Policing* (New York: McGraw-Hill, 1990), pp. 140–141. Used with permission of McGraw-Hill.

BOX 3–2

Problem Solving: Guide to Collaboration

GENERAL BACKGROUND

1. Develop personal networks with members of other agencies who can give you information and help you with problems on which you may be working.
2. Become familiar with the workings of your local government, private businesses, citizen organizations, and other groups and institutions that you may need to call on for help in the future.
3. Develop skills as a negotiator.

GETTING OTHER AGENCIES TO HELP

1. Identify agencies that have a role (or could have a role) in addressing the problem early in the problem-solving process.
2. Determine whether these other agencies perceive that there is a problem.
   a. Which agency members perceive the problem and which do not?
   b. Why is it (or isn't it) a problem for them?
   c. How are police perceptions of the problem similar to and different from the perceptions of members of other agencies?
3. Determine whether there is a legal or political mandate for collaboration.
   a. To which agencies does this legal mandate apply?
   b. What are the requirements needed to demonstrate collaboration?
   c. Who is checking to determine whether collaboration is taking place?
4. Look for difficulties that these other agencies face that can be addressed through collaboration on this problem.
   a. Are there internal difficulties that provide an incentive to collaborate?
   b. Are there external crises affecting agencies that collaboration may help address?
5. Determine how much these other agencies use police services.
6. Assess the resource capabilities of these agencies to help.
   a. Do they have the money?
   b. Do they have the staff expertise?
   c. Do they have the enthusiasm?
7. Assess the legal authority of these other agencies.
   a. Do they have special enforcement powers?
   b. Do they control critical resources?

8. Determine the administrative capacity of these agencies to collaborate.
   a. Do they have the legal authority to intervene in the problem?
   b. What are the internal procedures and policies of the stakeholders that help or hinder collaboration?

WORKING WITH OTHER AGENCIES

1. Include representatives from all affected agencies, if possible, in the problem-solving process.
2. Look for responses to the problem that maximize the gains to all agencies and distribute costs equitably.
3. Reinforce awareness of the interdependence of all agencies.
4. Be prepared to mediate among agencies that have a history of conflict.
5. Develop problem information sharing mechanisms, and promote discussion about the meaning and interpretation of this information.
6. Share problem-solving decisions among stakeholders, and do not surprise others with already-made decisions.
7. Develop a clear explanation as to why collaboration is needed.
8. Foster external support for collaborative efforts, but do not rely on mandates to further collaboration.
9. Be prepared to negotiate with all involved agencies as to their roles, responsibilities, and resource commitments.
10. When collaborating with agencies located far away, plan to spend time developing a working relationship.
11. Try to create support in the larger community for collaborative problem solving.

WHEN COLLABORATION DOES NOT WORK

1. Always be prepared for collaboration to fail.
2. Have alternative plans.
3. Assess the costs and benefits of unilateral action.
4. Be very patient.

Source: Adapted from John E. Eck, "Implementing a Problem-Oriented Approach: A Management Guide," mimeo, draft copy (Washington, D.C.: Police Executive Research Forum, 1990), pp. 69–70.

BOX 3–3

Methods for Convincing Others to Accept Responsibility for Community Problems

- Educating others regarding their responsibility for the problem
- Making a straightforward informal request of some entity to assume responsibility for the problem
- Making a targeted confrontational request of some entity to assume responsibility for the problem
- Engaging another existing organization that has the capacity to help address the problem
- Pressing for the creation of a new organization to assume responsibility for the problem

- Shaming the delinquent entity by calling public attention to its failure to assume responsibility for the problem
- Withdrawing police services relating to certain aspects of the problem
- Charging fees for police services related to the problem
- Pressing for legislation mandating that entities take measures to prevent the problem
- Bringing a civil action to compel entities to accept responsibility for the problem

---

numbers of arrests, levels of reported crime, response times, clearance rates, citizen complaints, and various workload indicators, such as CFS and the number of field interviews conducted.[24]

Several of these measures may be helpful in assessing the impact of a problem-solving effort; however, a number of nontraditional measures will shed light on whether a problem has been reduced or eliminated[25]:

- Reduced instances of repeat victimization
- Decreases in related crimes or incidents
- Neighborhood indicators (including increased profits for businesses in the target area, increased usage of the area, increased property values, less loitering and truancy, and fewer abandoned cars)
- Increased citizen satisfaction regarding the handling of the problem, determined through surveys, interviews, focus groups, electronic bulletin boards, and so on
- Reduced citizen fear related to the problem

Assessment is obviously key in the S.A.R.A. process; knowing that we must assess the effectiveness of our efforts emphasizes the importance of documentation and baseline measurement. Supervisors can help officers assess the effectiveness of their efforts.

If the responses implemented are not effective, the information gathered during analysis should be reviewed. New information may need to be collected before new solutions can be developed and tested.[26]

Working partnerships with residents to create safer and more secure neighborhoods are vital in community policing.

Courtesy Keith Richards, City of Charlotte, North Carolina.

It is also important to distinguish between evaluation and assessment. Evaluation is an overarching scientific process for determining if a problem declines and if the solution caused the decline; it begins at the moment the problem-solving process begins and continues throughout the effort. Though assessment is the final stage of both evaluation and problem solving, critical decisions about the evaluation are made throughout the process.

Figure 3–6 shows the relationship between the problem-solving process and critical evaluation questions that should be asked at each stage. The left side of the figure shows the S.A.R.A. process while the right side lists critical questions to address to conduct an evaluation. We discuss assessment (evaluation) in greater depth in Chapter 4.

DIFFICULTIES WITH PROBLEM SOLVING

Notable community policing and problem-solving researcher and author John Eck has bluntly offered a number of caveats with respect to problem solving. Given his pioneering involvement with and stellar reputation in the field, his musings are certainly worthy of mention.

First, Eck argues that POP suffers from appearing to be simple—beginning with the term "problem solving" itself. It is one of those ubiquitous terms that are used in countless business, mathematics, computer,

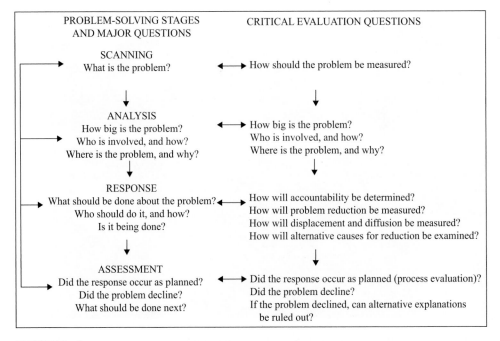

FIGURE 3–6
The Problem-Solving Process and Evaluation

Source: John Eck, *Assessing Responses to Problems: An Introductory Guide for Police Problem-Solvers* (Washington, D.C.: U.S. Department of Justice, Office of Community Oriented Policing Services, 2004), p. 6.

psychology, and many other books. Another problem is that the term suggests that for every difficulty there is a solution that is easy, cheap, permanent, and 100 percent effective.[27]

Eck also bluntly maintains that several explanations have been offered for why problem-solving efforts are not always successful. Most of these explanations (but not all, he argues) are inadequate[28]:

- *Police officers do not have the analytical skills required to analyze problems.* Eck believes that while more problem-solving training certainly could be given to officers, it should not be assumed that we even know *how* to train police in problem solving, especially in its nuances. (See, however, Chapter 9 on training for COPPS, which includes discussion of the new Police Training Officer [PTO] program.)
- *Police managers and supervisors do not know how to foster problem solving.* Eck believes this is probably true. Can supervisors discriminate between quality problem solving and superficial problem solving? The answer is no.
- *Police agencies resist change.* Eck argues that despite a large body of literature on policing and COPPS, there is little practical advice that research can provide police executives. Resistance to change is to be expected if research cannot provide practical guidance on how to behave with a new approach.
- *Police workloads prevent anything but superficial analysis.* One thing is clear: Problem solving—which requires days, weeks, even months—has a different time frame than responding to calls, which is measured in minutes

and hours. Eck is of the opinion that difficulty with time is not how much is available but how much time the police are willing to devote.

- *There is too little involvement of communities.* There is also merit to this argument. Neighborhoods usually cover much larger areas than most problems, even the most engaged communities are aware of problems, and citizens are often in the dark about how to systematically analyze and fix problems, Eck states.

- *Little is known about what works under what circumstances.* Eck believes this statement is also true. He says that the police and community can therefore experiment with solutions or systematically record and organize their problem-solving experiences; then they can share them with each other. Neither approach is adequate, however. Experimentation is a slow process, while few problem-solving efforts result in a formal evaluation.

COMMUNITY ORIENTED POLICING AND PROBLEM SOLVING: COPPS

Basic Principles

As we mentioned in Chapter 2, our view is that the two concepts of community policing and problem oriented policing are separate but complementary strategies that work together hand-in-glove. And as we emphasized in Chapter 2, the police are severely hampered when attempting to solve neighborhood and community problems without the full cooperation—a partnership and collaboration—with the community and other resources.

The two concepts of community oriented policing and problem oriented policing share some important characteristics: (1) decentralization (to encourage officer initiative and the effective use of local knowledge); (2) geographically defined rather than functionally defined subordinate units (to encourage the development of local knowledge); and (3) close interactions with local communities (to facilitate responsiveness to and cooperation with the community).[29]

Herman Goldstein did not see POP as an alternative to community policing or in competition with it. However, he asserted that much of what is occurring in community policing projects begs for application of all that has been described under the label of problem oriented policing.

Definition

What exactly is COPPS? How does it function? How would we know it if we saw it? Following is a definition we feel accurately captures the essence of this concept:

> Community oriented policing and problem solving (COPPS) is a proactive philosophy that promotes solving problems that are criminal, affect our quality of life, or increase our fear of crime, as well as other community issues. COPPS involves identifying, analyzing, and addressing community problems at their source.

One of the strongest advocates of this kind of approach to policing is the California Department of Justice, which has published several monographs on the subject and has taken the following position:

> Community Oriented Policing and Problem Solving is a concept whose time has come. This movement holds tremendous promise for creating effective police-community partnerships to reclaim our communities and keep our streets safe. COPPS is not "soft" on crime; in fact, it is tougher on crime because it is smarter and more creative. Community input focuses police activities; and, with better information, officers are able to respond more effectively with arrests or other appropriate actions. COPPS can unite our communities and promote pride in our police forces.[30]

In order for COPPS to succeed, however, the following measures are required[31]:

- Conducting accurate community needs assessments
- Mobilizing all appropriate players to collect data and brainstorm strategies
- Determining appropriate resource allocations and creating new resources where necessary
- Developing and implementing innovative, collaborative, comprehensive programs to address underlying causes and causal factors
- Evaluating programs and modifying approaches as needed

CHOICE OF APPROACH: TAILORING STRATEGIES TO NEIGHBORHOODS

Which Strategy Where?

Some interesting research has been done on whether or not COPPS can work in different types of neighborhoods; one study suggests that COPPS should have similar benefits in different types of neighborhoods.[32] Furthermore, a theoretical framework has been developed by Nolan et al. to help police decide which type of COPPS strategy to employ in specific neighborhoods.[33] First, it is important to remember—as noted in Chapter 3 discussions of communitarianism, social capital, mobilization, and alliances—that the level of responsibility for neighborhood safety and problem solving is important and relates to a community's level of crime. Some authors have termed this "collective efficacy": the cohesion among residents combined with shared expectations for the social control of public space that predicts both crime and disorder.[34] Some researchers argue that neighborhood-level collective efficacy is the most significant predictor of crime.

In a related vein, research has indicated that a neighborhood can exist in one of three identifiable stages[35]:

1. *Dependence*. Community members depend on the police to solve problems related to public order, and officers are willing to do so. Most residents view

officers as competent and respect them, and officers view the neighborhood as unable or unwilling to care for itself.

2. *Conflict.* Here, officers cannot address community problems or provide safety because residents have become dissatisfied with the police and with each other; they see the police as having primary responsibility for order maintenance in the neighborhoods but consider the police to be ineffective. In defending themselves, officers may initiate high-visibility foot or bicycle patrols or other methods in order to appease residents. To move out of this stage, officers must give up the notion that they alone can address crime and disorder in neighborhoods.

3. *Interdependence.* Once the police and the community have come to recognize their mutual responsibilities for restoring order and safety, development of social networks begins to occur. Officers play a less prominent role in order maintenance and develop a more trusting relationship with the community.

Differing Types of Neighborhoods

Obviously, neighborhoods will differ in their ability to move along these stages of development. Some are stronger than others and have more resources to help them evolve. There are four basic types of neighborhoods[36]:

1. *Strong.* Strong communities experience low levels of crime and have residents who interact or organize themselves on issues of community disorder.

2. *Vulnerable.* Vulnerable neighborhoods also have low rates of crime and disorder, but they have minimal levels of development as well. Residents depend on the police to deal with disorder.

3. *Anomic.* Anomic communities have high rates of crime and disorder and low levels of neighborhood development. Residents are dependent on officers to take care of safety problems and are dissatisfied because of the officers' lack of success.

4. *Responsive.* Responsive neighborhoods have high levels of crime and disorder, but residents work with the police to resolve problems.

Effective policing involves not only reducing crime and disorder but also facilitating neighborhood development. The police must strive to move the community along two dimensions: low levels of crime and disorder, and high levels of integration and collective efficacy (interdependence). Therefore, matching the policing style to the neighborhood type represents only the first step in the process.

Figure 3–7 shows **situational policing** in motion. The right side of the figure lists policing strategies that will help to move a community toward the responsive and then to the strong quadrants. If crime is high and the citizens are independent (stage one), police should use a professional service-oriented approach as the logical and preferred first step. The dotted line at the bottom of the figure indicates the direction the police usually want to follow based on the utopian idea that given increased resources or more efficient responses to calls for service, they could reduce

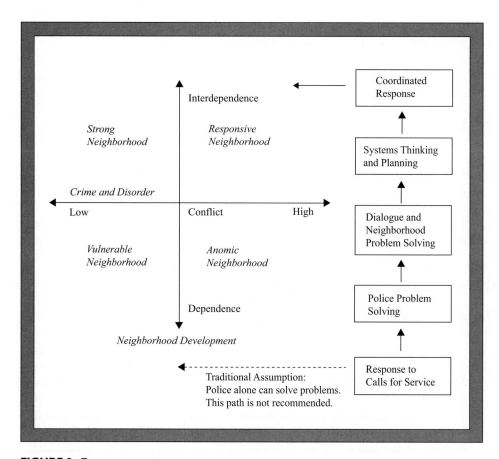

FIGURE 3–7
Situational Policing in Motion

Source: FBI Law Enforcement Bulletin.

crime without collective effort. This assumption has proved fictional over the years because the police do not have the resources needed to eliminate crime and disorder through more or better services.

After an initial stage of stepped-up law enforcement, a second wave of activity might include problem solving. At first, the police might do problem solving on their own, without the help of residents. But as officers establish dialogue with residents and as relationships and communication build, police and citizens must reach a shared realization that officers alone cannot fix neighborhood problems and keep residents safe. With this understanding, activities may begin to take place that move the neighborhood toward the responsive quadrant, where residents are ready to organize and plan for addressing crime and disorder.[37]

In sum, situational policing may very well bridge the philosophical gap between traditional policing and COPPS by identifying situations where each style is appropriate. It provides a desired end state at which the police can aim and against which competing strategies can be evaluated.

A Winning Example: The Oakland Airport Motel Program

To illustrate COPPS and S.A.R.A. in action, it would be helpful to see how the Oakland (California) Police Department addressed a serious motel problem near its local airport. This project won the coveted Herman Goldstein Award for Excellence in Problem-Oriented Policing, conferred at the annual International Problem Oriented Policing Conference. The Oakland Police Department followed the S.A.R.A. model[38]:

- *Scanning.* Located along a major gateway to the city of Oakland, the Oakland Airport Motel (OAM) is situated in a commercial area comprising lodging, restaurants, and fast-food outlets; it is also situated about two miles from Oakland's professional baseball, football, and basketball franchises. An analysis complainant working at the motel for several weeks informed an Oakland Police Department (OPD) officer that prostitutes soliciting sex had approached him nightly, prostitutes "had the run of the place," there were loud parties and disturbances each night around the clock, junked vehicles littered the parking lot, and the smell of marijuana came through his window nightly.

- *Analysis.* After consulting with city zoning and attorney's offices concerning applicable laws, an officer reviewed the property owner information and determined that a large corporation owned the motel, there was not a policy of limiting the duration of guest stays, and a disproportionately high number of narcotics arrests had occurred over the previous two years. The officer made a site visit, photographing and documenting his observations and interviewing tenants and the motel staff. He noted that a corner of the motel parking lot was used as an illegal freelance auto repair business, that rooms were routinely rented to minors, and that prostitution activity was rampant. A review of police incidents over three years revealed that the motel had an astounding 900 percent higher number of police incidents than comparable area lodging facilities.

- *Response.* A response plan was developed. Phase one involved working with the motel manager to clean up the property and to deal with problem tenants. A policy was implemented to restrict renting rooms to persons age 21 or older, to evict problem tenants in a timely manner, to monitor the parking lot to prevent junked vehicles from being dumped there, and to fire employees caught renting out rooms "under the table" and using their passkeys. Corporate officials balked at several of these initiatives, however, so the officer sent a drug nuisance abatement notification letter to the motel. Police surveillance revealed that motel security guards were not taking affirmative steps to keep nuisances out of the parking lot and that frequent prostitution and hand-to-hand drug transactions continued to occur. An undercover officer rented rooms at the motel; on two occasions, motel managers changed the room lock and took the undercover officer's property left in the rooms so as to double-rent the rooms. Given this lack of improvement, phase two involved meeting with the motel's corporate officials. A document was prepared covering the criminal activity at the motel over a three-year period, a comparison of the motel's problems with those of the five adjacent motels, and descriptions and photographs of the prostitution and violent crimes occurring at the site. The document also outlined the legal consequences and costs of not complying with relevant legal, health, and safety codes. It was requested that the motel be closed for 90 days to improve the physical aspects and to retrain motel staff in their proper duties, post a $250,000 performance bond, and repay OPD for investigative costs. Corporate officials promised swift change; again, however, there was little improvement in the conditions at the motel after two weeks had passed. Phase three of the project was then launched: preparation of lawsuits and negotiations. Police continued surveillance of activities at the motel, and a drug nuisance abatement lawsuit was prepared for filing and sent to the home of the chief executive officer in France. At a meeting with the motel chain's vice president of operations, an additional document summarized continuing problems. Finally, after seven hours of negotiations, corporate officials agreed to post the performance bond and to pay the city $35,000 in fees and expenses incurred to date. Furthermore, barbed wire was installed along all fence lines to discourage fence climbing, area lighting was upgraded, room rates were increased by 50 percent to improve its clientele, room rentals for more than 30 days were prohibited, foot and vehicle traffic was stopped for identification by security guards, a "no-rent" list was developed for banned guests, cleaning and painting of the property were accomplished, rigorous background checks were performed on new employees, and problem employees were terminated.

- *Assessment.* Seven months after these corrective activities were launched, calls for service to the motel dropped by 59 percent. Two years later, there had been only one call for police service. Overall crime and nuisance activities were also on par with the other five adjacent motels.

▲ SUMMARY

This chapter and the discussion of community in Chapter 2 constitute the heart and soul of this book and have set out the basic principles and strategies of the COPPS concepts. This combined approach of COPPS is, we believe, the best philosophy and strategy for the future of policing. We also believe that blending these two concepts results in a better, more comprehensive approach to providing quality police service—combining the emphasis on forming a police-community partnership to fight crime with the use of the S.A.R.A. process to solve problems.

As we noted in the summary of Chapter 2, it is essential for the reader to have a firm, fundamental understanding of these two chapters, as they lay the foundation for what follows in the remaining chapters. Subsequent chapter topics elaborate on COPPS and the problem-solving process and include a large number of examples of COPPS in real-life situations. Furthermore, some chapters, particularly those addressing such topics as crime prevention, information technology, and crime analysis, bear heavily on the S.A.R.A. problem-solving process.

ITEMS FOR REVIEW

1. Explain what is meant by problem oriented policing and how it differs from traditional reactive, incident-driven policing.
2. Briefly describe the four steps of the S.A.R.A. problem-solving process.
3. Review in detail what kinds of activities are involved in the analysis stage of the S.A.R.A. process.
4. Delineate the three elements of the problem analysis and graffiti problem triangles.
5. List the three types of roles of third parties in the problem analysis triangle.
6. List the five potential solutions to problems.
7. Describe five potential difficulties with problem solving.
8. Explain what is meant by COPPS, and provide an example of how it might function in a situation involving neighborhood disorder.
9. Review some of the considerations in tailoring problem-solving strategies to neighborhoods.

◆ NOTES

1. Herman Goldstein, *Policing a Free Society* (Cambridge, Mass.: Ballinger, 1977).
2. Herman Goldstein, *Problem-Oriented Policing* (New York: McGraw-Hill, 1990).
3. Herman Goldstein, "Problem-Oriented Policing." Paper presented at the National Institute of Justice Conference on Policing: State of the Art III, Phoenix, Arizona, June 12, 1987.
4. *Ibid.,* p. 4.
5. *Ibid.,* pp. 5–6.
6. John Eck and William Spelman, "A Problem-Oriented Approach to Police Service Delivery," in Dennis Jay Kenney (ed.), *Police and Policing: Contemporary Issues* (New York: Praeger, 1989), pp. 95–111.
7. Quoted in Roland Chilton, "Urban Crime Trends and Criminological Theory," in Chris W. Eskridge (ed.), *Criminal Justice: Concepts and Issues* (Los Angeles: Roxbury, 1993), pp. 47–55.
8. *Ibid.,* p. xvii.
9. Samuel Walker, *The Police in America: An Introduction* (2nd ed.) (New York: McGraw-Hill, 1992), p. 177.
10. Goldstein, *Problem-Oriented Policing,* pp. 38–40.
11. Goldstein, "Toward Community-Oriented Policing: Potential, Basic Requirements, and Threshold Questions," *Crime and Delinquency* 33 (1987):6–30.
12. *Ibid.,* p. 21.
13. *Ibid.,* pp. 43–52.
14. Goldstein, *Problem-Oriented Policing,* p. 18.

15. U.S. Department of Justice, Office of Community Oriented Policing Services, *Problem Solving Tips: A Guide to Reducing Crime and Disorder Through Problem-Solving Partnerships* (Washington, D.C.: Author, 2002), p. 10.

16. Karl E. Weick, "Small Wins: Redefining the Scale of Social Problems," *American Psychologist,* 39 (1) (1984):40–49.

17. John Eck, *A Dissertation Prospectus for the Study of Characteristics of Drug Dealing Places* (Dissertation, College Park, Md.: University of Maryland–College Park, 1992).

18. Marcus Felson, "Linking Criminal Career Choices, Routine Activities, Informal Control, and Criminal Outcomes," in Derek Cornish and Ronald Clarke (eds.), *The Reasoning Criminal: Rational Choice Perspectives on Offending* (New York: Springer-Verlag, 1986).

19. Lawrence E. Cohen and Marcus Felson, "Social Change and Crime Rate Trends: A Routine Activity Approach," *American Sociological Review* 44 (August 1979):588–608.

20. Eck, *A Dissertation Prospectus for the Study of Characteristics of Drug Dealing Places,* p. 5.

21. Rana Sampson, "Problem Solving," in *Neighborhood-Oriented Policing in Rural Communities: A Program Planning Guide* (Washington, D.C.: U.S. Department of Justice, Office of Justice Programs, Bureau of Justice Assistance, 1994), p. 4.

22. William Spelman and John E. Eck, "Problem-Solving," *Research in Brief* (January 1987):6.

23. Michael Scott and Herman Goldstein, *Shifting and Sharing Responsibility for Public Safety Concerns* (Washington, D.C.: U.S. Department of Justice, Office of Community Oriented Policing Services, August 2005), pp. 2–5.

24. Darrel Stephens, "Community Problem-Oriented Policing: Measuring Impacts," in Larry T. Hoover (ed.), *Quantifying Quality in Policing* (Washington, D.C.: Police Executive Research Forum, 1995).

25. U.S. Department of Justice, Office of Community Oriented Policing Services, *Problem Solving Tips,* p. 20.

26. Sampson, "Problem Solving," p. 5.

27. John E. Eck, "Why Don't Problems Get Solved," in Wesley G. Skogan (ed.), *Community Policing: Can It Work?* (Belmont, Calif.: Wadsworth, 2004), pp. 185–206.

28. *Ibid.,* pp. 190–193.

29. Mark H. Moore and Robert C. Trojanowicz, *Corporate Strategies for Policing* (Washington, D.C.: U.S. Department of Justice, National Institute of Justice, 1988), p. 11.

30. California Department of Justice, Attorney General's Office, *Community Oriented Policing and Problem Solving: Definitions and Principles* (Sacramento, Calif.: Author, 1993), p. iii.

31. *Ibid.*

32. See W. G. Skogan, S. M. Hartnett, J. DuBois, J. T. Comey, M. Kaiser, and J. H. Lovig, *Problem Solving in Practice: Implementing Community Policing in Chicago* (Washington, D.C.: U.S. Department of Justice, National Institute of Justice, 2000).

33. James J. Nolan, Norman Conti, and Jack McDevitt, "Situational Policing," *FBI Law Enforcement Bulletin* (November 2005):1–9.

34. R. J. Sampson and S. W. Raudenbush, "Systematic Social Observation of Public Spaces: A New Look at Disorder in Urban Neighborhoods," *American Journal of Sociology* 105 (3) (1999):603–651.

35. *Ibid.,* pp. 3–4.

36. *Ibid.,* pp. 4–5.

37. *Ibid.,* pp. 7–9.

38. "The Oakland Airport Motel Program: Eliminating Criminal and Nuisance Behavior at a Motel," in U.S. Department of Justice, National Institute of Justice (ed.), *Best Practices in Problem-Oriented Policing: Winners of the 1999 Herman Goldstein Award for Excellence in Problem-Oriented Policing* (Oakland, Calif.: Oakland Police Department, 2003), pp. 1–7.

Crime Prevention

Creating Safe Communities

Key Terms and Concepts _____

Crime displacement

Crime opportunity

Crime prevention through
    environmental design (CPTED)

Designing out crime

Evaluation

Second-generation CPTED

Situational crime prevention (SCP)

Learning Objectives _____

As a result of reading this chapter, the student will:

- Know how crime prevention evolved
- Understand how crime prevention relates to community oriented policing and problem solving (COPPS)
- Be able to describe crime prevention through environmental design (CPTED) as well as some of the obstacles to adopting it
- Comprehend the meaning and value of situational crime prevention
- Be aware of the displacement of crime
- Know (based on cited studies) which crime prevention strategies work, do not work, and hold promise
- Be able to list the principles of crime opportunity

> I don't see much improvement in man's heart. The whole thing is in man's heart: his desire, his greed, his lust, his pride, his ego.
>
> *—Billy Graham, 2006*

> The test of police efficiency is the absence of crime and disorder, not the visible evidence of police action dealing with them.
>
> *—Sir Robert Peel's ninth principle of policing, 1829*

INTRODUCTION

Crime prevention has been defined by the Crime Prevention Coalition of America this way:

> A pattern of attitudes and behaviors directed both at reducing the threat of crime and enhancing the sense of safety and security to positively influence the quality of life in our society and to help develop environments where crime cannot flourish.[1]

Crime prevention once consisted primarily of exhorting people to "lock it or lose it" and giving out advice by the police on door locks and window bars for their homes and businesses. It typically was (and often still is) an add-on program or appendage to the police agency, which normally included a few officers who were trained to go to citizens' homes and perform security surveys or engage in public speaking on prevention topics.

But times have changed dramatically in this respect—especially since 9-11. We also know that attempting to investigate and solve crimes and prosecuting and punishing offenders are much more expensive than preventing the offense from occurring in the first place. We are also aware that as the costs of public safety have skyrocketed, governments are extremely hard-pressed to continue to afford to build, staff, and operate more jails and prisons. In an era of decreasing resources, crime prevention offers a cost-effective means of making communities safer. Therefore, crime prevention now involves the police and government seeking to influence the civil behavior of individuals, corporations, businesses, and others that are responsible for the creation of criminal opportunities or motivation.[2]

This chapter examines the multifaceted domain of what contemporary crime prevention has become. We begin with a brief history of how crime prevention evolved and then discuss how today's police are shifting their emphasis to that of crime prevention as an agency-wide philosophy. Then the essential role of the community in preventing crime is explored, followed by an overview of how crime prevention relates to community oriented policing and problem solving (COPPS) (examined in Chapter 3).

Two very important components of crime prevention and COPPS are then analyzed: crime prevention through environmental design and situational crime prevention. Following that, we review several issues and problems that can accompany crime prevention efforts: the implementation of crime interventions, the displacement of crime when interventions are undertaken, and the evaluation of results. Finally, we view which crime prevention strategies work, do not work, and hold promise.

Throughout the chapter, the emphasis or the common thread—from strategy to strategy, community to community—is the acknowledgment by the police that they alone cannot prevent or address crime and disorder; the community *must* be engaged in a collaborative effort if the physical and social problems that plague the community are to be reduced or eliminated.

Under COPPS, crime prevention
is evolving to more comprehensive
situational and environmental
intervention strategies. This photo
depicts a Neighborhood Watch sign
vandalized by local gangs.

A Brief History

Crime prevention is not a new idea. Humans have long known that crime is not simply a matter of motivation; it is also a matter of opportunity. Indeed, for as long as people have been victimized, there have been attempts to protect one's self and family. The term "crime prevention," however, has only recently come to signify a set of ideas for combating crime.[3]

Our earliest ancestors maximized lighting from the sun and moon and employed defensive placement of homes on the side of cliffs, with only one entrance and exit.[4] Cave dwellers established ownership of a space by surrounding it with large boulders; later the Romans developed and enforced complex land laws. Walled cities and castles exist throughout the world. It is a natural human impulse to claim and secure an area to prevent problems.[5]

A more contemporary form of early preventive action was the Chicago Area Project (CAP), based on the research of Shaw and McKay in the 1930s and 1940s, which concerned the altering of the social fabric. Crime and delinquency were concentrated in the central areas of Chicago. Identifying a high level of transiency and an apparent lack of social ties in these areas as the root cause of the problems, Shaw and McKay labeled the problem as "social disorganization," meaning that the constant turnover of residents resulted in the inability of the people to exert any informal social control over the individuals in the area. Consequently, offenders could act with some degree of impunity in these neighborhoods.[6]

Shaw's proposed solution to the problem was to work with the residents to build a sense of pride and community, thereby prompting people to stay and exert control over the actions of the people in the area. CAP was founded in 1931 and generated community support by using volunteers and existing neighborhood institutions.[7]

The 1970s saw the rise of community-based crime prevention programs, such as the Neighborhood or Block Watch. These programs used the same premise as physical design approaches—potential offenders will not commit a crime if they perceive citizen activity, awareness, and concern in an area. The focus is on citizen surveillance and action (such as cutting back bushes, installing lighting, removing obstacles to enhance sight lines, organizing security surveys, and distributing crime and crime prevention news). Signs of resident activity and cohesion should work to protect the neighborhood. The police also recognized that they could not stop crime or solve problems on their own; they needed the help of the citizenry.[8]

Crime prevention experienced perhaps its biggest boost, however, with the emergence of physical design as a topic of debate. Led by the work of Oscar Newman in 1972, flaws in the physical environment were identified as causes of, or at least facilitators for, criminal behavior. In 1969 Newman first coined the term "defensible space," which in his mind did not mean ugly fortress-like buildings where occupants were prisoners. (Table 4–1 depicts Newman's suggestions for defensible space.) Rather,

TABLE 4–1

Oscar Newman's Defensible Space Suggestions
1. Reduce the size of a housing estate or block.
2. Reduce the number of dwellings sharing an entrance way.
3. Reduce the number of stories in a building block.
4. Arrange dwellings in groups to encourage social contact.
5. Minimize the degree of shared public space inside and near blocks.
6. Make the boundaries between public and private space very clear.
7. Make public areas clearly visible to nearby housing.
8. Use external rather than internal corridors in blocks of housing so that they are visible.
9. Make entrances flush with the street rather than set back.
10. Do not have entrances facing away from the street because they are not open to surveillance.
11. Avoid landscaping and vegetation that impede surveillance.
12. Reduce escape routes (elevators, staircases, and multiple exits) for criminals.

Source: U.S. Department of Housing and Urban Development, *Crime Prevention Brief,* "Crime Prevention Through Environmental Design" (no date), p. 2.

buildings that are properly designed promote a sense of safety and power to their occupants, making them less afraid and vulnerable.[9]

Newman, an architect, argued that the physical characteristics of an area have the potential to suggest to residents and potential offenders either that the area is well cared for and protected or it is open to criminal activity. Design features conducive to criminal behavior—allowing offenders to commit a crime and escape with minimal risk of detection—would include common entrances for a large number of people, poorly placed windows inhibiting casual surveillance of grounds and common areas, hidden entrances, easy access for illegitimate users, and isolated buildings.[10]

Then in the 1970s and 1980s, theories of crime were developed that gave added importance to the role of **crime opportunity.** L. E. Cohen and M. Felson's routine activity theory seeks to explain how physical and social environments create crime opportunities by bringing together in one place at a particular time a "likely" offender, a "suitable" target, and the absence of a "capable guardian" against crime (e.g., a police officer or security guard).[11] Routine activity theory was used to explain how large increases in burglary rates occurred in the United States in the 1960s and 1970s

The glass stairwell in this parking garage demonstrates how natural surveillance can be designed into a facility. People using the stairwell are easily seen by passers-by, thus reducing the likelihood of victimization.

because (1) home electronic goods became lighter, and (2) women increasingly entered the labor force, resulting in more empty homes during the day that could be entered by burglars.

Another opportunity theory is the rational choice perspective, which holds that all crime is purposive behavior designed to benefit the offender.[12] In committing an offense, the offender makes the choice to balance the effort, risks, and rewards with the costs and benefits of alternative legal means of achieving an end.

James Q. Wilson and George Kelling's 1982 "broken windows" theory extended Oscar Newman's focus on housing projects to entire neighborhoods. "Broken windows" refers to physical signs that an area is unattended: There may be abandoned vehicles and buildings in the area, trash and litter may be present, and there may be broken windows and lights and graffiti.[13] In addition to these physical indicators are social manifestations of the same problems, such as loitering youths, public drunkenness, prostitution, and vagrancy. Both the physical and social indicators are typically referred to as signs of "incivility" that attract offenders to the area.[14]

The most recent movements in crime prevention focus efforts and interventions on attacking specific problems, places, and times. Ronald V. Clarke

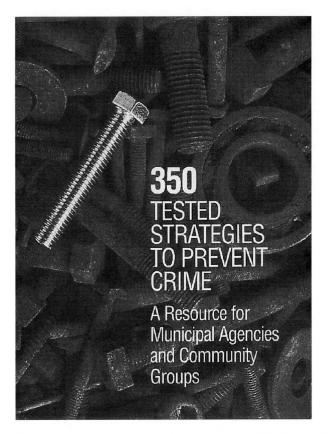 

Comprehensive crime prevention resource guides for municipal and rural agencies are available through the National Crime Prevention Council at http://www.ncpc.org.

Courtesy National Crime Prevention Council.

proposed "situational prevention" as "measures directed at highly specific forms of crime that involve [environmental changes that] reduce the opportunities for crime and increase its risk."[15] Examples of situational prevention include the installation of surveillance equipment in a parking lot experiencing vandalism, erecting security screens in banks to stop robberies, altering traffic patterns in a drug market neighborhood, using electronic tags for library materials, and using caller ID for obscene phone calls.[16] The physical environment as it relates to crime prevention is discussed shortly. Next we discuss the contemporary crime prevention–based philosophy.

TODAY'S SHIFTING EMPHASIS

A simple but profound shift in thinking in contemporary times may help American police organizations to realize new gains in reducing crime, victimization, and fear. Many police agencies now conceive of prevention as the overarching goal of policing rather than as a set of activities. We discuss the following benefits of crime prevention[17]:

- Deterrence of specific kinds of crimes
- Mobilization of residents
- Development of physical and social environments inhospitable to crime

The concept of prevention shifts a police organization's purpose. Police agencies that are operating in a prevention framework must be organized to prevent the next problem from occurring. This reflects Herman Goldstein's call for replacing efficiency with effectiveness as the goal of policing. Once the question becomes "How can we prevent the next crisis?" all kinds of approaches become possible. Police departments and their partners will find themselves embracing approaches that would have been unimaginable under the traditional reactive policing model.[18]

The Boston Police Department, for example, partners with probation officers to conduct joint curfew checks on gang members and other high-risk probationers. As the police commissioner noted, "First we tried conventional, police heavy enforcement tactics. Then we realized we needed a better strategy. We realized the kids needed jobs and opportunities. At that point we gained a new appreciation of our mission."[19]

Understanding prevention as the strategic goal of the policing process rather than as a set of activities for police officers puts into practice Sir Robert Peel's ninth principle of policing, quoted at the beginning of this chapter.[20] Today prevention means more than simply warning citizens about crime; it means strategically maximizing police resources and those of the community for tangible outcomes.

The core mission of the police is simply to preserve the peace, but they cannot do so alone. Crime prevention is much broader than the confines of the police station house. Still, there is much important work for the police to do in the area of crime prevention. As the International Association of Chiefs of Police Crime Prevention Committee has stated, "Community safety is everyone's responsibility, and crime prevention is everyone's business."[21] The mission is clear: "Establish the prevention of crime as fundamental to a free and safe society; anchor crime prevention in each department's organizational policy."[22]

NEEDED: COMMUNITY PARTNERSHIPS

As we saw in Chapter 2 and the discussion of communitarianism, it is essential for the entire community to take responsibility for itself, actively participating and giving time, energy, and money.[23] We noted that communitarians support processes such as crime prevention and community policing, taking matters into their own hands and closing off streets and creating other physical barriers to disrupt the drug trade, working to overcome problems of homelessness and panhandling, and so on. Communitarians recognize that many of the answers to community problems lie not with government but in the community at large. Volunteerism can also provide a much-needed boost for the police, building a sense of community and breaking down barriers between people. Finally, visionary leaders are needed to provide a voice and an example.[24]

In addition to the partnership between the police and the community, another area of partnering that is being viewed as more and more critical in this post–9-11 era involves the public and private police. In fact, the federal Office of Community Oriented Policing Services sees the need to improve the working relationship between local law enforcement and private security as so important that it funded a national summit between the two entities, held in January 2004 in Arlington, Virginia.

Noting that 85 percent of the nation's critical infrastructure is protected by private security, the need for complex coordination, extra staffing, and special resources after a terrorist attack—coupled with the general demands of crime prevention—make absolutely essential the boosting of partnership. The nation's 800,000 sworn law enforcement officers and the estimated 2 million security officers (who are employed in 90,000 security organizations), according to speakers at the summit, must make a formal commitment to cooperate, share information, and educate each other about their capabilities. Given law enforcement's stretched resources and added burdens, there is no better time to develop this relationship.[25]

CRIME PREVENTION AND COPPS

COPPS argues that the police and the community must stop treating the symptoms of the problem. COPPS requires a new age of prevention—as well as improvement of prevention efforts.

Altering physical designs of buildings, for example, is not in itself generally sufficient for altering the level of crime; physical design changes cannot stop a truly motivated offender. Furthermore, altering the physical environment does not guarantee that residents will become involved and take action. Direct efforts to enhance active citizen involvement are necessary.[26]

Crime prevention and COPPS are therefore close companions, attempting to define a problem, identify contributing causes, seek out the proper people or agencies to assist in identifying potential solutions, and work as a group to implement the solution. The problem drives the solution.[27]

At its heart, COPPS is about preventing crime. COPPS and crime prevention are linked in several areas. Crime prevention efforts provide information and skills that are essential to community policing. Furthermore, crime prevention and community policing have six major points in common[28]:

1. *Each deals with the health of the community.* They acknowledge the many interrelated issues that contribute to crime.
2. *Each seeks to address underlying causes and problems.* Although short-term and reactive measures (such as personal security and response to calls for service) are necessary, they are insufficient if crime is to be significantly reduced. Looking beyond symptoms to treat the causes of community problems is a strategy that both, at their best, share in full measure.
3. *Each deals with the combination of physical and social issues that are at the heart of many community problems.* An abandoned building may attract drug addicts; bored teens may become area burglars. Both approaches examine the broadest possible range of causes and solutions.
4. *Each requires active involvement by community residents.* Both have the chief task of enabling people to make themselves and their communities safer by helping them gain appropriate knowledge, develop helpful attitudes, and take useful actions.
5. *Each requires partnerships beyond law enforcement to be effective.* Both efforts can and have involved schools, community centers, civic organizations, religious groups, social service agencies, public works agencies, and other elements of the community.
6. *Each is an approach or a philosophy rather than a program.* Neither is a fixed system for delivery of a specific service; instead, each is a way of doing business and involves the development of an institutional mind-set.

Crime prevention provides knowledge about ways to involve the entire community in reducing crime, both individually and collectively; community policing practices can spread that knowledge. Community policing officers need to understand and apply techniques to educate and motivate citizens; crime prevention offers these techniques. Because crime prevention addresses both physical and social aspects of neighborhoods, it offers numerous ways for community policing officers to gain entry into community circles. Crime prevention offers resources to help change community attitudes and behaviors.

Exhibit 4–1 provides an example of crime prevention and community policing working hand-in-hand to address a serious set of problems in Bridgeport, Connecticut.

EXHIBIT 4–1

Crime Prevention and Community Policing in Bridgeport, Connecticut

Once a major industrial center on the shore of Long Island Sound, Bridgeport, Connecticut, lost a great deal of its tax base during the 1970s and 1980s. By 1991 the city had filed for bankruptcy. The population of 143,000 included a highly diverse population of 54 separate ethnic groups. The city also faced a major crime crisis, with the highest homicide rate in New England—50 to 60 per year. Many of the victims were juveniles. Drug markets were blatant. There was a long history of police–resident animosity. The police department decided to focus efforts on the toughest area of the city—Eastside, a 1.75-square-mile, high-density area of burned buildings, plagued nightly by automatic weapons gunfire. Gang members walked around openly. Almost half of Eastside's residents were under age 18; most families were too poor to relocate. The police department initiated an outreach to the community, based on community policing and emphasizing that the police wanted to hear residents' concerns. Meanwhile, police stepped up enforcement and surveillance in the area, curbing narcotics traffic by disrupting both sellers and buyers and rescheduling officers to provide for more intensive patrolling in the critical period, 7:00 P.M. to 3:00 A.M. Eventually, community meetings were drawing as many as 200 people. Residents began to more readily report suspicious activities and call 911 or page community officers to report crimes. Community policing was implemented on a neighborhood-by-neighborhood basis, and the emphasis was placed on eradicating blight. Seventy abandoned houses in Eastside were boarded up and vacant lots and graffiti were cleaned up. Crime prevention through environmental design (CPTED), [discussed elsewhere in this chapter] tactics were employed, including the installation of concrete diverters and low curbs (to prevent easy access to drug markets by suburban junkies). A sense of community developed, and new programs sprang up from the community policing efforts (such as the group of seniors who conduct a life-skills course for girls ages 13 to 14). Between 1993 and 1997, crime declined 40 percent overall and 75 percent in Eastside; murder rates were down by one-third, as were robberies, burglaries, stolen cars, and fired shots—figures that are even more remarkable because reporting rates in Eastside have increased.

Source: U.S. Department of Justice, Bureau of Justice Assistance, *Crime Prevention and Community Policing: A Vital Partnership* (Washington, D.C.: U.S. Government Printing Office, 1997), pp. 8–9.

CRIME PREVENTION THROUGH ENVIRONMENTAL DESIGN

Role of Designing Out Crime

Crime prevention through environmental design (CPTED) is defined as the "proper design and effective use of the environment that can lead to a reduction in the fear and incidence of crime, and an improvement in the quality of life."[29] At its core are three principles that support problem-solving approaches to crime[30]:

1. *Natural access control.* Natural access control uses elements such as doors, shrubs, fences, and gates to deny admission to a crime target and to create a perception among offenders that there is a risk in selecting the target.

2. *Natural surveillance.* Natural surveillance includes the proper placement of windows, lighting, and landscaping to increase the ability of those who care to observe intruders as well as regular users, allowing them to challenge inappropriate behavior or report it to the police or the property owner.

3. *Territorial reinforcement.* Using such elements as sidewalks, landscaping, and porches helps distinguish between public and private areas and helps users exhibit signs of "ownership" that send hands-off messages to would-be offenders.

Ironically, in the past the police were not involved in design planning, whereas fire departments have promulgated and enforced national fire codes for about a half-century. Today, in cities such as Tempe, Arizona, if the police are not involved in the preliminary stages of planning a building, they often become very involved afterward, when crimes are committed in or around the structure.[31]

Cities such as Tempe have become leaders in expanding policing's new role in **designing out crime.** In the late 1900s Tempe enacted an ordinance requiring that no commercial, park, or residential building permit be issued until the police department had approved it, ensuring that the building fully protected its occupants.

Tempe's CPTED officers advocate that walls around the perimeter of a building be at least eight feet high to make them more difficult to scale. River rocks are banned from parking lots, as they can be used as weapons. Natural surveillance, which can be obtained from proper lighting and window placement, helps people to oversee nearby activities. Transparent

This gated storage facility uses an electronic keyed gate for access control.

fences are better than walls to monitor activities. Light switches in rest rooms should be keyed or remotely controlled to prevent tampering, thus perhaps facilitating a possible hiding place for an attacker; rest rooms should not be located at the ends of hallways where they are isolated. Defensive architecture includes "target hardening" through quality dead-bolts and other mechanical means and includes proper landscaping (e.g., thorny bushes help to keep burglars away).[32]

Five types of information are needed for CPTED planning[33]:

1. *Crime analysis information.* This can include crime mapping, police crime data, incident reports, and victim and offender statistics.
2. *Demographics.* This should include resident statistics such as age, race, gender, income, and income sources.
3. *Land use information.* This includes zoning information (such as residential, commercial, industrial, school, and park zones) as well as occupancy data for each zone.
4. *Observations.* These should include details of parking procedures, maintenance, and residents' reactions to crime.
5. *Resident information.* This includes resident crime surveys and interviews with police and security officers.

Exhibit 4–2 shows other successful CPTED case studies.

Second-Generation CPTED

As emphasized in Chapter 2 and stated by Greg Saville and Gerry Cleveland, "what really counts is a sense of community."[34] In that vein, a **second-generation CPTED** has more recently been developed that, again in the words of Saville and Cleveland, "recognizes that the most valuable aspects of a safe community lie not in structures of the brick and mortar type, but rather in structures of family, of thought, and, most importantly, of behavior."[35]

In addition to the basic elements such as access control and natural surveillance, second-generation CPTED looks at several *social* aspects of how neighborhoods work[36]:

- *Size of the district, population density, and differentiation of buildings.* There is an environmental influence on social interaction. We have relied for too long on large systems for survival. It is difficult to get to know one's neighbors when the neighborhood consists of 100 homes, an apartment building has over 300 units, a high school has more than 3,000 students. Size can affect the alienation of a place. We need to live in smaller, locally based neighborhoods, near where we work, go to school, and socialize. We must develop ways to encourage more local contacts for social, economic, and political interaction. (This brings us full circle to the Chicago studies of the 1930s, discussed above.)
- *Urban meeting places.* Providing meeting places is an absolute necessity in neighborhoods, and the lack thereof can make urban spaces empty and dangerous—which is why regional shopping malls fail to become places of community gathering.

EXHIBIT 4–2

Successful CPTED Case Studies

Following are brief descriptions of three successful applications of CPTED strategies for solving problems.

Knoxville, Tennessee's "Deal Street," as the name implies, was the locus of drive-through drug dealing for as many as 1,200 cars per day. Based on the neighborhood analysis, the following programs and activities were adopted:

- Cleaning up the area and replacing broken street lights and fixtures
- Closing streets, creating cul-de-sacs, and adding speed bumps in the neighborhoods
- Redesigning parks and rescheduling recreational activities to encourage the use of park facilities
- Training police officers to work with other city staff toward CPTED objectives, and training volunteers in how to conduct security surveys

The result was that only 50 cars per day came into the neighborhood, and children now cross the streets safely to get to and from school.

Richmond, Virginia, had one branch of a bank in a declining area that contained numerous vacant properties and abandoned businesses. The bank installed bullet-resistant enclosures for tellers inside the bank. Another problem arose, however; ATM patrons were being robbed an average of once a month. Robbers would come to the bank after hours and hide around the corner from the ATM, under cover of the darkened drive-up teller area. When a patron conducted the ATM business on foot, the offender would jump from cover and rob the patron. After the bank's officers rejected a number of expensive options for addressing the problem, one of the bank's employees suggested a very simple and cost-effective solution: construction of a fence at the corner of the building to remove any opportunity to jump out and surprise ATM patrons. The bank installed an 8-feet tall, 16-feet long ornamental aluminum picket fence at a cost of $800, totally eliminating robberies at the location.

Gainesville, Florida, was faced with a tremendous increase in the number of convenience store robberies. The police department carried out an evaluation of the problems and possible solutions, finding that nearly every store in the community (96 percent) had been robbed more than once. The city commission enacted an ordinance that required store operators to remove signs from windows to offer clear views to and from cash registers, locate the sales area and cash registers in a place visible from the street, post signs declaring limited cash availability, provide lighted parking areas, install security cameras, and train all employees in robbery prevention. Afterward, the city enjoyed a 64 percent decrease in convenience store robberies.

Source: National Crime Prevention Council, *Designing Safer Communities: A Crime Prevention Through Environmental Design Handbook* (Washington, D.C.: Author, 1997), pp. 7–8.

- *Youth clubs.* Again, the creation of youth clubs has been a crime prevention and community-building strategy since the aforementioned Chicago Area Project of the 1930s and can provide activities, meeting places, and life skills training.

Saville and Cleveland emphasize that such activities must have residents' support and participation. If residents are too busy or overworked, are quite elderly and perhaps fearful of unsupervised youths in the neighborhood, or have their own network of friends, they may not participate in community life.

Advertising obstructions create poor natural surveillance and may contribute
to a location's being an attractive target to offenders.

Second-generation CPTED also involves the idea of an ecological threshold, or what is called the neighborhood "tipping point." The fundamental idea is that a neighborhood, just like a natural ecosystem, has the capacity to contain only so much; too much of something and the system will collapse.

A study of neighborhood bars and taverns serves as an example. For those persons who are harmed by alcohol-related behavior, for the police who respond to alcohol-related calls for service, and other municipal officials who attempt to control these establishments, too many bars in too small an area can create an excessive amount of crime and disorder. The bars can lead to a drain on municipal services, especially the police, and the neighborhood may reach its tipping point. Studies show that the number of bar seats located in a neighborhood has a multiplier effect on the police calls for service, and at some point the police, social services, and city resources become exhausted, and the situation can no longer be tolerated.[37] More research is certainly warranted concerning this tipping point concept.

Obstacles to Adopting CPTED

It may be said that the goal of CPTED is to design and build safer, less fortress-type environments that promote security, reduce costs and liability, and improve our quality of life.[38] There are, however, several significant challenges associated with the adoption of CPTED[39]:

- Lack of knowledge of CPTED by environmental designers, land managers, and the community
- Resistance to change, and skepticism by people who reject the research that supports CPTED

- Perception that CPTED is the panacea for crime instead of being a complementary tool
- Many existing areas not built with CPTED that would require expensive or politically difficult changes to conform with the CPTED environment

SITUATIONAL CRIME PREVENTION

Situational crime prevention (SCP) draws from the aforementioned rational choice and routine activities theories and departs radically from most criminology in its orientation. It is focused on the settings for crime and the prevention of crime rather than on persons committing criminal acts. It seeks to forestall the occurrence of crime rather than to detect and sanction offenders. It seeks not to eliminate criminal or delinquent tendencies through improvement of society or its institutions but merely to make criminal action less attractive to offenders.[40]

SCP is a targeted means of reducing crime. It provides an analytical framework for strategies to prevent crime in varying settings. It is an "environmental criminology" approach that seeks to reduce crime opportunity by making settings less conducive to unwanted or illegal activities, focusing on the environment rather than the offender.[41] The commission of a crime requires not merely the offender but, as every detective story reader knows, also the opportunity for crime.[42]

Because "opportunity makes the thief," seven principles of crime opportunity have been developed, some of which draw on the above theories[43]:

1. Opportunities play a role in all crime.
2. Crime opportunities are highly specific (e.g., the theft of cars for joyriding has a different pattern of opportunity than theft for car parts).
3. Crime opportunities are concentrated in time and space (dramatic differences are found from one address to another, even in high-crime areas, and shift by time, hour, and day of week).
4. Crime opportunities depend on everyday movements of activity (e.g., burglars visit houses in the daytime when occupants are away).
5. One crime produces opportunities for another (e.g., a successful burglary may encourage the offender to return in the future, or a youth who has his bicycle stolen may feel justified in stealing someone else's).
6. Some products offer more tempting crime opportunities (e.g., easily carried items such as electronic equipment and jewelry are attractive).
7. Social and technological advancements produce new opportunities (products are most sought after in their new "mass-marketing" stages, when demand for them is greatest; most products reach a saturation stage where most people have them and they are unlikely to be stolen).

Although the concept of SCP was British in origin, its development was influenced by two independent, but nonetheless related, strands of policy research in the United States: defensible space and crime prevention through

Signage at the entrance to this apartment complex and high school parking lot serves to remove offenders' excuses for loitering and trespassing.

environmental design—both of which preceded SCP and were discussed earlier in the chapter. Because of the trans-Atlantic delay in the dissemination of ideas, however, there was no stimulus for the development of SCP.[44]

SCP is a problem-oriented approach that examines the roots of a problem and identifies a unique solution to the problem. Experience has shown that successful SCP measures must be directed against specific crimes and must be designed with a clear understanding of the motives of offenders and their methods. SCP relies on the rational choice theory of crime, which asserts that criminals choose to commit crimes based on the costs and benefits involved with the crime. For example, a potential offender will commit a high-risk crime only if the rewards of the crime outweigh the risks.[45]

Ronald V. Clarke divided crime prevention goals into five primary objectives, each of which is designed to dissuade the criminal from committing the offense by making the crime too hard to commit, too risky, or too small in terms of rewards to be worth the criminal's time.[46] We discuss each of these five objectives:

1. *Increasing the effort needed to commit the crime.* Crimes typically happen because they are easy to commit. A person might see an easy opportunity to commit a crime and do so. Casual criminals are eliminated by increasing the effort needed to commit a crime. Following are different methods for increasing the effort needed to commit a crime:

   a. *Hardening targets.* Install physical barriers (such as locks, bolts, protective screens, and mechanical containment and antifraud devices to impede an offender's ability to penetrate a potential target).

   b. *Controlling access.* Install barriers and design walkways, paths, and roads so that unwanted users are prevented from entering vulnerable areas.

   c. *Deflecting offenders.* Discourage crime by giving people alternate legal venues for their activities (such as decreasing littering by providing litter bins or separating fans of rival teams after athletic events).

   d. *Controlling facilitators.* Facilitators are accessories who aid in the commission of crimes. Controlling them is achieved by universal measures (such as firearms permit regulations) and specific measures (metal detectors in community centers).

2. *Increasing the risks associated with the crime.* Increasing the risks associated with a crime reduces the incidence of that crime, because criminals believe they will not be caught; offenders who believe that they will be caught are less likely to offend. For example, if a video camera monitors all entrances and exits to a convenience store or bank, potential robbers who know of such surveillance will be less likely to rob such establishments.

   a. *Entry and exit screening.* Screening methods include guest sign-ins or a required display of identification; they ensure that residents and visitors meet entrance requirements.

   b. *Formal surveillance.* Using security personnel and hardware (such as CCTV and burglar alarms) is a deterrent to unwanted activities.

   c. *Informal surveillance.* The presence of building attendants, concierges, maintenance workers, and attendants increases site surveillance and crime reporting.

   d. *Natural surveillance.* The surveillance can be provided by people as they go about their daily activities, making potential offenders feel exposed and vulnerable.

3. *Reducing the rewards.* Reducing the rewards from crime makes offending not worthwhile to offenders. Methods of reducing rewards include making targets of crime less valuable by the following means:

   a. *Removing targets.* Eliminate crime purposes from public areas. Examples include having a no-cash policy and keeping valuable property in a secure area overnight.

    b. *Identifying property.* Use indelible marks, establishing ownership and preventing individuals from reselling the property.

    c. *Removing inducements.* Related to target removal, this involves removing temptations that offenders have not targeted in advance but that are likely to become the targets of a spontaneous crime (such as vacant houses or other living units or broken windows and light fixtures).

4. *Reducing the provocations.* The environment or manner in which places are managed (e.g., busy bars and unmonitored drinking) may provoke crime and violence. Studies show that certain lighting improves people's mood and morale in the workplace. Additional seating and soothing music, measures to avoid long waiting lines, and other such options may reduce people's frustrations in crowded public places.

5. *Removing the excuses.* Many offenders say, "I didn't know any better" or "I had no choice." This strategy involves informing individuals of the law and rules and offers them alternatives to illegal activity by eliminating their excuses for committing crime. For example, a "no trespassing" sign is enforceable if posted. It also involves rule setting, such as clearly stating the rules of a housing development, which establish the procedures of punishment for violators. Such methods prevent offenders from excusing their crimes by claiming ignorance or misunderstanding.

Table 4–2 presents a situational crime prevention matrix for CPTED, specifically for the five CPTED objectives discussed. Included are organized (procedural measures), mechanical (provision or removal of certain physical objects), and natural (use of native aspects of the environment) means of facilitating each.

ISSUES AND PROBLEMS

Next we look at three areas that can be problematic for crime prevention: implementation of programs, crime displacement, and evaluation of results.

Implementation of Programs

A key issue for any type of intervention is the degree to which it is adequately implemented. Unless implemented properly, interventions have a good chance of failure. For example, a Neighborhood Watch initiative in a crime-ridden, ethnically divided area that gains participation from only 20 percent of the residents, and that number from only one of three ethnic groups, could not be expected to have much of an impact on the entire neighborhood or community.

Another potential problem is the possibility that key agencies, actors, or community members will only halfheartedly participate. The police and public might develop a "we-versus-them" attitude, there may be a sense that the police have the necessary training and the public does not, or there might be a fear of a return to vigilante justice. Breaking through

TABLE 4–2

Situational Crime Preventiion Matrix				
INCREASE THE EFFORT	INCREASE THE RISKS	REDUCE THE REWARDS	REDUCE THE PROVOCATIONS	REMOVE THE EXCUSES
1. **Harden targets** immobilizers in cars antirobbery screens	6. **Extend guardianship** cocooning Neighborhood Watch	11. **Conceal targets** gender-neutral phone directories off-street parking	16. **Reduce frustration and stress** efficient queueing soothing lighting	21. **Set rules** rental agreements hotel registration
2. **Control access to facilities** alley gating entry phones	7. **Assist natural surveillance** improved street lighting Neighborhood Watch hotlines	12. **Remove targets** removable car radios prepaid public phone cards	17. **Avoid disputes** fixed cab fares reduce crowding in pubs	22. **Post instructions** "No parking" "Private property"
3. **Screen exits** tickets needed electronic tags for libraries	8. **Reduce anonymity** taxi driver IDs "How's my driving?" signs	13. **Identify property** property marking vehicle licensing	18. **Reduce emotional arousal** controls on violent porn prohibit pedophiles working with children	23. **Alert conscience** roadside speed display signs "Shoplifting is stealing"
4. **Deflect offenders** street closures in red light district separate toilets for women	9. **Utilize place managers** train employees to prevent crime support whistle-blowers	14. **Disrupt markets** checks on pawn brokers licensed street vendors	19. **Neutralize peer pressure** "Idiots drink and drive" "It's OK to say no"	24. **Assist compliance** litter bins public lavatories
5. **Control tools/weapons** toughened beer glasses photos on credit cards	10. **Strengthen formal surveillance** speed cameras CCTV in town centers	15. **Deny benefits** ink merchandise tags graffiti cleaning	20. **Discourage imitation** rapid vandalism repair V-chips in TVs	25. **Control drugs/alcohol** Breathalyzers in pubs alcohol-free events

Source: Ronald V. Clarke and Derek Cornish, "Opportunities, Precipitators, and Criminal Decisions: A Reply to Wortley's Critique of Situational Crime Prevention." In M. Smith and D. B. Cornish (eds.), Theory for Situational Crime Prevention. *Crime Prevention Studies*, Vol. 16 (Monsey, N.Y.: Criminal Justice Press, 2003).

such attitudes and fears is not easy, but cooperation between the police and the public is essential for successful crime prevention programs.[47]

We discuss planning and implementation of COPPS in Chapter 6; many of those same methods, considerations, and approaches can be applied to crime prevention as well.

Displacement of Crime

An issue that emerges in any serious discussion of crime prevention is **crime displacement,** which refers to the idea that rather than eliminate crime, interventions simply result in the movement of crime to another area, shift offenders to new targets in the same area, alter the methods used to accomplish a crime, or prompt offenders to change the type of crime they commit.[48] Displacement has, therefore, been the Achilles' heel of crime prevention in general. Efforts to control drug dealing and crime in neighborhoods and places are often criticized for having displaced the offending behavior instead of reducing it. If crime or drug dealing has only been moved around without any net reduction in harmful behavior, then that would be a valid criticism.

Research indicates, however, that displacement is not inevitable but is contingent on the offender's judgments about alternative crimes. If these alternatives are not viable, the offender may well settle for smaller criminal rewards or for a lower rate of crime. Few offenders are so driven by need or desire that they have to maintain a certain level of offending, whatever the cost. For many, the elimination of easy opportunities for crime may actually encourage them to explore noncriminal alternatives.[49] There are six commonly recognized types of displacement[50]:

1. *Time*. Offenders change the time when they commit crimes (e.g., switching from dealing drugs during the day to dealing at night).
2. *Location*. Offenders switch from targets in one location to targets in other locations (e.g., a dealer stops selling drugs in one community and begins selling them in another community).
3. *Target*. Offenders switch from one type of target to another type (e.g., a burglar switches from apartment units to detached single-family homes).
4. *Method*. Offenders change the way they attack targets (e.g., a street robber stops using a knife and uses a gun).
5. *Type*. Offenders switch from one form of crime to another (e.g., from burglary to check fraud).
6. *Perpetrator*. New offenders replace old offenders who have been removed by police enforcement (e.g., a dealer is arrested and a new dealer begins business with the same customers).

A review of the evidence for displacement shows that when attempts to detect displacement have been made, it is often not found, and if found, it is far less than 100 percent.[51] John Eck found that of 33 studies that looked for displacement effects, only 3 found evidence of much displacement.[52] Eck concluded, "There is more reason to expect no displacement than a great deal. A reasonable conclusion is that displacement can be a threat, but that it is unlikely to completely negate gains due to an enforcement crackdown or a crime prevention effort."[53]

Research has shown that offenders generally begin offending at places they are familiar with and explore outward into increasingly unfamiliar areas.[54] If opportunities are blocked (by increased enforcement, target hardening, or some other means) close to a familiar location, then displacement to other targets close to familiar areas is most likely. Displacement usually occurs in the direction of familiar places, times, targets, and behaviors. Offenders may desist for varying periods of time, or they may even stop offending, depending on how important crime is to their lives.[55]

Although studies have indicated that displacement may not pose a major threat to crime prevention efforts, it is still a phenomenon that police officials must take into account. Ignoring this problem can lead to inequitable solutions to problems; this is particularly true of problem-solving tactics designed to displace offenders from specific locations. Efforts must be made to track those individuals to ensure that they do not create a problem somewhere else.[56]

Evaluation of Results

Crime prevention also suffers from the same malady from which many other interventions suffer: poor or nonexistent **evaluation.** The evaluation component of many programs is poorly conceived, marginally funded, and short-lived. A useful form of evaluation is an outcome or impact evaluation to determine whether the intervention accomplished the expected result. Assessments of this type require more planning and effort, and consideration must be given to the selection of comparison groups, time frames, outcome variables, potential confounding factors, and analytic techniques.[57] (Evaluations are discussed more thoroughly in Chapter 8.)

Giving community leaders and residents an indication of the success or failure of crime prevention efforts is critical to maintaining strong ties, ensuring their continued participation, and documenting that headway is being made in efforts to improve the safety and quality of neighborhoods.[58] (See the following discussion of what works and does not work in crime prevention.)

CRIME PREVENTION: WHAT WORKS AND WHAT DOESN'T

Many crime prevention programs work; others do not. Most programs have not yet been evaluated with enough scientific evidence to draw conclusions. Enough evidence is available, however, to create tentative lists of what works, what does not work, and what is promising.

Following are the major conclusions of a report to Congress, based on a systematic review of more than 500 scientific evaluations of crime prevention practices by the University of Maryland's Department of Criminology and Criminal Justice.[59] This is the first major evaluation of crime prevention programs, resulting in much attention and debate in the field. There are some surprising findings, particularly in the list of programs that do not hold promise—several of which have become pet projects of police agencies and political leaders.

What Prevents or Reduces Crime

The following are programs that researchers believed with reasonable certainty would prevent crime or reduce risk factors for crime. These programs are thus likely to be effective in preventing some form of crime:

- Providing extra police patrols in high-crime hot spots
- Monitoring known high-risk repeat offenders to reduce their time on the streets and returning them to prison quickly
- Arresting employed domestic abusers to reduce repeated abuse by these suspects
- Offering rehabilitation programs for juvenile and adult offenders that are appropriate to their risk factors to reduce their rates of repeat offending
- Offering drug treatment programs to prison inmates to reduce repeat offending after their release

What Does Not Appear to Be Successful

Sufficient evidence indicated to the University of Maryland researchers that the following programs failed to reduce crime or reduce risk factors:

- Gun buyback programs failed to reduce gun violence in cities (as evaluated in St. Louis and Seattle).
- Neighborhood Watch programs organized with police failed to reduce burglary or other target crimes, especially in higher-crime areas where voluntary participation often fails.
- Arrests of unemployed suspects for domestic assault caused higher rates of repeat offending over the long term than nonarrest alternatives.
- Increased arrests or raids on drug markets failed to reduce violent crime or disorder for more than a few days, if at all.
- Storefront police offices failed to prevent crime in the surrounding areas.
- Police newsletters with local crime information failed to reduce victimization rates (as evaluated in Newark, New Jersey, and Houston, Texas).
- Correctional boot camps using traditional military training failed to reduce repeat offending after release compared to similar offenders serving time on probation and parole, for both juveniles and adults.
- "Scared Straight" programs that bring minor juvenile offenders to visit maximum-security prisons to see the severity of prison conditions failed to reduce the participants' reoffending rates and may increase crime.
- Shock probation, shock parole, and split sentences, in which offenders are incarcerated for a short period of time at the beginning of the sentence and then supervised in the community, did not reduce repeat offending compared to the placement of similar offenders only under community supervision, and they increased crime rates for some groups.
- Home detention with electronic monitoring for low-risk offenders failed to reduce offending compared to the placement of similar offenders under standard community supervision without electronic monitoring.
- Intensive supervision on parole or probation did not reduce repeat offending compared to normal levels of community supervision.

What Holds Promise

Researchers determined that the level of certainty for the following programs is too low for there to be positive generalizable conclusions, but

Although both adult and juvenile military-style boot camps increased in number in the 1990s, they had poor results in reducing repeat offending.

Courtesy Washoe County, Nevada, Sheriff's Office.

some empirical basis exists for predicting that further research could show positive results:

- Problem-solving analysis is effective when addressed to the specific crime situation.
- Proactive arrests for carrying concealed weapons in gun crime hot spots, using traffic enforcement and field interrogations, can be helpful.
- Community policing with meetings to set priorities reduced community perceptions of the severity of crime problems in Chicago.
- Field interrogations of suspicious persons reduced crime in a San Diego experiment.
- Gang offender monitoring by community workers and probation and police officers can reduce gang violence.
- Community-based mentoring by Big Brothers/Big Sisters of America substantially reduced drug abuse in one experiment, although evaluations of other similar programs showed that it did not.
- Battered women's shelters were found to reduce at least the short-term (six-week) rate of repeat victimization for women who take other steps to seek help.

Many more impact evaluations using stronger scientific methods are needed before even minimally valid conclusions can be reached about the impact of programs on crime. Again, as previously noted, there is much debate in the field about the research findings. The Maryland report to Congress, however, has raised the consciousness of the crime prevention discipline and will, it is hoped, bring about much more needed research and inquiry.

▲ SUMMARY

It is clear that the field of crime prevention has matured from its earlier forms, originally involving strategic placement of rocks by early cave dwellers and more recently having to do primarily with target hardening one's home with better locks. This chapter has shown its various elements as well as the results of research efforts concerning what good can occur when measures are taken to prevent crimes. The police are realizing that they alone cannot prevent or address crime and disorder and that a partnership with the community is essential if the physical and social problems that plague communities are to be reduced or eliminated.

ITEMS FOR REVIEW

1. Describe briefly the history of crime prevention.
2. Explain the relationship between crime prevention and COPPS.
3. Define what is meant by CPTED, what its second generation includes, and what some potential obstacles to implementing it are.
4. Explain what is meant by situational crime prevention, and list its five goals.
5. Review what is meant by crime displacement, and discuss how it relates to crime prevention.
6. Explain briefly which crime reduction or prevention activities have been shown by researchers to work, to not work, and to hold promise.

NOTES

1. Crime Prevention Coalition of America, *Crime Prevention in America: Foundations for Action* (Washington, D.C.: National Crime Prevention Council, 1990), p. 64.
2. Ronald V. Clarke, *Situational Crime Prevention: Successful Case Studies* (2nd ed.) (Monsey, N.Y.: Criminal Justice Press, 1997), p. 2.
3. Steven P. Lab, "Crime Prevention: Where Have We Been and Which Way Should We Go?" in Steven P. Lab (ed.), *Community Policing at a Crossroads* (Cincinnati, Ohio: Anderson, 1997), pp. 1–13.
4. Cynthia Scanlon, "Crime Prevention Through Environmental Design," *Law and Order* (May 1996):50.
5. U.S. Department of Housing and Urban Development, "Crime Prevention Through Environmental Design," in *Crime Prevention Brief* (Washington, D.C.: Author, no date), p. 2.
6. Lab, "Crime Prevention," p. 5.
7. *Ibid.*
8. *Ibid.*, p. 7.
9. Scanlon, "Crime Prevention Through Environmental Design," p. 50.
10. Lab, "Crime Prevention," p. 6.
11. L. E. Cohen and M. Felson, "Social Change and Crime Rate Trends: A Routine Activity Approach," *American Sociological Review* 44 (1997):588–608.
12. D. B. Cornish and R. V. Clarke, *The Reasoning Criminal: Rational Choice Perspectives on Offending* (New York: Springer-Verlag, 1986).

13. James Q. Wilson and George Kelling, "Broken Windows," *The Atlantic Monthly* 211 (1982):29–38.

14. Lab, "Crime Prevention," p. 6.

15. Ronald V. Clarke, "Situational Crime Prevention: Its Theoretical Basis and Practical Scope," in Michael Tonry and Norval Morris (eds.), *Crime and Justice: An Annual Review of Research* (Vol. 4) (Chicago: University of Chicago Press, 1983), pp. 225–256.

16. Lab, "Crime Prevention," pp. 8–9.

17. U.S. Department of Justice, Bureau of Justice Assistance, *Crime Prevention and Community Policing: A Vital Partnership* (Washington, D.C.: U.S. Government Printing Office, 1997), p. 4.

18. Jim Jordan, "Shifting the Mission: Seeing Prevention as the Strategic Goal, Not a Set of Programs," in *Subject to Debate* (Washington, D.C.: Police Executive Research Forum, December 1999), pp. 1–2.

19. *Ibid.,* p. 3.

20. *Ibid.*

21. Quoted in Julian Fantino, "Taking Crime Prevention Back to the Future!" *The Police Chief* (May 1999):18.

22. *Ibid.*

23. Rob Gurwitt, "Communitarianism: You Can Try It at Home," *Governing* 6 (August 1993):33–39.

24. Fantino, "Taking Crime Prevention Back to the Future!" p. 20.

25. U.S. Department of Justice, Office of Community Oriented Policing Services, *National Policy Summit: Building Private Security/Public Policing Partnerships to Prevent and Respond to Terrorism and Public Disorder* (Washington, D.C.: Author, 2004), pp. 1–12.

26. Lab, "Crime Prevention," p. 6.

27. *Ibid.,* p. 8.

28. U.S. Department of Justice, Bureau of Justice Assistance, *Crime Prevention and Community Policing,* p. 3.

29. C. R. Jeffrey, *Crime Prevention Through Environmental Design* (Beverly Hills, Calif.: Sage, 1971), p. 117.

30. National Crime Prevention Council, *Designing Safer Communities: A Crime Prevention Through Environmental Design Handbook* (Washington, D.C.: Author, 1997), pp. 7–8.

31. "Building a More Crime-Free Environment: Tempe Cops Have the Last Word on Construction Projects," *Law Enforcement News* (November 15, 1998):7.

32. Scanlon, "Crime Prevention Through Environmental Design," pp. 51–52.

33. *Ibid.,* p. 3.

34. Greg Saville and Gerry Cleveland, "2nd Generation CPTED: An Antidote to the Social Y2K Virus of Urban Design." Paper presented at the Third Annual International CPTED Conference, Washington, D.C., December 14–16, 1998.

35. *Ibid.,* p. 1.

36. *Ibid.*

37. Gregory Saville, "New Tools to Eradicate Crime Places and Crime Niches." Paper presented at the Conference of Safer Communities, Melbourne, Australia, September 10–11, 1998, pp. 9–10.

38. Robert A. Cizmadia, "Influences of CPTED on Urban Design and Security Planning," *Security Insider* (January 2004):30.

39. Matthew B. Robinson, "The Theoretical Development of CPTED: 25 Years of Responses to C. Ray Jeffery," http://www.acs.appstate.edu/dept/ps-cj/vitacpted2.html (Accessed March 7, 2006).

40. Clarke, "Situational Crime Prevention," p. 230.

41. U.S. Department of Housing and Urban Development, "Situational Prevention," *Crime Prevention Brief* (Washington, D.C.: Author, no date), p. 1.

42. Clarke, "Situational Crime Prevention," p. 231.

43. U.S. Department of Justice, Center for Problem-Oriented Policing, "The 10 Principles of Crime Opportunity," http://www.popcenter.org/about-situational.htm (Accessed March 7, 2006).

44. Clarke, "Situational Crime Prevention," p. 236.

45. *Ibid.*

46. *Ibid.*

47. *Ibid.,* pp. 254–258.

48. Lab, "Crime Prevention," p. 12.

49. Clarke, "Situational Crime Prevention," p. 237.

50. Robert Barr and Ken Pease, "Crime Placement, Displacement, and Deflection," in Michael Tonry and Norval Morris (eds.), *Crime and Justice: A Review of Research* (Vol. 12) (Chicago: University of Chicago Press, 1990), pp. 146–175.

51. John E. Eck, "The Threat of Crime Displacement," *Criminal Justice Abstracts* 25 (3) (1993):529.

52. Pat Mayhew, Ronald V. Clarke, A. Sturman, and J. M. Hough, *Crime as Opportunity* (Home Office Research Study No. 34) (London: Her Majesty's Stationery Office, 1976); J. Lowman, "Prostitution in Vancouver: Some Notes on the Genesis of a Social Problem," *Canadian Journal of Criminology* 28 (1) (1997):1–16; Barry Poyner and Barry Webb, "Reducing Theft from Shopping Bags in City Center Markets," in Ronald V. Clarke (ed.), *Situational Crime Prevention: Successful Case Studies* (Albany, N.Y.: Harrow and Heston, 1992).

53. Eck, "The Threat of Crime Displacement," pp. 534–536.

54. *Ibid.,* p. 537.

55. *Ibid.*

56. *Ibid.,* pp. 541–542.

57. *Ibid.*

58. William Spelman and John E. Eck, "Problem-Solving: Problem Oriented Policing in Newport News," *Research in Brief* (January 1987):8.

59. Lawrence W. Sherman, Denise C. Gottfredson, Doris L. MacKenzie, John Eck, Peter Reuter, and Shawn D. Bushway, "Preventing Crime: What Works, What Doesn't, What's Promising." *Research in Brief* (Washington, D.C.: National Institute of Justice, 1998), pp. 1–27.

Information Technology

Tools for the Task

Key Terms and Concepts _____

CompStat

Computer-aided dispatch (CAD)

Crime analysis

Geographic information system
  (GIS)

Geomapping

Geographic profiling

Global Positioning System (GPS)

Hot spot

Mobile computing

Records management system (RMS)

Street-level criminology

Learning Objectives _____

As a result of reading this chapter, the student will:

- Understand the function of the three basic aids for crime analysis: computer-aided dispatch (CAD), mobile computing, and records management systems (RMS)
- Know the difference between strategic and tactical crime analysis
- Comprehend how crime patterns can be geomapped
- Be able to trace the development, purposes, and methods of CompStat, and understand how it can function today in agencies of all sizes
- Understand geographic profiling and hot spots
- Be able to explain Global Positioning Systems (GPS) with regard to using police resources
- Know how the Internet and an intranet apply to policing and crime analysis
- Understand the kinds of knowledge, skills, and abilities needed to be a crime analyst

> God hath made man upright; but they have sought out many inventions.
>
> *–Ecclesiastes 7:29*

INTRODUCTION

According to the National Commission of Law Observance and Enforcement in 1931 (best known as the Wickersham Commission), the advent of the radio-equipped patrol car brought a new era where "the roving patrol car, fast, efficient, stealthy . . . [was] just as liable to be within 60 feet as 3 miles of the crook plying his trade . . . who is coming to realize that a few moments may bring them down about him like a swarm of bees—this lightning swift angel of death."[1] And thus was police technology born, with the introduction of the radio-controlled patrol car hailed as the technological innovation that would turn the tide against criminals.

For more than four decades, the police have been employing myriad technologies to gather, store, and share information. In addition, today's police officers are on a cell phone, deploy a TASER instead of a six-shot revolver, use a defibrillator from the patrol car trunk to resuscitate heart attack victims, send latent fingerprints to an automated database for matching, use digital photographs and other identification means to see if someone is telling the truth, and utilize many other kinds of databases and tools of the trade (many of which are discussed later in this chapter) that would boggle the minds of such pioneers as August Vollmer and O. W. Wilson. Today technology can help the police to better serve their communities by automating time-consuming tasks, dispatching personnel more efficiently, and improving an agency's ability to collect and analyze data as well as disseminate it to both internal and external audiences.

This chapter examines the current use of technology as it can be applied to community oriented policing and problem solving (COPPS); specifically, we look at how it can generally assist with analyzing crime information. We begin with a consideration of the function of crime analysis in the problem-solving concept and list several criteria that must be met for analysis to succeed. Then we consider what we call the basic systems of analysis: computer-aided dispatch, mobile computing, and records management. Next is a section where we briefly distinguish between strategic and tactical crime analysis. Following that is a look at how geomapping is used to reveal crime patterns.

Then we turn to a concept that often represents a higher level of accountability for crime analysis: CompStat. This involves the collection and analysis of a number of types of data, and we provide examples of how CompStat evolved and what its functions are. Then we look at applications of geographic profiling, the mapping of hot spots, and Global Positioning Systems. Next we review how use of both the Internet and an intranet can assist the police in engaging the community as well as in doing analysis, and then we briefly consider how surveys are used in this same regard. After a brief look at counterterrorism, the chapter concludes with a discussion of the kinds of knowledge, skills, and abilities that should be possessed by today's professional crime analyst.

CRIME ANALYSIS

Street-Level Criminology

Integral to the process of problem solving, discussed in Chapter 3, is **crime analysis,** which may be simply defined as "the collection and analysis of data pertaining to a criminal incident, offender, and target."[2]

The importance of analysis in this era of COPPS can be summed up in the following statement: "Community policing can be distinguished from professional policing because it calls for information from domains that had previously been neglected and for more complex analysis of that information."[3] Indeed, the more that important data is collected, analyzed, and related to all components of the crime triangle (victim, offender, and location, as discussed in Chapter 4), the better equipped police will be to develop innovative solutions that include the full spectrum of suppression, intervention, and prevention options.[4]

It is very important for officers who are engaged in problem solving to understand how, when, where, and why criminal events occur rather than merely responding to them. In this vein we do not mean to say that patrol officers should develop expertise in understanding the mental processes and theories that are involved in a person's choosing to commit crimes (although criminology or psychology courses at a college or university would certainly benefit the problem-solving officer); rather, we are referring to what might be termed **street-level criminology.** This matter is relatively new to policing at the street level, and it requires that we learn more about crime occurrences through analysis and experimentation with the problem-solving process.

An important note of caution must be stressed, however. Crime analysis will only be as good as the data or information that is collected. There are three essential criteria for crime analysis that police agencies should use when designing data collection processes and interpreting the meaning of information gleaned from crime analysis[5]:

1. *Timeliness.* Does the pattern or trend presented reflect a current problem or issue, or does it represent a previous situation? Deployment decisions with respect to both prevention and offender apprehension efforts must be based on current information to the extent that is possible.
2. *Relevancy.* Do the measures used in the analysis accurately reflect what is intended? For example, whether a pattern is based on calls for service data or incident data can be a very important determination depending on what the police manager is trying to understand.
3. *Reliability.* Would the same data, interpreted by different people at different times, lead to the same conclusions?

The Basics: Computer-Aided Dispatch, Mobile Computing, and Records Management

Here we briefly describe the computer-aided dispatch system, mobile computing, and records management system. While there are other police information technologies (several of which are discussed below), these are described in detail because they are the primary technologies for offering *core* data management capabilities for COPPS, such as data capture and entry; search, retrieval, and display; messaging; and linkages between data elements.[6]

Computer-Aided Dispatch (CAD).   **Computer-aided dispatch (CAD)** has become an indispensable technology in policing, designed to handle all information related to receiving and dispatching emergency calls for service (CFS). CAD is often the first point of data entry, whether processing an emergency 911 CFS or managing an officer-initiated car stop. CAD fully automates the call-taking and dispatching functions; used with automated vehicle location (AVL) systems that track patrol vehicle status, CAD can help to prioritize CFS and make recommendations for unit and resource dispatching based on beats, zones, closest resources, and/or current unit activities. Some CAD systems can also provide the number and type of prior calls that were made at the location, whether there are existing warrants for residents, or if there are specific hazards related to the location.[7] Exhibit 5–1 provides an example of how CAD works.

Mobile Computing.   **Mobile computing** has become the catchall phrase for outfitting an officer's vehicle or person with the technology that, in effect, allows him or her to be a "mobile office." Mobile computing is actually composed of several law enforcement hardware and software technologies working together to allow officers to access, receive, create, and exchange information wirelessly in the field. Officers can proactively query local, state, and national databases; receive and initiate CAD events; view unit

EXHIBIT 5–1

Computer-Aided Dispatch: How It Works

Assume a 911 call for service (CFS) is received by a police dispatcher. The automatic name index (ANI) and automatic location information (ALI) come on the CAD screen, and the dispatcher adds additional call details to CAD. The computer assigns a priority rating to the call based on the information entered, checks the validity of the address using the geofile, and searches for historical location information (previous CFS, hazardous conditions, weapons, warrants); it then makes recommendations about dispatching available officers and units (cars, foot/bike patrol, etc.) to the scene based on unit proximity and availability. The dispatcher can use a radio or silently dispatch the call to officers via mobile computers (laptops) in their patrol cars. The system constantly updates unit and call status for the dispatcher and officers to view. The computer automatically maintains status information, listing all vehicles that work on a specific tour of duty, their status and their current assignment. Response times are documented and reports are captured.

Source: U.S. Department of Justice, Office of Community Oriented Policing Services, *Law Enforcement Tech Guide: How to Plan, Purchase, and Manage Technology (Successfully!)* (Washington, D.C.: Author, 2002), p. 248.

EXHIBIT 5–2

Mobile Computing: How It Works

After receiving dispatch information via the mobile laptop computer, the officer responds to the incident, running queries and other inquiries against databases remotely. When the incident is closed, the officer completes a required report via laptop or handheld unit. The report information is electronically forwarded to a supervisor for approval via a wireless communications network. The supervisor decides whether to approve the report. If not approved, the report is sent back to the officer for corrections; if approved, the report is electronically submitted to the records unit. Once it is received by the records unit, records staff performs quality assurance on the report prior to submitting it electronically to the records management system.

Source: U.S. Department of Justice, Office of Community Oriented Policing Services, *Law Enforcement Tech Guide: How to Plan, Purchase, and Manage Technology (Successfully!)* (Washington, D.C.: Author, 2002), p. 248.

status; send e-mail; prepare and file incident reports; issue citations; capture field interview information; access department policies and procedures; research penal codes; and perform many other functions. In sum, they are able to do nearly everything they could do in the station house.[8] Exhibit 5–2 discusses how mobile computing works in the field.

Records Management System (RMS).   Today a **records management system (RMS)** is a key asset to effective policing, offering robust analytical tools and the ability to seamlessly share information, developing complex linkages between myriad data and information, and assisting in effective management strategies. In its simplest form, an RMS captures, maintains, and analyzes all police agency and incident-related information and is vital for tracking and managing criminal and noncriminal events, investigations, and personnel information. An RMS automates the daily practice of entering, storing, retrieving, retaining, archiving, viewing, and exchanging records, documents, data, information, or files related to persons, vehicles, incidents, arrests, warrants, traffic accidents, citations, pawn tickets, civil process papers, gun registration investigations, property, and evidence.[9] Exhibit 5–3 provides an example of how an RMS works.

Together, CAD and RMS can produce most of the data in CompStat (discussed below) with a touch of a button. Otherwise, a data entry clerk or crime analyst must enter the details of *every* incident reported, arrest effected, summons issued, case cleared, and other such information into a spreadsheet or database to produce the reports.[10]

Strategic and Tactical Crime Analysis

The collection and analysis of data spanning a long period of time result in strategic crime analysis. This type of analysis is research focused because

EXHIBIT 5–3

Records Management System: How It Works

Officers prepare reports via desktop or mobile computer and submit them electronically to a supervisor, who reviews them. Once the supervisor's approval is given, a report is automatically added to the RMS. If property or evidence has been received, it can be bar coded and linked directly to the recorded data in the RMS. Information stored in the RMS becomes available to agency users, such as detectives, crime analysis and COPPS divisions, command staff, and others. A public interface is built into most RMS systems to provide information to the community, and appropriate RMS data and information can be shared and exchanged with other justice systems.

Source: U.S. Department of Justice, Office of Community Oriented Policing Services, *Law Enforcement Tech Guide: How to Plan, Purchase, and Manage Technology (Successfully!)* (Washington, D.C.: Author, 2002), p. 248.

it includes the use of statistics to make conclusions. This analysis can be useful to departments in terms of forecasting crime trends or estimating future crime based on past trends. (*Note:* Although we will not delve into it at this point, it should be mentioned that the Microsoft Word Excel function is very useful for making forecasts of crime trends; this task can be accomplished fairly easily.)

While strategic crime analysis involves the review of data spanning generally a year or more, tactical crime analysis uses real-time data spanning several days. One of its principal uses involves problem identification, or the pattern detection of multiple offenses over a short period of time that have common characteristics, such as the type of crime, modus operandi, and type of weapon used.[11] One example of tactical crime analysis that is discussed later in this chapter is geographic profiling, which can be used to suggest the likelihood of where an offender resides based on the pattern of where victims and offenses occur. Linkage analysis involves connecting a suspect to a series of incidents based on commonalities in modus operandi and suspect descriptions as well as known offenders who live in close proximity to a given area. For example, many states search their databases of registered sex offenders when a series of sexual offenses is identified.[12]

Crime Pattern Geomapping

Mapping crime patterns has become increasingly popular among law enforcement agencies and is given high visibility at the federal level, in the media, and among the largest police departments in the nation. A **geographic information system (GIS)** is an automated system for the capture, storage, retrieval, analysis, and display of spatial data. It has been said that "GIS technology is to geographical analysis what the microscope, the telescope, and computers have been to other sciences."[13]

Replacement for Pin Maps. The traditional crime map was a jumbo representation of a jurisdiction with pins stuck in it. These maps were useful for showing where crimes occurred, but they had several limitations as well: As they were updated, the prior crime patterns were lost; the maps were static, unable to be manipulated or queried; they could be quite difficult to read when several types of crime were mixed together.[14] Consequently, during the 1990s pin maps largely gave way to desktop computer mapping, which has now become commonplace and fast, aided by the availability of cheap color printers.[15]

The importance of **geomapping** is evidenced by the fact that the National Institute of Justice has established a Crime Mapping Research Center (CMRC) to promote research, evaluation, development, and dissemination of GIS technology for criminal justice research and practice. The CMRC holds annual conferences on geomapping to provide researchers and practitioners an opportunity to gain both practical and state-of-the-art information on the use and utility of computerized geomapping. The CMRC Web site address is http://www.ojp.usdoj.gov/cmrc.[16]

GIS for COPPS. GIS has revolutionized the way in which COPPS is conducted internationally. This is largely due to the ability of the police to now overlay seemingly diverse types of data that all contribute to a true understanding of a particular problem.

For example, a series of burglaries taking place between the hours of 1 A.M. and 3 A.M. might be the first thing visually displayed on a crime map. This would correspond with the scanning phase of the S.A.R.A. problem-solving process described in Chapter 3. However, getting at the underlying causes of the burglary problem requires deeper probing and innovative thinking. In this case, the crime analyst might overlay the burglary incident data with available data about land usage in the area and might then learn that the burglaries are occurring within walking distance of an area high school.[17]

Although this might seem to be an obvious linkage to many, individuals often overlook such connections. By visually displaying overlays of various potential data combinations, GIS can play a critical role in jumpstarting the analysis process. With the above burglary example, the police manager might begin to develop a theory related to the fact that the burglaries might be caused by youths who are truant from school. Looking forward, in addition to now having a large pool of individuals from which investigators might begin seeking information about the incidents, analysts may eventually be led to a collaborative project with the school to develop responses that increase truancy enforcement.[18]

GIS pattern analysis can also indicate a broader understanding of a problem. For example, assume that a pattern is indicated of disorderly conduct and assaults in an area. An overlay with available liquor stores and bars in the area may present the analyst with some ideas as to what factors might be driving the problem. An additional benefit of GIS is that it

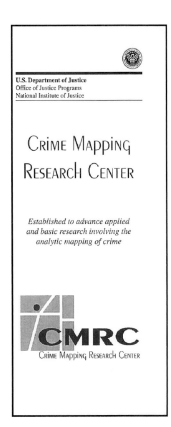

U.S. Department of Justice
Office of Justice Programs
National Institute of Justice

CRIME MAPPING
RESEARCH CENTER

*Established to advance applied
and basic research involving the
analytic mapping of crime*

CMRC
CRIME MAPPING RESEARCH CENTER

The Crime Mapping Research Center (CMRC) is a national clearinghouse for information about crime analysis and mapping.

U.S. Department of Justice, National Institute of Justice, Crime Mapping Research Center (Washington, D.C.: Author, 1999).

is compatible with statistical analyses to further refine an analyst's examination of a problem; for example, simple statistical analyses may link disorderly conduct and assaults in a city to the overall density of alcohol availability or other possibilities.[19]

Exhibit 5–4 discusses interactive geomapping on the Internet. In a related vein, Figure 5–1 is the initial screen that appears when the user chooses "vehicle and traffic incidents" from the San Diego County Web site, providing information about auto thefts and burglaries as well as traffic accidents. Figure 5–2 shows the Austin, Texas, map viewer; Figure 5–3 provides an example of geomapping of street gang–motivated homicide in Chicago.

Geomapping can greatly increase the accountability of a police agency by visually demonstrating incident patterns for which the agency's administrators can hold commanding officers accountable over time. A proactive police manager should use GIS and other problem-solving tools described in this chapter to create sound strategic and tactical decisions related to such things as officer deployment, resource allocation, and partnerships with other agencies for sustained crime reductions.[20]

The CompStat model of the New York Police Department (NYPD), discussed below, institutionalized the use of GIS for departmental planning purposes. The program was such a success that similar versions of CompStat have been implemented in departments across the country.

EXHIBIT 5–4

Interactive Geomapping on the Internet

Following are two examples of interactive geomapping efforts on the Internet in San Diego County, California, and Austin, Texas. Use of such systems not only enables citizens to obtain much more information than was previously available, but it precludes their having to make formal requests for information while freeing crime analysts to devote more time to analyzing crime instead of providing reports to the public.

In 1970, San Diego County's Automated Regional Justice Information System (ARJIS) began allowing all law enforcement agencies in the county to maintain and access crime and arrest information. Recently, however, ARJIS developed the first multiagency interactive geomapping Web site in the nation. Now anyone in the world can query and view certain crime, arrest, call, and traffic data for the county. Searches can be by geographic location (street, neighborhood, police beat, or city) as well as by time of day or day of week. ARJIS serves as a model for making interactive crime maps available to the public on the Internet. People access ARJIS for a variety of purposes: data on crime in their area, a grant proposal, support for a debate on an issue, citizen patrol data and real estate agent information.

Austin, Texas, unveiled a similarly unique approach to geomapping on the Web, tripling the amount of information that was previously available and providing aggregated data by patrol areas, ZIP codes, census tracts, and neighborhood associations. Citizens can also see crime totals within 500 feet of any user-inputted address.

Source: Adapted from *Crime Mapping News* [a Police Foundation newsletter] 3 (Summer 2001):1–6.

CompStat

Key Elements of CompStat. Unfortunately, today it seems the NYPD crime control model **CompStat** (computer-driven crime statistics) is often oversimplified to refer to aggressive or data-driven policing, where police commanders are frequently grilled about crimes in their areas of responsibility—and they are even castigated, transferred, or demoted after a lifetime of service if they failed to do something about it. According to police scholar Phyllis McDonald, this perception of CompStat "does a disservice to its management principles and its potential for other jurisdictions."[21]

The key elements of CompStat are as follows[22]:

- Specific objectives
- Accurate and timely intelligence
- Effective tactics
- Rapid deployment of personnel and resources
- Relentless follow-up and assessment

Prior to CompStat, NYPD generally had a reporting lag of three to six months for crime statistics—and even then, any meaningful analysis was impossible. Headquarters was not systematically tracking crime activity

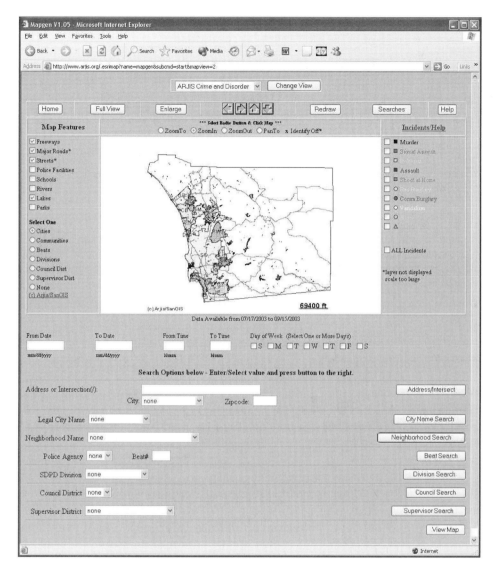

FIGURE 5–1

San Diego County's Interactive Crime Map

Source: http://www.arjis.org/esrimap?name=mapgen&subcmd=start&mapview=2.

in the precincts, let alone using such information to evaluate the performance of its commanding officers. As a result, the commanders did not view crime reduction as a primary job responsibility. As was common to departments across the country, reactive, incident-driven patrol was seen as more important, and detective and patrol bureaus rarely collaborated and even directly clashed over territorial concerns.[23]

CompStat was devised as a means of reforming these organizational issues by pushing all precincts to generate weekly crime activity reports so

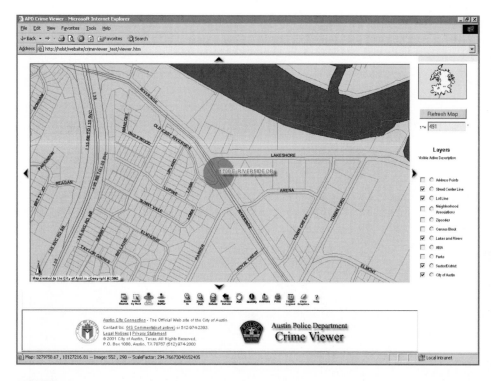

FIGURE 5–2

The Austin, Texas, Crime Mapping Viewer

Source: Al Johnson, "The Austin Police Department's Crime Mapping Viewer," *Crime Mapping News* (Washington, D.C.: Police Foundation, Summer 2001), p. 5.

that they could be held accountable for the achievement of several objectives. Over time, crime data was readily available, computerized, and compiled into the "CompStat Book," offering up-to-date information that was then compared at city, precinct, and patrol levels. Commanders quickly realized that their role had changed and that they had to stop simply responding to crime and start proactively thinking about ways to deal with it in terms of suppression, intervention, and prevention. To solidify this message, NYPD headquarters began to hold regularly scheduled meetings in which the commanders and their staff meet with top brass to discuss crime trends and issues. In a very intimidating environment, commanders stand before a lectern in front of three large video screens that flash GIS-generated maps of recent crime patterns. The commanders are then asked what tactics they have tried to address the patterns, what resources they have and need, and with whom they have collaborated. Brainstorming problem-solving sessions ensue about proactively responding to the crime problems, and suggestions for strategies are made at subsequent meetings, with relentless follow-up by top brass to further ensure accountability.[24]

Over time, CompStat has evolved to include other data: census demographics, arrest and summons activity, average response time, domestic violence incidents, unfounded radio runs, personnel absences, and even

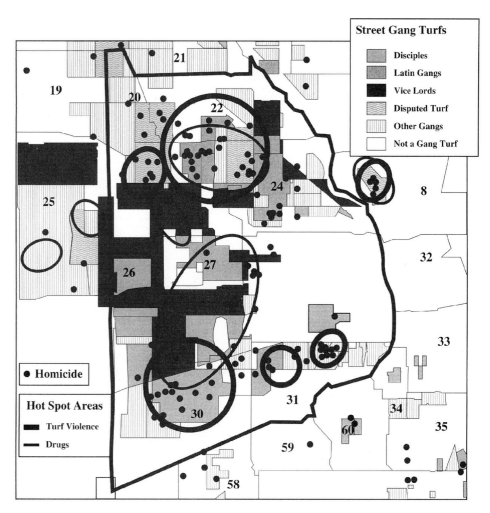

FIGURE 5–3

A Crime Map of Street Gang–Motivated Homicide, Chicago

Source: Carolyn Rebecca Block and Richard Block, *Street Gang Crime in Chicago*
(Washington, D.C.: National Institute of Justice, 1993), p. 5.

citizen complaints and charges of officer misconduct. Scholars and practitioners have argued that CompStat has played a prominent role in the significant crime reductions in New York City following its implementation.
True or not, the impact CompStat has had on police management practices cannot be denied. Certainly another benefit has been the significant
increases in job satisfaction found by those who feel empowered by the
problem-solving process (see Figure 5–4).[25]

Use of CompStat Data: An Example.   Next we provide some fundamen-
tals about how to present, compare, and map data. Although some of this
information may well be beyond the training of some readers (e.g., the section that discusses descriptive statistics), we feel it is important to at least

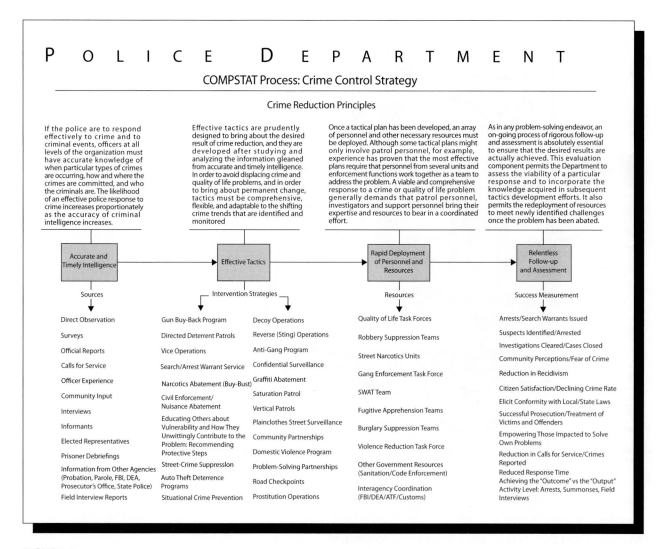

FIGURE 5–4
CompStat Crime Control Strategy

Source: Jon M. Shane, "The Compstat Process," *FBI Law Enforcement Bulletin,* (April 2004), p. 19.

present the process, as well as an overview of what is available with CompStat analyses. Here are the three steps[26]:

1. The first step involves descriptive statistics, or presenting the data so that everyone, from commanders down to patrol officers, can readily understand the relevant information. Data may be presented and described in a number of ways: aggregate increase or decrease; simple percentages (including increase or decrease over previous time frames); ratio and rates; incidents compared to population; mean, median, and mode; pie charts, line charts, bar charts, histograms; and so on. Figure 5–5 shows the means by which data may be presented.

2. The second step in presenting data, comparing, is designed to reveal the relationship between two or more crimes. These statistics are called measures of association, and

Appropriate Statistics					
Descriptive Analysis	Maximum	Minimum	Mean	Median	Mode
	Violent and nonviolent crime summary		Aggregate increase or decrease		Standard deviation
Frequency Distribution	Percentage increase or decrease	Proportion across categories	Ratio and rates Incidents to population Performance to police officers		
Organization and Presentation of Data	Pie charts (for percentage of total)		Bar charts (for aggregate data or rate; e.g., incidents per 100,000 people)		
	Line charts (frequency polygon); add trend lines to establish direction		Histograms with a normal curve (e.g., response time analysis)		Cross-tab charts

FIGURE 5–5
Means of Data Presentation

Source: Jon M. Shane, "Compstat Design," *FBI Law Enforcement Bulletin,* (May 2004), p. 14.

they enable crime analysts to quantify the strength and direction of a relationship—to uncover the connections between crimes and to make predictions. For example, suppose a crime analyst was interested in seeing if a relationship existed between calls for service (CFS) pertaining to drug sales and shootings. After gathering the appropriate data, by calculating the measure of association (such as a Pearson's r), the analyst can determine the strength of the relationship and its direction. Suppose a strong positive relationship was found between these two variables (i.e., the two crimes of drug sales and shootings); one might infer that the two crimes were closely related, so as one of the crimes increased, the other would also. A prediction could then be made that as there are more CFS for drug sales, a higher number of shootings might be expected as well. The analyst would do well to remember, however, that this strong positive relationship does not automatically prove such a connection exists, but this association would serve as an important clue about causation. Comparing the data allows analysts and commanders to consider adjusting or compensating for shifts in trends or patterns. Appropriate charts should display the information for each beat, zone, or precinct, as well as city- or county-wide areas, including the aggregate difference and percentage change in reported incidents (see Figure 5–6). The data should also be depicted in temporal (time) distribution so that commanders can see when crimes occur.

3. The final step, mapping data (called spatial analysis), can detect where criminals travel. Officers can create overlays of CFS with arrests effected, unsolved burglaries with known burglars' residences, or CFS with abandoned buildings. Analysis can create specialty maps, such as sex offenders' residences, recovered guns, recovered stolen autos, and thefts of auto parts. Most important, maps can display data to show hot spots, or areas of concentrated crime (discussed more fully below); then the police can develop appropriate intervention strategies.

Data Comparison

				Diff.	% +/–
Day to day	One chart for each week of the CompStat period				
Week to week	Current week	vs.	Previous week	+5	+3%
Month to month	March 2007	vs.	April 2007	–18	–27%
Quarter to quarter	Jan, Feb, Mar	vs.	Apr, May, Jun	+32	+44%
Half year to half year	1st 6 months	vs.	2nd 6 months	–63	–40%
Year to year	2006	vs.	2007	–27	–2%
Year to date	January 1, 2007, to present date			Aggregate	
Last 12 months	March 15, 2006, to March 14, 2007			Aggregate	
Custom date	Any time period (days, weeks, months, quarters, years, decades)				

Comparisons for each period against the prior period

Week	Current week 2007	vs.	Same week 2006
Month	Current month 2007	vs.	Same month 2006
Quarter	Jan, Feb, Mar 2007	vs.	Jan, Feb, Mar 2006
Half year	1st 6 months 2007	vs.	1st 6 months 2006
Year	Jan 1, 2007, to present	vs.	Jan 1, 2006, to present
12 months	Jan 18, 2006, to Jan 17, 2007	vs.	Jan 18, 2005, to Jan 17, 2006
Custom	Any custom date period compared with the prior date period		

FIGURE 5–6
Data Comparison Chart

Source: Jon M. Shane, "Compstat Design," *FBI Law Enforcement Bulletin,* (May 2004), p. 16.

Figure 5–7 is a matrix showing the kinds of intervention strategies that might be used to address crime that is experiencing different temporal (time) and spatial (space) occurrences. For example, in the lower-left corner of the matrix, it shows where crimes are being committed and when they are heavily concentrated in terms of time of day/week at a particular hot spot, so the police would want to use surveillance, arrest squads, CCTV, and unmarked police cars.

Future of CompStat.   The future of CompStat does not lie in its survival as a tool of upper management but as a tool of the street officer. All of the principal reform movements in policing—from the now-antiquated management by objectives (MBO) through today's community policing era—have relied on line-level officers and investigators having current, ongoing knowledge of the criminal activity in their beat. Agencies have been improving their internal information management and communications infrastructure for this purpose, making it possible for any member of any police agency to create CompStat-like analyses at their discretion. CompStat belongs at the line level and has evolved from a simple file name to a technique and a belief system. It must therefore be understood by management and then pushed down to both supervisors and rank-and-file police officers.[27]

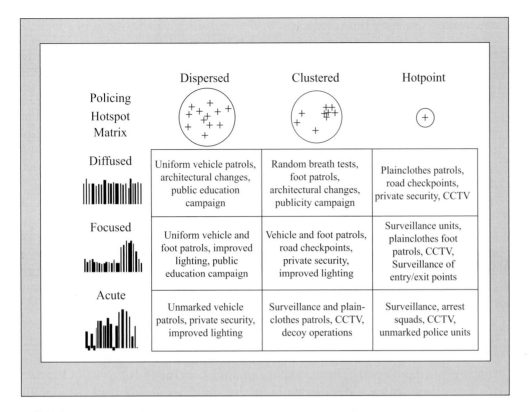

FIGURE 5–7
Intervention Strategies Matrix

Source: Jon M. Shane, "Compstat Design," *FBI Law Enforcement Bulletin,* (May 2004), p. 18.

Other Applications: Geographic Profiling and Hot Spots

Geographic Profiling.   **Geographic profiling,** or the combined use of geography, psychology, and mathematics to identify the location of an offender, is most commonly associated with tracking down serial killers, rapists, and arsonists. However, it is a useful investigative tool in any case in which an individual offender has committed criminal activity across a series of locations. Geographic profiling suggests investigative alternatives based on the "hunting behavior" of the offender. Leading geographic profiler Kim Rossmo argues that criminals are no different in their pattern of carrying out their offenses than ordinary citizens are in going about their day-to-day activities.[28]

Following this principle, geographic profiling uses the nearness principle as a key rule. The nearness principle argues that offenders will remain within a limited range that is comfortable to them when committing their offenses, just as animals will forage within a limited range from their base. This principle has led to the creation of a computerized geographic profiling workstation that includes statistical analyses, GIS features, and database management to aid in calculating investigative suggestions. Crime scenes are broken down by type and entered by location, and addresses of suspects can be evaluated based on their probability of being the actual offender. This can help investigators sort through existing records, such as registered sex offenders, and other information.[29]

Hot Spots.   The term **hot spot** refers to the theory that crime is not spread randomly but tends to cluster in certain places. The significance of place in relation to crime has long been the subject of research, is described as "a discrete location in space and time," and can include "stores, homes, apartment buildings, street corners, addresses, and subway stations."[30] (A related concept, routine activity theory, was discussed in Chapter 4.)

Generally described as areas or places with a relatively high concentration of crimes, hot spots can be readily identified through the use of spatial statistical software. This software can provide a colored electronic overlay, resembling a thermal image, with the colors indicating the degree of intensity. Hot spot identification has become increasingly popular under COPPS and is now generally considered an essential GIS tool. Coupled with the other kinds of analyses that the police can perform, this provides a more holistic approach to crime prevention, whereby social, environmental, and demographic factors are all considered before an appropriate response is developed. These responses might include (but are not limited to) targeting police patrol activity at hot spot locations and at specific times, providing crime prevention advice to victims or community groups on crime reduction strategies (target hardening), advising on the placement of closed-circuit televisions in public places, or a myriad of other situational crime prevention techniques. The identification of hot spots can also provide valuable insight into emerging crime trends and predictive patterns of behavior by looking at the modus operandi of the offenders.[31]

Global Positioning System (GPS)

Global Positioning Systems (GPS) have been used to enhance the tracking of offenders and officer deployments. GPS use satellite-based technologies for the purpose of tracking the movement of patrol cars or specially equipped stolen vehicles. In some cases, an officer's cell phone can be equipped with GPS technology, providing an alternative to conventional address matching for an officer responding to a call. GPS technology has also proven to significantly enhance aerial photography of crime incident locations, allowing for greater visualization of the complete context of a situation. Some states have capitalized on the surveillance capacity of GPS to monitor the real-time location of high-risk offenders released from prison.[32]

Internet/Intranet and COPPS

The Internet has also proven to be an important mechanism for furthering police agencies' COPPS objectives. Important features that are used by many departmental Web sites in reaching their citizens include the following[33]:

- Libraries devoted to crime prevention and safety tips (including information about known scam cases operating within the jurisdiction)
- Virtual tours of the department
- Recent jurisdictional and neighborhood crime statistics (including crime maps)
- Departmental wanted lists and upcoming court cases
- Capability for citizens to anonymously report crime or complaints about officer conduct

Many agencies are also establishing an intranet for their employees. Through the intranet, a department is able to supply a number of important informational needs through access to the following[34]:

- *Problem-solving system.* A searchable database of problems that officers have worked on over the past few years can be accessed.
- *Property evidence system.* A searchable database on property and evidence in the department's custody can be used.
- *Calls for service.* A searchable database on CFS by several categories would be accessible.
- *Records management system.* There would be online access to RMS and a wide range of search capabilities for offense reports.
- *Computer-aided dispatch system.* Online access to CAD system records, including active call information, would be available.
- *Gang database.* There would be online access to the agency's gang information.

Surveys

Not to be overlooked in crime analysis is the use of community surveys to identify or clarify problems. For example, an officer may canvass all the business proprietors in shopping centers on his or her beat. One variation on this theme occurred in Baltimore when an officer telephoned business owners to update the police department's after-hours business contact files. Although the officer did not conduct a formal survey, he used this task to also inquire about problems the owners might want to bring to police attention.

On a larger scale, a team of officers may survey residents of a housing complex or neighborhood known to have particular crime problems. The survey could assist in determining residents' priority concerns, acquiring information about hot spots, and learning more about residents' expectations of police.[35] Residents will also be more likely to keep the police abreast of future problems when officers leave their cards and encourage residents to contact them directly.

Another approach to the survey process involves developing a beat profile. In Tempe, Arizona, COPPS officers began by conducting a detailed profile of a target beat. This involved both door-to-door surveys of residents and businesses and detailed observations of the environment. A survey instrument was developed and pilot-tested, and all survey team members were trained and given a uniform protocol to follow. The instrument contained questions about sociodemographic characteristics of residents, observed crime and drug problems, fear of crime, perception of city and police services, willingness to participate in and support community policing objectives, and other information. Survey team members also recorded information about the surroundings—condition of buildings, homes, streets, and yards; presence of abandoned vehicles; possible zoning and other code violations; and existence of graffiti, trash, loiterers, gang members, and other signs of disorder.[36]

Counterterrorism Analysis

In the wake of attacks by terrorists on U.S. soil, the role and function of crime analysts have become even more crucial. Crime analysts' approach to counterterrorism involves two major areas—investigation and prevention[37]:

- *Investigation.* Terrorists operate according to rules and principles that can be identified, analyzed, and predicted. Although they can be fanatical and fiendish, they behave in a logical fashion, picking their targets with precision. This makes them more vulnerable in the sense that analysts can predict their behavior and disrupt their efforts. Analysts must never work alone, however; they must coordinate with the appropriate federal agency, most often the Federal Bureau of Investigation (FBI).
- *Prevention.* Prevention is accomplished by denying the terrorist the opportunity to attack in the first place. The process begins with a threat assessment of the jurisdiction: identifying and evaluating the risk of targets, and constructing countermeasures by using the S.A.R.A. process. Analysts can *scan* for vulnerabilities, *analyze* these methods of attack to determine countermeasures, *respond* by allocating the necessary police resources to try to thwart an attack, and *assess* by performing periodic readiness tests and exercises to determine effectiveness.

WANTED: THE "RIGHT STUFF" TO BE A CRIME ANALYST

This chapter has certainly proved that certain kinds of knowledge, skills, and abilities are essential in order for one to become a crime analyst. The mere possession of a badge and police experience will likely not suffice, at least not without prior specialized training and education. The items in the following list have been shown in this chapter to be important for conducting crime and problem analyses; ideally, an analyst would possess all of them, but that is nearly impossible. Therefore the following is more of a job description for an analyst's position[38]:

- *Criminological theory.* We noted earlier in this chapter that one must be a "street-level criminologist"; one does not need to know all of the criminological theories in depth but should possess a working knowledge of theories that contribute the most to understanding the local crime and disorder problems (e.g., situational crime prevention, repeat victimization, rational choice theory, and routine activities theory).

- *Literature.* The crime analyst should be aware of both classic and current research literature related to community policing and problem solving and the aforementioned theories, as well as statistics and research methods. Goldstein's concepts of problem oriented policing and problem solving—both in theory and in practice—are essential, as is the history of policing and how it has evolved.
- *Research methods.* Basic research design, sampling methods, modes of observation (experiment, field research, surveying, evaluation), data collection, process and impact evaluation, and ethics are important here.
- *Statistics.* Knowledge of measures of descriptive and inferential statistics, as well as forecasting, is important.
- *Geographic information systems (GIS) and spatial analysis.* These are important because of the influence of geography on crime, on problem solving, and on crime prevention.
- *Technology.* A crime analyst should know the advantages and limits of technology for both data collection and analysis.

▲ SUMMARY

This chapter has examined what might be fairly said to be the heart of the COPPS strategy: analysis of crime data. This discussion included the kinds of methods and technologies—including various forms of computer hardware and software—that are now in the analyst's quiver and are being applied to COPPS.

It should be abundantly clear now, after reading this chapter, that these are most certainly challenging times for those persons who are charged with trying to determine the who, what, when, where, why, and how of crime; for example, the traditional reliance on a giant pin map that showed criminal locations would provide little in the way of sufficiency for addressing today's criminal element. Indeed, compared to today's computer-generated analytical tools, the pin map of not too long ago (which, by the way, is probably hanging on the walls and in use by some law enforcement agencies today) seems about as high tech as the tube-type patrol car radios of yore. It has also made clear that the attributes needed for today's crime analyst are probably much different and more sophisticated than they were even a decade ago.

■ ITEMS FOR REVIEW

1. What is the function of the three basic aids for crime analysis (computer-aided dispatch, mobile computing, and records management systems)?
2. What is the difference between strategic and tactical crime analysis?
3. Describe how crime patterns can be geomapped.

4. Trace the development, purposes, and methods of CompStat, and discuss how it can function today in all sizes of agencies.

5. Describe geographic profiling and mapping of hot spots.

6. Distinguish between the Internet and an intranet in terms of how they apply to policing and crime analysis.

7. List and explain some of the knowledge, skills, and abilities that are needed to be a crime analyst.

NOTES

1. National Commission of Law Observance and Enforcement, *Report on Police* (Washington, D.C.: Government Printing Office, 1931), p. 140.

2. Philip Canter, "Using a Geographic Information System for Tactical Crime Analysis," in Victor Goldsmith, Philip G. McGuire, John H. Mollenkopf, and Timothy A. Ross (eds.), *Analyzing Crime Patterns: Frontiers of Practice* (Thousand Oaks, Calif.: Sage, 2000), pp. 3–10.

3. Timothy C. O'Shea and Keith Nicholls, *Crime Analysis in America: Findings and Recommendations* (Washington, D.C.: U.S. Department of Justice, Office of Community Oriented Policing Services, March 2003), p. 7.

4. Heath J. Grant and Karen J. Terry, *Law Enforcement in the 21st Century* (Boston, Mass.: Allyn & Bacon, 2005), pp. 329–330.

5. *Ibid.,* p. 330.

6. U.S. Department of Justice, Office of Community Oriented Policing Services, *Law Enforcement Tech Guide: How to Plan, Purchase, and Manage Technology (Successfully!)* (Washington, D.C.: Author, 2002), p. 247.

7. *Ibid.,* p. 248.

8. *Ibid.,* p. 250.

9. *Ibid.,* p. 252.

10. Jon M. Shane, "CompStat Design," *FBI Law Enforcement Bulletin* (May 2004), p. 17.

11. Canter, "Using a Geographic Information System for Tactical Crime Analysis," p. 5.

12. Grant and Terry, *Law Enforcement in the 21st Century,* p. 331.

13. D. Cowen, "Why Is GIS Important?" http://www.env.duke.edu/lel/enn351/images/uoi.txt/ (Accessed May 4, 2006).

14. U.S. Department of Justice, National Institute of Justice, Crime Mapping Research Center, *Mapping Crime: Principle and Practice* (Washington, D.C.: Author, 1999), p. 1.

15. *Ibid.,* p. 2.

16. U.S. Department of Justice, National Institute of Justice, *Crime Mapping Research Center* (Washington, D.C.: Author, 2000), pp. 1–3.

17. Grant and Terry, *Law Enforcement in the 21st Century,* p. 332.

18. *Ibid.,* pp. 332–333.

19. *Ibid.,* p. 333.

20. *Ibid.*, p. 335.
21. Phyllis McDonald, *Managing Police Operations: Implementing the New York Crime Control Model—CompStat* (Belmont, Calif.: Wadsworth, 2002), p. 1.
22. Grant and Terry, *Law Enforcement in the 21st Century,* p. 336.
23. *Ibid.,* p. 337.
24. *Ibid.*
25. *Ibid.,* p. 339.
26. Jon M. Shane, "CompStat Design," *FBI Law Enforcement Bulletin* (May 2004), pp. 17–18.
27. Michael E. Buerger, "COMPSTAT: A Strategic Vision," *The Associate* (January-February 2005), pp. 18–23.
28. A. Onion, "Coordinates of a Killer: A Mathematical Method Can Help Investigators Locate Killers," http://www.abcnews.com (Accessed October 8, 2002).
29. Grant and Terry, *Law Enforcement in the 21st Century,* p. 340.
30. John Eck, Jeffrey Gersh, and Charlene Taylor, *Mapping Hotspots of Crime and Related Events* (New York: New York Police Department, Spatial Analysis of Crime Conference, City University of New York Centre for Applied Studies of Environment and Centre for Urban Research, 1997).
31. Peter Branca, "Police News: Mapping Crime Hotspots," http://www.wapolun.org.au/010236.htm (Accessed May 4, 2006).
32. Grant and Terry, *Law Enforcement in the 21st Century,* p. 343.
33. *Ibid.,* pp. 346–347.
34. Darrel W. Stephens, "IT Changes in Law Enforcement," in Ronald W. Glensor and Gerard R. Murphy (eds.), *Issues in IT: A Reader for the Busy Police Chief Executive* (Washington, D.C.: Police Executive Research Forum, 2005), pp. 7–29.
35. For an example of this type of survey process, see William H. Lindsey and Bruce Quint, *The Oasis Technique* (Fort Lauderdale, Fla.: Florida Atlantic University/Florida International University Joint Center).
36. Barbara Webster and Edward F. Connors, "Community Policing: Identifying Problems" (Alexandria, Va.: Institute for Law and Justice, March 1991), pp. 14–15.
37. Dan Helms, "Closing the Barn Door: Police Counterterrorism After 9-11 from the Analyst's Perspective," *Crime Mapping News* 4 (Winter 2002):1–5.
38. Rachel Boba, "Problem Analysis in Policing: An Executive Summary," *Crime Mapping News* 5 (1) (Winter 2003):4.

From Recruit to Chief

Changing the Agency Culture

Key Terms and Concepts

"Bombshell" technique
Change agent
First-line supervisor
Lewin's process model for change

Middle manager
Recruitment for COPPS
Service orientation
Time management

Learning Objectives

As a result of reading this chapter, the student will:

- Understand a process that police organizations can employ in order to effect change
- Recognize some pitfalls and types of resistance to change
- Know the roles of key police leaders serving as change agents
- Understand how police agencies can and must capture time for their officers to engage in COPPS activities
- Realize the importance of recruiting and hiring individuals into policing who possess a service orientation—the core of COPPS

> Where there is no vision, a people perish.
>
> —*Ralph Waldo Emerson*

INTRODUCTION

Police agencies have a life and culture of their own. Powerful forces have a much stronger influence over how a department conducts its business than do managers of the department, courts, legislatures, politicians, and members of the community. As Herman Goldstein observed, "Against this background, many of the exhortations for change do, indeed, look naive, and the elaborate schemes for 'improving the police' unlikely to succeed."[1] Nonetheless, willingness to change is a fundamental requirement of community oriented policing and problem solving (COPPS); police agencies must modify their culture from top to bottom. This chapter addresses that agency imperative. Change is never easy, however, because there is so much uncertainty accompanying it.

We open this chapter with a discussion of change in police organizations, beginning with a look at some lessons learned and how change must occur to accommodate COPPS. The roles of three key leaders in this process—chief executives (and their precarious political position as innovators), middle managers, and rank-and-file officers—are then covered, including how sufficient time may be allocated for the latter to engage in problem-solving activities. In this vein we also examine some methods and challenges involved with recruiting problem solvers under the COPPS philosophy. We conclude the chapter with some case studies of agencies that have modified their culture for adopting the COPPS approach.

CHANGE THEORIES

Formula for Change

Organizational change occurs when an organization adopts new ideas or behaviors.[2] Any change in the organization involves an attempt to persuade employees to change their behavior and their relationships with one another. Therefore, it is not surprising that most people find change uncomfortable. Studies on change in organizations have shown that only about 10 percent of the people in most organizations will actively embrace change; approximately 80 percent will wait to be convinced or wait until the change is unavoidable, and the remaining 10 percent will actively resist change. For these people, change is very upsetting; they may even seek to subvert or sabotage the process.[3]

This resistance to change is reflected in the "change equation"—Discomfort (the case for change) plus vision plus steps must be greater than resistance to change[4]:

$$D + V + S > R$$

D includes those compelling reasons for and against change in an agency or community, such as existing supports for and barriers against change. *V* requires the leadership to consider changes that will have to occur with respect to related public institutions, management practices, individual behaviors, organizational culture, and the community at large. *S* includes those steps that must be developed in order to leverage supports and overcome barriers to change.[5]

Usually when change is proposed, an innovative idea is introduced and behavioral changes are supposed to follow. Consequently, the ultimate success of any organizational change depends on how well the organization can alter the behavioral patterns of its employees. Employee behavior is influenced by factors such as leadership styles, motivational techniques, informal relationships, and organization and job design. To bring about timely change, managers need to consider why people resist change and how resistance can be overcome.[6]

As indicated earlier, probably the most common characteristic of change is people's resistance to it. Generally, people do not like to change their behavior, and adaptation to a new environment or methods often results in feelings of stress or other forms of psychological discomfort. Resistance to change is likely when employees do not clearly understand the purpose, mechanics, or consequences of a planned change because of inadequate or misperceived communication. If employees are not told how they will be affected by change, rumors and speculation will follow, and resistance and even sabotage can ensue.[7]

Those who resist change are sometimes coerced into accepting it. Although coercion may be immediately effective and lead to compliance, the long-range results will certainly be harmful. Change in police agencies, particularly major changes, are frequently characterized by the use of centralized decision making and coercive tactics. Management and employees often have an adversarial relationship. Management might assume that because many employees do not understand the need for the change and will resist it anyway, there is no need to involve them in the process, and they must be forced to go along. Some managers might even hope that those persons resisting the change will retire or resign. These are inappropriate assumptions; coercion should be used as a last resort.[8]

By using task forces, ad hoc committees, group seminars, and other participatory techniques, employees can become directly involved in planning for change. By thoroughly discussing and debating the issues, an accurate understanding and unbiased analysis of the situation are likely to result.[9]

Lewin's Process Model for Change

Psychologist Kurt Lewin is often considered the father of modern organizational change theory. He coined the term "group dynamics" and was one of the first people to observe that leader behavior could shape culture during organizational change. Working with anthropologist Margaret Mead during World War II, Lewin established the concept of participative management: People are more likely to modify their own behavior and carry out decisions when they participate in problem analysis and solution.

Decentralized decision making is key to the success of COPPS.

Fort Lauderdale, Florida, Police Department.

Lewin's process model for change has three phases: unfreezing, changing, and refreezing (see Table 6–1). He believed that people are naturally resistant to change, but meanwhile the environment is changing. To create change, "unfreezing" the organization is necessary; this includes overcoming the negative forces that cause people to resist change through new or disconcerting information. "Changing" is the change in attitudes, values, feelings, and behaviors of the people, and it occurs when people discuss and plan new actions. "Refreezing" occurs when the organization reaches a new status quo, with the support mechanisms in place to maintain the desired behaviors.

Any police executive contemplating change should do so in a manner that offers the greatest possibility of success. As Charles Swanson, Leonard Territo, and Robert Taylor noted:

> Conventional wisdom about change states that the way to change an organization is to bring in a new top executive, give the individual his or her head (and maybe a hatchet), and let the individual make

TABLE 6–1

Lewin's Process Model for Change		
UNFREEZING	CHANGING	REFREEZING
The process by which people become aware of the need for change	The movement from the old way of doing things to a new way	The new behaviors now relatively permanent and resistant to change

the changes that he or she deems necessary. What the conventional wisdom overlooks are the long-term consequences of unilateral, top-down change.[10]

The problem, then, with radical and unilateral change is the possibility of a severe backlash in the organization; a complementary problem for changes that are made very gradually is that after many months or a few years of meetings, discussions, and planning sessions, nothing much has actually happened in the organization. Finding an appropriate pace for change to occur—neither too quickly and radically nor too slowly and gradually—is one of the most critical problems of planned organizational change. The readiness of the organization for change is a problem for which no easy resolutions are available.[11]

Sometimes a great deal can be learned by studying the success and failure patterns of organizations that have undertaken planned change. A survey of 18 studies of organizational change found the following successful change patterns[12]:

- They were spread throughout the organization.
- They produced positive changes in line and staff attitudes.
- They prompted people to behave more effectively in solving problems.
- They resulted in improved organizational performance.

CHANGE IN POLICE ORGANIZATIONS

Lessons Learned

Change is difficult for any organization and is particularly so for police departments, which are paramilitary, bureaucratic, and somewhat socially isolated from the community. How did change come about in those many agencies that have adopted COPPS?

A general transition process appears to have emerged: First, the agencies recognized that traditional approaches did not succeed; second was a change in attitude about the functions of administrators, line personnel, and citizens; third, community assessments were performed to identify new police responsibilities; fourth, new organizational and operational approaches were conceived to meet the newly defined police responsibilities; and fifth, the community was enlisted to work cooperatively with the police to achieve the desired results.[13]

Lessons were also learned about the political environment in which police administrators managed change and included the following eight points:

1. There must be a stimulus for change. A leader must have a vision, be willing to take the first step in challenging the status quo, involve people at all levels, and maintain that commitment (reallocating resources, amending policies and procedures, experimenting with new ideas).

2. Change must be grounded in logical and defensible criteria as opposed to effecting change just to "shake things up" in the organization.

3. There must be sufficient time for experimentation, evaluation, and fine-tuning of new ideas.

4. Major change might require a generation; people tend to be impatient, but resocialization of employees and citizens is a long-term endeavor requiring patience and stamina.

5. Not everyone will buy into new ideas.

6. Flexibility in a view of change is necessary. Many ideas are "losers," so a leader must maintain the freedom to fail, even though in U.S. culture success is often mandated.

7. Change carries risks, and change agents might be placed on the hot seat to explain new endeavors; in short, a leader's political neck may be on the line.

8. Organizational personnel evaluation systems must measure and reward effective involvement in change. Benefits do not have to be monetary, but they can include such things as positive reinforcement, creative freedom, and awards or commendations.

"Bombshell" Technique

Police organizations develop considerable inertia and can develop a resistance to change. Having a strong personal commitment to the values with which they have "grown up" in the organization, patrol officers may find any hint of proposed change in the department extremely threatening. Therefore, the chief executive who simply announces that COPPS is now the order of the day—the **"bombshell" technique**—without a carefully designed plan for implementing that change is in danger of "losing traction" and of throwing the entire force into confusion. Additionally, the chief executive confronts a host of difficult issues: What structural changes, if any, are needed? How do we get the people on the beat to behave differently? What should we tell the public, and when? How fast can we bring about this change? Do we have enough external support?[14]

Change in Organizational Values

A related subject is that of values in police organizations. All organizations have values, the beliefs that guide an organization and the behavior of its employees.[15] Police departments are powerfully influenced by their values, and policing styles reflect a department's values.

COPPS reflects a set of values rather than a technical orientation toward the police function. There is a service orientation, which means that citizens are to be treated with respect at all times. When riding in patrol vehicles, supervisors and managers must listen for the "talk of the department" to determine whether values expressed by officers reflect those of the department.

The Honolulu Police Department displays its values—"Integrity/Respect/Fairness"—
on its vehicles.

Honolulu, Hawaii, Police Department.

Also, values are no longer hidden but serve as the basis for citizen
understanding of the police function, judgments of police success, and
employee understanding of what the police agency seeks to achieve.[16] Values are a guidepost by which the agency will provide service to the community and a means by which the community can evaluate the agency.

CHANGE TO COPPS

Potential for Resistance and Conflict

As Fresno, California, Police Chief Jerry Dyer has observed, managing
change in police agencies is not working as it should, for a variety of reasons: Officers and labor unions block change by claiming memorandum of
agreement violations, filing grievances, utilizing their political influence
with council members, or making calls to local news media outlets. Such
obstacles may prevent many police leaders from seeking change in their
organizations.[17] (Fresno's reorganization effort, and that of the Boston
Police Department, are discussed in the Case Studies section of the chapter, below.)

In the many jurisdictions where COPPS has been implemented and
is flourishing and succeeding, however, the traditional orthodoxy of policing, rooted in military command and scientific management theory, had
to be changed. In short, the traditional orthodoxy became "taboo."[18] This

included management style, performance measures (as one author put it, "Bean-counting performance measures have little meaning in such a system"[19]), and disciplinary measures.[20] The new required leadership style meant (1) a shift from telling and controlling employees to helping them develop their skills and abilities; (2) listening to the customers in new and more open ways; (3) solving problems, not just reacting to incidents; (4) trying new things and experimenting, realizing that risk taking and honest mistakes must be tolerated to encourage creativity and achieve innovation; and (5) avoiding, whenever possible, the use of coercive power to effect change.[21]

A Washington State University graduate student determined that there were three significant reactions by Spokane officers to the shift to community policing[22]:

1. *Meaning.* Some officers saw community policing as a way of validating who they were, allowing them to do the kind of policing they believed they should have been doing all along.

2. *Resistance.* Community policing, being a philosophy rather than a program, made it more difficult for management to describe, so some officers who were said to be resistant were merely trying to determine what community policing meant in relation to how they were currently doing their jobs.

3. *Sabotage.* Some employees went beyond resistance, engaging in sabotage and being obstructionist; some supervisors would wait until a ranking officer was out of earshot and then proceed to tell their staff "how it's really going to be."

"We're Too Busy to Change"

It is not uncommon for consultants to go into police agencies to assist in implementing or training COPPS and be told, "We're too busy for community policing and problem solving." As William Geller and Guy Swanger noted, it may be true in some organizations that people are too busy to change. They said:

> [This may be the case] if the senior leadership insists that middle managers continue doing all the old things they shouldn't be doing plus all the new things they should. The classic problem here is being too busy bailing out the boat to fix the hole in the hull.[23]

Indeed, preoccupation with the task at hand prevents people from pausing to reflect critically on whether what they are doing has any value. As Price Pritchett and Ron Pound observed, "Ditch those duties that don't count much, even if you can do them magnificently well."[24] Beliefs that police are too busy to change can be compounded by fears that COPPS will only intensify the workload. But when the community is an organized, active partner in problem solving, the problem-solving process is not as labor-intensive for the police as some have asserted.[25] (Exhibit 6–1 shows how one police department got the community involved in its change to COPPS.)

EXHIBIT 6–1

Time for a Change in Santa Clara

The following text is taken from the "Community Policing Tutorial" home page of the Santa Clara, California, Police Department. It presents the reasons the department believes it is time to change to COPPS:

- Public safety is a citywide concern. Crime and disorder in our neighborhoods, parks, and business districts cause citizen frustration, uneasiness, and fear.
- Traditionally, police respond to calls, investigate crimes, and make arrests. This process alone does not reduce crime.
- Crime and public safety issues are community problems. They require the commitment of the community and the police to solve them together.
- The police department is committed to developing a strong relationship with the citizens of Santa Clara through community policing.

Source: Santa Clara, California, Police Department, "What Is Community Policing?" http://www.scpd.org/community_policing_pg5 .htm (Accessed January 7, 2004).

ROLES OF KEY LEADERS

Earlier in this chapter, we discussed briefly the roles of chief executives, middle managers, and first-line supervisors in the implementation of COPPS. Here we briefly examine their respective roles in the change process.

Chief Executives

Of course, the police chief executive is ultimately responsible for all of the facets of COPPS, from implementation to training to evaluation. Therefore, what is needed are chief executives who are willing to do things that have not been done before, or as one writer put it, "risk takers and boat rockers within a culture where daily exposure to life-or-death situations makes officers natural conservators of the status quo."[26] These are chief executives who become committed to getting the police and neighborhoods to work together to attack the roots of crime. For them, "Standing still is not only insufficient . . . it is going backwards."[27]

Therefore, a police executive must be a viable **change agent.** In any hierarchy the person at the top is responsible for setting both the policy and tone of the organization. Within a police agency, the chief or sheriff has the ultimate power to make change, particularly one as substantive as COPPS. The chief executive must be both visible and credible and must create a climate conducive to change. Under COPPS, chief executives must focus on the vision, values, mission, and long-term goals of policing in order to create an organizational environment that enables officers, government officials, and community members to work together. By building consensus, they can establish programs, develop timelines, and set priorities. They should honor the good work done in the past but exhibit a sense of urgency about implementing change while involving people from the community and the department in all stages of the transition. The chief executive's roles and responsibilities during the change to COPPS include the following:

- Articulating a clear vision to the organization
- Understanding and accepting the depth of change and time required to implement COPPS
- Assembling a management team that is committed to translating the new vision into action
- Being committed to removing bureaucratic obstacles whenever possible

Many police organizations boast talented and creative chief executives who, when participating in the change process, will assist in effecting change that is beneficial and lasting. James Q. Wilson put it this way:

> The police profession today is the intellectual leadership of the criminal justice profession in the United States. The police are in the lead. They're showing the world how things might better be done.[28]

Middle Managers

Middle managers—lieutenants and captains—also play a crucial role in the operation of a COPPS philosophy. The COPPS emphasis on problem solving necessitates that middle managers draw on their familiarity with the bureaucracy to secure, maintain, and use authority to empower subordinates, helping officers to actively and creatively confront and resolve issues, sometimes using unconventional approaches on a trial-and-error basis.

There are many really significant contributions middle managers can make to the changing culture of the agency to embrace and sustain COPPS. First, they must build on the strengths of their subordinates, capitalizing on their training and competence.[29] They do so by treating people as individuals and creating talented teams.[30] They must "cheerlead," encouraging supervisors and patrol officers to actually solve the problems they are confronting.[31] It is also imperative that middle managers *not* believe they are serving the chief executive's best interests by preserving the status quo. The lieutenants are the gatekeepers and must develop the system, resources, and support mechanisms to ensure that the officers, detectives, and supervisors can perform to achieve the best results. The officers and supervisors cannot perform without the necessary equipment, resources, and reinforcement.[32]

Middle managers, like their subordinates, must be allowed the freedom to make mistakes—and good middle managers protect their subordinates from organizational and political recrimination and scapegoating when

COPPS is not soft on crime—and first-line supervisors are key to its success.

Courtesy Washoe County, Nevada, Sheriff's Office.

things go wrong. Put another way, middle managers cannot stand idly by while their people are led to the guillotine, and they must protect their officers from the political effects of legitimate failure.[33] They must not allow their problem-solving officers to revert to traditional methods. They must be diplomats and facilitators, using a lot more persuading and negotiating (toward win-win solutions) than they did under the traditional "my way or the highway" management style.

The roles and responsibilities of middle managers during the change to COPPS include the following:

- Assuming responsibility for strategic planning
- Eliminating red tape and bottlenecks that impede the work of officers and supervisors
- Conducting regular meetings with subordinates to discuss plans, activities, and results
- Assessing COPPS efforts in a continuous manner

The position of middle managers in a COPPS environment was well described by Kelling and Bratton:

> The idea that mid-managers are spoilers, that they thwart project or strategic innovation, has some basis in fact. Mid-managers improperly directed can significantly impede innovation. Yet, ample evidence exists that when a clear vision of the business of the organization is put forward, when mid-managers are included in planning, when their legitimate self-interests are acknowledged, and when they are properly trained, mid-managers can be the leading edge of innovation and creativity.[34]

First-Line Supervisors

It is widely held that the most challenging aspect of changing the culture of a police agency lies in changing the attitudes and beliefs of **first-line supervisors.** The influence of first-line supervisors is so strong that their role warrants special attention.

The primary contact of street officers with their organization is through their sergeant, so the quality of an officer's daily life is often dependent on his or her immediate supervisor. Most officers do not believe their sergeants are sources of guidance and direction but rather are authority figures to be satisfied (by numbers of arrests and citations, manner in which reports are completed, officer's ability to avoid citizen complaints, and so on). There is just cause for the reluctance of first-line supervisors to avoid change. Herman Goldstein stated it this way:

> Changing the operating philosophy of rank-and-file officers is easier than altering a first-line supervisor's perspective of his or her job, because the work of a sergeant is greatly simplified by the traditional form of policing. The more routinized the work, the easier it is for the sergeant to check. The more emphasis placed on rank and the symbols of position, the easier it is for the sergeant to rely on authority—rather than intellect and personal skills—to carry out [his or her] duties. . . . [S]ergeants are usually appalled by descriptions of the freedom and independence suggested in problem oriented policing for rank-and-file officers. The concept can be very threatening to them. This . . . can create an enormous block to implementation.[35]

Supervisors must be convinced that COPPS makes good sense in today's environment, and they should possess the characteristics of a good problem-oriented supervisor, as shown in Exhibit 6–2.

The roles and responsibilities of first-line supervisors during a change to COPPS include the following:

- Understanding and practicing problem solving
- Managing time, staff, and resources
- Encouraging teamwork
- Helping officers to mobilize stakeholders
- Tracking and managing officers' problem solving
- Providing officers with ongoing feedback and support

Another matter implicating police supervisory personnel concerns the amount of time required for patrol officers to engage in problem-solving activities. We examine that issue next.

Ways to "Recapture Officers' Time" for Problem Solving

One of the ongoing controversies with respect to COPPS—as noted in the "We're Too Busy to Change" section earlier—concerns whether police officers can garner the time required to engage in problem-solving activities.

EXHIBIT 6–2

Characteristics of a Good Problem-Oriented Supervisor

1. Allowing subordinates freedom to experiment with new approaches.
2. Insisting on good, accurate analyses of problems.
3. Granting flexibility in work schedules when requests are appropriate.
4. Allowing subordinates to make most contacts directly and paving the way when they are having trouble getting cooperation.
5. Protecting subordinates from pressures within the department to revert to traditional methods.
6. Running interference for subordinates to secure resources, protect them from criticism, and so forth.
7. Knowing what problems subordinates are working on and whether the problems are real.
8. Knowing subordinates' beats and important citizens in it, and expecting subordinates to know it even better.
9. Coaching subordinates through the process, giving advice, helping them manage their time.
10. Monitoring subordinates' progress and, as necessary, prodding them along or slowing them down.
11. Supporting subordinates even if their strategies fail, so long as something useful is learned in the process and the process was well thought through.
12. Managing problem-solving efforts over a long period of time; not allowing efforts to die simply because they get sidetracked by competing demands for time and attention.
13. Giving credit to subordinates and letting others know about their good work.
14. Allowing subordinates to talk with visitors or at conferences about their work.
15. Identifying new resources and contacts for subordinates and making them check them out.
16. Stressing cooperation, coordination, and communication within the unit and outside it.
17. Coordinating efforts across shifts, beats, and outside units and agencies.
18. Realizing that this style of policing cannot simply be ordered; officers and detectives must come to believe in it.

Source: Police Executive Research Forum, "Supervising Problem-Solving" (Washington, D.C.: Author, training outline, 1990).

On the one hand, officers complain that they are going from call to call and have little time for anything else; on the other hand, administrators say there is plenty of time for problem solving because calls account for only 50 to 60 percent of an officer's time.

Who is right? According to Tom McEwen, both sides are correct.[36] Table 6–2 describes a hypothetical workload during a unit's shift. In the example shown in the table, the unit starts the shift at 4:00 P.M. and receives an accident call at 4:14 P.M., which takes until 4:44 P.M. (30 minutes). The next call (robbery) comes in at 5:02 P.M., which means 18 minutes elapsed between calls. The pattern continues throughout the shift, alternating between handling calls for service and having time for other activities. In total, the unit devotes 4 hours 46 minutes (286 minutes) to calls, with the remaining 3 hours 14 minutes (194 minutes) available for other activities.

TABLE 6–2

Example of a Unit's Workload During a Shift				
ACTIVITY	TIME DISPATCHED	TIME CLEARED	TIME ON CALL	TIME TO NEXT CALL
Start of shift	4:00 P.M.			14 minutes
Accident	4:14	4:44 P.M.	30 minutes	18
Robbery	5:02	5:18	16	17
Suspicious activity	5:35	6:38	63	32
Family problem	7:10	7:40	30	28
Theft	8:08	8:26	18	10
Alarm	8:36	8:46	10	47
Emotionally disturbed person	9:33	11:21	108	17
Unwanted person	11:38	11:49	11	11
End of shift	12:00 A.M.			
Total			286 minutes	194 minutes

The time between calls is the key element of the argument as to whether officers have time for problem solving. In this example, more than 3 hours are available for other activities. An administrator would be correct in pointing out that there is plenty of time available; however, the available time is spread throughout the shift, varying from 10 minutes between calls to 47 minutes. If we assume a problem-solving project takes 45 minutes, then the officer in this unit has only one block of uninterrupted time for an assignment. (*Note:* Clearly not all problem-solving projects take 45 minutes each day. Some days, all that is needed is 10 minutes to complete a phone call to, perhaps, a building inspector. On other days, such as Friday or Saturday nights, no work will be done on problem oriented policing (POP). POP projects have no due dates; therefore, problem-solving efforts might be best thought of as being accomplished in bits and pieces, not over the course of a day but over the course of a longer period of time. Departments, however, should be striving to find uninterrupted time for officers so that they can increase their proactive responsibilities.) The average time between calls is 21 minutes. Officers believe they are going from call to call with no time for anything else because of the relatively short periods of time between calls.

Of course, not all units or shifts will have the same experience as in this example. Time between calls varies considerably depending on the number of calls for a particular shift, the types of calls, and the time they require. One or two fewer calls can make a big difference in whether there will be stretches of uninterrupted time.

Obviously, citizen calls are important and cannot be ignored, but the aim should be to handle citizen calls in an expeditious manner. The following four methods of **time management** can be used to overcome the problem of finding time for problem solving while still handling calls effectively:

1. *Allow units to perform problem-solving assignments as self-initiated activities.* Under this approach, a unit would contact the dispatcher and go out of service for a problem-solving assignment. The unit would be interrupted only for an emergency call in its area of responsibility; otherwise, the dispatcher would hold nonemergency calls until the unit becomes available or send a unit from an adjacent area after holding the call for a predetermined amount of time.

2. *Schedule one or two units to devote a predetermined part of their shift to problem solving.* As an example, a supervisor could designate one or two units each day to devote the first half of their shift or even only one hour to problem solving. Their calls would be handled by other units so that they have an uninterrupted block of time for problems. Of course, this approach means that the other units will be busier. The trade-off is that problem solving gets done and the supervisor can rotate the units designated for these activities.

3. *Take more reports over the telephone.* Many departments take certain nonemergency complaints by telephone rather than dispatch a patrol unit. The information about the incident is recorded on a department report form and entered in the department's information system as an incident or crime. The average telephone report taker can process four times as many report calls per hour compared to a field unit. The department might increase the types of calls handled by telephone, or the staffing for a telephone report unit can be increased to cover more hours of the day.

4. *Review the department policy on assist units.* In some departments, several units show up at the scene of a call even though they are not needed. Some units assist out of boredom or curiosity. The units may initiate themselves out of service to assist, or the dispatcher may send several units to the scene. This problem is particularly acute with alarm calls. Many departments have a policy of dispatching two or more units to alarms, even when the source has a long history of false alarms. A department should undergo a detailed study on the types of calls for which assist units are actually appearing, with the aim of reducing the number of assists and discouraging officers from assisting other units unless it is necessary.

As a more general approach, a department should review its patrol plan to determine whether units are fielded in proportion to workload. Time between calls is a function not only of the number of incoming calls but also of the number of units in the field. More units result in more time between calls.

Indeed, we can calculate the number of units needed to ensure that the time between calls averages, for example, 35 minutes. A department may also want to consider changes in officer schedules to facilitate overlapping during busy times of the day; however, adjustments within a shift may be the more effective approach. Delaying response time to calls for service can also provide more time for officers. For example, by refining the manner in which 911 calls are dispatched in non-life-threatening cases, responses may be significantly reduced annually.[37]

Response time research implied that rapid responses were not needed for most calls. Furthermore, dispatchers can advise citizens of an officer's arrival time. Slower police responses to nonemergency calls has been found satisfactory to citizens if dispatchers tell citizens an officer might not arrive right away. Managers have also garnered more time for officers by having nonsworn employees handle noncrime incidents.[38] Time between calls is an important, but frequently overlooked, element of any problem-solving strategy. The overall aim should be to provide officers with uninterrupted amounts of time for problem-solving assignments. There are many ways to accomplish this aim, but they require a concerted planning effort by the department.

Box 6–1 shows the 15-step exercise developed for police managers to recapture officers' time while working in a problem-solving framework.

BOX 6–1

A 15-Step Exercise for Recapturing Officers' Time

1. Assemble a group of patrol officers and emergency communications center personnel representing each shift.

2. Have each of them write down three to five locations where the police respond regularly to deal with the same general problem and people repeatedly.

3. Determine the average number of responses to those locations per month and approximately how long the problem has existed.

4. Determine the average number of officers who respond each time to those incidents.

5. Determine the average length of time involved in handling the incidents.

6. Using the information from 3, 4, and 5, determine the total number of staff hours devoted to each of these problem locations. Do this for the week, month, and year.

7. Identify all the key players that either participate in or are affected by the problem—all direct and indirect participants and groups such as the complaining parties, victims, witnesses, property owners and managers, and bystanders.

8. Through a roundtable discussion, decide what it is about the particular location that allows or encourages the problem to exist and continue.

9. Develop a list of things that have been done in the past to try to deal with the problem, and a candid assessment of why each has not worked.

10. In a free-flowing brainstorming session, develop as many traditional and nontraditional solutions to the problem as possible. Try to include alternative sources like other government and private agencies that could be involved in the solution. Encourage creative thinking and risk taking.

11. After you have completed the brainstorming session, consider which of those solutions are (a) illegal, (b) immoral, (c) impractical, (d) unrealistic, or (e) not affordable.

12. Eliminate all those that fall in categories a and b.

13. For those that fall in categories, c, d, and e, figure out if those reasons are because you are thinking in conventional terms like "We've never done it this way," "It won't work," "It can't be done." If you are satisfied that those solutions truly are impractical, unrealistic, or not affordable, then eliminate them, too. If there is a glimmer of hope that some may have merit with just a little different thinking or approach, then leave them.

14. For each remaining possible solution, list what would have to be done and who would have to be involved to make it happen. Which of those solutions and actions could be implemented relatively soon and with a minimum of difficulty?

15. If the solution were successful, consider the productive things officers could do with the time that would be recaptured from not having to deal with the problem anymore.

Source: Jerald R. Vaughn, *Community Oriented Policing: You Can Make It Happen* (Clearwater, Fla.: National Law Enforcement Leadership Institute, no date), pp. 6–7. Used with permission.

If during the recapturing time exercise a police manager finds potential ways to effectively solve problems and recapture time lost to repetitive incidents, then problem oriented policing may be a smart approach.

Federal Guidance.   This issue of time for COPPS activities is of such importance that the federal Office of Community Oriented Policing Services recently developed a guidebook to show agencies ways and means of freeing up officer time for COPPS functions; this 100-page guidebook—which discusses such topics as using call intake strategies, managing call responses, and collecting and analyzing call data—should be a part of the COPPS agency's "toolbox" for sustaining these efforts. It discusses in detail all the time-related subjects we have mentioned in this chapter section.[39]

ROLE OF THE RANK-AND-FILE OFFICERS

All experts on the subject of police innovation and change emphasize the importance of empowering and using the input from the street officers. Next we discuss these key personnel, including the unique nature of their recruitment, the need to give them a sense of ownership in their work, and the means by which they can progress.

A recruitment poster illustrates the department's diversity, values, and belief that one person can make a difference.

Courtesy Broken Arrow, Oklahoma, Police Department.

Recruitment for COPPS

Times have changed greatly in hiring police personnel, especially in the area of **recruitment for COPPS.** This shift in philosophy and practice has important implications for how we select police recruits, requiring a reevaluation of past practices and the development of more positively oriented selection criteria and procedures.[40]

As shown in Exhibit 6–3, the hiring of patrol officers under COPPS can be quite removed from traditional means where officers are problem solvers; as seen in the exhibit, even the federal government is willing to invest in funding and developing formal mechanisms for hiring COPPS officers with a **service orientation.**

 EXHIBIT 6–3

Hiring in the Spirit of Service: The Detroit Experience

Hiring in the Spirit of Service (HSS) is a federally funded project in designated communities for recruiting and hiring service-oriented individuals with the skills and abilities to engage the community—the core of COPPS. The Detroit Police Department, with 3,800 officers, was one of the HHS sites. Following are some of the methods developed and used in Detroit to recruit and hire COPPS officers:

- A marketing firm used eight focus groups consisting of citizens and police officers to define what service-oriented officers do; it was concluded that on-the-job performance and interpersonal relations best defined such officers, that they should perform job duties in a safe manner, work well as team members, have the ability to de-escalate situations, treat other people and each other with respect, be polite, show compassion and empathy, get to know their public, and interact with citizens in a positive manner.

- A second focus group helped to develop a recruitment and marketing campaign to depict policing in Detroit as a fulfilling, life-changing, and rewarding career. Recruitment campaign materials were developed (called "Give Back, Get More") that emphasized the department was serious about recruiting community-minded officers, and media support was elicited.

- The department met weekly with a range of community groups to discuss what is involved in becoming a police officer; the department also included the community in the oral board interviews and CompStat meetings (CompStat is discussed in Chapter 5). The oral board interviews now include a series of questions that relate specifically to service orientation.

- More structure was provided to the background investigation, with investigators encouraged and trained to seek information relative to service when conducting reference checks.

- The department added service-oriented questions to the psychological/social history questionnaire, eliciting information about hobbies, volunteer and charity work, and work with community nonprofit institutions.

- A point system is used to rank each candidate to include credit for earlier volunteer experiences, residency in the community, and previous employment in a service-oriented industry such as social work.

It was recently reported that candidate applications reached 1,500, which represents unprecedented growth in interest for the position of police officer in the city of Detroit.

Source: Ellen Scrivner, *Innovations in Police Recruitment and Hiring: Hiring in the Spirit of Service* (Washington, D.C.: U.S. Department of Justice, Office of Community Oriented Policing Services, 2006), pp. 1–4.

Selection favors those who are interested in creating solutions rather than applying learned rules. Furthermore, there is an emphasis on practical intelligence—the ability to quickly analyze key elements of a situation and identify possible courses of action to reach logical conclusions. It is difficult to neatly delineate separate problem-solving elements. A patrol officer might witness, for example, neighborhood youth painting graffiti on a wall. The officer has to analyze the situation and define the problem. Another scenario might be a patrol officer assigned to a beat in which automobiles are smashed and vandalized each night. In order to formulate a response, the officer must define the problem and address the motivations of the offenders.[41]

Under COPPS, the patrol officer is expected to recognize when old methods are inadequate and new and different solutions are needed; he or she is expected to display many of the skills demanded in higher-level personnel such as detectives—being creative, flexible, and innovative; working independently; and maintaining self-discipline. Communication skills are also vital. The officer must possess the ability to work cooperatively with others, to solve problems, and to listen.[42]

Today there are private corporations that specialize in assisting police organizations in identifying candidates who will become effective officers for community policing. An examination can be administered that assesses more of the whole person, in addition to traditional measures such as accuracy of observation, short-term memory, reading comprehension, and written communication. Such tests of one's community policing abilities additionally measure one's service orientation, accountability, ethics, and problem-solving orientation.[43] Many police agencies inform their applicants on their Web page and other recruitment materials that they have implemented COPPS and are thus interested in hiring people who can perform under that philosophy.[44]

CASE STUDIES

Following are examples of how three police organizations approached some aspects of needed change with the COPPS philosophy.

Fresno, California: Departmental Reorganization

The Fresno, California, Police Department undertook a reorganization effort to completely transform its structure, systems, and processes; the purposes of reorganizing included increasing the agency's effectiveness and efficiency, establishing higher levels of trust by the community, allowing for stronger management and accountability, enhancing communication flow, and decentralizing control of authority. The process began with an informational gathering phase to assess the department's status in these areas.

An initial step was to unify the staff and to build a strong management team. A management psychologist interviewed each staff member and conducted a series of team-building exercises, including an analysis of behavioral styles and personality profiles and a three-day retreat.

To gain greater community trust, a chief's advisory board was established to share community concerns and enhance communications, a professional standards unit was established to audit police operations and monitor citizen-officer interactions, demographic data was collected to address concerns of racial profiling, new recruiting strategies were employed to focus on a broader candidate pool, and the agency began going through an accreditation process to ensure its compliance with national standards. Other changes during this year of reorganization included a new vision and mission, a flattened organizational structure, and decentralization of resources into policing districts. The department's labor unions were involved in each step of the process and provided input; the media were apprised of changes.

The department learned during this process, however, that there are several potential major costs involved in undertaking significant change that must be minimized if possible[45]:

- *Loss of seasoned professionals*. Some employees may not feel included in the change plan, take early retirement, lose confidence in leadership, or not accept new assignments.
- *Productivity losses*. There can be miscommunication between divisions, inadequate policies and procedures as guidelines, disorganization from change itself, and delay in employees assuming new roles.
- *Lack of clarity in purpose or mission*. Some employees might hate change or refuse to change without substantial preparation or opportunity for input; they might also need a real connection to community feedback to make change stick.

Boston, Massachusetts: Revitalization of the Force

In the early 1990s, when a mayoral commission called for major managerial reforms for the Boston, Massachusetts, Police Department, then-chief William Bratton asked an organizational psychologist to assist with this challenge. Now, more than a decade later, Boston has evolved into one of the country's premier community policing agencies. The psychologist introduced a focus on systemic change, integrating adult learning models into management training and paying greater attention to the nuances of organizational structure. Each initiative, involves systemic changes related to basic policing practices, business processes, technology, and management and leadership development.

A strategic planning initiative used a long-term planning process to address crime, quality of life, and management issues, with 350 people (police, elected officials, clergy, and other officials) working in 17 teams over a six-month period to carve out action plans for each of the city's 11 police districts. It was determined in these meetings, for example, that the traditional system of officer rotations, transfers, and shift changes ran counter to community policing's philosophy of building relationships with the community; structural changes were then made so that officers worked in neighborhood-focused beat teams.

The department has learned that complex problem solving and systemic change are less difficult when traditional views—such as those involving officers' response to calls for service—are minimized or eliminated.[46]

Hayward, California: Hiring, Training, and Evaluation of Personnel

After making the decision to change its policing philosophy, a systems change was required that would greatly affect personnel. Therefore, the initial focus was on personnel systems such as recruiting, hiring, training, performance appraisals, and promotability guidelines. To transform the recruiting and hiring processes, the Hayward, California, Personnel Department and Police Department began exploring the following three questions:

1. Overall, what type of candidate, possessing what types of skills, should be recruited?
2. What specific knowledge, skills, and abilities reflect the COPPS philosophy—particularly regarding problem-solving abilities and sensitivity to community needs?
3. How can these attributes best be identified in the initial screening process?

The department also analyzed the city's demographics, finding that it had a diverse ethnic composition. To promote cultural diversity and sensitivity to the needs of the community, a psychologist was employed to develop a profile of an effective COPPS officer in Hayward. These considerations became an integral part of the department's hiring process.

Next the training and performance evaluation systems were reappraised. All personnel, both sworn and civilian, had to receive COPPS training to provide a clear and thorough understanding of the history, philosophy, and transition to COPPS. The department's initial training was directed at management and supervisory personnel and was designed to assist these employees in accomplishing the department's goals of reinforcing COPPS values, modifying the existing police culture, strategically transitioning the organization from traditional policing to the new philosophy, and focusing on customer relations. Rank-and-file officers were given 40-hour blocks of instruction.

Performance and reward practices for personnel were modified to reflect the new criteria. Emphasizing quality over quantity (e.g., arrest statistics, number of calls for service, response times), new criteria included an assessment of how well a call for service was handled and what type of problem-solving approach was used to reach a solution for the problem. Other mechanisms were developed to broadcast and communicate successes, including supervisors' logs, a COPPS newsletter, and city-wide recognition of extraordinary customer service efforts.

The department's promotional process was also retooled; a new phase was added to the department's promotional test—the "promotability" phase—to evaluate the candidate's decision-making abilities, analytical skills, communication skills, interpersonal skills, and professional contributions.[47]

▲ SUMMARY

This chapter has been about change: It can be quite difficult in organizations—especially those police agencies with the traditional entrenched culture and management styles. The chapter also discussed the roles of key police leaders and rank-and-file officers in effecting change.

This chapter underscores the importance and means of changing the culture of the police agency, from recruit to chief, to accommodate the new philosophy and the operation of COPPS. Also called for is a requisite radical change in the way the police organization views itself, hones its values, and conducts its affairs. The chief executive must be a risk taker, and all employees, sworn and civilian, must believe that change is needed within the organization, if COPPS is to succeed. This modified approach to policing is also required in the view and latitude given to the middle managers and first-line supervisors and especially to the very important problem-solving street officer. We also emphasized the need to examine—and probably shift—the organization's means for recruiting people as police problem solvers.

■ ITEMS FOR REVIEW

1. Describe why change must occur within police organizations in order to accommodate COPPS, and review some of the common forms of potential resistance to such change.

2. Explain the roles of three key leaders in the change process—chief executives, middle managers, and rank-and-file officers.

3. Review some of the major means by which sufficient time may be obtained for officers to engage in problem-solving activities.

4. Describe some methods for recruiting and hiring people who will have the knowledge and skills to engage in problem-solving activities under the COPPS philosophy.

◆ NOTES

1. Herman Goldstein, *Problem-Oriented Policing* (New York: McGraw-Hill, 1990), p. 29.

2. J. L. Pierce and A. L. Delbecq, "Organization Structure, Individual Attitudes and Innovation," *Academy of Management Review* 2 (1977):27–37.

3. Community Policing Consortium, *Curricula: Module Four: Managing Organizational Change* (Washington, D.C.: Author, August 2000), pp. 4–5.

4. *Ibid.,* p. 6.

5. *Ibid.,* pp. 6–7.

6. Roy R. Roberg and Jack Kuykendall, *Police Management* (2nd ed.) (Los Angeles: Roxbury, 1997), p. 370.

7. *Ibid.,* pp. 370–371.

8. *Ibid.,* pp. 375–376.

9. *Ibid.,* p. 376.

10. Charles R. Swanson, Leonard Territo, and Robert W. Taylor, *Police Administration: Structures, Processes, and Behavior* (3rd ed.) (New York: Macmillan, 1993), p. 668.

11. *Ibid.,* pp. 668–669.

12. L. E. Greiner, "Patterns of Organization Change," *Harvard Business Review* 45 (1967):124–125.

13. David L. Carter, "Community Police and Political Posturing: Playing the Game." Policy paper for the Regional Community Policing Training Institute, Wichita State University, Wichita, Kansas, 2000.

14. Malcolm K. Sparrow, "Implementing Community Policing," *Perspectives on Policing* 9 (November 1988):1–2.

15. Thomas J. Peters and Robert H. Waterman Jr., *In Search of Excellence* (New York: Harper & Row, 1983), p. 15.

16. Robert Wasserman and Mark H. Moore, "Values in Policing" (Washington, D.C.: U.S. Department of Justice, National Institute of Justice, November 1988), pp. 6–7.

17. Jerry Dyer and Keith Foster, "Managing Change: Reorganizing and Building Community Trust," in symposium paper "Risk Management Issues in Law Enforcement," http://www.riskinstitute.org (Accessed May 28, 2003).

18. Mark H. Moore and Darrel W. Stephens, *Beyond Command and Control: The Strategic Management of Police Departments* (Washington, D.C.: Police Executive Research Forum, 1991), pp. 1, 3–4.

19. Gordon Witkin and Dan McGraw, "Beyond 'Just the Facts, Ma'am,'" *U.S. News & World Report* (August 2, 1993):29.

20. Malcolm K. Sparrow, Mark H. Moore, and David M. Kennedy, *Beyond 911: A New Era for Policing* (New York: Basic Books, 1990), p. 149.

21. California Department of Justice, Attorney General's Office, Crime Prevention Center, *COPPS: Community Oriented Policing and Problem Solving* (Sacramento, Calif.: Author, November 1992), pp. 67–68.

22. Lunell Haught, "Meaning, Resistance, and Sabotage—Elements of a Police Culture," *Community Policing Exchange* (May/June 1998):7.

23. William A. Geller and Guy Swanger, *Managing Innovation in Policing: The Untapped Potential of the Middle Manager* (Washington, D.C.: Police Executive Research Forum, 1995), p. 41.

24. Price Pritchett and Ron Pound, *A Survival Guide to the Stress of Organizational Change* (Dallas, Tex.: Pritchett and Associates, 1995), p. 12.

25. Warren Friedman, "The Community Role in Community Policing," in Dennis P. Rosenbaum (ed.), *The Challenge of Community Policing: Testing the Promises* (Thousand Oaks, Calif.: Sage, 1994), p. 268.

26. Mike Tharp and Dorian Friedman, "New Cops on the Block," *U.S. News & World Report* (August 2, 1993):23.

27. *Ibid.,* p. 24.

28. James Q. Wilson, "Six Things Police Leaders Can Do About Juvenile Crime," *Subject to Debate* (September/October 1997):1.

29. Geller and Swanger, *Managing Innovation in Policing*, p. 105.

30. *Ibid.,* p. 131.

31. *Ibid.,* p. 109.

32. *Ibid.,* p. 112.

33. *Ibid.,* pp. 137–138.

34. George L. Kelling and William J. Bratton, "Implementing Community Policing: The Administrative Problem," *Perspectives on Policing* 17 (1993):11.

35. Goldstein, *Problem-Oriented Policing*, p. 29.

36. Tom McEwen, "Finding Time for Problem Solving," *Problem Solving Quarterly* 5 (Spring 1992):1, 4.

37. Lee P. Brown, "Community Policing: Bring the Community into the Battle Against Crime." Speech at the 19th Annual Lehman Lecture Series, Long Island University, Brookville, New York, March 11, 1992.

38. John Eck and William Spelman, "A Problem-Oriented Approach to Police Service Delivery," in Dennis Jay Kenney (ed.), *Police and Policing: Contemporary Issues* (New York: Praeger, 1989), pp. 95–111.

39. U.S. Department of Justice, Office of Community Oriented Policing Services, *Call Management and Community Policing: A Guidebook for Law Enforcement* (Washington, D.C.: Author, February 2003).

40. Eric Metchik and Ann Winton, "Community Policing and Its Implications for Alternative Models of Police Officer Selection," in Peter C. Kratcoski and Duane Dukes (eds.), *Issues in Community Policing* (Cincinnati, Ohio: Anderson, 1995), pp. 107–123.

41. *Ibid.,* p. 116.

42. *Ibid.,* pp. 119–120.

43. "Community Police Officer Pre-Employment Exam," *Law and Order* (December 2000):125.

44. See the Redding, California, Police Department's Web site, http://ci.redding.ca.us/personnel/porec.htm.

45. Dyer and Foster, "Managing Change," pp. 1–3.

46. Joan Sweeney, "Revitalizing Boston's Police Force," http://www.apa.org/monitor/jun02/revitalizing.html (Accessed February 21, 2003).

47. Joseph E. Brann and Suzanne Whalley, "COPPS: The Transformation of Police Organizations," in California Department of Justice, Attorney General's Office, Crime Prevention Center, *COPPS: Community Oriented Policing and Problem Solving* (Sacramento, Calif.: Author, 1992), p. 72.

Planning and Implementation

Translating Ideas into Action

Key Terms and Concepts

Environmental scanning
Modeling behavior
Needs assessment
Planning cycle

Strategic management
Strategic planning
Strategic thinking

Learning Objectives

As a result of reading this chapter, the student will:

- Know what is meant by strategic thinking and strategic management and why they are important for today's police executives
- Be able to list the primary elements of strategic planning and the planning process
- Understand what is involved in a planning cycle and a needs assessment
- Comprehend the roles of chief executives, middle managers, first-line supervisors, detectives, and patrol officers in the planning and implementation of COPPS
- Know why labor unions pose a challenge for leadership and administration in the implementation of COPPS
- Be able to delineate several possible obstacles that can militate against, and undermine, the implementation of COPPS

Alice:	Cheshire Puss, would you tell me, please, which way I ought to go from here?
Cheshire Cat:	That depends a good deal on where you want to get to.
Alice:	I don't much care where . . .
Cheshire Cat:	Then it doesn't matter which way you go.

—Lewis Carroll, in Alice's Adventures in Wonderland, *1865, Chapter 6*

INTRODUCTION

Having identified the core components and elements of community oriented policing and problem solving (COPPS) in previous chapters, we now look at how to strategically plan for and implement this concept. To help conceptualize strategic planning, one might view it as maintaining the tension on the line while fishing—if you reel it in too fast, the line might snap; but if you go too slowly, the fish will not be landed. The strategic plan that the police agency "holds in its hands" outlines bold milestones spread over the next several years.[1]

This chapter begins with a look at the general need for strategic thinking and the need for police managers and organizations to engage in the strategic planning process. This section also discusses the planning cycle and how to assess local needs and develop a planning document.

Then we shift to the implementation of COPPS per se, considering some principal components: leadership and administration, human resources, field operations, and external relations. All of this is then brought fully into focus by use of examples, with a view of actual agency strategic planning processes. We conclude the chapter by considering several general obstacles to implementation and by delineating ten ways that COPPS can be undermined.

STRATEGIC THINKING

In order for a chief executive to engage in strategic planning (strategic management is discussed below), he or she must first become engaged in **strategic thinking** and then assist the organization in thinking strategically. This means seeing both the big picture and its operational implications. As Herocleous observed, the purpose of strategic thinking is to discover novel, imaginative strategies "that can rewrite the rules of the competitive game and to envision potential futures significantly different from the present."[2] Strategic thinking refers to a creative, divergent thought process. It is a mode of strategy making that is associated with reinventing the future.[3]

Strategic thinking is, therefore, compatible with strategic planning (see Figure 7–1). Both are required in any thoughtful strategy-making process and strategy formulation. The creative groundbreaking strategies emerging from strategic thinking still have to be operationalized through convergent and analytical thought (strategic planning). Thus, both strategic thinking and strategic planning are necessary, and neither is adequate without the other for effective strategic management.[4] Herocleous stated:

> It all comes down to the ability to go up and down the ladder of abstraction, and being able to see both the big picture and the operational implications, which are signs of outstanding leaders and strategists.[5]

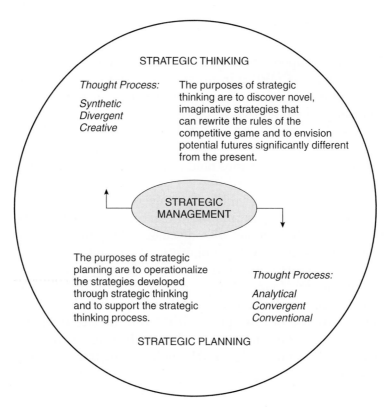

FIGURE 7–1
Strategic Thinking and Strategic Planning

Source: Loizos Heracleous, "Strategic Thinking or Strategic Planning?"
Long Range Planning 31 (June 1998):485. Used with permission.

STRATEGIC MANAGEMENT

Police executives know that community policing, external and internal environments, political influences, homeland security, and new technologies are molding the profession into a highly complex structure. To be successful in this environment, executives should also know that they need to set their course with strategic management.[6]

Strategic management is a systems management approach that uses active leaders in the organization to move change across organizational boundaries. A small team of personnel is assembled to analyze operational functions, identify inefficiencies, review systems integration, and detect gaps in management communications that hinder performance. Major transformation within an organization cannot rest with one person but should be guided by teams under the direction of strategic managers—command and support staff members who have the expertise, credibility, and competence to get the job done.[7]

STRATEGIC PLANNING

Basic Elements

Strategic planning is a leadership tool and a process; furthermore, as with most tools, it is primarily used for one purpose: to help an organization do a better job—to focus its energy, ensure that members of the organization are working toward the same goals, and assess and adjust an organization's direction in response to a changing environment. In short, strategic planning is a disciplined effort to produce fundamental decisions and actions that shape and guide what an organization is, what it does, and why it does it, with a focus on the future.[8]

The history of strategic planning begins in the military, in which strategy is the science of planning and directing large-scale military operations. Although our understanding of strategy as applied to management has been transformed, one element remains: aiming to achieve competitive advantage. Strategic planning also includes the following elements[9]:

- It is oriented toward the future and looks at how the world could be different five to ten years in the future. It is aimed at creating the organization's future.
- It is based on thorough analysis of foreseen or predicted trends and scenarios of possible alternative futures.
- It thoroughly analyzes the organization, both its internal and external environment and its potential.
- It is a qualitative, idea-driven process.
- It is a continuous learning process.
- When it is successful, it influences all areas of operations, becoming a part of the organization's philosophy and culture.

Excellent examples of strategic planning abound; for example, see the strategic plan of the U.S. Department of Justice.[10]

For police leaders, strategic planning holds many benefits. It can help an agency anticipate key trends and issues facing the organization, both currently and in the future. The planning process explores options, sets directions, and helps stakeholders make appropriate decisions. It facilitates communication among key stakeholders who are involved in the process and keeps organizations focused on outcomes while battling daily crises. Planning can be used to develop performance standards to measure an agency's efforts. Most important, it helps leaders facilitate and manage change (which was the subject of Chapter 6).

Planning Cycle

A **planning cycle** is used for strategic planning—the initial steps to be taken in the process—with appropriate involvement by all stakeholders.

The process is not fixed, however; it must be flexible enough to allow rapid revision of specific strategies as new information develops:

1. Identify the planning team: Include the involvement of several key stakeholders, both internal and external to the organization.
   a. *Department and city leadership.* Police chief executives and other office-holders should be involved.
   b. *Department personnel.* Supervisors, officers, nonsworn staff members, and all members of the department should be included.
   c. *The community.* The plan must be developed in partnership with the community it is designed to serve.
   d. *Interagency partners.* These include both staff and other government agencies and representatives of key social welfare agencies.
2. Environmental scanning: Conduct a needs assessment (discussed later).
3. Development of a planning document (discussed later).

The steps in the planning cycle are presented in Figure 7–2.

Environmental Scanning: A Needs Assessment

Environmental scanning is a part of the planning cycle that deserves special attention because it refers to the collection and analysis of information required to determine the nature and extent of crime in a community, community residents' perceptions of crime and how they are affected by it, and information about the environment or conditions of a community. The purpose of the **needs assessment** is to determine and exchange information about specific types of community crime and disorder problems, their causes and effects, and the resources available to combat them. The needs assessment provides the foundation for a community's entire COPPS effort.

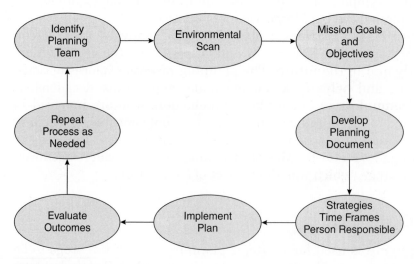

FIGURE 7–2
Planning Cycle

Therefore, in order to develop a comprehensive implementation plan for community policing, a needs assessment should be completed at the earliest possible time for several reasons:

- To list in order of priority and clarify the existing crime and drug problems
- To provide a view of resident perceptions about the crime and drug problems, and to provide an excellent means of involving the community in problem identification
- To provide information to the public about problems
- To provide initial direction for developing a work plan, and to assist in setting program goals, strategies, and objectives
- To provide baseline data for evaluation

Needs assessment is ultimately a process conducted for outlining the current issues of the community and the resources needed to resolve those issues. This document will do the following:

- Result in a clearer picture of community needs and resources
- Allow the planning team to develop a strong rationale for decision making

Information sources for needs assessment include:

- City planning reports
- Newspaper articles
- Police reports (including local crime analysis and dispatch calls for service [CFS] data, as well as police officers' knowledge of the community, the Federal Bureau of Investigation's *Uniform Crime Reports,* and other related sources)
- Interviews with community leaders
- Community surveys (see "Community Survey in Fort Collins, Colorado," in Appendix B)
- Employment, housing, education, and health information

PLANNING DOCUMENT: A GUIDE
FOR IMPLEMENTATION

Elements and Issues

Strategic planning is both a document and a process. A written document or plan is the product of a planning team's efforts, is helpful for organizing key objectives, and serves as a guide for those persons involved in the implementation process. The detail and structure of a plan may vary greatly: It may be highly detailed and cover goals, objectives, tasks, and timelines, or it may be less formal, identifying general areas targeted for change.

The structure and formality of a plan will depend largely on the needs and capacity of the organization (based on the environmental scanning and needs assessment). Large organizations with funding and staff support may desire a more comprehensive plan to keep track of the many details and numbers of people involved in implementation. Conversely, smaller police

Montgomery County, Maryland's multiyear strategic plan was designed for adaptability and continual evaluation.

Courtesy Montgomery County, Maryland, Police Department.

organizations may be capable of implementing change with less detailed plans (see Exhibit 7–1).

Following are some format and content issues for the planning process and the development of a planning document:

1. Develop statements of vision, mission, and values:
   a. Vision is a scenario or description of how the agency and community will change if the plan is successful.
   b. Mission defines the "business" of COPPS. The statement can be expected to include both traditional aspects of policing (such as public safety, enforcement, "protect and serve") and aspects of COPPS philosophy (community engagement, shared responsibility for public safety).
   c. Values guide decisions and actions. Prioritize and develop a short list of key principles that people who are involved in COPPS implementation should consider.
2. Identify primary objectives that define critical outcomes anticipated from the change to COPPS.
3. Select strategies from among various options outlined during the process that clearly outline the primary avenues and approaches that will be used to attain objectives.
4. Set goals that are general statements of intent. They are the first step in translating a mission statement into what can realistically be attained. Goals should be obtainable and measurable, often beginning with such phrases as "to increase," "to reduce," or "to expand."
5. Set objectives, specific statements of what must be done to achieve a goal or desired outcomes. Usually, several objectives are developed for each goal. A meaningful and well-stated objective should be:
   a. Specific: stating precisely what is to be achieved
   b. Measurable: answering how much, how many, how well
   c. Time-bound: indicating when results will be achieved
6. Set activities, detailed steps necessary to carry out each strategy; they should be time-framed and measurable.
7. Identify a responsible person for every task.
8. Set timelines for the completion of tasks.

EXHIBIT 7–1

Small Town, Large Strategic Planning Effort: Durham, New Hampshire

The Durham, New Hampshire, Police Department has 18 sworn officers and serves about 12,000 residents, but it is also home to the University of New Hampshire, with 12,000 students. Each officer responds to about 1,100 calls for service annually. Concern arose when it was discovered that residents saw the department as distant from the people in the community; the decision was made to launch a strategic planning initiative. The first step was to conduct a community survey wherein citizens could rate the department. An internal survey of officers and staff was also developed. Next, a one-day strategic planning session was conducted, bringing together officers, community leaders, and other citizens for a frank discussion about contemporary and future police services. Armed with findings from the surveys and this session, the department set out to draft its strategic plan, which evolved into seven long-term objectives—maintaining accredited status, reducing crime, increasing quality of service and customer satisfaction, obtaining grants and other funding, replacing equipment as needed, maintaining an acceptable workload for officers, and providing high-quality training for all personnel. Each objective had a performance indicator, target dates, and strategies for achieving it. Copies of the plan were disseminated to the town council and key session participants as well as made available for public viewing. The community and department now have a better understanding of the police mission, values, goals, and strategies.

Source: David L. Kurz, "Strategic Planning and Police-Community Partnership in a Small Town," *Police Chief* (December 2000):28–36.

IMPLEMENTATION OF COPPS—METHOD

Since COPPS came into being, most police executives have implemented the strategy throughout the entire agency; some executives, however, have attempted to implement the concept by introducing it in a small unit or in an experimental district and often in a specific geographic area of the jurisdiction.

It is strongly argued that COPPS be implemented on a department-wide basis because the introduction of a "special unit" seems to exacerbate the conflict between community policing's reform agenda and the more traditional outlook and hierarchical structure of the agency. A perception of elitism is created—a perception that is ironic because COPPS is meant to close the gap between patrol and special units and to empower and value the rank-and-file patrol officer as the most important functionary of police work.

The key lesson from research on implementation, however, is that there is no "golden" or "bright line" rule or any universal method to ensure the successful adoption of COPPS. Two general propositions are important, however, for consideration in implementing the concept: the role of the rank-and-file officer and the role of the environment (or "social ecology") in which COPPS is to be implemented.[11] The social ecology of COPPS includes both the internal/organizational and external/societal environments. Both of these factors are discussed later in the chapter.

We also believe that total quality management (TQM) supports putting the responsibility for implementation of COPPS at the door of everyone in the organization. If rank-and-file officers are able to show positive results with COPPS projects, their success can become difficult to criticize among those with whom the philosophy is unpopular.[12]

IMPLEMENTATION OF COPPS—PRINCIPAL COMPONENTS

Moving an agency to COPPS is a complex endeavor. Four principal components of implementation profoundly affect the way agencies do business: leadership and administration, human resources, field operations, and external relations.[13]

Leadership and Administration

Management Approaches.   COPPS requires changing the philosophy of leadership and management throughout the entire organization. This begins with the development of a new vision/values/mission statement, as noted earlier. Leadership should be promoted at all levels, and a shift in management style from controller to facilitator is necessary. The organization should invest in information systems that will assist officers in identifying patterns of crime and support the problem-solving process. Progressive leaders will need to prepare for the future by engaging in long-term strategic management and developing continuous evaluation processes, but at the same time these leaders should be flexible and comfortable with change. Finances and resources will no longer be firmly established within boxes in the organizational chart; rather, they will be commonly shared across the organization, with other city departments and the public engaged in neighborhood problem solving.

Chief Executives.   It is essential that chief executives communicate the idea that COPPS is department-wide in scope. To get the whole agency involved, the chief executive must adopt four practices as part of the implementation plan[14]:

1. Communicate to all department members the vital role of COPPS in serving the public. Executives must describe why handling problems is more effective than simply handling incidents.
2. Provide incentives to all department members to engage in COPPS. This includes a new and different personnel evaluation and reward system as well as positive encouragement.
3. Reduce the barriers to COPPS that can occur. Procedures, time allocation, and policies all need to be closely examined.
4. Show officers how to address problems. Training is a key element of COPPS implementation. The executive must also set guidelines for innovation. Officers must know they have the latitude to innovate.

Springfield, Massachusetts, Police Chief Ed Fynn "walks the talk" of COPPS by appearing at neighborhood clean-up efforts to show his support to residents and officers.

Courtesy Springfield, Massachusetts, Police Department.

The top management of a police agency must consciously address these four concerns. Failure to do so will result in the COPPS approach being conducted by a relatively small number of officers; as a result, relatively few problems will be addressed.

The general task of the chief executive is to challenge the fundamental assumptions of the organization, its aspirations and objectives, the effectiveness of the department's current technologies, and even the chief's own self-perception. This is an awkward stage in the life of the organization. It seems to be a deliberate attempt by the chief to upset the agency. The remedy lies in the personal commitment of the chief and his or her senior managers and supervisors. Ensuing surveys may well find that morale improves once it becomes clear that the change in direction and style was more than a "fleeting fancy," that the chief's policies have some longevity.[15]

Middle Managers.   In the early twentieth century, a powerful midlevel management group emerged that extended the reach of chiefs throughout the department and became the locus of the practice and skill base of the occupation. As such, middle managers—captains and lieutenants— became the leading edge in the establishment of decentralized control over police departments' internal environment and organizational operations.[16]

Furthermore, in the past one of the basic functions and practices of middle managers was to forestall creativity and innovation.

Times have changed in this regard, however; today these middle managers play a crucial role in planning and implementing COPPS as well as encouraging their officers to be innovative, to take risks, and to be creative.[17] As George Kelling and William Bratton observed, "Ample evidence exists that when a clear vision of the business of the organization is put forward, when mid-managers are included in planning, when their legitimate self-interests are acknowledged, and when they are properly trained, mid-managers can be the leading edge of innovation and creativity."[18]

First-Line Supervisors.   Research has provided additional information for leaders to consider when implementing a COPPS philosophy. To begin, first-line supervisors and senior patrol officers seem to generate the greatest resistance to community policing, largely because they have long-standing working styles cultivated from years of traditional police work and because these officers can feel disenfranchised by a management system that takes the best and brightest out of patrol and (they often believe) leaves them behind. The press of 911 calls also makes it difficult to meet the need for community outreach, problem solving, and networking with other agencies. Officers may become concerned about the size of the area for which they are responsible; community policing beats are typically smaller than those of radio patrols.

The role of middle managers and first-line supervisors is covered in greater detail in Chapter 6, on changing the culture of the organization.

Examination of the Organization.   An important aspect of COPPS is that its implementation occurs not over a period of days or weeks but more likely over many months or even years. The bigger the organization, the longer it will take to change. Also, throughout the period of change, the office of the chief executive is going to be surrounded by turbulence. An executive may be fortunate enough to inherit an organization that is already susceptible to change; however, the executive who inherits a smoothly running bureaucracy, complacent in the status quo, has a tougher job.

With regard to the organization, one of the first steps the executive and managers must take is an analysis of existing policies and procedures. Although a need remains for some standing orders and some prepared contingency plans and procedures, in the past such manuals have been used more to allocate blame retrospectively after some error has been discovered. It is not surprising that street officers have adopted a mind-set of doing things "by the book." Many executives have deemphasized their policy and procedure manuals in implementing community policing. As an extreme example, the manual of an English police force had grown to four volumes, each more than three inches thick, totaling more than 2,000 pages of instructions. Under COPPS, the manual was discarded in favor of a one-page "Policy Statement" that gave 11 brief "commandments." These commandments related more to initiative and "reasonableness of action" than to rules and regulations. Each officer was issued a pocket-size laminate copy of the policy statement.[19]

The organization should conduct an in-depth analysis of the existing departmental rank structure, which itself can be a principal obstacle to the effective communication of new values and philosophy throughout the organization. A large metropolitan police force may have ten or more layers of rank. The chief executive must talk with the officers; therefore, it is necessary to ensure that the message not be filtered, doctored, or suppressed.[20]

Human Resources

Human resources constitute the basis of organizational culture. Developing COPPS as a part of daily police **modeling behaviors** and practices presents a major challenge. To accomplish this requires that the mechanisms that motivate, challenge, reward, and correct employees' behaviors comport with the principles of COPPS. They include recruiting, selection, training, performance evaluations, promotions, honors and awards, and discipline, all of which should be reviewed to ensure that they promote and support the tenets of COPPS.

Modeling Behaviors.   Recruiting literature should reflect the principles of COPPS. Agencies should actively recruit students, minorities, and women into their organization (community groups may be helpful in this respect). Advertisements in newspapers or on television and radio shows that target certain populations are also wise.

COPPS should be integrated into academy training, field training programs, and in-service training. As was discussed in previous chapters, it is also important to provide training and education to the other city agencies and community, business, and social service organizations so that they understand COPPS. Performance evaluations and reward systems should reflect new job descriptions and officers' application of their COPPS training.

Promotion systems should be expanded from their usual focus on tactical decision making to include knowledge of the research on community policing, and they should test an officer's ability to apply problem solving to various crime and neighborhood problems.

Labor Relations.   Another challenge for leadership and administration in the implementation of COPPS centers is labor unions. Since the 1960s police unions and associations have evolved quickly, making great strides in improving wages, benefits, and working conditions. Yet there is a concern about police administrators' ability to run their agencies and the impact of unions on police-community partnerships. Unions are often viewed by administrators and the public as a negative force, focusing only on financial gain and control over administrative policy making without regard for the department or community.

Does COPPS conflict with the philosophy of police unions? It is understandable that this approach could be construed as antithetical to union interests. For example, COPPS asks officers to assume a proprietary interest in the neighborhoods where they work and to be flexible and creative in their work hours and solutions to problems. This approach often conflicts with collective bargaining contracts in which unions have negotiated for stability of work hours and compensation when working conditions are altered. The idea of civilianization, reductions of rank, and decentralized investigations can also be viewed as a threat to officers' lateral mobility, promotional opportunities, and career development. Labor organizations are also concerned with any proposed changes in shifts, beats, criteria for selection, promotion, discipline, and so on.

It is wise to include labor representatives in the planning and implementation process from the beginning. When the unions are excluded from the planning process, officers perceive the implementation of COPPS as a public relations gimmick in management's interests. It is also important that union leaders understand management's concerns and collaborate in planning an agency's future.

Remember, COPPS is important from both the labor and management perspectives. Both sides are interested in creating a quality work environment for employees. This translates to a healthy and productive workforce. COPPS provides officers the opportunity to use their talents, and it removes layers of management and quota-driven evaluations that are often opposed by officers.

Field Operations

Decentralized Services.　The need for available time to engage in problem solving presents a supervisory challenge that begins with managing CFS. This requires comprehensive workload and crime analyses, call prioritization, alternative call handling, and differential response methods (discussed in Chapters 4 and 6). This information helps an agency when its managers are considering a decentralized approach to field operations that involves assigning officers to a beat and shift for a minimum of one year to learn more about a neighborhood's problems. It is also helpful in reconstructing beat boundaries to correspond more closely with neighborhoods.

Decentralized service is an important part of the general scheme of COPPS. Under the traditional incident-driven style of policing, officers have little permanent territorial responsibility. They know that they may be dispatched to another area at any time and that they are not responsible for anything that occurs on their beat when they are off duty. This responsibility for their area only during a specific period of time reinforces the officer's focus on incidents rather than on long-term area problems.

When the chief executive says to the officer, "This area is yours, and nobody else's," however, the territory becomes personalized. The officer's concern for the beat does not end with a tour of duty; concerned officers will want to know what occurred on their beat while they were off duty and will often make unsolicited follow-up visits, struggling to find causes of incidents that would otherwise be regarded as inconsequential.[21]

Detectives.   A matter that relates to field operations and COPPS involves detectives. The detective division may easily view the introduction of COPPS as a matter strictly for the patrol officers; the detectives might believe that "Our job is still to solve crime."[22] Detectives might maintain that attitude until they are removed from the group that reinforces that perception. They have to be incorporated into the COPPS context (see Exhibit 7–2). Valuable intelligence information gained by detectives through investigations can be fed to the patrol division. Also, detectives must believe that crime prevention is their principal obligation and not the exclusive responsibility of the patrol force.

Detectives have opportunities to establish and enhance positive working relationships with victim advocacy groups, civic organizations, police district advisory councils, and other stakeholders in the system. Detectives, like patrol officers, attend regular community meetings and impart valuable knowledge relating to criminal activities, trends, and patterns; in addition, quicker, easier investigative responses can be realized.

An excellent recent example of bringing detectives into COPPS is that of El Paso, Texas, which witnessed a problem of repetitive violent acts of domestic violence. After analyzing the problem—and examining the

EXHIBIT 7–2

Investigations in the COPPS Context

One problematic issue for police departments that are implementing COPPS is the appropriate organization of investigative functions. How can agencies structure investigations to best support these approaches? Who in the organization should conduct which types of investigations? Should agencies decentralize investigative functions? Should there be a separate command structure for detectives?

A group of chiefs leading organizations through the change process first identified this whole issue. The National Institute of Justice will fund a research project surveying 900 law enforcement agencies, all those serving populations of at least 50,000 and having at least 100 sworn personnel. The Police Executive Research Forum will ask these agencies about their status with respect to COPPS, as well as detailed questions about the structure of their investigative functions. Researchers will then develop several models of the investigative function in the COPPS context.

Source: Workshop presentation, Mary Ann Wycoff, Police Executive Research Forum, "The 8th Annual International Problem Oriented Policing Conference: Problem Oriented Policing 1997," November 16, 1997, San Diego, California.

environment of the offenses, including victims' family situations, economics, and social pressures involved in lack of prosecutions—detectives worked with the patrol division to encourage victims to follow through with prosecutions, engage in follow-up investigations, and even devise a rudimentary witness protection unit, with impressive outcomes.[23]

Top Priority: Patrol Personnel.　There is one very important positive aspect of considering whether to implement a COPPS philosophy, one that all chief executives should remember: It encourages many of the activities that patrol officers would like to do, that is, to engage in more inquiry of crime and disorder and get more closure from their work. When asked why they originally wanted to enter policing, officers consistently say that they joined in order to help people.[24] By emphasizing work that addresses people's concerns and giving officers the discretion to develop a solution, COPPS helps make police work more rewarding.

Among the most frequent complaints voiced by patrol officers, however, are that patrol officers are given little support, they are accorded low esteem by their organization, and they are simply a pool of employees from which to draw for other special assignments. For COPPS to be successful, the agency must ensure that patrol staffing is maintained and that its officers believe that their work is most important to the organization's success.

Allowing officers to identify and resolve neighborhood problems can improve morale by making the job more rewarding.

Courtesy Community Policing Consortium.

External Relations

In Chapter 4 we discussed the various stakeholders and partners that police will find in the community for assistance in the COPPS initiative. Enlisting the assistance of the community is often a more complex undertaking than one might assume.

Collaborative responses to neighborhood crime and disorder are essential to the success of COPPS. This requires new relationships and the sharing of information and resources among the police and community, local government agencies, service providers, and businesses. Also, police agencies must educate and inform their external partners about police resources and neighborhood problems using surveys, newsletters, community meetings, and public service announcements. The media also provide an excellent opportunity for police to educate the community. Press releases about collaborative problem-solving efforts should be sent to the media, and news conferences should be held to discuss major crime reduction efforts.

Another essential consideration of implementing COPPS is the solicitation and establishment of political support for the concept. The political environment varies considerably, say, with the strong mayor and council-manager forms of government. These and other rapidly changing political environments make the implementation of COPPS more difficult—especially when we add to the cauldron the at-will employment of most police executives.

Exhibit 7–3 shows how Sacramento, California, approached external relations by providing neighborhood services.

Elected officials must provide direction and support through policy development and resource allocation. This may be accomplished in several

 EXHIBIT 7–3

External Relations: Neighborhood Services in Sacramento

Recently Sacramento, California, decided to reorganize its city services into four geographically based system areas. This configuration mirrored the Sacramento police department's (SPD) patrol deployment boundaries. A new city department called Neighborhood Services was developed that included such elements as recreation, housing and building inspections, nuisance abatement, community centers, planning, parks, human services, and code enforcement. The four area managers of this new department and the four SPD patrol captains cooperated to implement new levels of problem solving. The increased contact between the departments and community members occurred simultaneously at several levels. Problem solving is a collaboration among the SPD, Neighborhood Services, and the community, facilitating the dissemination of information and enabling them to identify issues quickly. Community mobilization has spread from community associations to business associations, recreation programs, political action committees, and redevelopment project boards. With this increase of community input, a variety of responses enhances and continues the problem-solving cycle.

Source: Workshop presentation, Mike Busch, Sacramento Police Department, "The 8th Annual International Problem Oriented Policing 1997," November 16, 1997, San Diego, California.

ways. For instance, in Tempe, Arizona, the city council passed a resolution that established guidelines for the creation of a Neighborhood Assistance Office. The program's goal was "fostering a partnership among the city council, city staff and residents, and the creation of an environment in which citizens are afforded an opportunity to participate in city affairs in an advisory or advocacy role."[25] In essence, the Neighborhood Assistance Office was to be a conduit for communication between the city government and citizens:

> Implementation of the Neighborhood Associations included several important steps on the part of the City: maintaining a register and mailing list of existing organizations and their officers and bylaws; mailing newsletters for Neighborhood Associations; providing insurance coverage for use of school facilities for neighborhood meetings; coordinating annual citywide informational meetings; arranging for city staff and officials to speak at association meetings; and responding to concerns and questions raised by individual associations.[26]

Synthesis of Principal Components

Figure 7–3 ties together these four key areas—leadership and administration, human resources, field operations, and external relations—illustrating the principal components of implementation.

An Example: Montgomery County, Maryland

Exhibits 7–4 and 7–5 show the Montgomery County, Maryland, Department of Police Strategic Implementation Plan for moving to COPPS. Exhibit 7–4 provides the plan's vision statement, mission statement, and values statement; Exhibit 7–5 includes the statement of problem-solving goals, objectives, and strategies for implementing problem solving.

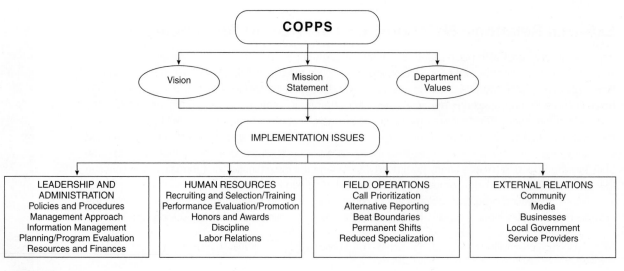

FIGURE 7–3
Principal Components of Implementation

EXHIBIT 7–4

Montgomery County Strategic Plan: Vision, Mission, and Values

VISION STATEMENT

The Montgomery County Police will provide the highest quality of police services by working in partnership with the community to improve the quality of life within Montgomery County, while at the same time maintaining respect for individual rights and human dignity. The Department recognizes the value and importance of its employees and will ensure that all employees are treated equitably and fairly. The Department is committed to providing its members with the quality of leadership, training, and equipment necessary to perform its mission.

MISSION STATEMENT

We, the Montgomery County Department of Police, are committed to providing the highest quality of police services by empowering our members and the community to work in partnership with the goal of improving the quality of life within Montgomery County, while at the same time maintaining respect for individual rights and human dignity.

ORGANIZATIONAL VALUES

Partnership

We are committed to working in partnership with the community and each other to identify and resolve issues which impact public safety.

Respect

We are committed to respecting individual rights, human dignity, and the value of all members of the community and the department.

Integrity

We are committed to nurturing the public trust by holding ourselves accountable to the highest standards of professionalism and ethics.

Dedication

We are committed to providing the highest quality of professional law enforcement service to the community with the goal of enhancing the quality of life within Montgomery County.

Empowerment

We are committed to empowering our members and the community to resolve problems by creating an environment that encourages solutions that address the needs of the community . . . pride in our community, pride in our department, pride in ourselves.

Source: Montgomery County, Maryland, Department of Police, *Strategic Implementation Plan: Transition to Community Policing* (Montgomery County, Md.: Author, 2000).

To further demonstrate the implementation process, Box 7–1 shows the specific sequential steps taken by the Baltimore, Maryland, Police Department toward implementation of its COPPS philosophy, following the development of appropriate vision, mission, and values statements for the department.

EXHIBIT 7–5

Montgomery County Strategic Plan: Goals, Objectives, and Strategies

Community policing emphasizes the need for a problem solving approach to reduce the incidence and the fear of crime. In many instances, it will be more effective and efficient to spend several hours (or even days) to thoroughly address and eliminate a problem than it will be to repeatedly dispatch cars to the same call day after day, week after week, month after month, and in some cases, year after year.

Problem solving requires that officers be allowed to not only try the safe and proven traditional solutions, but also new, imaginative, and even unorthodox solutions. Not all solutions will be successful, as with any solution there is the risk of failure.

Risk taking is a necessity in community policing. Problem solving requires that the Department not only accept risk taking but encourage it. Employees should be commended for their successes and not chastised for their failures. A common axiom in community policing is "zero risk equals zero success."

GOAL

The analysis of a recurring problem to determine its cause and to devise solutions to permanently eliminate it. Problem solving also includes implementing the chosen solution. Problem solving involves risk taking.

OBJECTIVES

2.1 Reduce fear of crime and conditions that contribute to crime and disorder through community policing strategies.

2.2 Reallocate individual and unit workloads to facilitate innovation and problem solving opportunities.

2.3 Establish a permanent planning unit to support and facilitate current and future departmental planning strategies.

2.4 Identify changes needed to existing laws and ordinances and propose new legislation to facilitate community policing strategies.

STRATEGIES		TIME FRAME (YEARS)	FISCAL IMPACT	ASSIGNMENT OF RESPONSIBILITY
2.1.1	Institute a training program to train all members of the department in the concepts and philosophies of community policing. CALEA 33.6.2	Ongoing	Yes	Office of Comm. Policing Training
2.1.2	Develop a training manual for problem solving techniques. CALEA 33.6.2	Completed	No	Field Svcs. Bureau Office of Comm. Policing Training

Strategies	Time Frame (Years)	Fiscal Impact	Assignment of Responsibility
2.1.3 Assign beat officers the responsibility of identifying problems within their beat and developing plans to remedy the problem. CALEA 41.2.1, 41.2.5, 54.2.4, 54.2.5	Immediate	No	Field Svcs. Bureau District Commanders
2.1.4 Increase district crime analysts' interaction with beat officers by jointly identifying crime patterns or problem areas through analysis. CALEA 15.1.6	Ongoing	No	Field Svcs. Bureau Central Crime Analyst District Crime Analysts District Commanders
2.1.5 Expand and publicize the Neighborhood Watch Programs. CALEA 45.2.2	1–2	Yes	Field Svcs. Bureau District Commanders Community Svcs. Section District Comm. Svcs. Officer
2.1.6 Reinstitute and publicize "Operation ID." CALEA 45.2.2	1–2	Yes	Field Svcs. Bureau District Commanders Crime Prevention Section District Comm. Svcs. Officer
2.1.7 Train patrol officers in specific skill areas of investigations and innovative investigative techniques. CALEA 33.6.2	1–2	Yes	Training Investigative Svcs. Bureau
2.1.8 Develop and maintain a Community Services Section within each district. This section will coordinate community meetings and serve as a liaison. CALEA 45.2.1	Completed	No	Field Svcs. Bureau District Commanders
2.1.9 Implement a training program to educate resident managers and rental property owners. CALEA 33.7.1	2–3	No	District Comm. Svcs. Officer

Source: Montgomery County, Maryland, Department of Police, *Strategic Implementation Plan: Transition to Community Policing* (Montgomery County, Md.: Author, 2000).

BOX 7–1

Implementation in Baltimore, Maryland

Several implementation issues had to be addressed. The values statement was widely disseminated across the community and the department. The public was challenged to come forth when they believed a value standard had been violated. The policing strategy became neighborhood-based and officers were shown that they were respected for the enormous contributions they could and did make to the community. Restructuring of the department, especially the Operations Bureau, was necessary. Each commander was given total responsibility for policing the neighborhoods in that district. There were a number of other important steps in the implementation sequence:

- *Fiscal support:* A commitment by the city was necessary to provide the department with the capital needed for maximum effectiveness, as well as a commitment by the department that resources would be carefully and effectively utilized.

- *Organizational structure and management systems:* The organizational hierarchy was flattened so that there was a minimum of supervisory and management levels between the police commissioner and the officers assigned to field service delivery in the city's neighborhoods. Investigative functions were decentralized as well, and civilianization was increased.

- *Community policing district deployment model:* Decisions had to be made concerning such matters as duties and job descriptions of COPPS officers, functions to be performed, staffing levels, and neighborhood boundaries.

- *Internal and external marketing:* The philosophy had to be marketed in order to succeed. All members of the department had to be oriented to the philosophy and massive changes had to be undertaken with regard to the department's handling of 911 CFS. The city council, other government agencies, and citizens were made fully aware of the changes proposed and positive results to be expected.

- *Deployment:* A new set of district and post boundaries were created that matched the major neighborhood areas of the city, ensuring that key "activity" centers (those areas generating the greatest number of CFS) were in the middle of districts and posts, thus providing for strong accountability for policing those areas. Patrol staffing was given the highest priority in the department.

- *Training:* COPPS training was developed for patrol officers and detectives, based on nationally recognized, state-of-the-art police problem-solving methodology. To support the curricula, new materials were developed reflecting the department's new orientation. Lieutenants, sergeants, and patrol officers were trained in facilitation and COPPS skills.

- *Interagency support:* A problem-solving methodology was developed to link all levels of the department with other agencies of government.

- *Quality control:* A new system was developed for evaluating police success at all levels—as a department, within a district, and on individual posts. A new set of performance standards was developed.

- *Recruitment and personnel management:* A new recruitment strategy was initiated that attracted young men and women to join the department, desiring to serve the community and become neighborhood COPPS officers. This ensured that the department remained on a "fast track" toward guaranteeing that the diversity of the community was reflected in all ranks.

- *Profiling neighborhoods:* Officers in each neighborhood of the city profiled their post, developing a "picture" of the neighborhood's priorities, resources, institutions, and problems of crime, fear, and violence. They also developed an action plan to address the neighborhood's concerns, in collaboration with local residents and businesspeople.

Source: Baltimore Police Department, *Implementation Task Force Report: Assessment of the Department* (Baltimore, Md.: Author, no date), pp. 10–12.

GENERAL OBSTACLES

Several possible obstacles that can militate against the implementation of COPPS have been identified[27]:

1. *Police leadership.* Many police executives pride themselves on being hard-line disciplinarians, unbending in the governance of their organizations. They may rule through coercion, fear, and intimidation. Their officers may be legalistic in style and reactive in nature. There may be a distinct separation between labor and management, as well as an "us-versus-them" schism between the police and the public.

2. *Police organization.* Traditional crime-fighting organizational values provide a strong barrier to COPPS because in order for implementation of COPPS to occur, the very core of the organization's culture must change (discussed in Chapter 8). There also exists in some organizations what has been termed a "small cadre of nonproductive, abusive malcontents." Not until police officers at all levels begin to clean house will the community accept them as trusting, civil, sensitive, and responsive representatives, which is a vital step toward implementing COPPS.

3. *Political leadership.* Politics are involved in every aspect of policing in America. Every jurisdiction is beholden to some extent to elected politicians, who in turn serve at the pleasure of their constituents. Politicians set the tone for the policing of a community.

4. *Community diversity.* Until officers can fully embrace our diverse communities, it is not likely that the concept can be implemented in those neighborhoods.

Notwithstanding these conceivable obstacles, the potential for their coming into play and creating problems for COPPS implementation will be minimized if the guidelines provided earlier in this chapter are followed.

TEN WAYS TO UNDERMINE COPPS

In closing this chapter on implementation, Exhibit 7–6 offers, to the tradition-bound police chief, John Eck's "ten things you can do to undermine COPPS"—a prescription for preventing COPPS from gaining a foothold for many years to come.[28] Many of these tactics are being practiced today, sometimes out of ignorance and sometimes intentionally. With apologies to the U.S. Surgeon General, we issue a prefatory warning: "Practicing these techniques in a police department may be hazardous to the health of community policing and problem solving."

EXHIBIT 7–6

Ten Ways to Undermine COPPS

1. *Oversell it:* COPPS should be sold as the panacea for every ill that plagues the city, the nation, and civilization. Some of the evils you may want to claim COPPS will eliminate are crime, fear of crime, racism, police misuse of force, homelessness, drug abuse, gangs, and other social problems. COPPS can address some of these concerns in specific situations, but by building up the hopes and expectations of the public, the press, and politicians, you can set the stage for later attacks on COPPS when it does not deliver.

2. *Don't be specific:* This suggestion is a corollary of the first principle. Never define what you mean by the following terms: community, service, effectiveness, empowerment, neighborhood, communication, problem solving. Use these and other terms indiscriminately, interchangeably, and whenever possible. At first, people will think the department is going to do something meaningful and won't ask for details. Once people catch on, you can blame the amorphous nature of COPPS and go back to what you were doing before.

3. *Create a special unit or group:* Less than 10 percent of the department should be engaged in this effort, lest COPPS really catch on. Since the "grand design" is possibly the return to conventional policing anyway (once everyone has attacked COPPS), there is no sense in involving more than a few officers. Also, special units are popular with the press and politicians.

4. *Create a soft image:* The best image for COPPS will be a uniformed female officer hugging a small child. This caring and maternal image will warm the hearts of community members suspicious of police, play to traditional stereotypes of sexism within policing, and turn off most cops.

5. *Leave the impression that COPPS is only for minority neighborhoods:* This is a corollary of items 3 and 4. Since a small group of officers will be involved, only a few neighborhoods can receive their services. Place the token COPPS officers in areas like public housing. With any luck, racial antagonism will undercut the approach. It will appear that minority, poor neighborhoods are not getting the "tough on crime" approach they need.

6. *Divorce COPPS officers from "regular" police work:* This is an expansion of the soft image concept. If the COPPS officers do not handle calls or make arrests, but instead throw block parties, speak to community groups, walk around talking to kids, visit schools, and so on, they will not be perceived as "real" police officers to their colleagues. This will further undermine their credibility and ability to accomplish anything of significance.

7. *Obfuscate means and ends:* Whenever describing COPPS, never make the methods for accomplishing the objective subordinate to the objective. Instead, make the means more important than the ends, or at least put them on equal footing. For example, to reduce drug dealing in a neighborhood, make certain that the tactics necessary (arrests, community meetings, etc.) are as important as, or more important than, the objective. These tactics can occupy everyone's time but still leave the drug problem unresolved. Always remember: The means are ends, in and of themselves.

8. *Present community members with problems and plans:* Whenever meeting with community members, officers should listen carefully and politely and then elaborate on how the department will enforce the law. If the community members like the plan, go ahead. If they do not, continue to be polite and ask them to go on a ride-along or witness a drug raid. This avoids having to change the department's operations while demonstrating how difficult police work is, and why nothing can be accomplished. In the end, they will not get their problems solved, but will see how nice the police are.

9. *Never try to understand why problems occur:* Do not let officers gain knowledge about the underlying causes of the problems; COPPS should not include any analysis of the problem and as little information as possible should be sought from the community. Keep officers away from computer terminals; mandate that officers get permission to talk to members of any other agency; do not allow COPPS officers to go off their assigned areas to collect information; prevent access to research conducted on similar problems; suppress listening skills.

10. *Never publicize a success:* Some rogue officers will not get the message and will go out anyway and gather enough information to solve problems. Try to ignore these examples of effective policing and make sure that no one else hears about them. When you cannot ignore them, describe them in the least meaningful way (item 2). Talk about the wonders of empowerment and community meetings. Describe the hours of foot patrol, the new mountain bikes, or shoulder patches. In every problem solved, there is usually some tactic or piece of equipment that can be highlighted at the expense of the accomplishment itself. When all else fails, reprimand the COPPS officer for not wearing a hat.

Source: John E. Eck, "Helpful Hints for the Tradition-Bound Chief," *Fresh Perspectives* (Washington, D.C.: Police Executive Research Forum, June 1992), pp. 1–7.

▲ SUMMARY

This chapter has shown how police executives can plan and implement the COPPS concept after assessing community needs and developing a planning document. Four keys to successful implementation—leadership and administration, human resources, field operations, and external relations—were examined, and we considered several obstacles that can undermine COPPS.

It should be evident that there is no substitute for having a well-thought-out, well-laid-out plan of implementation for the COPPS philosophy. As with any new venture, there must be a "road map" to show the executive and the agency how to travel the "highway" in order to reach the ultimate destination.

■ ITEMS FOR REVIEW

1. Explain what is meant by strategic thinking and strategic management, and set forth why it is important for today's police executives to engage in them.
2. List the primary elements of strategic planning.
3. Define what is involved in a planning cycle and a needs assessment.
4. Explain the roles of chief executives, middle managers, and first-line supervisors in the planning and implementation of COPPS.

5. Delineate why labor unions pose a challenge for leadership and administration in the implementation of COPPS.

6. Review the roles of detectives and patrol personnel in COPPS planning and implementation.

7. List the four possible obstacles that can militate against the implementation of COPPS.

8. List and explain ten ways that a police executive can undermine COPPS, per Eck.

◆ NOTES

1. Robert Trojanowicz, quoted in Harry Sloan, Grand Rapids, Michigan, Police Department Web page, http://www.grpolice.grand-rapids.mi.us/default.htm (Accessed October 20, 2000), p. 1.

2. Loizos Heracleous, "Strategic Thinking or Strategic Planning?" *Long Range Planning* 31 (1998):481–487.

3. Eton Lawrence, "Strategic Thinking: A Discussion Paper," Research Directorate, Policy, Research, and Communications Branch, Public Service Commission of Canada, Ottawa, Ontario, Canada, April 27, 1999, pp. 6–7.

4. *Ibid.*

5. Heracleous, "Strategic Thinking or Strategic Planning?" p. 482.

6. Kim Charrier, "The Role of the Strategic Manager," *The Police Chief* (June 2004):60.

7. *Ibid.*

8. Internet Nonprofit Center, "What Is Strategic Planning?" (San Francisco, Calif.: Author, 2000), p. 1.

9. "Brief History of Strategic Planning," http://www.des.calstate.edu/glossary .html (Accessed September 24, 2000), p. 2.

10. U.S. Department of Justice, "Information Technology Strategic Plan," http://www.usdoj.gov/jmd/irm/imss/2002itplan/strategic_plan.htm (Accessed September 12, 2006).

11. Gregory Saville and D. Kim Rossmo, "Striking a Balance: Lessons from Community-Oriented Policing in British Columbia, Canada" (unpublished manuscript, 1993), pp. 29–30.

12. Charles S. Bullock and Charles M. Lamb (eds.), *Implementation of Civil Rights Policy* (Monterey, Calif.: Brooks/Cole, 1984).

13. Ronald W. Glensor and Kenneth J. Peak, "Implementing Change: Community-Oriented Policing and Problem Solving," *FBI Law Enforcement Bulletin* 7 (July 1996):14–20.

14. John E. Eck and William Spelman, *Problem-Solving: Problem-Oriented Policing in Newport News* (Washington, D.C.: Police Executive Research Forum, 1987), pp. 100–101.

15. Malcolm K. Sparrow, "Implementing Community Policing," *Perspectives on Policing* 9 (November 1988):2–3.

16. George L. Kelling and William J. Bratton, "Implementing Community Policing: The Administrative Problem," *Perspectives on Policing* 17 (July 1993):4.

17. *Ibid.*, p. 9.

18. *Ibid.*, p. 11.

19. Sparrow, *Implementing Community Policing*, pp. 4–5.

20. *Ibid.*, p. 5.

21. *Ibid.*, p. 6.

22. *Ibid.*, p. 7.

23. Sylvia Aguilar, "Detectives and Community Oriented Policing," *Law and Order* (September 2002):222–225.

24. Jesse Rubin, "Police Identity and the Police Role," in Thomas J. Sweeney and William Ellingsworth (eds.), *Issues in Police Patrol: A Book of Readings,* (Kansas City, Mo.: Kansas City Police Department, 1973); John Van Maanen, "Police Socialization: A Longitudinal Examination of Job Attitudes in an Urban Police Department," *Administrative Science Quarterly* 20 (1975): 207–228.

25. Don Cassano and Carol Smith, *Establishing and Sustaining Political Support for Problem Oriented/Community Policing* (Tempe, Ariz.: Tempe City Council Representatives, 1992), p. 74.

26. *Ibid.*, pp. 74–75.

27. Adapted from George E. Rush, "Community Policing: Overcoming the Obstacles," *The Police Chief* (October 1992):50, 52, 54–55.

28. John E. Eck, "Helpful Hints for the Tradition-Bound Chief," in *Fresh Perspectives* (Washington, D.C.: Police Executive Research Forum, June 1992), pp. 1–7.

Evaluation of COPPS Initiatives

Key Terms and Concepts

Effectiveness

Efficiency

Equity

Evaluation

Evaluative criteria

Impact evaluation

Process evaluation

Qualitative measure

Quantitative measure

Rating scale

Survey

Learning Objectives

As a result of reading this chapter, the student will:

- Understand the general rationale for evaluation in COPPS
- Know the kinds of criteria and measures to be used in evaluating COPPS
- Comprehend the role of evaluation in problem solving
- Be aware of the kinds of criteria that might be employed for assessing the individual officer's problem-solving skills
- Know how surveys of the community, neighborhoods, and individual patrol officers can assist in evaluative efforts.

All things have two handles: beware of the wrong one.

—*Ralph Waldo Emerson*

Not everything that counts can be counted; and not everything that can be counted counts.

—*Albert Einstein*

INTRODUCTION

A 75-year-old woman rose to her feet at a town meeting in a midwestern city to offer a suggestion on how an open-air drug market problem might be addressed. "You know," she said, "if you add one more streetlight per block, you might just get rid of these thugs selling drugs. They're like rats. They prefer the dark." The city manager's office and the police department designated the 16-block neighborhood as a test zone, used Community Development Block Grant money to purchase three new streetlights per block for the high-crime area, and gathered data on reported crimes and drug trafficking. After three months (and still a year later), there were significant decreases in all monitored crimes for the area. The desired outcomes were achieved.[1]

This case study shows that the police, citizens, community leaders, and evaluators, working together—with community oriented policing and problem solving (COPPS) strategies—can create and evaluate change. With sound techniques and measurable results, communities can solve problems and demonstrate that the solutions employed were effective.

This chapter begins by discussing the general rationale for evaluating COPPS. Next we examine the kinds of criteria to be used in evaluating COPPS, including several different types of measures. Then we review the role of evaluation in problem solving, including some of the questions that might be asked prior to commencing this task. Next is a review of criteria that might be employed for assessing the individual officer's problem-solving skills, and we include a rating scale. Following is the use of surveys—of the community, neighborhood, and individual patrol officers—to obtain input for evaluative purposes. We conclude the chapter with two case studies of COPPS evaluations (other examples of evaluative efforts are provided throughout the chapter as well).

This chapter provides only rudimentary coverage of response evaluation; this is a challenging undertaking, one that is best accomplished by people who are specially trained in this function and who understand evaluation research methodology. Those persons who are interested in engaging in further inquiry should read *Assessing Responses to Problems: An Introductory Guide for Police Problem-Solvers,* published by the federal Office of Community Oriented Policing Services; some of the information provided in this chapter draws from that booklet.

RATIONALE FOR EVALUATION

Rigorous **evaluation** is an essential component of the problem-solving process (S.A.R.A., discussed in Chapter 3). Contrary to what many people believe, however, an evaluation is seldom performed to prove the success or failure of a strategy or program; rather, evaluation provides continuing feedback, so that methods and practices can be adjusted as necessary.[2] Program evaluation is also used to inform decision makers, clarify options, reduce uncertainties, and provide feedback to decision makers and stakeholders about the program being evaluated. It is, therefore, decision oriented and focuses on what is intended and accomplished.[3]

Furthermore, evaluations provide knowledge; key decision makers in the jurisdiction need a gauge of the strategy's impact and cost-effectiveness. Assessing progress will inform top management whether necessary changes in the culture and in support systems are indeed taking place. Until rigorous evaluations are completed, there will be no clear verdict on whether the COPPS approach makes a difference in controlling crime and disorder. An evaluation also helps ascertain whether a crime prevention initiative has achieved such goals as reducing crime and the fear of crime, raising the community's quality of life, and determining whether it is worthy of continued funding.[4]

It should be noted that few police agencies possess persons adequately trained and educated for conducting program evaluations. Therefore, it is normally best to go outside the agency to obtain the services of an evaluator—one who understands the complexity of the task, often someone with an academic orientation.[5] The police need good research because there is a demand for outcomes. It is no longer good enough for the police to say they made X number of arrests or wrote thousands of tickets. There are thus occasions when the police agency should acquire the services of one who is well grounded in research methodology.[6]

USE OF PROPER CRITERIA

Old Versus New

The **evaluative criteria** employed in the professional policing model, such as crime rates, clearance rates, and response times, have been problematic when applied to the professional model itself and are even less appropriate for the COPPS model. These measures do not gauge the effect of crime prevention efforts and do not capture much of the work that police do or how they do it. A decrease in the reliance on these quantitative measures of police success is also important because communities differ in the services they desire, depending on their particular individual characteristics.[7] Evaluating COPPS requires measurements that better reflect the objectives of this strategy.[8]

Some new indicators for success include identifying and solving local crime and disorder problems through a police-community consultation process; using higher reporting rates both for traditional crime categories and for nontraditional crime and disorder problems; reducing the number of repeat calls for service (CFS) from repeat addresses; improving the satisfaction with police services by public users of those services, particularly with victims of crime; increasing the job satisfaction of police officers; increasing the reporting of information of local crime and disorder problems by community residents and increasing the knowledge of the community and its problems by local beat officers; and decreasing the fear of personal victimization.[9]

An officer's efforts to improve overall safety in a shopping mall may decrease crime and increase safety and profits for merchants.

Courtesy Community Policing Consortium.

Three General Criteria

According to the Community Policing Consortium, three major criteria can assist in evaluating a problem-solving effort: effectiveness, efficiency, and equity.

Effectiveness.   The **effectiveness** of a COPPS strategy has a positive impact on reducing neighborhood crime, allays citizen fear of crime, and enhances the quality of life in the community. It accomplishes this by combining the efforts and resources of the police, the local government, and the community.[10] Assessing the effectiveness of problem-solving efforts includes determining whether problems have indeed been solved and how well the managers and patrol officers have used the community partnership and problem-solving components of COPPS.

Assessment should focus not only on whether the problem has been effectively eradicated or reduced but also on the manner in which this was accomplished. Solving problems does not always involve making arrests.[11] Improved quality of life is difficult to measure (and define), but it is an important goal of COPPS. Everyone desires a safe environment in which families can live and work. COPPS helps identify the fears, concerns, and needs at the neighborhood level. The factors that may determine quality of life may differ from neighborhood to neighborhood; removing signs of disorder—drunks, panhandlers, prostitutes, gang members—will enhance the quality of life. The absence of previous signs of neglect—abandoned vehicles, derelict buildings, garbage, and debris—offers a tangible indication that COPPS is working.[12]

Efficiency.   **Efficiency** means getting the most impact from available resources. Evaluation measures determine whether available resources—including the police agency, the local government, private agencies, citizen groups, and the business community—are being used to their fullest to solve any given problem.[13] If COPPS is to be successful, staunch partnerships and collaborative efforts must be established within the community.[14]

Employee job satisfaction also takes on a new significance in a COPPS organization. Patrol officers function more efficiently and effectively as catalysts and mobilizers of community support if they are highly motivated, given the necessary support, and appropriately rewarded for their efforts.[15] The need to survey the officers becomes evident in an organization where employee morale and satisfaction take on a greater level of meaning and importance.

Equity.   **Equity,** the third major criterion for judging progress, has the most comprehensive impact on the success of COPPS. Equity is especially important because officers work closely with the community and may be increasingly confronted with moral and ethical dilemmas.[16]

Equity has three separate dimensions in COPPS: (1) equal access to police services by all citizens, (2) equal treatment of all individuals according to the Constitution ("respect for dignity is incompatible with needless confrontation, excessive force, or discrimination"[17]), and (3) equal distribution of police services and resources among communities (it is critical that one community not be given preference over another).[18]

EVALUATION'S ROLE IN PROBLEM SOLVING

Right Questions

It is important to remember that evaluation and assessment are different. Evaluation is a scientific process for determining if a problem declined and if the solution caused the decline. Assessment occurs at the final stage of the S.A.R.A. problem-solving process. Evaluation begins at the moment the S.A.R.A. problem-solving process begins and continues through the completion of the effort.[19] Critical decisions about the evaluation are made throughout the process, as indicated in Figure 8–1. The left side of the figure shows the standard S.A.R.A. process and some of the most basic questions asked at each stage. It also draws attention to the fact that the

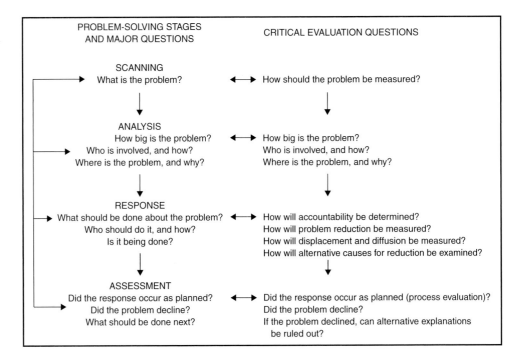

FIGURE 8–1
The Problem-Solving Process and Evaluation

Source: John E. Eck, *Assessing Responses to Problems: An Introductory Guide for Police Problem-Solvers* (Washington, D.C.: U.S. Department of Justice, Office of Community Oriented Policing Services, 2002), p. 6.

assessment may produce information requiring the problem solver to go back to earlier stages to make modifications. The right side of Figure 8–1 lists critical questions to address to conduct an evaluation.

Types of Evaluations

There are two types of evaluations, process and impact. Both should be conducted because they complement each other.

Process evaluations ask the following questions: Did the response occur as planned? Did all the response components work? A hypothetical example will assist in understanding process evaluations. A problem-solving team of officers, after a careful analysis, determines that in order to curb a street prostitution problem, after a crackdown in an area of town they will ask the city's traffic engineering department to make a major thoroughfare one-way to create several dead-end streets to thwart cruising by "johns." Convicted prostitutes will be given probation under the condition that they do not enter the target area for a year. Finally, a nonprofit organization will help prostitutes who want to leave their line of work to gain the necessary skills for legitimate employment. The police, prosecutor, local judges, probation office, and traffic engineering departments all agree to this plan.

A process evaluation will determine whether the crackdown occurred, and if so, how many arrests police made; whether the traffic engineering department altered street patterns as planned; and how many prostitutes asked for job skills assistance and found legitimate employment. The process evaluation will also examine whether everything occurred in the planned sequence. Note that the process evaluation does *not* answer the question "What happened to the problem?"

To determine what did in fact happen to the problem, an **impact evaluation** is needed. An impact evaluation asks the following questions: Did the problem decline? If so, did the response cause the decline? Continuing with the prostitution example, assume that during the analysis stage vice detectives conduct a census of prostitutes operating in the target area. They also ask the traffic engineering department to install traffic counters on the major thoroughfare and critical side streets to measure traffic flow. This is done to determine how customers move through the area. The vice squad makes covert video recordings of the target area to document how prostitutes interact with potential customers. All of this is done before the problem-solving team selects a response, and the information gained helps the team to do so.

After the response is implemented, the team decides to repeat these measures to see if the problem has declined. They discover that instead of the 23 prostitutes counted in the first census, only 10 can be found. They also find that there has been a slight decline in traffic on the major thoroughfare on the weekends, but not at other times; however, there has been a substantial decline in side street traffic on Saturday nights. New covert video recordings show that prostitutes in the area have changed how they approach vehicles. In short, the team has evidence that the problem has declined after response implementation.[20] When conducting impact evaluations, it is important to remember that such efforts have two parts: measuring the problem and systematically comparing changes in measures by using an evaluation design to provide the maximum evidence that the response was the primary cause of the change in the measure. It is best to decide during the scanning stage how to measure the problem. There are both quantitative and qualitative measures.

Quantitative measures involve numbers (e.g., the number of burglaries in an apartment complex during a period of time) and allow one to use math to estimate the response's impact (such as burglary rates drop 10 percent from before the response to after the response). Such measures can be counted before and after the response.

Qualitative measures allow comparisons but do not involve any math. For example, suppose there is gang-related violence in a neighborhood. Analysis shows that much of the violence stems from escalating turf disputes and that graffiti is a useful indicator of intergang tensions. The number of reported gunshots and injuries are counted the year before and the year after the response. These are quantitative measures. Photos are also taken monthly of gang graffiti hot spots both before and after the response. By comparing the photos, it is noted that before the response, graffiti was quite common; after the response, there is little graffiti. This qualitative information reinforces the quantitative information by indicating that the response may have reduced gang tension or that gangs have declined.[21]

USE OF SURVEYS

Social scientists and political pollsters use **surveys** of the public to learn about social relations and predict future events. Government agencies survey people to learn how they will react to new policies. In criminal justice, researchers use surveys to get a better understanding of crime and the fear of crime.[22]

This section discusses three types of surveys that police managers find increasingly useful: surveys of the community, surveys of the neighborhoods, and surveys of the officers who are engaged in the work of COPPS. We do not include an in-depth discussion of survey research methodology; instead, we provide citations of some helpful resources in the Notes section at the end of the chapter.

Many agencies use neighborhood meetings as a method to evaluate their performance and to identify residents' needs and priorities.

Courtesy Arlington County, Virginia, Police Department.

Community Surveys

Rationale.   The public's perception of crime in the community should be an important part of any measurement of community life and of police performance within a given community.[23] No other sector of government in our society has more frequent and direct contact with the public than the police:

> Whatever the citizen thinks of the police, they can hardly be ignored. Whereas other public bureaucrats are often lost from the public's view, locked in rooms filled with [computers] and anonymity, police officers are out in the world—on the sidewalks and in the streets and shopping malls, cruising, strolling, watching, as both state protectors and state repressors.[24]

Surveys are a vital part of a COPPS strategy. About one-fourth of local police departments, employing 50 percent of all officers, survey citizens in their jurisdiction.[25] Furthermore, as shown in Figure 8–2, citizen survey information is used for a variety of purposes—primarily to provide information to patrol officers, evaluate program effectiveness, and prioritize crime and disorder problems. Given their position, role, and function in the community, it is all the more important that police agencies attempt to "feel the pulse" of their communities. The importance of surveying community needs cannot be overstated. Public opinion surveys provide vital information and feedback in the matter of the public's perception of officer performance and can assess the effectiveness of police department communication with the public. The mood of the public should be a vital consideration when the police make public policy decisions.[26]

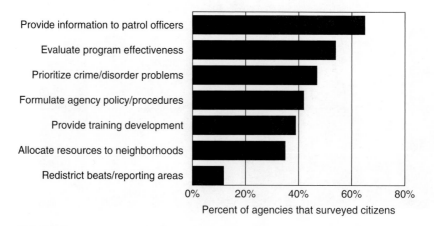

FIGURE 8–2
Uses of Citizen Survey Information by Local Police Departments, 2000

Source: U.S. Department of Justice, Bureau of Justice Statistics, *Local Police Departments 2000* (Washington, D.C.: Author, January 2003), p. 17.

Police agencies have long used citizen surveys to measure performance and assess the quality of their work. Surveys have been used to evaluate random patrolling, rapid response to CFS, patrol deployment schemes, and community policing strategies. Thus, although direct use of police surveys is relatively new, the application of survey research to management and policy questions is quite extensive.[27] In recent years, carefully developed surveys have been used to great advantage for measuring citizen attitudes toward police and citizen satisfaction with police services.

Methods and Issues.   Those persons who are about to conduct community surveys will find a very valuable resource in a joint publication by the federal Bureau of Justice Statistics and the Office of Community Oriented Policing Services: *Conducting Community Surveys: A Practical Guide for Law Enforcement Agencies.*[28] This is a very good primer on the use of surveys by police agencies, discussing survey development and administration and ways to analyze and interpret survey results. Many other books have been written that are devoted exclusively to the subject of evaluation.[29] Individuals who are contemplating COPPS evaluations can review these texts to determine the best method to use given the nature of their operation. Following are several key issues to resolve before developing a questionnaire[30]:

- *What are the specific purposes of the survey, and what kinds of questions are most likely to yield responses that are consistent with those purposes?* It is important to clarify the goals of the survey project to minimize the number of questions asked. Without clear goals, the number of questions tends to mushroom. This increases the amount of time required to administer each survey, which is a burden on both interviewer and interviewee. In short, fight the temptation to include everyone's "pet" question.
- *How will the survey be administered—by mail, by telephone, or in person?* There are three basic types of strategies: A questionnaire can be mailed to everyone in the sample to complete and return; the sampled respondents can be interviewed by telephone; or they can be interviewed in person (at home, in the office, on the bus, or wherever they are). Mail surveys are an inexpensive method of obtaining a large sample.[31] There are advantages and disadvantages to each type of survey that should be explored prior to determining which type is to be used.
- *How much time will it take to complete the survey, and is this a reasonable amount of time to impose on respondents?* Remember that completion of a survey is an intrusion on the time of others. Most people will allow such intrusion if the cause is worthwhile and the time burden is not too onerous. About 10 to 15 minutes to complete a questionnaire is reasonable, but if examining, say, problems involving drugs and violence, 30 to 40 minutes might be reasonable. The key is to be considerate about demands on others.

Neighborhood Surveys

Neighborhood surveys are often employed by police officers in problem solving; usually such surveys are informal, but they can provide large amounts

The closure of a home can affect residents' feelings about safety and their overall quality of life.

of information that are not available in crime statistics. Some evidence even suggests that door-to-door surveys by officers are enough to reduce crime and fear and to enhance citizen attitudes toward police, independent of any information they gain or what the police do with it. Surveys can help measure the characteristics of neighborhood residents, the background of crime victims, or the background of offenders. Surveys also seek information on the "mental state" of the community, and they frequently address issues such as these:

- Attitudes toward police performance
- Fear of crime
- Future plans and intentions
- Concerns about specific problems
- Suggestions for police actions

Surveys are useful for gathering data on individuals' behaviors and experiences. Common topics addressed in surveys of this type include[32]:

- Crime prevention actions taken
- Experiences as victims of crime
- Experiences with the police
- Experiences with problems

Surveys are also useful in revealing characteristics of groups of people[33]:

- Characteristics of people living in a neighborhood
- Background of victims of crimes
- Personal history of offenders

In short, surveys can be used to achieve four goals[34]:

1. Gather information on the public's attitudes toward the police and about neighborhood priorities
2. Detect and analyze problems in neighborhoods or among special population groups
3. Evaluate problem-solving efforts and other programs
4. Control crime and reduce fear of crime

There are many alternative sources of information as well. For example, census data provides a great deal of information about neighborhoods. Characteristics of victims can be obtained from offense reports, and offender background information can be obtained from arrest reports.

Officer Surveys

Under COPPS, patrol officers become key decision makers and catalysts, and as we commented earlier, employee morale and job satisfaction take on a new significance in a COPPS organization. Patrol officers function more efficiently and effectively as catalysts and mobilizers of community support if they are highly motivated, given the necessary support, and appropriately rewarded for their efforts. Job satisfaction will both affect and result from the success of the COPPS philosophy. Former Montgomery County, Maryland, and Portland, Oregon, Police Chief Charles A. Moose and his coauthors noted:

> With added responsibilities for police officers, job satisfaction becomes critical. If they are satisfied, they perform better and are able to support their agency's mission. Employee job satisfaction is not simply an indicator of success in community policing—it is a goal of community policing.[35]

Therefore, intraagency surveys can be invaluable for providing a look at the big picture of a COPPS initiative: the attitudes, opinions, and impressions of officers toward their jobs, the department, and the COPPS philosophy.

Officers can be asked a wide variety of questions concerning their knowledge and application of COPPS. Following is a sample of the subjects and questions that might be posed to officers.[36] Note that these items are only a sample of general and topical questions that might be considered. Actual questions should be carefully written for use in a survey and for the particular venue, and some sort of Likert scale is needed to assess the direction and strength of feeling for each question. Here is the sample officer survey:

Role of the Police

- What is the role of the police in a community?
- Do you believe the increase in administrative responsibilities and paperwork has stripped you of your ability to expand COPPS initiatives? If yes, how?

Proactive Action

- In what ways does your department emphasize proactive action, reactive action, or a blend of the two?

Public Expectations

- In what manner does your community want its police force, first and foremost, to focus on reactive tasks? To respond rapidly to all calls for service? To reduce the fear of crime? Does the public want to be educated on crime prevention? To work with the police to solve problems of crime and disorder? (*Note:* This subject area has any number of possible items that could be included.)

Work Activities

- How much of your duty time is spent conducting administrative or paperwork functions? Responding to calls for service? Explaining crime prevention techniques to citizens? Working with citizens to solve underlying causes of crime? Coordinating with other governmental agencies to improve police service or solve problems? (*Note:* This subject area also has a wide range of possible questions.)

Perceptions of COPPS

- What have you been told about the purpose of COPPS (or how valuable was the academy training in this regard)?
- What have you been told concerning the implementation of COPPS?
- How would you rate the quality of your department's in-service training concerning COPPS?
- Does COPPS increase, decrease, or have no impact on the risk of corrupt behavior by police?
- Will COPPS increase, decrease, or have no effect on the amount or seriousness of excessive force incidents?[37]

Coworkers' Attitudes

- How do your coworkers feel about implementing COPPS? Working with citizens to solve crimes? Preventing crime? Reducing the fear of crime? Sharing information with the community regarding police activities? Using the proactive style of policing?

Other Selected Issues

- To what extent do your citizens understand the problems of the police?
- Describe the kinds of discretion you are given to carry out COPPS initiatives.
- Explain why you believe the investigative division or other specialized units are or are not more "elite" than the patrol division.
- Are COPPS activities and conventional policing activities given equal weight?
- How have the performance appraisal and promotional processes of your department been made appropriate for a COPPS philosophy?

Analysis of Data

To handle large sets of survey data (many questions answered by many respondents), a computer will probably be needed. Today computers are inexpensive, and user-friendly software programs are available for analyses. Also, police agencies can partner with local colleges and universities for assistance with data analysis. Someone will have to read each questionnaire, note how each question was answered, determine the code for each answer, and enter the codes into a data file. This must be done with care to minimize data entry errors.[38] Once the data has been entered, there are four types of analyses to be performed[39]:

1. *The characteristics of the sample must be determined.* During this most basic stage of data analysis, the frequency, central tendency (the average or typical response to a question, which includes the mean, median, and mode), and dispersion of responses (i.e., standard deviation or variance) to each question are calculated.

2. *A determination is needed of how representative of the population being studied the sample really is.* The principal method for checking representativeness is by comparing answers to a few of the questions with information known about the population. If there are no substantial differences, the sample is likely representative of the entire population under study. It may not always be possible to make such a comparison, however.

3. *An investigator may want to make inferences from the sample to the population it represents.* There are two types of inferences that can be made about the population based on sample data. First, characteristics of the population can be determined from what is learned from the sample. Second, one can determine whether there are relationships among the characteristics of members of the population (e.g., whether the age and sex of a person have an influence on fear of crime).

4. *The investigator may want to determine whether there are relationships among the attitudes, behaviors, and characteristics identified in the sample population.* When analyzing relationships, social scientists usually talk about variables. Two variables can be noncausally or causally related. A noncausal relationship means that neither variable causes the other; they merely happen to be associated, perhaps because a third variable is causing both of them. In a causal relationship, one variable is causing the other. In statistical analysis, the causes are called *independent* variables, and the effects are the *dependent* variables.

OFFICER PERFORMANCE EVALUATIONS

A major need of police agencies that have adopted COPPS is a performance evaluation system that is specifically intended for the street officer who is applying COPPS skills to crime and disorder issues. Exhibit 8–1 shows six steps for revising a police performance evaluation system. Next

EXHIBIT 8–1

Steps for Revising Police Performance Evaluation Systems

Step 1. *Decide on the purpose(s) of the evaluation.* The purpose(s) to be served by an evaluation system will dictate both what and how officer behavior is measured.

Step 2. *Identify performance criteria.* Traditional measures of police performance do not capture the entirety of the community policing officer's role. New performance evaluations must reflect the work that the administration desires. A job analysis, identifying tasks typically performed by an employee (such as learning about beat problems and area residents, and developing means of problem solving), might be included. Related activities (such as conducting neighborhood meetings or analyzing crime data) might also be performed.

Step 3. *Define effective behavior.* Each police agency must define effectiveness individually as it relates to its own vision, mission, values, goals, and objectives. Input from officers, supervisors, and citizens may be required to determine what effective policing is, depending on realistic expectations of what they can accomplish.

Step 4. *Decide who should be evaluated.* Several officers and supervisors may be jointly responsible for a certain geographic area or beat, working as a team to solve problems therein. The extent to which officers are working in teams or groups must be considered for evaluation.

Step 5. *Decide who will participate in the evaluation process.* Many different constituencies may provide input to the evaluation of community policing officers, with supervisors being the primary source of evaluation. Other officers who in rank are equal to, above, or below the officer to be evaluated may provide input. Citizen feedback should also be considered.

Step 6. *Develop or revise instrumentation and rating scales.* Remember that much of the community policing officer's work is of a qualitative nature and thus not easily reduced to numbers. As performance criteria change and community policing "behaviors," such as communication and innovation, are modified, so should the performance evaluation instrument and the rating scales.

Source: Adapted from Meghan S. Chandek, "Meaningful and Effective Performance Evaluations in a Time of Community Policing," *Journal of Community Policing* 2 (Spring 2000):7–24. This article includes examples of sample tasks and activities, definitions of effectiveness, quantifiable community policing activities, and an officer performance evaluation scale.

we discuss ten performance criteria for rating officers' skills and a rating scale that might be used to evaluate their efforts.

COPPS Skills, Knowledge, and Abilities

While not yet being done on a large scale (presently only about 14 percent of local police agencies, which employ about 35 percent of all officers, include problem-solving projects in the performance evaluation criteria for patrol officers),[40] supervisors should measure how well officers perform problem-solving functions during the course of their tour of duty. If officers are not familiar with the problem-solving process, their performance will be deficient. Supervisors should work with officers to correct any deficiencies regarding the following performance ten criteria[41]:

1. *Time management.* Use uncommitted time to scan neighborhoods and identify problems; balance problem-solving efforts with other responsibilities.

2. *Awareness.* Have knowledge of problems in assigned areas; take steps to stay informed via citizen contact; be familiar with current events; review departmental information; share information with colleagues.

3. *Communication.* Elicit information from colleagues, supervisors, and citizens to facilitate problem solving; convey information in a clear, concise manner.

4. *Analysis.* Be able to relate symptoms to underlying circumstances; identify factors that cause incidents to occur and know what questions to ask.

5. *Judgment.* Identify legitimate alternatives that can be used as responses in addressing problems; select the best alternative based on resource availability, ease of implementation, and perceived effectiveness of response.

6. *Goal seeking.* Distinguish between short- and long-term goals of response; identify goals that are measurable; relate the goals to the problem.

7. *Planning.* Prepare a legitimate action plan to implement a response; identify responsibilities of participants, appropriate procedures, and a timetable.

8. *Coordination.* Demonstrate competency in organizing efforts of participants involved in implementing responses.

A guide for evaluating COPPS officers' performance was developed by the Community Policing Consortium in Washington, D.C.

Courtesy Police Executive Research Forum.

9. *Initiative.* Be self-motivated and engaged in the problem-solving process, identifying and addressing problems; help others when appropriate.

10. *Assessment.* Identify the proper variables to assess; know the types of information to collect to assess results; describe the implications of results attained.

Rating Scale

The supervisor's rating of subordinates' COPPS efforts must be accurately reflected on a **rating scale.** Five value descriptions have been developed to help establish reliability in this regard[42]:

1. *SUPERIOR skill performance.* Officer's skill performance is consistently excellent as to quality, accuracy, thoroughness, and technical excellence. Officer has superior understanding of what skills to use to accomplish assigned responsibilities. Officer initiates and completes responsibilities without prompting from supervisor, and there is no doubt as to officer's exercise of sound judgment. Supervisor and officer work in consultation with each other when appropriate.

2. *STRONG skill performance.* Performance exhibited is above average. Work performed and skills displayed regularly exceed basic requirements. Officer demonstrates advanced ability to apply skills to various responsibilities and projects and makes conscientious effort to adhere to procedures and standards. Sound judgment is always exercised, and officer is always willing to perform skills to do the work—without instructions or directions from supervisor.

3. *EFFECTIVE skill performance.* Performance in response to each skill is acceptable. Officer has demonstrated ability to perform problem skills effectively and efficiently in consistent manner. Officer applies knowledge and skills while using sound judgment and is usually desirous and willing to perform skills with minimum instructions and directions from supervisor.

4. *MARGINAL skill performance.* Performance is barely satisfactory, and skill performance is marginal. There is limited ability to perform skill in association with appropriate activities. Officer frequently disregards performing skill properly or does not adhere to standards governing skill and only occasionally exercises sound judgment in skill performance. Supervisor is often required to observe officer performing skill; instructions are usually needed. Performance is sufficient, inconsistent, and occasionally effective, but only to a minimally acceptable degree.

5. *POOR skill performance.* Officer's skill performance causes supervisor great concern about officer's capabilities. Demonstration of skill is weak, leading one to question officer's understanding of what is expected and ability to perform with consistent competency. Officer demonstrates signs of going through the motions and tends to act quickly, without regard to effects or consequences of actions. Supervisor spends inordinate amount of time correcting officer's actions or telling officer what must be done.

Figure 8–3 shows the Columbia, South Carolina, Police Department's monthly performance evaluation report form based on the preceding criteria.

COLUMBIA POLICE DEPARTMENT
MONTHLY PERFORMANCE EVALUATION REPORT

Supervisor's Name: _____ Time/Date: _____

Officer's Name: _____ Assignment/Shift: _____

Use the following criteria to assess an officer's ability to perform problem solving skills to address crime and disorder within assigned neighborhoods.

A B I L I T Y

	Poor		Marginal		Effective		Strong		Superior	
Time Management	1	2	3	4	5	6	7	8	9	10
Awareness	1	2	3	4	5	6	7	8	9	10
Communication	1	2	3	4	5	6	7	8	9	10
Analysis	1	2	3	4	5	6	7	8	9	10
Judgment	1	2	3	4	5	6	7	8	9	10
Goal Seeking	1	2	3	4	5	6	7	8	9	10
Planning	1	2	3	4	5	6	7	8	9	10
Coordination	1	2	3	4	5	6	7	8	9	10
Initiative	1	2	3	4	5	6	7	8	9	10
Assessment	1	2	3	4	5	6	7	8	9	10

Grand Total: _____

Final Classification

Check:

_____ Category 1: Poor.............................. 10 - 19
_____ Category 2: Marginal .... 20 - 49
_____ Category 3: Effective .... 50 - 69
_____ Category 4: Strong............................ 70 - 89
_____ Category 5: Superior........................ 90 - 100

_____	_____	_____	_____
Supervisor's Signature	Date	Officer Signature	Date

FIGURE 8–3

Columbia Police Department Monthly Performance Evaluation Report

Source: Columbia, South Carolina, Police Department.

CASE STUDIES

The following two case studies provide views of COPPS evaluations for Chicago, Illinois, and Lawrence, Massachusetts.

Chicago, Illinois

The Chicago Alternative Policing Strategy (CAPS) initiative was field-tested in 1993 in five selected districts (and later implemented on a city-wide basis) to cultivate problem solving and to reorganize policing around the city's 279 police beats. By 1995 researchers had found that perceived crime problems had decreased significantly in all five districts; furthermore, physical decay had declined in three districts, and citizen assessments of police had improved significantly.[43]

A more recent evaluation of CAPS was conducted in 2004 by the Chicago Community Policing Evaluation Consortium. Some of the findings were as follows[44]:

- Chicagoans have attended more than 550,000 beat meetings. Attendance for these meetings is generally highest where it is needed the most; attendance is usually worse in areas with bad housing, high levels of crime, and poor schools. Meetings have improved with respect to the adoption of clear procedures, model agendas, informative materials to be covered, training for officers, and special training for beat sergeants.
- Positive opinions of the Chicago police increased steadily between 1993 and 1999, before leveling off at a new high in the 2000s.
- Many categories of crime in Chicago have declined since 1991; violent crime declined by 49 percent and property crimes by 36 percent. Burglaries of residences dropped by 46 percent; rapes, 45 percent; and aggravated assault and battery, 41 percent.
- Fear of crime was reduced by 20 percent, mostly among the highest fear groups—African Americans, women, and older residents of Chicago.

Lawrence, Massachusetts

Lawrence, Massachusetts, is a dense urban center of 70,000 people, 28 miles north of Boston, whose residents live in an area of only 7 miles. In the 1980s the Massachusetts Criminal Justice Training Council submitted a critical report concerning the operations of the Lawrence Police Department. A wide gap existed between the police and the public. The department's budget was cut as well. The department began to explore new philosophies to deliver police service and to generally reform its operations.

The police chief and a nine-member management team began rethinking their basic strategies. First, the police chief adopted total quality management (TQM). Then a bilingual community questionnaire was designed to identify crime and disorder issues important to citizens. Next, a citizen advisory committee was established to get more direct input about the needs of the customers.[45] The management team then began to develop a vision for the department; from this process, new mission and values statements were written.

The department began to explore how to strategically address problems. The team chose the Arlington neighborhood, a 45-square-block area consisting mostly of multiple-family residential units, with relatively little single-family housing. A team of six community police officers (CPOs) was assigned to Arlington to seek citizen input, analyze problems, and develop intervention strategies. Questionnaires were again used to identify problems and concerns in the area. Return of these questionnaires produced a lot of valuable information on drug dealers' operations and also raised the fear levels of dealers. A public education campaign was launched in the area, and police activity was enhanced.

The department believed it was important to develop an objective means of evaluating whether the strategy was worth the effort. A pre-post citizen survey approach was adopted with a random sample of households, using a 60-item questionnaire distributed to 3,676 households (with a 30.3 percent response rate). Responses to each question were given a numerical weight, and an average score was computed. The following formula was developed and helped obtain a fear index for the neighborhood[46]:

$$\frac{(\text{\# increased} \times 5) + (\text{\# same} \times 3) + (\text{\# decreased} \times 0)}{\text{Total responses}}$$

A disorder index was developed from the survey, based on the following formula:

$$\frac{(\text{\# big problem} \times 5) + (\text{\# problem} \times 3) + (\text{\# no problem} \times 0)}{\text{Total responses}}$$

Using this procedure, a summary measure of disorder for each neighborhood was obtained.

The findings indicated that Arlington residents experienced substantial reductions in their fear and perceptions of crime and disorder. The close attention to involvement of both staff and managers in the organizational change process and the carefully planned community intervention strategy make Lawrence an important case study in the systematic implementation of COPPS in a medium-size city.[47]

 ## SUMMARY

This chapter emphasized the fact that the evaluation of the impact of COPPS is critical; without such scrutiny this initiative may be jeopardized in the long term. Although there is no one evaluation process that will work for all communities, this chapter offered some reasons, methods, and criteria for evaluating such a social intervention. The chapter also provided several examples of successful evaluations. The philosophy and methods under COPPS are quite different from those of traditional policing and obviously require different measurements of performance.

ITEMS FOR REVIEW

1. Discuss the general rationale for evaluating COPPS.
2. Explain the kinds of criteria to be used in evaluating COPPS, including types of measures to be used.
3. Review the role of evaluation in problem solving, including some of the questions that might be asked prior to commencing this task.
4. Describe the criteria that might be employed for assessing the individual officer's problem-solving skills, including an overview of the rating scale.
5. Explain the benefits of using surveys—of the community, neighborhood, and individual patrol officers—to obtain input for evaluative purposes.

 ## NOTES

1. Adapted from the National Crime Prevention Council, *How Are We Doing? A Guide to Local Program Evaluation* (Washington, D.C.: Author, 1998), p. 5. This is a valuable resource for COPPS evaluations, including many examples of forms that may be used in the evaluation process (see, for example, Chapter II, "A Toolkit for Evaluation Design"), and other types of information not commonly found in evaluation textbooks (such as communicating findings and results for maximum results).
2. Carter McNamara, "Some Myths About Program Evaluation," http://www .managementhelp.org/evaluatn/fnl_eval.htm#anchor1575679 (Accessed September 18, 2006).
3. *Ibid.,* p 3.
4. U.S. Department of Justice, Bureau of Justice Assistance, Community Policing Consortium, *Understanding Community Policing: A Framework for Action* (Washington, D.C.: Author, 1993), p. 82.
5. Gloria Laycock, "Becoming More Assertive About Good Research," *Subject to Debate* 14 (July 2000):1.
6. *Ibid.,* p. 3.
7. Community Policing Advisory Committee, *Community Policing Advisory Committee Report* (Victoria, British Columbia, Canada: Author, March 1993), p. 61.
8. Barry Leighton, "Visions of Community Policing: Rhetoric and Reality in Canada," *Canadian Journal of Criminology* (July/October 1991):75–87.
9. *Ibid.*
10. U.S. Department of Justice, Bureau of Justice Assistance, Community Policing Consortium, *Understanding Community Policing*, p. 86.

11. *Ibid.*, pp. 87–89.

12. *Ibid.*, p. 90.

13. *Ibid.*, p. 91.

14. *Ibid.*, pp. 92–93.

15. *Ibid.*, p. 93.

16. *Ibid.*, p. 97.

17. Edwin Delattre and Cornelius Behan, quoted in *ibid.*, p. 99.

18. *Ibid.*, pp. 101–102.

19. John E. Eck, *Assessing Responses to Problems: An Introductory Guide for Police Problem-Solvers* (Washington, D.C.: U.S. Department of Justice, Office of Community Oriented Policing Services, 2002), p. 5.

20. *Ibid.*, pp. 7–9.

21. *Ibid.*, pp. 13–14.

22. Police Executive Research Forum, *A Police Practitioner's Guide to Surveying Citizens and Their Environment: Monograph* (Washington, D.C.: U.S. Department of Justice, Bureau of Justice Assistance, 1993), p. 1.

23. Richard D. Morrison, "What Effect Is Community Policing Having on Crime Statistics?" *Law Enforcement Technology* (October 1998):26.

24. N. D. Walker and R. J. Richardson, *Public Attitudes Toward the Police* (Chapel Hill, N.C.: Institute for Research in Social Science, 1974), p. 1.

25. U.S. Department of Justice, *Law Enforcement Management and Administrative Statistics* (Washington, D.C.: Author, 2003), p. 17.

26. Mervin F. White and Ben A. Menke, "A Critical Analysis on Public Opinions Toward Police Agencies," *Journal of Police Science and Administration* 6 (1978):204–218.

27. *Ibid.*, p. 1.

28. Deborah Weisel, *Conducting Community Surveys: A Practical Guide for Law Enforcement Agencies* (Washington, D.C.: U.S. Department of Justice, Bureau of Justice Statistics, Office of Community Oriented Policing Services, 1999).

29. See, for example, Carl A. Bennett and Arthur A. Lumsdaine, *Evaluation and Experiment* (New York: Academic Press, 1975); Ronald Roesch and Raymond R. Corrado (eds.), *Evaluation and Criminal Justice Policy* (Beverly Hills, Calif.: Sage, 1981); Malcolm W. Klein and Katherine Teilmann Van Dusen, *Handbook of Criminal Justice Evaluation* (Beverly Hills, Calif.: Sage, 1980); Richard H. Price and Peter E. Politser, *Evaluation and Action in the Social Science Environment* (New York: Academic Press, 1980).

30. See, for example, Ken Peak, "On Successful Criminal Justice Survey Research: A 'Personal Touch' Model for Enhancing Rates of Return," *Criminal Justice Policy Review* 4 (3) (Spring 1992):268–277; Don A. Dillman, *Mail and Telephone Surveys: The Total Design Method* (New York: John Wiley & Sons, 1978); Arlene Fink and Jacqueline Kosecoff, *How to Conduct Surveys: A Step-by-Step Guide* (Beverly Hills, Calif.: Sage, 1985); Floyd J. Fowler, *Survey Research Methods* (Newbury Park, Calif.: Sage, 1988); Abraham Nastali Oppenheim, *Questionnaire Design, Interviewing, and Attitude Measurement* (New York: St. Martin's Press, 1992); Charles H. Backstrom and Gerald Hursh-Cesar, *Survey Research* (2nd ed.) (New York: Macmillan, 1981).

31. Police Executive Research Forum, *A Police Practitioner's Guide,* p. 22.

32. *Ibid.,* p. 8.

33. *Ibid.,* pp. 8–9.

34. *Ibid.*

35. Charles A. Moose, Wendy Lin-Kelly, Steve Beedle, and Brian Stipak, "Evaluating Community Policing with Employee Surveys," *The Police Chief* (March 2000):44.

36. Adapted from the Royal Canadian Mounted Police, Community Policing Branch, *R.C.M.P. Community Policing: Blending Tradition with Innovation* (Ottawa, Canada: Author, 1992).

37. Police Foundation, "Abuse of Police Authority in the Age of Community Policing: What Police Say," http://www.policefoundation.org/docs/recentresearch. html (Accessed May 27, 2003).

38. For a more detailed introduction to analyzing data in policing, see John Eck, *Using Research: A Primer for Law Enforcement* (Washington, D.C.: Police Executive Research Forum, 1984).

39. Adapted from Police Executive Research Forum, *A Police Practitioner's Guide,* pp. 31–34.

40. U.S. Department of Justice, Bureau of Justice Statistics, *Law Enforcement Management and Administrative Statistics: Local Police Departments 2000* (Washington, D.C.: Author, January 2003), p. 17.

41. Adapted from Columbia, South Carolina, Police Department, *Columbia Patrol Officer Performance Evaluation Workbook* (Columbia, S.C.: Author, March 1997), pp. 6–7; also see Timothy N. Oettmeier and Mary Ann Wycoff, *Personnel Performance Evaluations in the Community Policing Context* (Washington, D.C.: Community Policing Consortium, 1997).

42. *Ibid.,* pp. 8–9.

43. Chicago Community Policing Evaluation Consortium, *Community Policing in Chicago, Year Ten* (Chicago: Author, April 2004), pp. i–x.

44. *Ibid.,* pp. i–vi.

45. Allen W. Cole and Gordon Bazemore, "Police and the 'Laboratory' of the Neighborhood: Evaluating Problem-Oriented Strategies in a Medium Sized City," *American Journal of Police* 18 (1994):119–147.

46. *Ibid.,* p. 124.

47. *Ibid.,* p. 131.

Training for COPPS

Approaches and Challenges

Key Terms and Concepts _____

Adult learning

Andragogy

Case study

COPPS curriculum

Distance learning

E-learning

Field training officer (FTO)

Generalist

Higher education

In-service training

Learning organization

Needs assessment

Police training officer (PTO)

Problem-based learning (PBL)

Recruit academy

Roll call training

Specialist

Training technology

Learning Objectives _____

As a result of reading this chapter, the student will:

- Know how the concepts of adult and problem-based learning apply to training for COPPS
- Understand why it is important for police agencies to become learning organizations
- Be familiar with the unique challenges that are involved with training police officers
- Be able to explain why the police should be trained as neither generalists nor specialists
- Understand how knowledge is imparted at the basic recruit academy and with the postacademy, in-service, and roll call methods
- Have a grasp of why higher education can be beneficial for officers engaged in COPPS
- Know the kinds of technologies that exist in police training
- Have a fundamental understanding of how to determine officers' training needs
- Know the kinds of topics that are covered in a COPPS curriculum

> A man can seldom—very, very seldom—fight a winning fight against his training: the odds are too heavy.
>
> *–Mark Twain*

INTRODUCTION

As we have noted in previous chapters, the movement toward community oriented policing and problem solving (COPPS) involves a change in the philosophy and the organizational structure of the police agency. A philosophical shift is critical to the development of new skills, knowledge, and abilities, as well as to a reorientation of perceptions and a refining of current skills. This is a difficult challenge for those involved in the training and education of police officers.

This training is of utmost importance, and the challenge greatly enhanced, because the successful implementation of COPPS requires the training of *every* employee inside the agency as well as an orientation for a number of people and organizations outside the police department. Indeed, police administrators, federal and state criminal justice planning officials, and criminal justice policy advisory groups have rated training as the primary need in order for COPPS to reach its fullest potential. Furthermore, it is important that the police educate the public and other public and private agencies and organizations in the concept because they will be required, at times, to help carry out the COPPS effort. This chapter analyzes COPPS training from these disparate yet related perspectives.

We begin this chapter with a look at the concepts of adult and problem-based learning, and the important contributions they make to COPPS training, as well as the need to create a learning organization. Next we consider why having police officers in the classroom constitutes another sort of challenge and the various means by which training is provided to these individuals (including the recruit academy and via field training, in-service, roll call, and specialized means); included in this section is a brief description of training technologies.

Then we focus on a combined program for accomplishing COPPS training; this comprehensive section includes the extent to which such training is occurring nationally, the methods for determining officers' training needs, the components of a COPPS curriculum, and the various audiences that should be exposed to COPPS training.

The chapter concludes with a sample training program. Exhibits containing examples of police training initiatives are provided throughout the chapter.

Key Considerations: Adult and Problem-Based Learning

Before examining the training of police officers specifically in the COPPS strategy, it is important to consider how adults learn best. Next we briefly discuss adult learning, problem-based learning, and the learning organization.

First, in order for adult training to succeed, the following conditions for **adult learning** should be borne in mind:

- Adults must be partners in their own educational plans and evaluations.
- The material must be relevant.
- Adult learning should be problem centered rather than content oriented.

Based on these ends, the writings of Malcolm Knowles and Benjamin Bloom are important. Knowles's theory of **andragogy** was developed specifically for adult learners. Andragogy emphasizes that adults are self-directed and need to be free to direct themselves; teachers must actively involve class participants in the learning process and serve as facilitators for them through such means as allowing presentations and group leadership. Knowles wrote that adults are characterized by the following[1]:

- Adults have life experiences and knowledge that may include work-related activities, family responsibilities, and previous education. They need to connect learning to this base, so try to draw out their experience and knowledge that are relevant to the topic.
- Adults are goal oriented and appreciate an educational program that is organized and has clearly defined elements. Instructors should explain how their course assists participants in obtaining their goals.
- Adults are relevancy oriented and must see a reason for learning something; learning must be applicable to their work or other purposes to be of value to them. Therefore, when possible, allow participants to choose projects that reflect their own interests.
- Adults need to be shown respect, and teachers should treat them as equals in experience and knowledge and allow them to voice their opinions freely in class.

Benjamin Bloom's taxonomy is also helpful. Bloom's cognitive domain for learning emphasizes intellectual outcomes. Bloom's taxonomy of six learning activities, in ascending order, is as follows[2]:

1. Knowledge—remembering or recalling previously learned material
2. Comprehension—understanding meaning, and explaining and restating ideas
3. Application—applying learned material in new and different situations
4. Analysis—categorizing material into segments and demonstrating their relationships
5. Synthesis—grouping or combining the separate ideas to form a new whole and establishing new relationships
6. Evaluation—evaluating the material for appropriate outcomes based on established criteria

Problem-based learning (PBL) is a learning process that also has application to COPPS training, as it stimulates problem solving, critical thinking, utilization of nontraditional resources, and team participation. Like the adult learning theory discussed above, the purpose of PBL is to make learning relevant to real-world situations. In PBL, the trainee engages in self-teaching; trainees begin with a problem rather than follow the traditional approach whereby a class is given a problem to solve at the end of the class.[3]

The aim of PBL is not solely to solve the problem but rather to help the students fill gaps in their knowledge and to involve them in self-directed learning techniques. The students are guided by instructors and facilitators so that they can ultimately learn what they are supposed to learn. PBL departs from traditional learning models by beginning with the presentation of a real-world problem that the trainee must attempt to solve. The trainee follows a path of inquiry and discovery whereby he or she expresses initial ideas about how to solve the problem, lists known facts, decides what information is needed, and develops a course of action to solve the problem. This approach to learning teaches the trainees to look at problems from a broader perspective. It encourages trainees to explore, analyze, and think systemically, while they also collaborate with peers, open lines of communication, and develop resources for solving future problems.

PBL is therefore both a curriculum and a process. The curriculum consists of carefully selected problems that demand from the learner acquisition of critical knowledge, problem-solving proficiency, and team participation skills. The process involves resolving problems or challenges that are encountered in life and careers. With PBL, students assume increased responsibility for their learning, giving them more motivation and feelings of accomplishment. Adult learning and PBL are essential for creating a learning organization, which is discussed next.

Officers receive in-service computer training to expand their capabilities.

FBI Law Enforcement Bulletin.

THE LEARNING ORGANIZATION

Peter Senge's increasingly influential concept of **learning organizations** certainly applies to COPPS training and is very important for training adult learners. Senge feels that the organization must allow its employees to continually expand their capacity to nurture new and expansive patterns of thinking, allow their collective aspiration to be set free, and continually learn to see the whole picture.

To help effect change in their organizations, police administrators are increasingly turning to Senge's writings, which evolved into a book that popularized the concept, *The Fifth Discipline*.[4] Senge states:

> Learning organizations are those where people continually expand their capacity to create the results they truly desire, where new and expansive patterns of thinking are nurtured, where collective aspiration is set free, and where people are continually learning to see the whole together.[5]

Senge also feels that organizations need to "discover how to tap people's commitment and capacity to learn at all levels."[6] Certain basic disciplines must be mastered[7]:

- *Systemic thinking*. People need to focus on the whole rather than the parts of the organization and to remember that people learn from personal experiences.
- *Personal mastery*. Organizations learn only through individuals who learn, continually clarifying and deepening their personal vision, focusing their energies, and seeing reality objectively.
- *Mental models*. Deeply ingrained assumptions and generalizations influence how people understand the world, so people need to rigorously scrutinize them so that they can learn new skills and develop new orientations.
- *Shared vision*. People must have the capacity to hold a shared picture of the future in order to excel and learn (the development of a police organizational vision for COPPS was discussed in Chapter 7).
- *Team learning*. The process of developing the capacities of the team creates results that its members truly desire.

In sum, the learning organization requires a new view of leadership; leaders are responsible for building organizations where people continually expand their capabilities to understand complexity, clarify vision, and improve shared mental models. Leaders do not teach but foster learning.

How does COPPS relate to learning organizations? As police organizations implement COPPS and assess its efficacy, they can learn better to distinguish between "conceptual failures" and "implementation failures." If an initiative failed because the basic strategy was flawed or because the approach works only in very limited circumstances, that is possibly due to its not being properly conceptualized. But if a sound and accepted concept such as COPPS is found to not have met its goals, it is likely due to implementation failure. Thus, a learning organization capitalizes on its own and others' experiences—successes as well as failures—to continually hone strategies, tactics, operations. A learning organization learns to measure what really matters, for it understands that what we want to measure is taken more seriously.[8]

TRAINING OF POLICE OFFICERS

Unique Challenges

Anyone who undertakes to train police officers must be mindful of the challenge at hand. Michael E. Buerger provided food for thought concerning police training:

> Training is usually discussed in terms of a benefit provided to the rank-and-file. From the perspective of those receiving it, however, training is easily divided into two main categories: the kind officers like, and the kind they despise. What they like fits into their world view; what they despise is "training" that attempts to change that view.[9]

There are challenges in training officers in the COPPS strategy. First, because policing often attracts action-oriented individuals, officers tend to be more receptive to hands-on skills training, such as arrest methods, weaponless defense, pursuit driving, firearms proficiency, and baton usage. Certainly these measures are needed from time to time, and for that reason (and because of the specter of liability) police personnel must receive training in those areas. As many studies have demonstrated, however, only a small fraction of the typical officer's work routine involves the use of weapons, defensive tactics, high-speed chases, and so forth. If training is to help officers do their jobs better, it must focus on what they need to know in order to do their job well. It should also be driven by the mission of the agency.

It must also be remembered that police training is best conducted—and is better received by the officers—when it reflects skills with immediately recognizable application to the job and when that message is constantly reinforced throughout training. Thus, it is not surprising that officers prefer to be instructed by persons who both possess expertise in the activity and have "walked the walk" of police patrol, that is, other police officers.[10] It is also worthwhile to remember that an environment that is conducive to learning, with a clearly stated outcome that inspires learners' physical and mental engagement, and activities that precipitate critical thinking and problem solving are important training processes as well.

Generalists or Specialists?

There is also some debate concerning whether police officers should be trained as **generalists** or as **specialists.** The trend toward generalization grew out of the late 1970s when the team policing concept was devised to bridge the chasm between the police and their communities and to give officers more autonomy to address problems on their beats. Today many agency executives shy away from the belief that officers should be generalists, however, preferring to deploy specialists to one degree or another.

Some people believe, however, that the specialization model comes with a high price. Officers train extensively and in many specialties must certify at some level in order to conduct a highly technical investigation, such as arson, computer fraud, or homicide. It is becoming increasingly expensive to pay for the training required to do so efficiently. Other agencies, therefore, adhere to the generalist model, relying on state police or another investigative agency when facing investigations or other problems beyond the scope of their training or experience. For example, if an agency has no hit-and-run unit, no accident investigation unit, no K-9 unit, no community policing unit, and no gang unit, often the initiating officer follows up on all but the most complex and involved cases.

The best approach—and one that should work well in an agency practicing COPPS—is one that is balanced, a "generalist-specialist," where officers train in more than one specialty, such as crimes against persons or property. This allows for more diversity in officer knowledge and approaches to problems.[11]

NEW KNOWLEDGE AND RETENTION OF LEARNED SKILLS

Police training may be obtained through four primary means—recruit academy, postacademy field training/police training officer, in-service training, and roll call training—in addition to the many excellent conferences and workshops that also now exist to provide COPPS training. Each is extremely important for imparting values and information concerning the COPPS philosophy.

Recruit Academy

Academy training (the recruit or cadet phase) sets the tone for newly hired officers. It is at the **recruit academy** that new officers begin to develop a strong mind-set about their role as police. Ideally, academy training will provide comprehensive instruction in the two primary elements of COPPS—community engagement and problem solving—if the proper philosophical mind-set for recruits is to be formed. In many cases, this will require that traditional courses, such as those in history, patrol procedures, police-community relations, and crime prevention, be revamped to include the topics and information recommended in this chapter; this information will teach officers to be more analytical and creative in their efforts to address community crime and disorder. A primary emphasis on the nature of crime and disorder and problem-solving methods should be the foundation for this training.

In 1996, Maryland became the first state in the nation to initiate a community policing academy, with the goal of providing training in COPPS to officers in every local police agency. The academy serves as a central resource for providing agencies with continuing education as well as training in resource development and community involvement.

Field Training Officer (FTO) Program

The next phase of training for newly hired officers is the **field training officer (FTO)** program, which is provided immediately on leaving the academy. The field training program was begun in the San Jose, California, Police Department in 1972, and assists recruits in their transition from the academy to the streets while still under the protective arm of a veteran officer.[12] Most FTO programs consist of an introductory phase (where the recruit learns agency policies and local laws), training and evaluation phases (the recruit is introduced to more complicated tasks confronted by patrol officers), and a final phase (the FTO may act strictly as an observer and evaluator while the recruit performs all the functions of a patrol officer). This last phase of the recruit's training can obviously have a profound effect on his or her later career based on whether or not the neophyte officer is allowed to learn and put this strategy into practice.

Police Training Officer (PTO) Program

Many police executives have come to believe, however, that the traditional FTO approach that was implemented in 1972 is not relevant to the challenges of contemporary policing, especially those agencies that have adopted COPPS. Therefore, many police agencies are retooling their FTO programs to emphasize community policing and to better meet the needs of their officers with what is termed the **police training officer (PTO)** program.

The Reno, Nevada, Police Department—with assistance and about a half million dollars in funding from the Police Executive Research Forum and the federal Office of Community Oriented Policing Services—recently developed a model PTO program that recognizes the importance of problem-solving skills and critical thinking. PTO uses a number of tools that embrace the aforementioned adult- and problem-based learning concepts as well as a learning matrix that shows core competencies, which are specific knowledge, skills, and abilities that are essential for community policing and problem solving.

Exhibit 9–1 shows the learning matrix that is used with the Reno model. Each cell (A1 through D15) has a corresponding list of skills required to achieve competency in the areas listed. The learning matrix serves as a guide for trainees and trainers during the training period, and

A Problem-Based
Learning Manual
for Training and Evaluating
Police Trainees

pto
manual

COPS

The federal Office of Community Oriented Policing Services publishes a manual on the PTO approach for training new police officers.

U.S. Department of Justice, Office of Community Oriented Policing Services, 2005.

it demonstrates the interrelationships between the core competencies and daily policing activities.

Problem solving is woven throughout the training process, and the matrix assists trainees to determine what they have learned, what they

EXHIBIT 9–1

Reno PTO Learning Matrix

	PHASE A NONEMERGENCY INCIDENT RESPONSE	PHASE B EMERGENCY INCIDENT RESPONSE	PHASE C PATROL ACTIVITIES	PHASE D CRIMINAL INVESTIGATION
CORE COMPETENCIES				
Police Vehicle Operations	A1	B1	C1	D1
Conflict Resolution	A2	B2	C2	D2
Use of Force	A3	B3	C3	D3
Local Procedures, Policies, Laws, Philosophies	A4	B4	C4	D4
Report Writing	A5	B5	C5	D5
Leadership	A6	B6	C6	D6
Problem-Solving Skills	A7	B7	C7	D7
Community-Specific Problems	A8	B8	C8	D8
Cultural Diversity & Special Needs Groups	A9	B9	C9	D9
Legal Authority	A10	B10	C10	D10
Individual Rights	A11	B11	C11	D11
Officer Safety	A12	B12	C12	D12
Communication Skills	A13	B13	C13	D13
Ethics	A14	B14	C14	D14
Lifestyle Stressors/ Self-Awareness/ Self-Regulation	A15	B15	C15	D15
Learning Activities	Introduction of Neighborhood Portfolio Exercise	Continuation of Neighborhood Portfolio Exercise	Continuation of Neighborhood Portfolio Exercise	Final Neighborhood Portfolio Presentation
	Problem-Based Learning Exercise	Problem-Based Learning Exercise	Problem-Based Learning Exercise	Problem-Based Learning Exercise
Evaluation Activities	Weekly Coaching and Training Reports	Weekly Coaching and Training Reports	Weekly Coaching and Training Reports	Weekly Coaching and Training Reports

Source: Reno, Nevada, Police Department, *PTO Program: The Reno Model, 2004.*

need to learn to improve their performance, and which performance outcomes will be utilized to evaluate their performance. PTO covers two primary training areas: substantive topics (the most common activities in policing) and core competencies (the required common skills that officers use and that are required to utilize in the daily performance of their duties). As shown in the matrix, the four substantive topics that define the key phases of training are nonemergency incident response, emergency incident response, patrol activities, and criminal investigation. In addition, the 15 core competencies that are listed must be met under PTO; these are specific knowledge, skills, and abilities that have been identified as essential for good policing.

In-Service Training

In-service training provides an opportunity to impart information and to reinforce new skills learned in the academy and FTO program. In-service classes are useful for sharing officers' experiences in applying COPPS to a variety of problems as well as for their collaboration with other city agencies, social service organizations, or the community. In-service training is also one of the primary means of changing the culture and attitudes of personnel.[13]

Obviously, a tremendous challenge for large police departments is providing COPPS training for all of the many hundreds or even thousands of officers and civilians. Some large agencies have used videotaped or computer-assisted training. Many departments, using drug forfeiture funds, have also purchased high-technology equipment for use with training. In addition to COPPS courses and orientations, departmental newsletters can disseminate information to personnel on a regular basis. Also helping to meet this challenge are regional community policing institutes (RCPIs) (see Exhibit 9–2).

Roll Call Training

Roll call training is that period of time—from 15 to 30 minutes prior to the beginning of a tour of duty—in which supervisors prepare officers for patrol. Roll call sessions usually begin with a supervisor assigning the officers to their respective beats. Information about wanted and dangerous persons and major incidents on previous shifts is usually disseminated. Other matters may also be addressed, such as issuing officers court subpoenas, explaining new departmental policies and procedures, and discussing shift- and beat-related matters.

Roll call meetings afford an excellent opportunity for supervisors to update officers' knowledge and to present new ideas and techniques. This is particularly advantageous for small police agencies that have limited training staff and resources. For example, videotapes or problem-solving case studies can be used at briefing sessions to provide relevant information.

EXHIBIT 9–2

Regional Community Policing Institutes (RCPIs)

The federal Office of Community Oriented Policing Services (COPS) promotes and supports COPPS endeavors through problem-solving tactics and community-police partnerships, recognizing that this strategy brings about challenges and changes in the way the police are trained. Since 1994 the COPS Office has awarded approximately $8 billion to law enforcement agencies and its 27 regional community policing institutes (RCPIs) across the United States. The RCPIs have trained almost 350,000 officers and citizens across the nation; this includes more than 80,000 hours of training delivered in 174 curricula. Integral to this training is a national cadre of trainers, electronic dissemination of training sessions and content, and use of multimedia approaches.

Problem-solving training has also been conducted since 1989 at an annual International Problem-Oriented Policing Conference, attracting more than 1,500 participants from around the world; at this conference the prestigious Herman Goldstein Award for Excellence in Problem-Oriented Policing awards are presented.

Not to be overlooked is the fact that with the spread of COPPS across the United States many public and private universities and colleges offer courses specifically on COPPS, and some even have degree concentrations in this area.

Source: U.S. Department of Justice, Office of Community Oriented Policing Services, "COPS Fact Sheet: Regional Community Policing Institutes." http://www.cops.usdoj.gov (Accessed April 20, 2003).

The University of Delaware offers a "Certificate in Community Policing." Courses include the basic elements of COPPS: problem solving, strategic planning, ethics, and diversity.

Courtesy University of Delaware.

HIGHER EDUCATION

Certainly a feature of the COPPS strategy concerns **higher education** for officers. To begin with, from 1967 to 1986 every national commission that studied crime, violence, and policing in America was of the opinion that a college education could help the police to do their jobs better.[14] Advocates of higher education for the police maintain that it improves the quality of policing by making officers more tolerant of people who are different from themselves; in this view, educated officers are more professional, communicate better with citizens, are better decision makers, and have better written and verbal skills.

A ringing endorsement for higher education for the police came in 1985, when a lawsuit challenged the Dallas, Texas, Police Department's requirement that all applicants for police officer positions possess 45 credit hours and at least a C average at an accredited college or university. The Fifth Circuit Court of Appeals and eventually the U.S. Supreme Court upheld the educational requirement. The circuit court—in language that could be speaking of COPPS—said:

> A significant part of a police officer's function involves his ability to function effectively as a crisis intervenor, in family fights, teen-age rumbles, bar brawls, street corner altercations, racial disturbances, riots and similar situations. Few professionals are so peculiarly charged with individual responsibilities as police officers. Mistakes of judgment could cause irreparable harm to citizens or even to the community. The educational requirement bears a manifest relationship to the position of police officer. We conclude that the district court's findings . . . are not erroneous.[15]

There is abundant empirical evidence indicating that college-educated police officers are better officers, including the fact that these officers have more favorable attitudes toward community policing.[16] Certainly the kinds of abilities that are required for officers to work through the S.A.R.A. process (described in Chapter 3), as well as the skills needed by officers to communicate with citizens and to deal with them with respect and cooperation, would seem to result from having officers who have received higher education. Exhibit 9–3 underscores this benefit as it applies to COPPS.

TRAINING TECHNOLOGIES

As technology progresses, new and better methods of instruction and delivery of material continue to evolve. **Training technologies** include distance learning, interactive computer disks, satellite television, and even correspondence courses. On-demand learning allows students to receive their training without placing too great a burden on their personal or professional lives.[17] Online training can be self-paced, around-the-clock, and interactive and can contain one-on-one coaching and mentoring. Individuals as well as corporations, colleges, and universities now offer COPPS courses online.[18]

EXHIBIT 9–3

Higher Education and Officers' Work Habits

Are street smarts better than book smarts? In law enforcement training, there are still some instructors who criticize the recruitment of officers who have college degrees. A 2005 study was conducted in the Saint Paul, Minnesota, Police Department to determine whether the [educational] level of officers was a good predictor of their work habits. The data indicated that officers with a bachelor's of arts degree were above average in the frequency that they received commendations and below average in traffic collisions, sick time usage, and frequency of discipline. The authors reported that a bachelor's of arts degree emphasizes problem solving from a variety of viewpoints, develops understanding of how perceptions influence behavior, and increases a person's comfort level with ambiguity. With this style of thinking, individuals with bachelor's of arts degrees are likely *more comfortable with the notion that there is more than one way to solve a problem* [emphasis added].

Source: Matthew D. Bostrom, "The Influence of Higher Education on Police Officer Work Habits," *Police Chief* (October 2005): 18–25.

Distance learning is a method of training that does not require people to be physically present with the instructor. People may use written materials such as books and workbooks; videos, audiotapes, and CD-ROMs; or courses on the Internet to learn. Grading of papers and tests can be done by mail, fax, e-mail, the Internet, or videoconferencing over broadband network connections.

There is also a growing trend within distance learning called **e-learning,** or training online. Its advantages include documentation of the training, a testing component to establish successful completion of the training and retention of the information, and cost-effectiveness.

Instructor-based training will always exist in some form; to be effective, CD-ROM training may require a live instructor via telephone, on video, or in person to assist the student.[19] Nearly every state is changing its training curricula to reflect some form of interactive learning.[20] The key is that online or other technological training systems fit the department's needs. A system can provide the ability to do many things, but too much capability will often destroy a training program.[21] Exhibit 9–4 provides informational and training resources that are available on the Internet.

TRAINING PROGRAM

Training is at the heart of COPPS. Following is a breakdown of the components of such a training program, including an assessment of training needs, curricular content, and a number of topics that might be included in the training curriculum.

EXHIBIT 9-4

Use of the Internet for COPPS

The Internet provides police officers and trainers with a lower-cost means of communicating with their colleagues across the nation or abroad about policies and programs. Following are some Internet addresses where trainers can conduct research and gain information concerning virtually anything about law enforcement:

- *www.usdoj.gov.* U.S. Department of Justice (DOJ) site provides a link to all DOJ agencies and includes information about a wide range of research, training, and grants.
- *www.officer.com.* This directory is related to law enforcement issues.
- *www.census.gov.* U.S. Census Bureau site provides demographic information by jurisdiction.
- *www.ssc.msu.edu/~people.cp.* National Center for Community Policing center site at Michigan State University lists research, training, and information concerning community policing nationwide.
- *www.communitypolicing.org.* Community Policing Consortium site updates community policing topics monthly and includes an array of information such as training sessions and curricula.
- *www.usdoj.gov/cops/.* COPS Office site promotes policing strategies and offers a variety of grants, training, and education to state agencies and local communities nationwide.
- *www.ncjrs.org.* National Criminal Justice Reference Service site functions as a clearinghouse of publications and is an online reference service for a broad range of criminal justice issues.
- *www.nlectc.org.* National Law Enforcement and Corrections Technology Center site provides information about new equipment and technologies.
- *www.ojp.usdoj.gov/bjs.* Bureau of Justice Statistics site includes a variety of information about criminal justice statistics and provides links to other research Web sites.
- *www.ih2000.net/ira/ira.htm.* This site lists all federal, state, and local agencies on the Web.
- *www.policing.com/course1.* This site is representative of the kinds of online private training courses that are now provided.
- *police.sas.ab.ca/.* COPNET site provides information about police training, job opportunities, links to other agencies, and chat rooms about various subjects.

Also, the Police Executive Research Forum (PERF) (1120 Connecticut Avenue, Suite 930, Washington, D.C. 20036) manages an online resource known as POPNet that provides a library of successful problem-solving examples. PERF also has literally dozens of COPPS publications that can assist trainers. The Community Policing Consortium (1726 M Street N.W., Suite 801, Washington, D.C. 20036; e-mail: look@aspensys.com) publishes the *Information Access Guide,* a compilation of community policing practitioners, community organizers, and volunteers, updated and released the first week of every month.

Determination of Training Needs

Of primary importance is a **needs assessment** to provide the trainer with vital information about the new or veteran officers, including how they view their daily work and what obstacles exist that may prevent them from using COPPS training. It can also provide important information for changing officer performance evaluation systems, extending beyond such traditional assessments as traffic citations or numbers of arrests. The assessment is a tool to establish department-wide training needs and can be used for various purposes—academy training, in-service training, supervisory and nonsupervisory training, and so forth—to survey trainees prior to their receiving instruction.

Exhibit 9–5 provides a preliminary COPPS training needs assessment questionnaire. The exhibit shows the kinds of questions that could be used by a police agency to do a preliminary survey of its training needs. Obviously, question 3 of the survey is critical and will require considerable deliberation.

It is also important for COPPS curriculum development that (1) trainees be determined, (2) a task analysis be conducted, (3) performance measures be constructed by which trainees can be evaluated (to determine successful or unsuccessful course completion), (4) existing courses be identified that might address needs, and (5) the appropriate environment for the training be selected.

EXHIBIT 9–5

Needs Assessment Survey

1. Does our department currently have a community policing strategy or plan?

2. Which of the following best describes our department's community policing practice?
   a. All uniformed officers are/will be actively involved in community policing.
   b. All sworn officers are/will be actively involved in community policing.
   c. Only specifically assigned officers are/will be involved in community policing.
   d. The department does not use community policing.

3. What are our primary training needs related to community policing? (Responses might be wide-ranging, from community engagement issues to knowledge about crime prevention, the S.A.R.A. process generally, management of patrol time, resources and referrals, organizational change, responsibilities of administrators and supervisors, and so on.)

4. Have any of our officers received community policing training?
   a. Who presented/provided the training?
   b. What percentage of our officers received the training?

5. Does our department have at least one computer with a modem? Access to the Internet?

6. Does our department currently have a Web page?

7. Does our agency currently have e-mail external to the department?

8. Have our officers had any Internet training?

9. Which programs does our department currently have? (Responses might include Drug Abuse Resistance Education [DARE], Neighborhood or Business Watch, ride-alongs, Gang Resistance Education and Training [GREAT], and so forth.)

Source: Adapted from Andra J. Katz, *The Community Policing Needs Assessment in Kansas and Nebraska: Final Report* (Wichita, Kans.: Regional Community Policing Training Institute, December 1997).

Ideas for Curricular Content

The overall goal of COPPS training is to provide officers with a level of understanding that allows them to effectively apply community engagement and problem-solving techniques to their daily work. The objectives of such a **COPPS curriculum** include the following:

- Providing participants with an overview of the history of policing and research that serves as the foundation for the COPPS approach
- Providing participants with basic problem-solving skills and knowledge of the elements of community engagement
- Sharing with participants examples of case studies in jurisdictions where COPPS has been successful
- Providing participants with the opportunity to demonstrate the application of the problem-solving model to local problems
- Sharing with participants the benefits of collaborating with other government agencies, businesses, social service organizations, and the community in a COPPS approach
- Discussing the changes in leadership, management, and supervision styles required to develop an environment conducive to the implementation of COPPS
- Helping participants to identify the internal and external organizational barriers to COPPS and to implement problem oriented policing in their respective agencies
- Identifying other external individuals and groups, such as business leaders, other government agencies, social service organizations, and the media, that lend support to COPPS

These objectives are discussed in detail in the next sections, following which we examine some sample training curricula that are in use around the country. Note that references are frequently made to chapters of this book that contain information that can be applied to a training program.

Generally, problem solving requires that officers possess research skills, analytical abilities, and communications skills (including knowledge of group processes, such as running public meetings and working with teams).[22] It also requires a more in-depth understanding of situational crime prevention and CPTED (discussed in Chapter 4).[23]

Evolution of Policing. As indicated in Chapter 1, the evolution of policing toward COPPS has followed a logical progression. Policing, like other government organizations and private businesses, has developed new models for providing service based on past experiences and wisdom. It is important, therefore, that trainers begin their instruction on COPPS with an overview of the history and evolution of policing.

Chapter 1 of this book provides an outline for this instruction. It is important to include in this history a discussion of how our society is changing and what the police must do to confront these challenges (Chapter 2) as

The California Attorney General's Office offers a clearinghouse of COPPS resources for agencies that includes videos, curricula, Internet sources and links, and trainers and technical assistance.

California Attorney General's Office, Crime and Violence Prevention Center, Sacramento, California; Office of Community Oriented Policing Services, Regional Community Policing Institute, Sacramento, California, 2004.

well as the history of the local agency where the training is being conducted (to personalize the training and to facilitate better understanding of the material). This section of training should end by providing participants with clear definitions of the separate but complementary notions of community oriented and problem oriented policing.

Community Engagement.   In this phase of the training program, participants should be introduced to the concept of community policing and its primary components. This segment also provides an opportunity for the participants to interact with one another in examining why their agency is moving into such a method of policing and what changes are likely to occur by doing so. The desired outcomes for this part of the training are for the participants to be able to do the following:

- Define what is meant by the word "community" and the concept of "community policing" and its components
- Identify why police have a difficult time dealing with crime alone and how a collaborative approach to problem solving can lead to more effective crime control
- Know how to develop a community profile that analyzes its problems and identifies its leaders and available resources
- Know how to communicate and collaborate with the community (including other city or county departments, local businesses, social services agencies, and so forth), using approaches such as public meetings, newsletters, and contact with leaders, groups, and organizations representing the community
- Understand a community's cultural, ethnic, and racial diversity

- Discuss community-oriented government, including the concepts of "total quality" and "customer service" in policing
- Identify the changes that may arise, both for their agency and for themselves

Diversity Training. COPPS training should include, and provides an excellent opportunity for, a training strategy for policing in a multicultural society. As Chapter 2 described, we live in an increasingly diverse society with many new cultural mores and languages that pose new challenges for police. Policing these new communities requires understanding and new skills. (Chapter 10 addresses diversity, the history of police-minority problems, bias-based and racial policing, and ways COPPS can build bridges in these areas.) Especially given the current state of world affairs, it is important that police personnel be exposed to different cultures in order to generally make them better and more effective officers, assist in their problem-solving efforts, and hopefully prevent racial profiling.

In attempting to determine both the role of training in promoting policing in a manner that is culturally sensitive and responsive and an approach to training that will yield the greatest success, police agencies must remember the following six principles[24]:

1. Respect for and sensitivity to the diverse communities served are essential for effective policing.
2. Respect for and sensitivity to ethnocultural communities can best be achieved through a broad-based multicultural strategy.
3. Training must be an essential element of such a strategy.
4. Training must be ongoing and built into the experience of policing, that is, it must be more than a course or two on multiculturalism.
5. A multicultural strategy and the training that supports it will be most effective if they are perceived as integrated aspects of the philosophy and operations of policing.
6. A multicultural strategy and training program must be created in consultation with the ethnocultural communities served by the police.

Problem Solving: Basics and Exercises. The PBL concept was introduced earlier in this chapter. Here we discuss this approach more specifically as it relates to COPPS. The problem-solving session of training entails teaching officers the basics of conflict resolution, which is the focus of COPPS; it puts the COPPS philosophy into practice, or "walks the talk" of COPPS. The analysis of problems is the most important component of problem solving. In-depth analysis provides the information necessary for officers to develop effective responses. The S.A.R.A. (scanning, analysis, response, and assessment) problem-solving model (which was discussed in detail in Chapter 3) is presented through an interactive lecture and use of case studies. The desired outcomes for this segment include the following:

- Identifying each component and principal element of the S.A.R.A. process
- Learning the importance of in-depth analysis in the complete identification of a problem

- Learning to identify and apply a variety of responses to a problem
- Discussing the application of situational crime prevention and crime prevention through environmental design (CPTED) concepts on the environmental influences on crime and disorder
- Discussing the importance of both quantitative and qualitative evaluation measures of problem-solving efforts
- Discussing how accountability, empowerment, service orientation, and partnership fit into problem solving

Regarding the use of problem-solving exercises, participants should identify current problems in their assigned areas. Facilitators should divide the classes into small workgroups and ask them to examine each problem, developing strategies for analyzing, responding to, and assessing the effectiveness of their problem-solving efforts. Figures and tables throughout Chapter 3 can be used to lead officers through the process. Brainstorming should be discussed and used as an appropriate tool to foster innovative and creative thinking in the workgroups.[25] The desired outcomes for this segment include the participants' ability to do the following:

- Identify problems on the officer's beat
- Demonstrate an understanding of the problem analysis triangle
- Identify the diversity of resources available, the variety of strategies to address the problem, and some crime prevention techniques
- Evaluate the results using methods similar to those used in the analysis of the problem
- Discuss the advantages and disadvantages of the methods used

Once the problem-solving exercises are completed, each group will have the opportunity to present its problem to the entire class and explain each step of the S.A.R.A. model. Through these presentations, the participants will be exposed to the problem-solving efforts of the other groups. This method of instruction not only provides officers with a practical exercise but also gives them the opportunity to work through an actual problem on their beat. Their efforts in the classroom can easily be repeated in the field, providing them with their first COPPS projects.

Case Studies.   The session on **case studies** provides the trainer with an opportunity to use the S.A.R.A. model of problem solving in addressing an actual situation. Case studies are an excellent training mechanism because they allow the instructor to put the theory (or, as in this case, a problem-solving model) into practice. They also allow the trainer to demonstrate the flexibility of the model as well as emphasize important steps, such as analysis. The desired outcomes of this training segment include the participants' ability to do the following:

- Demonstrate the steps of S.A.R.A.
- Illustrate the importance of thoroughly analyzing a problem using a variety of informational resources and using the problem analysis triangle

- Discuss the methods and resources involved in problem solving
- Discuss the benefit of the problem-solving model over traditional incident-driven responses

As mentioned above, it is best to localize the case studies in order to provide a real-world flavor and to help trainees gain a better understanding of the material.

A new and extremely helpful addition to the body of COPPS training literature is the growing array of booklets in the Problem Oriented Guides for Police series, published by the COPS office. These guides—now with more than 20 different titles—summarize knowledge about how the police can address a variety of problems, including such crime and local problems as street prostitution, graffiti, panhandling, burglary and theft, rave parties, drug dealing, school bullying, false burglar alarms, loud car stereos, robberies at ATMs, and speeding. Appendix A also provides several case studies of problem-solving efforts by police agencies across the United States. These examples show how the S.A.R.A. process was applied to a variety of problems to formulate effective responses.[26]

Leadership and Middle Managers. Executive leadership and middle managers' support are critical to implementing the organizational changes required by the transition to COPPS. Chapters 6 and 7 discussed the roles of leadership and management as they relate to the implementation and cultural change of an organization adopting COPPS.

In many instances, the ultimate challenge to a police organization is to change its hierarchical paramilitary structure. Supervisors, managers, and executives working within a flattened COPPS-oriented organization would require new skills to ensure the successful adaptation and functioning of the police organization.[27] An example of one attempt to support leadership in its transition to COPPS is Seattle, Washington's Police Department (SPD), which has offered a three-day conference titled "Leadership Sessions to Support Problem Oriented Policing" for police supervisors, managers, and researchers. Topics included ethical challenges for leaders, politics inside and outside the organization (examining the organization from top to bottom to see how every system and structure supported problem oriented policing), and leadership. The course also includes adult learning theory, gender inclusiveness, and facilitation skills.[28]

First-Line Supervisor as Coach and Manager. As we pointed out in previous chapters, COPPS requires the support of the first-line supervisor. One of the most difficult hurdles for supervisors to overcome is the idea that giving officers the opportunity to be creative and take risks does not diminish the role or authority of the supervisor. Risk taking and innovation require mutual trust between supervisors and line officers.

Supervising in a COPPS environment means a change from being a "controller," primarily concerned with rules, to being a "facilitator" and "coach" for officers involved in problem solving. Supervisors must learn to encourage innovation and risk taking among their officers and be skilled in problem solving. Conducting workload analyses and finding the time for officers to problem-solve and engage with the community (discussed in Chapter 4) are important aspects of supervision. A supervisor must also be prepared to intercede and remove any obstacles to officers' problem-solving efforts.

Finding the time for officers to engage in problem solving and tracking their efforts are also challenges for first-line supervisors. Chapter 6 includes a section on "recapturing officers' time."

Barriers and Benefits.   A large group discussion may also be facilitated in which participants are asked to identify the internal and external organizational barriers to the success of COPPS. Following the identification of all barriers, strategies are discussed for removing or dealing with the barriers. This discussion helps prepare the trainers for the questions and concerns of the officers in attendance. It also gives the trainers the opportunity to recognize the many benefits of a COPPS approach to policing.

Support Personnel.   Support personnel provide officers with information that is vital to the success of COPPS. For example, it would be difficult for officers to engage in problem solving if the dispatcher, unaware of the COPPS philosophy, was concerned only with eliminating pending calls and continued to dispatch officers to low-priority calls.

Community and Business Leaders.   As we discussed at length in Chapter 2, the community plays a vital role in COPPS. There are a number of ways in which the department and officers can educate citizens about COPPS; these include newsletters, public service announcements, neighborhood meetings, and citizens' police academies. It is important that community and business leaders are oriented in the operation of COPPS. Experience has shown that involving the business community can contribute to the success of the COPPS approach. Business and industrial leaders can be valuable allies, maybe even providing financial support in causes they believe will help the community. Involving them can foster a cooperative relationship and can have any number of possible beneficial outcomes. Businesspeople might donate time and equipment or provide valuable information for problem-solving efforts.

Other Government Agencies.   Previous chapters have discussed how problem solving necessarily involves agencies other than the police or sheriff's departments. A large percentage of CFS handled by the police involve noncriminal matters that can be better handled by other city or county agencies. Furthermore, there is considerable overlap between

It is important to educate the public about community policing.

Courtesy Kris Solow, City of Charlotte, North Carolina.

agencies; a deteriorating neighborhood might involve the health, fire, zoning, prosecutor's, street, social services, or other departments as well as the police department. Thus, it is imperative that key persons in those organizations—active partners in problem solving—be trained in the philosophy and workings of COPPS and CPTED. This is community-oriented government, which is discussed thoroughly in Chapter 3.

Elected Officials.   Politicians must be involved and educated early in the planning of COPPS. They often have the final word on whether new ideas or programs will be implemented. The education of politicians regarding COPPS is important for understanding that this philosophy is unique. A police chief may be horrified to hear the mayor announce, in response to a recent tragedy, that henceforth the police would make every effort to arrive no later than 15 minutes after any CFS was received. Politicians must be taught that rapid response to calls is less effective at catching criminals than educating the public to call the police sooner after a crime is committed, and they should be informed that police response time is largely unrelated to the probability of making an arrest or locating a witness. They must also understand that personnel evaluations are to be conducted differently under this strategy and that reported crimes may well increase as the partnership between the police and the public grows.

A SAMPLE TRAINING PROGRAM

Next we look at a sample training program for preparing police personnel for their COPPS duties in Savannah, Georgia. The Savannah Police Department uses eight training modules, 38 hours in duration, for community oriented policing (COP):

Module I, "Participatory Decision-Making and Leadership Techniques for Management, Supervision, and Street Officers," is six hours long and is for upper-level supervisors. A professional facilitator presents this orientation, which is based largely on the concept of total quality management.

Module II, "Community-Oriented Policing," is an overview that lasts four hours. It begins with the distribution of an in-depth study of crime in Savannah and exacerbating conditions that are found in the same high-crime areas.

Module III is titled "Problem-Oriented Policing" (POP) (four hours). POP is viewed by the department as a major component of COP. Themes and advantages are discussed, as are the means by which certain problems can be identified and solved through a structured process (the S.A.R.A. process, discussed in Chapter 3). The resources of the entire community are considered in relation to solving recurring problems. Also discussed are the report forms involved in POP for the officers to use in their duties.

Module IV, "Referral System, Materials, City Ordinances" (eight hours), examines the use of referrals and the specific agencies available to help in problem solving. Relevant city codes are reviewed with officers. This block of instruction includes discussions of the several benefits of a good referral system, the key elements of a good referral, the sources for obtaining materials that explain referral services, and a crime victim brochure.

Module V, "Developing Sources of Human Information," focuses on communicating with citizens in a way that maximizes trust. Four hours in length, it focuses on problematic areas of field interviews and investigative detentions. Included are six barriers to effective communication, seven ways to enhance active listening, and a "citizen's internal checklist after a police-citizen contact." Reasons for conducting a field interview and the means for managing informant information are also included.

Module VI, "Neighborhood Meetings, Survey of Citizen Needs, Tactical Crime Analysis" (four hours), discusses how to organize and conduct neighborhood meetings and community surveys. Topics include identifying groups, formulating questions, pretesting, and gathering and analyzing data.

Module VII is "Crime Prevention Home and Business Surveys" (four hours). Crime prevention is examined in the context of community policing, and officers are trained to conduct security surveys of homes and businesses.

Module VIII, "Analyzing Data" (four hours), explores tactical crime analysis; it entails organizing and interpreting crime data, identifying crime trends, and disseminating data in a timely manner.

▲ SUMMARY

This chapter has presented some of the obstacles to learning, an overview of those persons and groups needing to receive COPPS training, and types and component parts of a COPPS training program.

COPPS must become a philosophy before it can become a practice. This change in thinking is the major challenge facing those involved in the training and education of police officers and the public. This challenge is enhanced because large numbers of police officers and citizens require orientation and training in COPPS.

Police executives who have implemented the COPPS strategy must give due consideration to the training issue—a major aspect of COPPS that is a sine qua non of this strategy. Without training, there is nothing.

▨ ITEMS FOR REVIEW

1. Explain how the concepts of adult and problem-based learning apply to training for COPPS.
2. Describe why it is important for police agencies to become learning organizations.
3. Delineate the unique challenges that are involved with training police officers.
4. Explain why the police should be trained as neither generalists nor specialists.
5. Review how knowledge is imparted at the basic recruit academy as well as with the postacademy, in-service, and roll call methods.
6. Describe the benefits of higher education for officers who are engaged in COPPS.
7. List some kinds of technologies that exist in police training.
8. Detail the means for determining officers' training needs.
9. List and explain the kinds of topics that might be covered in a COPPS curriculum.

◆ NOTES

1. Malcolm Knowles, *Andragogy in Action* (San Francisco: Jossey-Bass, 1981).
2. Benjamin S. Bloom, *Taxonomy of Educational Objectives, Handbook I: The Cognitive Domain* (New York: David McKay, 1956).
3. Howard Barrows and R. M. Tamblyn, *Problem Based Learning* (New York: Springer, 1980).
4. Peter M. Senge, *The Fifth Discipline: The Art and Practice of the Learning Organization* (London: Random House, 1990).

5. *Ibid.,* p. 3.

6. *Ibid.,* p. 4.

7. Mark K. Smith, "Peter Senge and the Learning Organization," http://www .infed.org/thinkers/senge.htm (Accessed July 14, 2002).

8. William A. Geller, "Suppose We Were Really Serious About Police Departments Becoming 'Learning Organizations,'" *NIJ Journal* 234 (December 1997):2–9.

9. Michael E. Buerger, "Police Training as a Pentecost: Using Tools Singularly Ill-Suited to the Purpose of Reform," *Police Quarterly* 1 (1998):32.

10. *Ibid.,* p. 39.

11. Carole Moore, "Should Officers Be Trained as Specialists?" *Law Enforcement Technology* (November 2003):56–60.

12. Roger G. Dunham and Geoffrey P. Alpert, *Critical Issues in Policing* (Prospect Heights, Ill.: Waveland Press, 1989), p. 112.

13. *Ibid.*

14. Gerald W. Lynch, "Why Officers Need a College Education," *Higher Education and National Affairs* (September 20, 1986):11.

15. *Davis v. City of Dallas*, 777 F.2d 205 (5th Cir. 1985).

16. For a comprehensive listing of studies of higher education for police officers, see Michael G. Aamodt, *Law Enforcement Selection: Research Summaries* (Washington, D.C.: Police Executive Research Forum, 2004), pp. 1–426.

17. Thomas Dempsey, "Cyberschool: Online Law Enforcement Classes," *FBI Law Enforcement Bulletin* (February 1998):10.

18. See, for example, the John Jay College of Criminal Justice School Safety and Security Professional Development course outline, "Community Policing in Schools," at http://www.jjay.cuny.edu/conference/teleconf/.

19. Richard D. Morrison, "Interactive Training," *Law Enforcement Technology* (January 2000):97.

20. Gregory May, quoted in *Ibid.*

21. Susan Reiswerg, "Distance Learning: Is it the Answer to Your Department's Training Needs?" *The Police Chief,* 72 (10) (October 2005):44–51.

22. Province of British Columbia, Ministry of Attorney General, Police Services Branch, *Community Policing Advisory Committee Report* (Victoria, Canada: Author, 1993), pp. 54–55.

23. *Ibid.,* p. 55.

24. Frum Himelfarb, "A Training Strategy for Policing in a Multicultural Society," *The Police Chief* (November 1991):53–55.

25. Nancy McPherson, "Problem Oriented Policing" (San Diego, Calif.: San Diego Police Department Training Outline, 1992), p. 2.

26. Tara O'Connor Shelley and Anne C. Grant (eds.), *Problem Oriented Policing: Crime-Specific Problems, Critical Issues, and Making POP Work* (Washington, D.C.: Police Executive Research Forum, 1999).

27. Province of British Columbia, Ministry of Attorney General, Police Services Branch, *Community Policing Advisory Committee Report,* p. 56.

28. Norm Stamper, *A Training Menu to Support Problem Oriented Policing* (Seattle, Wash.: Seattle Police Department, 1997).

Police
in a Diverse Society

Key Terms and Concepts _____

Bias-based policing
Cultural cue
Diversity
Hate crime

Police-community relations
Police-minority relations
Racial profiling

Learning Objectives _____

As a result of reading this chapter, the student will:

- Understand the historical background of police-minority relations
- Know whether or not the criminal justice system discriminates against minorities
- Comprehend what is meant by racial profiling (bias-based policing), and why it is a destructive practice
- Be aware of what constitutes hate crimes, and what the police can do to address them
- Realize how COPPS can assist in improving police-minority relations
- Know why it is important for the police to be aware of different cultural customs

No man will treat with indifference the principle of race. It is the key of history.

—Disraeli

INTRODUCTION

Immigration. Same-sex marriage. Hate crimes. 9-11. The war in the Middle East. Cultural, socioeconomic, ethnic, racial, religious, and language diversity. Racism and prejudice. Evolution versus intelligent design. This is one of the most difficult and issues-laden periods of time this nation has ever experienced. With a population that is becoming more and more diverse (see Chapter 2) comes greater divisiveness among its citizens. Of course, attempts by our government to protect the borders and the economy have contributed to an "us versus them" mentality. For example, attempts by Congress in mid-2006 to enact HR 4437—the Border Protection, Antiterrorism, and Illegal Immigration Control Act that sought to enact stricter penalties against illegal immigrants and the people who hired them and to construct a 700-mile-long fence along one-third of the U.S.-Mexico border—produced a number of protests nationwide. And certainly an escalated wariness since 9-11 toward people of alien citizenship, a huge rift in the country over a protracted war in the Middle East (which entails heightened security measures at our airports and borders), and the oft-controversial Patriot Act have contributed to this internal strife. Finally, not gone by any means are long-standing views and complaints by African Americans who feel that discrimination has remained a vestige of American daily life since slavery.

In sum, many people feel set apart from the fabric of the United States, most particularly those who view themselves as part of a struggling and disenfranchised minority group. Situated firmly in the middle of all this contemporary dissension are the police.

A minority group is a group or category of people who can be distinguished by special physical or cultural traits that can be used to single them out for differential and unequal treatment. We observed in Chapter 2 that U.S. society is rapidly becoming more diverse; it is a cornucopia of multicultural, multiracial, and ethnically rich people with different and competing norms, mores, values, languages, experiences, and expectations. This increase in cultural diversity and languages poses new challenges for the police—who must learn about the diverse cultures if they are to be successful in their objective of providing aid and assistance to all people.

This is not strictly a black and white issue; as indicated above, Latino/Hispanic Americans, Asian/Pacific Americans, and other ethnic minorities have had difficult relations with the police. Tensions have also arisen in the past because many racial and ethnic minorities, homosexuals, and women believed they had been prevented from entering the police field. The most serious problems in police-minority relations, however, have involved African Americans. We therefore devote a preponderance of this chapter's discussion to examining race relations between African Americans and the police.

We begin this chapter with a brief history of police-minority conflict. Then we examine whether criminal justice in the United States systematically discriminates against minorities; we include discussions of bias-based policing, racial profiling, and hate crimes. Then we consider some means by which police-minority relations can be enhanced, focusing on what community oriented policing and problem solving (COPPS) can do to facilitate that endeavor, including an understanding of cultural customs, differences, and problems.

Following that, we examine what works: innovative programs in several cities that have built bridges to their minority communities. Next is a discussion of some methods that can be used by police agencies to achieve greater diversity in their ranks. We conclude the chapter with some challenging scenarios involving ethnic customs that police officers might confront.

POLICE AND MINORITIES: A HISTORY OF CONFLICT

Modern-day attempts to "protect" America against people who came from other shores—including the Ku Klux Klan in the South who victimize blacks, the vigilantes who patrol the southwestern U.S. borders looking for illegal Mexican aliens, and people who engage in hate crimes against Muslims since 9-11—have their roots in the early twentieth century. Indeed, in 1900 the African American scholar and activist W. E. B. DuBois said the problem of the twentieth century is the problem of the color line. More than 100 years later we are still proving him right. In the past four decades many changes in society have influenced the nature of **police-minority relations:**

- The 1954 *Brown v. Topeka Board of Education*[1] decision of the U.S. Supreme Court declared that separate educational facilities were inherently unequal.
- The use of civil disobedience and nonviolent resistance increased in the 1950s and 1960s, and the Civil Rights Act was passed in 1964. Almost all of the riots in the 1960s were sparked by incidents involving the police.[2]
- The Equal Employment Opportunity Commission was established, and the 1972 Amendment to the Civil Rights Act became law.[3]

Collectively, these actions prohibited discrimination in education, hiring and promotion, voting, and use of public accommodations, among other things.

Of particular importance in the history of U.S. race relations are the events that occurred between 1960 and 1970, when police-minority encounters frequently precipitated racial outbursts. Specifically, Harlem, Watts, Newark, and Detroit all were scenes of major race riots during the 1960s. There were 75 civil disorders involving African Americans and the police in 1967 alone, with at least 83 people killed, mostly African Americans. In addition, many police officers and firefighters were killed or injured. Property damage in these riots totaled hundreds of millions of dollars.[4] The 1970s busing programs that were introduced to integrate schools resulted in white backlash and more interracial conflict.

In the late 1980s **police-community relations** appeared to worsen, with a major riot in Miami, Florida, in 1989. Also in the 1980s, affirmative action programs led to charges of reverse discrimination and more

A scene from the Walker Report of the 1968 Democratic National Convention in Chicago.

dominant-group backlash.[5] More recently, of course, there have been incidents of burning and looting in Miami, Los Angeles, Atlanta, Las Vegas, Washington, D.C., and St. Petersburg, Florida as well as other cities. These incidents have demonstrated that the same tensions that found temporary release on the streets of African American communities in the past still remain with us.

The police were involved in all the social changes described. At times the police have been used to prevent minority group members from demonstrating on behalf of civil rights, and on occasion the police have had to use force against protesting groups. At other times the police have been required to protect those same protesting minorities from the wrath of the dominant group and others who opposed peaceful demonstrations. Over time, alienation has developed from these contacts. Thus, members of both groups today have an uneasy coexistence with a good deal of "baggage" based on what they have seen, heard, or been told of their interactions throughout history. The phrase *"police-community relations,"* as Samuel Walker wrote, is really a euphemism for police-race relations:

> The police have not had the same kinds of conflicts with the white majority community as they do with racial minorities. The most serious aspect of the . . . problem involves *black Americans*. Similar problems exist with respect to other racial-minority groups. In areas with large numbers of *Hispanic Americans* . . . there are also serious conflicts with the police. *Native Americans* . . . have also had conflict with the police. Similar problems exist in cities with large *Asian-American* communities (emphases in original).[6]

Police-community problems are part of a larger problem of racism in our society. The highly respected National Academy of Sciences concluded

A scene from the Walker Report of the 1968 Democratic National Convention in Chicago.

nearly two decades ago that "black crime and the position of blacks within the nation's system of criminal justice administration are related to past and present social opportunities and disadvantages and can be best understood through consideration of blacks' overall social status."[7] Recent mass gatherings in Washington, D.C., engendered by such groups as the Southern Christian Leadership Conference and the Rainbow Coalition, have involved protests against racial profiling (discussed later), police brutality, and other perceived prejudices toward people of color; such assemblies would indicate that the Academy's statement is still valid today. Minority group members remain frustrated because the pace of gains in our society has not kept up with their expectations.

To many minorities the police are an "occupying force," more concerned with restricting their freedom than providing services to their community. From the police's point of view, minority neighborhoods have not always been supportive of their efforts to combat crime. Which perspective is more accurate? Perhaps that question cannot be answered; however, a key element in police-community relations—and one that is often overlooked—is how the police perceive the public.

MINORITIES AND THE CRIMINAL JUSTICE SYSTEM

Systematic Discrimination Against Minorities?

A highly influential study addressing whether the justice system discriminates against minorities by the RAND Corporation in 1983 found no consistent, statistically significant racial differences in the probability of arrest or in case processing, even though minority suspects were more likely than whites to be given longer sentences and to be put in prison instead of jail. RAND determined that the criminal justice system did not discriminate against minorities, who were not overrepresented in the arrest population *"relative to the number of crimes they actually commit"* (emphasis in original), nor were they more likely than whites to be arrested for those crimes.[8]

Recent studies in the late 1990s and the early 2000s, however, paint a different picture and challenge the RAND findings. Research on California's justice system in 1996 raised questions about that state's racial fairness, finding that 39 percent of its African American men in their 20s were in prisons, in jails, or on probation; the authors concluded that the system was discriminatory. African Americans were charged under California's "three strikes" law at 17 times the rate of whites, and at almost every stage of the justice process, whites fared better than African Americans or Latinos. A member of the National Association for the Advancement of Colored People (NAACP) Legal Defense Fund stated the report showed why the black community does not trust the justice system.[9] Even San Francisco's district attorney was compelled to observe that "The criminal justice system is putting an unfair burden on minorities."[10]

Then in 2003, the Leadership Conference on Civil Rights (LCCR) issued a report titled "Justice on Trial," observing that "in one critical area—criminal justice—racial inequality is growing, not receding."[11] The LCCR report bemoaned "unequal treatment of minorities [that] characterizes every stage of the process," and it noted that the majority of crimes are not committed by minorities, most minorities are not criminals, and disproportionate numbers of minority arrests perpetuate the belief that minorities commit more crimes, which in turn leads to racial profiling (discussed below).[12] In conclusion, and in complete opposition to the RAND report's findings two decades earlier, the LCCR determined that "our criminal justice system discriminates against minorities."[13]

Racial Profiling and Bias-Based Policing

The above studies would indicate that the American criminal justice system is indeed biased in its treatment of minorities. This has been and continues to be one of the most sensitive charges against the criminal justice system throughout its history, and differential treatment is our next topic of discussion.

Certainly in today's climate of **diversity** there is considerable pressure on the police to be watchful of certain minorities living in our nation who would do people harm. Indeed, since September 11, 2001, law enforcement's targeting of Arabs and Muslims, in their search for suspected terrorists, is viewed by two-thirds of Americans as "understandable."[14] Still, **racial profiling** has become a despised police practice in the new millennium. (Actually, a more inclusive term is "bias-based profiling," which includes unequal treatment of any persons on the basis of race, ethnicity, religion, gender, sexual orientation, or socioeconomic status.) At present, approximately half of the states have adopted legislation related to racial profiling, and similar legislation is pending in other states; most of these laws include data collection requirements (discussed below).[15]

Bias-based policing on the basis of race—also known as "driving while black or brown" (DWBB)—where a police officer, acting on a personal bias, stops a vehicle simply because the driver is of a certain race, is given no public support. Such incidents can take various forms, as demonstrated in the following accounts by people who were stopped by police on questionable grounds and subjected to disrespectful behavior or intrusive questioning[16]:

- A young black woman trades her new sports car for an older model because police have repeatedly stopped her on suspicion of possession of a stolen vehicle.
- An elderly African American couple returning from a social event in formal dress are stopped and questioned at length, allegedly because their car resembles one identified in a robbery.
- A prominent black lawyer driving a luxury car is frequently stopped on various pretexts.
- A Hispanic deputy police chief is stopped various times in neighboring jurisdictions on "suspicion."
- A black judge far from her hometown is stopped, handcuffed, and laid face down on the pavement while police search her car (they issue no citations).

This issue has driven a deep wedge between the police and minorities, many of whom claim to be victims of this practice. Indeed, the superintendent of the New Jersey State Police was fired by that state's governor in

Minority community members often believe they are unnecessarily detained and interviewed by police.

Courtesy Washoe County, Nevada, Sheriff's Office.

March 1999 for statements that were perceived as racially insensitive concerning racial profiling.

The best defense for the police may be summarized in two words: collect data. Collecting traffic stop data helps chiefs and commanders determine whether officers are stopping or searching a disproportionate number of minorities and enables them to act on this information in a timely fashion. Technology—including mobile data computers and wireless handheld devices—is available to the police for this purpose. Exhibit 10–1 shows what the Sacramento, California, Police Department has done to study and address racial profiling, although no such complaints had been reported in the city.

Recently the International Association of Chiefs of Police (IACP) issued a comprehensive policy statement on bias-based policing and data collection. The association "believes that any form of police action that is based solely on the race, gender, ethnicity, age, or socioeconomic level of an individual is both unethical and illegal" but that data collection programs "must ensure that data is being collected and analyzed in an impartial and methodologically sound fashion."[17] Next, another minority-related problem is discussed: hate crimes.

EXHIBIT 10–1

Sacramento Searches for Biased Policing

In the late 1990s the Sacramento, California, police department (SPD) began a study on racially biased policing, to determine the degree of intrusiveness of traffic stops, and whether or not such stops were indicative of racially biased policing. Even though there were no reported complaints of such policing, the SPD recognized the importance of responding to national concern toward the problem. The study, by the University of Southern California, and financed by $275,000 in grants from the federal Office of Community Oriented Policing Services and the state's highway patrol, began by collecting reports, editorials, and anecdotal information for insight into approaches taken by other agencies. Meetings were held with the community, civil rights organizations, the police union, and agency staff (officers were invited to provide input on how to conduct the study). Officers filled out data collection forms for each traffic stop, which included data on traffic patterns, type of crimes throughout the city, and officers' badge numbers, age, race, and unit assignments. To broaden the study, the SPD invited a number of stakeholders—including the American Civil Liberties Union, the Mexican American Legal Defense and Education Fund, and neighborhood associations, all of whom got a better understanding of police work—and who came to the vital realization that rarely could an officer identify the race of the driver or occupants of cars before they were actually stopped. The study did find that traffic stops involving African Americans occurred at a disproportionately higher rate than their overall population, so the study was extended for two years in order to examine whether systems existed that encouraged bias-based policing. Now, as part of its community policing "Police as Problem Solvers/Peacemakers Initiative," the SPD is providing technical assistance to other local police agencies interested in data collection on biased policing.

Source: Tammy Jones, "Sacramento Searches for Bias Policing." In *Community Links* (Washington, D.C.: Community Policing Consortium, February 2003), pp. 1–2.

RESPONSES TO HATE CRIMES

Hate crimes and hate incidents—those that are motivated by an offender's bias against an individual's or group's race, religion, ethnic/national origin, gender, age, disability, or sexual orientation[18]—are also major issues for the police because of these crimes' unique impact on victims and the community. Such crimes can have a special emotional and psychological impact. Hate violence can exacerbate racial, religious, or ethnic tensions in a community and lead to a cycle of escalating reprisals. Police executives must demonstrate a commitment to be both tough on hate crime perpetrators and sensitive to the impact of hate violence on the community.[19]

At present, 45 states and the District of Columbia have crime statutes that enhance the penalties for hate crimes and address hate violence. The 1990 Hate Crime Statistics Act requires the Department of Justice to collect and publish data on bias-motivated crimes across the United States. Furthermore, at the federal level hate crimes are investigated by the Federal Bureau of Investigation (FBI) Bias Crimes Unit and the Bureau of Alcohol, Tobacco, Firearms, and Explosives church arson and explosives experts.[20]

In 2005, 7,649 hate crimes were reported in the United States. Racial bias accounted for 52.9 percent of the single-bias incidents, religious intolerance led to 18.0 percent, bias about sexual orientation triggered 15.7 percent, and bias regarding ethnicity/national origin led to 12.7 percent of the incidents.[21]

There is much a law enforcement organization can do with respect to hate crimes to take a leadership role in the community: provide victims with a point of contact in the department to whom they can report hate crimes and express concerns, inform victims on case progress, participate in hate crime training as well as educate the public about these crimes, establish a zero tolerance of prejudice within the department, track the criminal activities of hate groups, and sponsor and participate in community events that promote tolerance and diversity.[22] A good example of a police agency's effort to fight hate crimes is that of Madison, Connecticut. At a departmental roll call, every officer receives a laminated hate crimes response card, which provides officers with important information for responding to hate crimes, working with victims, and pursuing perpetrators. The card includes the definition of a hate crime, questions responding officers should ask, and tips for recognizing signs of organized hate groups. In October 2002, the Anti-Defamation League took the effort further, distributing these cards to more than 7,500 police officers throughout Connecticut.[23]

The Justice Department has developed a new hate crime training curriculum for police officers, and the Anti-Defamation League has also produced a number of hate crime resources and prevention initiatives. See Exhibit 10–2 for more information.

EXHIBIT 10–2

Definition of a Hate Crime

A hate crime is a criminal offense committed against persons, property or society that is motivated, in whole or in part, by an offender's bias against an individual's or a group's perceived race, religion, ethnic/national origin, gender, age, disability or sexual orientation. Legal definitions of hate crimes vary. Check your state statutes for the definition of hate crime in your jurisdiction.

Hate incidents are those actions by an individual or group that, while motivated by bias, do not rise to the level of a criminal offense.

COMMUNITY TRAUMA

Hate crimes victimize the entire community and may involve

- Victimization projected to all community members
- Sense of group vulnerability
- Community fear/tension
- Possibility of reactive crimes or copycat incidents
- Community polarization
- Redirection of law enforcement resources
- Loss of trust in criminal justice institutions
- Public damage (e.g., buildings—such as churches)

VICTIM TRAUMA

Because the basis for the attack is the victim's identity, victim(s) may suffer

- Deep personal crisis
- Increased vulnerability to repeat attack
- Sense of community/system betrayal
- Acute shock and disbelief
- Extreme fear of certain groups
- Hopelessness
- Anger/desire for revenge
- Shame and humiliation

ACTION TO BE TAKEN AT THE SCENE:

- Explain to the victim(s) and witnesses the likely progression of the investigation
- Report the suspected hate crime to the supervisor on duty
- Refer media representatives to the public information officer or supervisor on duty
- Document the incident thoroughly on the department report forms, noting any particular hate crime indicators and quoting exact wording of statements made by perpetrators

Source: L. E. Technology, "Healing the Hate," p. 58; adapted as "Tear-Out Pocket Guide" by IACP, 515 N. Washington Street, Alexandria, Virginia 22314 (800 THE-IACP; www.theiacp.org).

IMPROVEMENT IN POLICE-MINORITY RELATIONS

Complicating Factors and Possible Solutions

Given its history and all of the previously mentioned exacerbating factors, we are left to wonder whether police-minority relations can ever be improved. Without question, some members of society believe the police have no redeeming qualities; to these people, police officers are, and will always be, symbolic agents of an entire system of injustice, never to be trusted under any circumstances. So long as the police have the duty to enforce the laws and the power to arrest and control the behavior of their fellows, there will be inherent problems in obtaining complete public support. "The most difficult of all police problems [is] how to make more palatable the basic regulatory nature of police work."[24]

James Baldwin's classic and powerful description of how the police are viewed in the ghetto illustrates the point:

> The only way to police a ghetto is to be oppressive. None of the Police Commissioner's men, even with the best will in the world, have any way of understanding the lives led by the people they swagger about in twos and threes controlling. Their very presence is an insult, and it would be, even if they spent their entire day feeding gumdrops to children. They represent the force of the white world, and that world's

Lasting improvements between the police and minorities require that both groups make necessary changes.

Courtesy Kris Solow, City of Charlotte, North Carolina.

criminal profit and ease, to keep the black man corralled up here, in his place. The badge, the gun in the holster, and the swinging club make vivid what will happen should his rebellion become overt. He moves through Harlem, therefore, like an occupying soldier in a bitterly hostile country, which is precisely what and where he is, and is the reason he walks in twos and threes.[25]

COPPS AND VARIOUS AGENCY INITIATIVES

Following are some examples of various activities some jurisdictions have undertaken to help address problems and bring about unity among their diverse populations.

Los Angeles: Establishment of Forums

Ethnic diversity defines the city of Los Angeles. To take advantage of that wealth of varied knowledge, the Los Angeles Police Department (LAPD) turned to the community for ideas, establishing six Community Forums to promote community policing with reliance on trust, respect, cooperation, and partnership. Each forum has about 25 members as well as direct access to the police chief. Following are brief descriptions of each[26]:

1. *Black Forum.* As a response to the forum's recent concerns about racial profiling, the LAPD published a pamphlet to improve relations between motorists and officers, explain procedures of traffic stops, and provide a means to commend officers and to lodge complaints.
2. *Hispanic Forum.* This forum's main concerns include immigration rights and LAPD's policy concerning undocumented aliens, and it attempts to ensure that police comply with a policy against initiating action for the sole purpose of determining a person's immigration status.
3. *Asian/Pacific Islander Forum.* This forum has developed a video on ethnic diversity.
4. *Gay/Lesbian Forum.* Concerns regarding arrests based on lewd conduct and the perceived use of police "baiting" to arrest gays are addressed, and the forum helps police to reduce hate crimes and to hire recruits who respect varied lifestyles.
5. *Religious Forum.* This forum promotes collaboration among the many religious groups in Los Angeles.
6. *Youth Forum.* This forum exposes young people to the scope of law enforcement so that they may better appreciate the importance of laws and justice in their lives.

Santa Ana, California: Hands-On Citizen Academy

The Santa Ana, California, Police Department has launched a unique 12-week citizen police academy that enhances its efforts in community policing by

Citizens' academies expose people to what it is like to be a police officer, and they help officers understand public concerns.

emphasizing problem solving and hands-on activities that expose students to what it is like to be a police officer.

Students are given a simulated burglary case, and they interview the victim and witnesses, investigate the case, and solve it. They dust for fingerprints, process evidence, and write reports of their activities. Graduates become "ambassadors" for the department; Cesar Dias and Alicia Ramos said the program is a vital source of information about COPPS, and they "go out and spread the word about law enforcement."[27]

Michigan City, Indiana: Kids and the Internet

Police in Michigan City, Indiana, were determined to befriend and help educate youths in the city's West Side, one of the city's poorer sections. Using a grant from a local group, the department created a new substation and stocked it with four computers, scanners, and printers as well as a reading library. Each computer has access to the Internet. School liaison and Drug Abuse Resistance Education (D.A.R.E.) officers were transferred to staff the center during weekdays, freeing community policing officers to continue their neighborhood work. Following a U.S. congressman's visit to the center, for which the police bought pizza, the center was packed with young people.

In addition to expanding the youths' minds, the center also provides children with a safe place to study and improves community relations.[28]

Lincoln, Nebraska: Services for Non-English-Speaking Populations

The Lincoln, Nebraska, Police Department (LPD) provides a host of services for residents who do not speak English as their primary language. The most common foreign languages spoken in Lincoln are Spanish and Vietnamese, so the LPD makes interpreters available to officers on the street when needed in those and virtually all languages. The LPD Web site contains information in Spanish and Vietnamese and has produced several bilingual videos on various topics for broadcast on cable television. Officers conduct training sessions for new immigrants on a number of topics as well, and LPD provides telecommunications device for the deaf (TDD) service to the deaf and hearing impaired; closed captioning is available for the city's public television programs.[29]

Office of Community Oriented Policing Services: Cultural Diversity Training

It should also be mentioned that the U.S. Department of Justice's Office of Community Oriented Policing Services (COPS) recognizes the need for cultural diversity training, which is provided through its 31 regional community policing institutes (RCPIs) across the nation. Specialized training is even being provided for communities that are experiencing rapid demographic changes.[30]

Discussion of the Issues

One of the problems with addressing police-minority relations issues is that police and people in general do not like to discuss the topic because "you step on somebody's toes or it's embarrassing."[31] The COPPS philosophy helps address this complex issue. In addition to getting the two groups talking with each other and, therefore, thwarting conflict, it enables police to pinpoint racial tension in their city. COPPS, by its very nature, encourages officers to find out exactly what is occurring in neighborhoods, including who is involved and what their motives are.

As we've discussed in earlier chapters, supervisors must support officers in this endeavor. Officers must be allowed to interact with different people rather than functioning as mere report takers. Through this interaction, officers begin to learn the cultural diversity of various racial, ethnic, and religious groups.

What can COPPS do to improve relations between the police and minorities? To begin with, at its most fundamental level COPPS tries to emphasize the interrelationship between the police and the community. COPPS dictates that officers understand their unique problem-solving relationship with the community as they execute the law. There is no denying that this is at times a huge task, given the history of problems between the two groups.

Indeed, many people are convinced that the U.S. criminal justice system *is* racist. Although COPPS cannot change the outcomes of the above studies by the LCCR and in California, it can humanize the justice system, showing a side of the police that is in stark contrast to these figures.

The acceptance and management of diversity, like the implementation of COPPS, cannot be simply a program or strategy. For either to succeed, there must be major personal, personnel, and policy changes from the top to the bottom of the organization.

The key to managing diversity and accommodating cultural differences is training and education. But training in both COPPS and diversity, if not conducted correctly and supported by changes in the organization, is better left undone. Gayle Fisher-Stewart notes:

> [Too often both COPPS and the management of diversity are introduced] with a "shot in the arm." A curriculum is developed, and the entire staff of the department is marched through for their inoculation. After the first dose, there are no boosters. The curriculum is not modified on the basis of rank ... officers are often viewed as the only ones who need training, because they are viewed as the ones causing problems in the community.[32]

In a related vein, Exhibit 10–3 contains 15 appropriately pointed questions compiled by Minneapolis, Minnesota, Chief of Police Robert K. Olson, to be considered by police agencies that are attempting to engage in "balancing crime strategies and democratic principles."

Understanding of Cultural Customs, Differences, and Problems

This section discusses the negative consequences of the police not understanding the cultural differences or discerning the **cultural cues** of the people they confront. Indeed, actions that are common in mainstream American culture can result in miscommunication and have dire consequences if the police do not recognize cultural nuances. As a fundamental example, it is not uncommon for an officer to get someone's attention by beckoning with a crooked index finger, repeatedly moving it back and forth; although this is an innocuous gesture to Americans, it is an insult to an Ethiopian man, who uses it to call a person a dog.[33]

A more serious example would be the custom of certain Asian cultures to exchange gifts at initial meetings. On meeting with members of such a

EXHIBIT 10–3

Self-Evaluation: Balancing Crime Strategies and Democratic Principles

1. Is your department really doing community-oriented policing: a continual discussion of implementation of crime control strategies involving the direct input of the citizens affected by police action?

2. Does your department routinely give detailed cultural awareness/diversity training to recruits, with follow-up in-services yearly to the rest of the police department?

3. Does your police department have a reputation in the minority community for taking swift internal discipline when serious police misconduct occurs?

4. Have you developed true school liaison and additional police interaction—other than enforcement—with young people?

5. Are there incentives or requirements for the chief and upper staff and/or other members of the department to reside in the city in which they are responsible for policing?

6. Has your department established strong community ties, particularly with the leadership of all relevant organizations representing people of color, so that when crisis happens—and it will—the department will have immediate access and assistance in dealing with it?

7. Has the department and its political leadership made clear to all its employees that racial intolerance will not be permitted, crushed at the slightest hint of its appearance, and that the public, particularly people of color, feel confident that their city will address those issues?

8. Who polices the police or chief in your community? Is there an alternative to internal affairs? Is the police chief held accountable by the appropriate elected body for [e]nsuring a corruption-free police department?

9. Is the chief executive clearly supported by mayor and council in their community policing and other activities designed to include, rather than exclude, all their constituents?

10. Does your department have a hiring process that will not only [e]nsure diversity within the ranks, but is fair and does not exclude people, and is designed to bring in candidates who wish to join for the spirit of service and not the spirit of adventure? Has your department created an internal atmosphere where people of color would want to become a member and have a rewarding 20-year career?

11. Does each department offer internal promotional and assignment opportunities equally to all? Do the promoted ranks clearly reflect the diversity of the whole organization and the community that it serves?

12. Is the community routinely involved in the discussion of all issues that affect policing within their neighborhoods?

13. Is your police organization structured to ensure there is accountability at every level for the performance and actions of each and every officer who encounters citizens in their daily work?

14. Does your department have consistent institutionalized citizen communication instruments that allow the department to not only keep the citizens informed of police activity, but to receive citizen input on a regular basis on a wide variety of issues?

15. Does your police department have a reasonable standard of behavior and protocol for the stopping of citizens, particularly in high crime areas? Are persons being stopped and clearly being advised of the reason for the stop? Are they being told exactly what the police are doing? Most particularly, does your police training include disengagement techniques—how to get out of a situation where, in fact, the officer may well have been wrong in their assumption, and must appropriately explain and apologize to the citizen for their inconvenience?

Source: List compiled by Chief Robert K. Olson of Minneapolis, Minnesota. Police Executive Research Forum, *Subject to Debate* 13(6) (June 1999):5. Used with permission.

Criminal justice agencies in the St. Paul, Minnesota, area developed a program to enhance citizens' understanding of the Hmong culture and to train Hmong people in the justice process.

Upper Midwest Community Policing Institute, Woodbury, Minnesota.

culture, the COPPS officer can be placed in an uncomfortable position at having to offend those persons whom he or she is there to serve either by not offering a gift or by refusing to accept a gift.[34] These are true ethical (if not legal) dilemmas that today's police officer—and his or her administrators and supervisors—must address. It has been stated that "law enforcement professionals need to develop cultural empathy."[35]

There are other cultural cues about which the police should be cognizant. For example, during an argument it would not be uncommon for a Mexican American to shout to his friend, "I'm going to kill you if you do that again." In the Anglo culture, this statement would clearly signal one's intent to do harm; however, in the context of the Latino/Hispanic culture, this simply conveys anger. Therefore, the Spanish word *matar* (to kill) is often used to show feelings, not intent. Another example is that Anglo Americans tend to assume that there is a short distance between an emotional verbal expression of disagreement and a full-blown conflict. For African Americans, though, stating a position with feeling shows sincerity. For most African Americans, threatening movements, not angry words, indicate the start of a fight. In fact, some would argue that fights do not begin when people are talking or arguing but rather when they stop talking.

Many possible breakdowns in verbal communication can cause difficulties for police officers and those of different cultures.[36] For example, for many Tongans, being handcuffed when arrested for minor crimes is a cultural taboo; that treatment is reserved for only the very worst offenders in their culture. To many Southeast Asians, being asked by an officer to assume a kneeling position with fingers interlocked behind the head is cause for rebellion; to them, this posture is a prelude to being assassinated. For the Chinese, causing someone to lose face through disrespect—such as not being able to use both hands to convey an object—is one of the worst things one person can do to another.[37]

For Latinos/Hispanics, the concept of masculine superiority is important, as are the dominance of the father in the family, the division of labor according to sex, and the belief that the family is more important than the individual. Arguing politics on street corners is an old tradition that, in its frenzy, might appear to be assaultive behavior. It is culturally taboo for a stranger to touch a small Hispanic girl. The use of surnames and last names may be confusing to some police officers. Latin custom dictates the use of the father's and the mother's last name (e.g., Jose Jesus Leon Flores). The legal name is the surname (Leon); the maternal name is the last name in the series (Flores).[38]

Native Americans, unfortunately, suffer severe social problems. Alcohol has been found to be a factor in 80 percent of all Native American suicides and in 90 percent of all homicides. Alcohol has also been found to play a part in the social, physical, psychological, economic, and cultural disruption experienced by Native Americans.[39]

In addition to the traits discussed above, other cultural differences that might be observed by the police include the following:

- *Body position.* A police sergeant relaxing at a desk with feet up, baring the soles of the feet, would likely offend a Saudi Arabian or Thai because the foot is considered the dirtiest part of the body.
- *Facial expression and expressiveness.* A smile is a source of confusion for police officers when encountering Asian cultures. A smile or giggle can cover up pain, humiliation, or embarrassment; on hearing something sad, an Asian may smile, appearing to be a "smart aleck." Whereas Latin Americans, Mediterranean Americans, Arab Americans, Israeli Americans, and African Americans tend to show emotions facially, other groups tend to be less facially expressive; officers may assume that these persons are not being cooperative.

Preservice and in-service police training should cover these cultural differences. At the very least, police officers should know what terms are the least offensive when referring to ethnic or racial groups. For example, most Asians prefer not to be called Orientals; they prefer their nationality of origin, such as Korean American. Many American Indians resent the term "Native American" because that term was invented by the U.S. government. They prefer to be called American Indian or to be known by their tribal ancestry (e.g., Crow, Winnebago). The terms "black American" and "African American" can usually be used interchangeably; however, the latter is more commonly used among younger people. Mexican Americans usually refer to themselves as Chicanos, whereas the term "Latino" is preferred by those from Central America.[40]

USE OF RECRUITING AND EMPLOYMENT TO CREATE DIVERSE POLICE DEPARTMENTS

Women and minorities are underrepresented in policing (see Exhibit 10–4 for one city's solution). The organizational culture of policing has been noticeably slow to change in this regard. Female officers may help improve the tarnished image of policing, improve community relations, and foster a more flexible, less violent approach to keeping the peace. Former Houston, Texas, police chief Elizabeth Watson stated, "Women tend to rely more on intellectual than physical prowess. From that standpoint, policing is a natural match for them."[41]

The recruitment of minority officers remains a difficult task. Probably the single most difficult barrier has to do with the image that police officers have among these groups. Unfortunately, for many African Americans and Latinos/Hispanics, police officers are symbols of oppression and have been charged with using excessive brutality; they are often seen as an army of occupation. Meanwhile, many women are reluctant to try to enter what they perceive as a male-dominated sexist occupation. They may also be aware of high turnover rates of female police officers and the glass ceiling that militates against the promotion of women.

Some very successful methods are being used by some law enforcement agencies to recruit women and minorities and to generally diversify their workforce. For example, the Philadelphia Police Department (PPD) has a very informative and easily navigable Web site, and officers visit all the minority communities and such organizations as the Latino Organization; minorities are offered a tour of the police academy to view the training.

The Omaha, Nebraska, Police Department's (OPD) Web site is extensive and takes the reader through the selection process, the command structure, the salary and benefits, and the Law Enforcement Code of Ethics. The OPD also works closely with local television and radio stations and newspapers to develop videos and publicity spots that highlight

EXHIBIT 10–4

Recruiting Women and Minority Officers in Philadelphia

The Philadelphia Police Department (PPD) has 7,000 sworn officers. In one decade, the percent of those sworn officers who were women rose from 14.7 percent to 24.2 percent. PPD has a very informative and easily navigable Web site, where each step of the selection process is explained. The recruiting staff believes that women and minority officers themselves are the best recruiting tool. Because PPD's deputy commissioner is female, higher visibility has been given to female officers' ability to rise in the ranks. Furthermore, when recruiting at colleges and universities, recruiters encourage students of all majors to consider a career in law enforcement. For example, theater majors would have important skills for undercover work, while computer science majors are needed to help support the computer network for the 7,000 officers and investigate computer and white-collar crimes. Recruiters describe the approximately 170 different units that compose the department. Visiting all the minority communities and such organizations as the Latino Organization, recruiters also offer tours of the police academy to allow prospective applicants to view the training. As part of their community policing and recruiting efforts, the police speak in the public schools, helping to increase the positive image of the department. Recruiters also ensure that prospective applicants are aware of the paid ten-month training period, during which they will learn how to minimize the risk of injury; knowing that they will receive extensive training in this area affords a greater degree of confidence to those individuals who have had little experience in physical or verbal confrontations.

Source: www.ppdonline.org/career_apply.php (Accessed September 16, 2006).

various aspects of police work and the department's recruiting efforts. Recruiting information and application forms are disseminated nationally to colleges, universities, community agencies, churches, health clubs, libraries, female- and minority-owned businesses, special-interest groups, and community leaders. Internet job announcements are posted on local, state, and national employment-related job sites, and recruiters attend numerous career fairs to not only disseminate information but also conduct mock interviews for interested candidates.

Similarly, the Chicago Police Department's (CPD) Web site carries a strong promotional message, offering minorities the opportunity to utilize the latest law enforcement methodologies and technological tools and describing some of the different career and promotional opportunities, benefits, and minimum qualifications as well as the hiring process. Applications can be downloaded. CPD's diverse recruiting division also visits community and college job fairs, military installations, community meetings, religious organizations, and neighborhood organizations, both in and out of state. CPD's recruiting effort, called the Ambassador Program, is advertised in military transition offices, on local television, in public service announcements, in newspapers, at movie theaters, at baseball fields, and in the mass transit system. A recent innovation is Recruitment Day, in which special invitations are

Agencies seek to employ a force that is as diverse as the population they serve.

Courtesy Fort Lauderdale, Florida, Police Department.

mailed to about 7,000 individuals who request them (unsolicited invitations to the general public are also sent).

Obviously, until more minority and female officers are promoted to administrative levels and can affect policy and serve as role models, there is a higher risk of their being treated unequally and having difficulty being promoted—a classic catch-22 situation. Nonetheless, as the United States generally becomes more diverse, police organizations must take measures to reflect the larger society.

ON THE STREET: FIVE PERPLEXING SCENARIOS

Following are five scenarios based on actual events that demonstrate some of the situations that COPPS officers might confront. For each scenario, we have provided some of the cultural beliefs and practices that might come into play. Try to consider how police officers might best handle each situation and the possible repercussions if they fail to recognize the nonverbal communication, beliefs, and practices that are at work in each. Also consider the need for cultural diversity to be incorporated into basic police academy training curricula.

> *Scenario 1.* An officer witnesses a traffic violation. When the officer stops the driver of the vehicle, he or she notices two things. First, the driver speaks with a heavy Spanish accent; second, he appears very nervous. The officer asks for his license and registration. When he

hands them over, the officer finds that he has also enclosed a $100 bill. The traffic offense carries a fine of $25, but now the offense of bribery has been committed. How would the officer handle this situation?[42]

Here, the officer might consider the fact that in some Latin American countries, the way to do business with any public official—especially the police—is to offer money. It is expected, and there are severe penalties for noncompliance. The offense of bribery has been committed, so the officer would be well within the law to arrest the driver. After further questioning the driver regarding his country of origin, the officer could explain that the exchange of money is a punishable offense in the United States and charge him only for the traffic offense.

> *Scenario 2.* An officer is summoned to a local school by the principal, who has been informed of a case of child abuse by a sixth-grade teacher. On arriving at the principal's office, the officer is shown a Vietnamese girl who had been absent from school for several days with a high fever. The girl has heavy bruising on the left side of her neck. The officer goes to the child's home and questions her father, who admits in broken English that he caused the bruising on the girl's neck. What is the officer's reaction?

In parts of Asia, a medical practice called "coining" involves rubbing the skin with a heated coin, leaving highly visible marks on the neck or back. This practice, intended to heal the child, may easily be misinterpreted as child abuse by police, school, or social service agencies. This is a good example of why police officers must avoid being ethnocentric or interpreting what they see through their own cultural "filters."

> *Scenario 3.* An officer is summoned to a murder scene involving a family picnic in a neighborhood park. On arriving, the officer learns that a Mexican woman had been involved in an extramarital affair and had been bragging about her activities in front of many extended-family members in the park. The woman also made comments about her new lover's sexual prowess and her husband's inability to satisfy her. Her husband then left the park. Returning shortly thereafter with a shotgun, he shot and killed his wife. He gives himself up. For what criminal charge should the defendant be convicted?

In probably all states, a case such as this would result in a minimum charge of second-degree murder against the defendant. However, in this actual case (in California), because the jury took into consideration the cultural background of this couple, the husband was convicted of a lesser charge of manslaughter. It was argued that the wife's boasting about her lover and the emasculation of her husband created a passion and emotion that completely undermined his "machismo," pride, and honor—what it means to be humiliated in the context of the Latin culture in front of one's family.[43]

> *Scenario 4.* While on foot patrol, a COPPS officer responds to neighbors' complaints. The scene is a brawl at a barbecue party in the backyard of a home where Samoans reside. How should the officer proceed?

The officer could immediately summon backup assistance, and together the officers could make a show of force, breaking up the fighting but also acquiring the undying disrespect of the Samoan community and widening the gap between the two groups. Alternatively, the police could locate the "chief" of this group and let that person deal with the problem in a manner in which he would handle it in Samoa. The chief has a prominent role to play and can serve as a bridge between the police and the community (and keep the matter out of court).[44]

> *Scenario 5.* A police officer stops a Nigerian cab driver, who moves close to the officer and ignores the officer's command to "step back." He also averts his eyes from the officer and begins defiantly "babbling to the ground" in a high-pitched tone of voice while making gestures. The officer believes that the cab driver is out of control, unstable, and possibly dangerous. How should the officer perceive this individual?

In Nigeria, the social distance for conversation is much closer than in the United States; it may be less than 15 inches. Furthermore, Nigerian people often show respect and humility by averting their eyes. What is perceived by the officer as "babbling" is actually the cab driver's way of sending a message of respect and humility. Most likely, the cab driver is not even aware that he is perceived as out of control, unstable, and possibly dangerous.

These case studies are not presented to question the rightness or wrongness of any group's values, beliefs, or practices, nor should they be interpreted to mean that serious crimes should be excused on cultural grounds. The point is to illustrate to the COPPS officer the importance of understanding cultural differences and individual backgrounds.

Obviously the police must take differences in nonverbal communication into account when dealing with people of different cultures. These case studies also reveal that discretion at the police level is much more important than that practiced at the court's level.

It would be unrealistic to expect all police officers to be aware of every possibility for miscommunication or cultural insult. Policing in a multicultural society, however, requires a humanistic approach through which differences are understood and accommodated rather than viewed as cause for conflict. Opponents of COPPS may believe that adding a multicultural focus will soften an allegedly already soft approach to crime prevention; however, not understanding cultural differences can and does result in officer or citizen injury as well as disorder and death.[45]

SUMMARY

This chapter focused on the often-fractured relations that have historically come between the police and the minority communities they serve. Ours is not a perfect world. The Constitution notwithstanding, people are *not* created equal, at least with respect to legal, social, political, and economic opportunities. This disparity creates confrontations, mistrust, and enmity between many citizens and the police.

As more studies point to systematic racism within our criminal justice system, the police must work even harder to heal the wounds of the past and to eliminate any vestiges of bias-based policing and vigorously pursue those who would commit hate crimes.

Policing also needs more women and minorities who are willing to assist as citizens or as police officers to join the cause as well as more culturally informed police training.

For these reasons, COPPS offers hope for improvement because this strategy fosters a partnership that is based on trust, communication, and understanding.

■ ITEMS FOR REVIEW

1. Explain the historical background of police-minority relations.
2. Review whether or not the criminal justice system discriminates against minorities.
3. Define what is meant by racial profiling (or bias-based policing), and explain why it is a destructive practice.
4. Define what constitutes hate crimes, and discuss what the police can do to address them.
5. Explain how COPPS can assist in improving police-minority relations.
6. Describe some of the cultural customs of people of different nationalities, and discuss why it is important for the police to be aware of those difference customs.

◆ NOTES

1. 347 U.S. 483 (1954).
2. Anthony M. Platt (ed.), *The Politics of Riot Commissions* (New York: Collier Books, 1971).
3. *Ibid.*, p. 272.
4. See, for example, Allen D. Grimshaw, *Racial Violence in the United States* (Chicago: Aldine, 1969), pp. 269–298; *Report of the National Advisory Commission on Civil Disorders* (New York: Bantam Books, 1968).
5. Steven M. Cox and Jack D. Fitzgerald, *Police in Community Relations: Critical Issues* (2nd ed.) (Dubuque, Iowa: William C. Brown, 1992), p. 129.
6. Samuel Walker, *The Police in America: An Introduction* (2nd ed.) (New York: McGraw-Hill, 1993), p. 224.
7. National Academy of Sciences, *A Common Déstiny: Blacks and American Society* (Washington, D.C.: National Academy Press, 1989), p. 453.
8. Joan Petersilia, "Racial Disparities in the Criminal Justice System: Executive Summary of RAND Institute Study, 1983," in Daniel Georges-Abeyle

(ed.), *The Criminal Justice System and Blacks* (New York: Clark Boardman, 1984), pp. 225–258.

9. Greg Krikorian, "Study Questions Justice System's Racial Fairness," *Los Angeles Times,* February 13, 1996. http://www.pdxnorml.org/LAT.racial.fairness (Accessed April 28, 2003).

10. "Racial Gap in Sentences Growing—New Figures Show Blacks Jailed More," *San Francisco Chronicle,* February 13, 1996. http://www.pdxnorml.org/LAT.racial.fairness (Accessed April 28, 2003).

11. Leadership Conference on Civil Rights, "Justice on Trial: Racial Disparities in the American Criminal Justice System," http://www.civilright.org/publications/reports/cj/ (Accessed April 28, 2003).

12. *Ibid.*

13. *Ibid.*

14. Scott Bittle and Jean Johnson, "Since Sept. 11: Racial Profiling of Arabs and Muslims," http://www.publicagenda.org/specials/terrorism/terror_pubopinion6.htm (Accessed April 28, 2003).

15. Lorie A. Fridell, *Racially Biased Policing: Guidance for Analyzing Race Data from Vehicle Stops—Executive Summary* (Washington, D.C.: Police Executive Research Forum and Office of Community Oriented Policing Services, 2005), p. 1.

16. Lorie Fridell, Robert Lunney, Drew Diamond, and Bruce Kubu, *Racially Based Policing: A Principled Response* (Washington, D.C.: Police Executive Research Forum, 2001), pp. 6–9.

17. G. Voegtlin, "Bias-Based Policing and Data Collection," *The Police Chief* (October 2001):8.

18. International Association of Chiefs of Police, *Responding to Hate Crimes: A Police Officer's Guide to Investigation and Prevention* (Arlington, Va.: Author, 2000), p. 27.

19. Michael Lieberman, "Responding to Hate Crimes," in *Community Policing Exchange* (Washington, D.C.: Community Policing Consortium, January/February 2000), p. 3.

20. Anti-Defamation League, "ADL Welcomes Release of FBI 2004 Hate Crimes Statistics," http://www.adl.org/PresRele/HatCr_51/4811_52.htm (Accessed April 11, 2006).

21. Federal Bureau of Investigation Press Release, "FBI Releases Hate Crimes Statistics," http://www.fbi.gov/pressrel/pressrel05/hatecrime111405.htm (Accessed April 11, 2006).

22. International Association of Chiefs of Police, "Responding to Hate Crimes: A Police Officer's Guide to Investigation and Prevention," http://www.theiacp.org/documents (Accessed April 28, 2003).

23. Madison, Wisconsin, Police Department, "Special Programs: ADL and Police Launch Statewide Effort to Fight Hate Crimes," http://www.madisonct.org/pdspcprog.htm (Accessed April 28, 2003).

24. A. C. Germann, Frank D. Day, and Robert R. J. Gallati, *Introduction to Law Enforcement and Criminal Justice* (Springfield, Ill.: Charles C Thomas, 1976), p. 241.

25. James Baldwin, *Nobody Knows My Name* (New York: Dial Press, 1961), p. 65.

26. Sharon K. Papa, "L.A. Brass Listens to the Forums," *Community Links* (March 2002):14.

27. Alan Caddell, "Citizen Academy: Hands-On Classes Stress Challenges, Responsibilities of Real Thing," *Community Links* (August 2002):1–2.

28. Matthew Zolvinski, "Police Help Kids to Roam," *Community Links* (March 2002):6–7.

29. "Lincoln Police Department Community Policing Projects," http://www.ci.lincoln.ne.us/city/police/pdf/cbpprog.html (Accessed April 28, 2003).

30. U.S. Department of Justice, Office of Community Oriented Policing Services, "COPS Fact Sheet: Regional Community Policing Institutes," http://www.cops.usdoj.gov (Accessed April 28, 2003).

31. Quoted in Patricia A. Parker, "Tackling Unfinished Business," *Police* (December 1991):19, 84.

32. Gayle Fisher-Stewart, "Multicultural Training for Police," *MIS Report* 26 (9) (1994):7.

33. *Ibid.*, p. 4.

34. *Ibid.*, p. 5.

35. Gary Weaver, "Law Enforcement in a Culturally Diverse Society," *FBI Law Enforcement Bulletin* 61 (September 1992):1–7.

36. *Ibid.*

37. Pamela D. Mayhall, *Police-Community Relations and the Administration of Justice* (3rd ed.) (Englewood Cliffs, N.J.: Prentice Hall, 1985), pp. 308–309.

38. *Ibid.*, pp. 312–313.

39. Ken Peak and Jack Spencer, "Crime in Indian Country: Another 'Trail of Tears,'" *Journal of Criminal Justice* 15 (1987):485–494.

40. Mayhall, *Police-Community Relations,* p. 6.

41. Jeanne McDowell, "Are Women Better Cops?" *Time* (February 17, 1992):70.

42. Fisher-Stewart, "Multicultural Training for Police," p. 8.

43. Adapted from Robert M. Shusta, Deena R. Levine, Philip R. Harris, and Herbert Z. Wong, *Multicultural Law Enforcement: Strategies for Peacekeeping in a Diverse Society* (Englewood Cliffs, N.J.: Prentice Hall, 1995), pp. 21–22.

44. *Ibid.*, p. 22.

45. Fisher-Stewart, "Multicultural Training for Police," p. 4.

COPPS on the Beat

Drugs, Gangs, and Youth Crimes

Key Terms and Concepts

Bullying

Clandestine drug lab

Gang

Graffiti

Hazardous materials (HAZMAT)

Intervention

Methamphetamine initiative

Office of Community Oriented
   Policing Services (COPS)

Open-air drug market

Raves

Suppression

Underage drinking

Youth crime

Learning Objectives

As a result of reading this chapter, the student will:

- Be aware of what COPPS can do to meet the challenges posed by the drug problem in America, including methamphetamine, clandestine drug labs, open-air drug markets, and rave parties
- Know how gangs and graffiti affect our quality of life, as well as some COPPS efforts toward identification, prevention, and suppression
- Understand how COPPS is addressing the problem of youth crime, including gun violence, disorderly conduct in public places, underage drinking, and school violence and bullying

A team is where a boy can prove his courage on his own. A gang is where a coward goes to hide.

—Branch Rickey

Drug misuse is not a disease, it is a decision, like the decision to step out in front of a moving car. You would call that not a disease but an error of judgment.

—Philip K. Dick

INTRODUCTION

How does community oriented policing and problem solving (COPPS) function in practice? While the preceding chapters have traced the origin, preparation, and methods of community policing and problem solving, this chapter (as well as the next chapter) demonstrates its practical application with a variety of problems of crime and disorder. It is quite necessary that we do so, for indeed the litmus test for COPPS is the degree to which it succeeds in our communities and neighborhoods. Included are several examples of this strategy's approaches and accomplishments.

This chapter focuses on three broad areas that are particularly troublesome or challenging for today's society. First we examine the problem of drug violations, including methamphetamine, clandestine drug labs, open-air drug dealing, and raves. Then we look at the entwined problems of gangs and graffiti. Finally, we consider problems involving our youth, which includes violence, use of firearms, disorderly behavior in public places, underage drinking, and school violence and bullying.

Emphasis for each of the areas is placed on describing the nature of the problem, the extent and nature of its effects on society, and several responses that have been used by the police for coping with the problem. A number of examples and exhibits demonstrate how police agencies and other stakeholders collaborate to take back their neighborhoods.

The success of these strategies, however, remains predicated on the police having laid the groundwork well: knowing what is going on in their beats, and using the S.A.R.A. (scanning, analysis, response, assessment) process (discussed in Chapter 3).

OUR NATION'S NIGHTMARE: DRUGS

Societal Conundrum

That the United States is in the throes of a grave drug problem is beyond doubt. About 1.75 million U.S. citizens are arrested for drug abuse violations per year.[1] That amount reflects only the tip of the iceberg in comparison to the actual levels of manufacturing, use, and trafficking. The social costs of drug abuse are inestimable; however, we know that drug violations have eroded the environment, created undesirable role models for many youth, given rise to a wide variety of related criminal acts, and resulted in innumerable gun-wielding gang members across the United States who are fighting to expand their turf.

Alcohol and drugs together are also major factors in crime and violence, with almost four in ten violent crimes involving alcohol. Half of convicted jail inmates were under the influence of drugs or alcohol at the time of the offense, and three out of every four convicted jail inmates were alcohol- or drug-involved at the time of their current offense.[2]

Drugs are clearly related to criminality in multiple ways. Most directly, it is a crime to use, possess, manufacture, or distribute drugs classified as having a potential for abuse. But drugs are also related to crime through the effects they have on the user's behavior and by the violence and other illegal activity in connection with drug trafficking they generate. Now methamphetamine has exploded onto the scene, with more than 12 million people age 12 and older reporting that they have used this relatively cheap, easy-to-make drug at least once in their lifetime.[3]

Methamphetamine Initiatives

Methamphetamine (meth) is a central nervous system stimulant often referred to as crack, speed, ice, or crystal. Developed in clandestine laboratories often located in remote areas, meth is cheap and addictive. Its negative effects can include physical addiction, psychotic behavioral episodes, and brain damage; chronic use can cause anxiety, confusion, insomnia, paranoia, and delusions. It is a serious health hazard to anyone who comes in contact with the precursor drugs used to produce it; they include police, medical, and fire personnel. Although meth use is a serious problem across the nation, it has been particularly prevalent in the West and Midwest.[4]

Since 1998, the federal **Office of Community Oriented Policing Services (COPS)** has invested more than $385 million nationwide to combat the spread of meth, supporting training, enforcement, and lab cleanup activities.[5] Indeed, training police officers in lab identification and removal

Operation Seaload, a joint effort of the NYPD, FBI, and U.S. Customs, ended with the seizure of 9.5 tons of marijuana and numerous arrests.

Courtesy NYPD Photo Unit.

is an important first step in any **methamphetamine initiative.** Training public works and hotel/motel staff is also successful in helping to identify meth lab operations. Drug courts are a beneficial option for the criminal justice system because they immediately expose meth-addicted individuals to treatment and provide them with a rigid structure with little tolerance for infractions. Another major part of meth initiatives involves establishing the partnerships that are essential for addressing the problem, such as those developed with prosecutors' offices, environmental protection agencies, agencies involved in cleaning up hazardous materials, child welfare and family services agencies, treatment centers, and federal drug enforcement agencies.[6]

Exhibit 11–1 shows some successful initiatives that have been undertaken in several communities to address their growing meth problem; note the commonalities of the approaches: reliance on training and assistance of outside agencies.

 EXHIBIT 11–1

What Works: Going After Meth

- *Oklahoma City, Oklahoma.* The Oklahoma City Police Department focused on increased enforcement and training as well as a partnership with a drug court to deal with meth problems. Officers used undercover buys, confidential informants, surveillance, and assistance from patrol officers making traffic stops to apprehend meth users and distributors. A 70 percent increase in meth labs seized occurred in the first year of the initiative. City-wide citizen training in meth use and identification was conducted; part of this training was focused on hotel/motel associations and natural gas employees—the latter responding to over 600,000 service calls in the city and having widespread and frequent access to properties and the potential for identifying lab locations.

- *Little Rock, Arkansas.* The police in Little Rock also focused on increased enforcement and training of all officers regarding meth identification and response. Other approaches included establishing a telephone hotline for citizens to call if they suspected meth activity, an information campaign for retailers of precursor chemicals (including giving the police license plate numbers of purchasers of large quantities), and interviews with jail detainees regarding meth use and manufacturing to better understand the meth market.

- *Salt Lake City, Utah.* The Salt Lake City Police Department used enhanced enforcement and prosecution, child endangerment laws, civil remedies to reduce neighborhood impacts, public awareness campaigns, and formation of a meth training team. More than 30 city, county, and federal agencies participated.

- *Minneapolis, Minnesota.* The police in Minneapolis first engaged in comprehensive data collection to obtain information about the extent and nature of the meth problem. Interviews with probationers and drug court clients were conducted (and confirmed police suspicions that meth users were more likely to be white and employed). The department also developed general training videos on lab identification and identification at traffic stops, and it trained community groups, police officers, and transit, housing, sanitation, and park employees who might come in contact with clandestine meth labs.

Source: U.S. Department of Justice, Office of Community Oriented Policing Services, *Combating Methamphetamine Laboratories and Abuse: Strategies for Success* (Washington, D.C.: Author, August 2003), pp. 7–9.

Clandestine Drug Labs

A problem that is closely related to meth manufacturing and sales is the clandestine drug labs (meth accounts for 80 to 90 percent of the labs' total drug production). Dealing with **clandestine drug labs** requires extraordinarily high levels of technical expertise. Responders must understand illicit drug chemistry—how to neutralize the risk of explosions, fires, fumes, and burns, and how to handle and dispose of **hazardous materials (HAZMAT).** They must also know the federal, state, and local laws governing chemical manufacturing and distribution, HAZMAT, and occupational safety. They must collaborate with fire officials, HAZMAT experts, chemists, public health officials, and social service providers.[7]

Cleaning up clandestine drug labs is an enormously complex, time-consuming, and costly undertaking. Seizing a lab potentially makes a police agency liable for some of the costs of cleaning up on-site hazardous materials. If the lab is in operation when found, it must first be safely neutralized so that it does not contaminate the environment; then the materials must be cleaned up and safely disposed of. The average cost of cleaning up these materials ranges from $2,500 to $10,000.[8]

Police responses to the problem of these drug labs involve much more than merely finding and seizing the small "mom and pop" labs, because they are so easy to set up that it seems impossible to find all or even most of them. Other responses include the following[9]:

- Using federal and state organized crime and racketeering statutes for dismantling more sophisticated "super labs," run by syndicates
- Searching the homes and vehicles of former lab operators who are on probation and parole regularly to determine if they have resumed operating a lab
- Seizing and filing for forfeiture of clandestine drug lab operators' assets (although this strategy is probably not effective with smaller labs)
- Enforcing environmental protection laws because the burden of proof under these laws is typically less than that required for criminal convictions
- Filing civil actions against persons who allow their properties to be used as clandestine drug labs as well as filing nuisance abatement actions and eviction actions
- Monitoring the sale and distribution of essential and precursor chemicals used in such labs, widely considered to be one of the most effective responses (although doing so requires effort at the local, state, national, and international levels)

Open-Air Drug Markets

Open-air drug markets represent the lowest level of the drug distribution network. These low-level markets need to be addressed, however, because of the risks that are posed to market participants and the harms that drug use can inflict on the entire community.

Open-air markets have several advantages for both buyers and sellers. Buyers know where to go in order to obtain the drugs they want and can weigh quality against price, and sellers are able to maximize customer access. Open-air markets also generate or contribute to a wide range of problems and disorder in the community, including traffic congestion, noise, disorderly conduct, loitering, prostitution, robbery, burglary, theft from motor vehicles, fencing of stolen goods, weapons offenses, assaults, and clandestine drug labs (discussed above).[10]

Dealing with open-air drug markets presents a considerable challenge for the police. Simply arresting market participants will have little impact in reducing the size of the market or the amount of drugs consumed. However, the nature of open markets means that market participants are vulnerable both to police enforcement and to dangers of buying from strangers, which may include rip-offs and robberies.

Whichever approach the police choose, it is unlikely that they will be able to eradicate open-air drug markets completely; furthermore, a police crackdown or sweep will be a deterrent only if appropriate sentencing is used. Following are some activities the police have engaged in[11]:

- *Policing the area in a highly visible fashion.* Visible policing (including foot patrol) may disrupt the drug market and make it inconvenient for sellers and buyers to engage in drug transactions.
- *Enforcing the law intensively.* The effect of such a crackdown is dependent on the drug market that is targeted and the amount of resources available. Methods include street surveillance and intelligence gathering, hotline for area residents, and increases in drug treatment services.
- *Using intelligence-led investigative work.* Information from drug hotlines and local residents can help to identify and analyze a problem. In addition, an arrest may produce information if officers debrief the offender, and drug buyers may lead undercover officers to drug locations.
- *Arresting drug buyers in "reverse stings."* This response serves to impact the demand side of the market and is most successful against new or occasional drug users. Police in Miami, Florida, found that the process of being arrested, charged, and forced to appear in court and having a vehicle impounded acted as a deterrent.

Exhibit 11–2 provides an example of COPPS strategies against open-air drug markets and residential drug dealing in Delray, Florida.

Raves

A serious problem that can involve serious drug abuse are **raves**—dance parties that feature fast-paced, repetitive electronic music and light shows. Drug use is intended to enhance ravers' sensations and boost their energy so that they can dance for long periods, usually starting late at night and going into the morning hours. Rave party problems are unique. They blend attitudes, drugs, and behaviors not found in other forms of youth culture. Dealing with raves is difficult for police. On the one hand, police often face pressure from society to put an end to raves, but on the other hand, raves are enormously popular among teenagers and adults,

◆ EXHIBIT 11–2

A Drug Problem in Delray, Florida

Delray Beach, Florida, experienced a drug problem that involved a variety of police tactics for resolution. A convenience store (Mario's Market) had been a problem for 20 years, generating hundreds of calls for service for robberies and drug dealing because 30 to 40 drug dealers, users, and robbers hung around the neighborhood. A nearby drug house contributed to the problem, and a T-shaped alley behind the store provided easy ingress and egress for buyers, both on foot and in vehicles. The lighting was poor, and pay phones in the store's front area were constantly used by traffickers. Officers began walking a beat in the area, made videos of the dealing, and made drug buys in the market. They contacted the owner of the drug house near Mario's, but the owner cared little about the problem. Officers initiated a nuisance-abatement suit against the house. They asked the utility company to install bulletproof security lights around and behind the market, and they erected barriers to prevent vehicles from entering and exiting the alleys. Mario agreed to install a chain-link fence behind the property. The drug dealing decreased because several dealers were sent to prison and others moved out. When dealers began scaling the chain-link fence, officers smeared axle grease on it ("Even drug dealers don't want to get their clothes dirty," an officer commented), slowing drug activity even further. Next, officers offered to paint the market, using paint purchased by Mario and the assistance of probationers. To ward off any remaining dealers, the officers installed a fake video camera at the market's entryway. Annual calls for service declined from more than 100 to 10, thus drastically improving this 20-year-old problem.

Source: Rana Sampson and Michael S. Scott, *Tackling Crime and Other Public Safety Problems: Case Studies in Problem Solving* (Washington, D.C.: U.S. Department of Justice, Office of Community Policing Services, 2000), pp. 23–26.

most of whom are law-abiding and responsible.[12] In addition, raves pose a number of concerns for police, including drug overdoses, drug trafficking, noise, driving under the influence, and traffic control. Of particular concern is that evidence suggests the drug most closely associated with rave parties—ecstasy (also known as MDMA, or "Eve")—can cause permanent brain damage when used habitually.

In order to understand the extent of the local rave problem, police should conduct an analysis that answers a number of questions concerning rave incidents, locations, and management. Some police responses that have met with success include regulating rave venues to ensure basic health and safety measures are in use, encouraging property owners to exercise control over raves, prohibiting juveniles and adults from being admitted to the same raves, applying nuisance abatement laws where appropriate, prosecuting rave operators and property owners for drug-related offenses, and educating ravers about the risks of drug use and overexertion.[13]

Summary

COPPS has wide applications to the problem of drugs. The traditional police approach to a citizen's call about suspected drug activity—showing up, taking a report, and leaving the area or perhaps making a misdemeanor arrest—is neither effective for the long term nor welcomed by COPPS; little analysis or measurement of results would occur under that approach.

Conversely, while a COPPS officer might also use a short-term response (such as an arrest), there would also be an analytical assessment of the situation to determine why the area was the scene of almost constant drug activity: What is the calls for service (CFS) pattern for the location? Are the arrestees youths who are truant from school? When is the activity occurring? Is lighting inadequate? Are grounds littered and vandalized? Are vacant apartments available to foster drug activity? Do abandoned vehicles provide convenient places for drug stashes? The S.A.R.A. process would likely be applied, with follow-up monitoring of the situation. We will examine some COPPS initiatives in jurisdictions that were not content with the traditional approach.

GANGS AND GRAFFITI

Gangs

Gangs have obviously been known to be a significant problem in this nation for several decades. What may not be so well known, however, is that the age range of gang members is broadening and becoming younger. The typical age range of gang members is about 14 to 24; youngsters generally begin hanging out with gangs at 12 or 13 years of age, join the gang at 13 or 14, and are first arrested at 14.[14] Furthermore, they have spread into rural areas. Also, the line between prison and street gangs is becoming muddled as gang members flow in and out of the correctional system.[15]

Gangs proliferate as well. According to estimates by the National Criminal Justice Reference Service, there are more than 24,500 gangs and more than 772,000 gang members in more than 3,300 jurisdictions in the United States. Nearly half of all gang members (48 percent) are African American youth, whereas Hispanic youngsters account for 43 percent and Asians total 5 percent.[16]

Street gangs can have a significantly damaging effect on a community. Gangs play a role in firearms transactions and violence, drug sales and use, home invasions, car thefts, homicides, and a number of other crime problems.

For COPPS activities, the police agencies must attempt a problem analysis of the involved street gangs. This is particularly important because no "cookie-cutter" approach will work; gangs are unique phenomena, particular to time and place. Failing to undertake a problem analysis of the crime problems at hand and the general gang landscape will likely result in a futile response strategy.[17]

The options available to the police when attempting to address a street gang problem(s) cover a wide spectrum with regard to both goals and

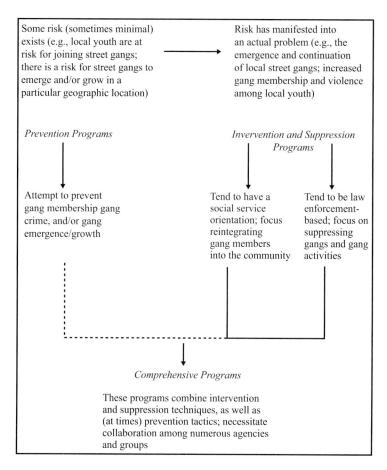

FIGURE 11–1

A Schematic of Prevention, Intervention, Suppression, and Comprehensive Programs

Source: Jean M. McGloin, *Street Gangs and Interventions: Innovative Problem Solving with Network Analysis* (Washington, D.C.: U.S. Department of Justice, Office of Community Oriented Policing Services, 2005), p. 3.

tactics (see Figure 11–1). Four programs represent the range of activities that exists for this purpose—prevention, intervention, suppression, and comprehensive strategies:

1. Prevention programs have the broadest audience of interest and are typically aimed at groups that pose some risk or, more broadly, at general populations. For example, a prevention program may focus on preschool children who reside in gang neighborhoods before they show any symptoms of having joined the gang life. Perhaps the best known of these programs is Gang Resistance Education and Training (G.R.E.A.T.). Although evaluation results of G.R.E.A.T. show no long-term impact on gang membership or delinquent behavior, they suggest positive short-term effects on gang-related behavior and attitudes.[18]

2. **Intervention** typically addresses individuals or places that have manifested some problem. In most cases, such intervention programs attempt to persuade gang members or gang-affiliated youth to abandon their current lifestyle or to reduce gang-related crime. At this stage, defining the type of gang of interest, the level of individual involvement in the gang, and the specific problem of focus becomes extremely important and integral to any success. Interventions may include a gang truce or the use of nonmembers to persuade gang members to leave gang life.

EXHIBIT 11–3

"Designing Out" Gangs

"Designing out" gang homicides and street assaults has been successful in Los Angeles. When a systematic pattern of opportunity was found—that the majority of drive-by shootings and violent gang encounters occurred in clusters on the periphery of neighborhoods linked to major thoroughfares—police closed all major roads leading to and from the identified hot spots by placing cement freeway dividers at the ends of streets that led directly to these roads. An evaluation determined that blocking opportunities reduced homicides and street assaults significantly and that crime was not displaced to other areas.

Source: James Lasley, *"Designing Out" Gang Homicides and Street Assaults* (Washington, D.C.: U.S. Department of Justice, National Institute of Justice Research in Brief, November 1998), pp. 1–4.

3. **Suppression** also has the aim of reducing gang activities, but suppression programs typically rely on the law as a guide and on criminal justice agencies as the primary (and often only) partners. Deterrence principles often include law enforcement task forces or units and sentencing enhancements. Their success hinges on developing a plan based on a problem analysis to understand the gang problem in the jurisdiction. When operating alone, however, suppression tactics are rarely successful in the long term. Even if a program appears successful in the short term, gangs tend to endure because the police can rarely eradicate them completely, nor do they have the resources to sustain such an intensive focus over time and across all gangs and gang members. In addition, crime may simply be displaced. Suppression tactics are important but appear to provide the most benefit when part of a larger comprehensive program.[19] (An example of a suppression tactic is shown in Exhibit 11–3.)

4. Comprehensive programs typically involve collaboration and include prevention, intervention, and suppression techniques and hinge on the collective work of a variety of agencies, from criminal justice to social service to mental health to faith-based groups. Though they often require intensive resources and time, such programs appear to have the most promise in areas that have an array of problems surrounding a gang problem and fit well within an existing COPPS philosophy. In addition, should a particular gang pose numerous problems, such as intense gang recruitment in schools, drug sales, and gang-related homicides, it may require a variety of techniques and partners to address the issues. Perhaps the best known comprehensive program is Boston's Operation Ceasefire (described in Exhibit 11–4).

Graffiti

A problem that is related to, and arises from gangs involves **graffiti,** which is another social harm that is associated with gangs (harms were discussed in Chapter 3). In addition to its being unsightly and being a general source

EXHIBIT 11–4

Boston's Operation Ceasefire

An innovative and successful gun project, Boston's Operation Ceasefire began as an attempt to address a dramatic increase in local youth violence, from 22 victims in 1987 to 73 victims in 1990. The partnerships that formed the base of this strategy included local, state, and federal criminal justice agencies (police, prosecution, probation) as well as social service agencies, academic researchers, and community groups. After an in-depth analysis of data, the project selected a strategy of focused deterrence that combined suppressive and social intervention techniques. In combination with a focus on shutting down the city's illegal firearms trafficking, a tactic of "pulling levers" was used. When a gang used violence, the relevant partners would pull every potential criminal justice sanction "lever" for that particular gang. At the same time, social services were made available to gang members to support an alternative to life in the gang. The operation resulted in declines in youth homicides, firearm assaults, and shots-fired CFS. Specifically, the gangs' drug market was disrupted, arrests were made for outstanding warrants, probation was strictly enforced, and federal sanctions were used. These penalties were borne by the whole gang, not just the shooter, and would be deployed within days of a violent event. Communicating regularly to the gangs served a number of purposes: to ensure that members knew of the new policy and to tell other gangs; to make cause and effect clear (e.g., that a particular drug raid was but a means to an end and was not about drugs but a penalty for violence); and to allow the creation of a fundamental balance of power between the authorities.

Source: David Kennedy, *Pulling the Levers: Getting Deterrence Right* (Washington, D.C.: National Institute of Justice Journal, July 1998), p. 6.

of irritation, graffiti depreciates property values, adds to the deterioration of neighborhoods, and contributes to economic and urban blight.

In the United States, the annual cost of graffiti is estimated to be between $10 and $12 billion. In New York City alone, the average cost of removing graffitti has increased from $300,000 to about $10 million. In a ten-year period, Los Angeles removed 162 million square feet of graffiti. A graffiti removal worker painting over a wall was fatally shot in Los Angeles in June 2004 by a man who police believe was angry because his gang's tags were being covered.[20]

Like New York and Los Angeles, most cities fight graffiti with their paintbrushes by quickly dispatching work crews to put on a fresh coat of paint over tagger or gang scribblings. Some experts, however, advocate photographing and filing graffiti markings because they represent actual communication and can be a valuable source of intelligence.

Five types of graffiti communication have been identified by researchers:

1. *Publicity.* Publicity graffiti (47 percent) is the most frequently found form and contains the name or abbreviation of the gang but does not include a threat and does not mark territory.
2. *Roll call.* Roll call graffiti (26 percent) identifies the gang name and a list of gang monikers (member nicknames).

Youths remove graffiti from a public wall.

Courtesy Washoe County, Nevada, Sheriff's Office.

3. *Territorial.* Territorial graffiti (17 percent) is identified by some sort of marking of a gang's territory, often in the form of an arrow pointing down.
4. *Threatening.* Threatening graffiti (9 percent) contains some sort of message aimed at a rival gang or perhaps at the police. It can include one gang crossing out another gang's graffiti.
5. *Sympathetic.* Sympathetic graffiti, the least observed form of graffiti (1 percent), is used to honor a slain gang member, usually in the form of an RIP (rest in peace).[21]

To combat the problem, some cities have enacted ordinances that require property owners to remove graffiti within a specified period of time. For example, in St. Petersburg, Florida, business owners are required to remove graffiti within 48 hours; in other areas, the city will paint over the graffiti for a set fee, usually $50 to $75. Box 11–1 shows an example of an antigraffiti ordinance.

The police must endeavor to eradicate the graffiti problem in order to diminish the gangs' sense of territory, improve the appearance of neighborhoods, and make a community statement that gang-type activities will not be tolerated. Following are some means by which the police and the public can attempt to reduce the rewards for and increase the detection of those who spread graffiti[22]:

- Detect graffiti rapidly and routinely (by monitoring graffiti-prone locations and increasing reporting).
- Remove graffiti rapidly.
- Increase natural observation of graffiti-prone locations through use of police, security personnel, and citizens.

BOX 11–1

Example of a Municipal Antigraffiti Ordinance

WHEREAS, property defaced by gang members is an act of vandalism and is against the law; and

WHEREAS, gang graffiti constitutes a public nuisance that causes depreciation of the value of the defaced property and the surrounding property and contributes to the deterioration of the neighborhood and the City in general; and

WHEREAS, depreciation of property values and deterioration of neighborhoods lead to economic blight and an increase in criminal activity and are injurious to the public health, safety, morals, and general welfare,

NOW, THEREFORE, BE IT ORDAINED BY THE CITY COUNCIL OF THE CITY OF LAKEWOOD, COLORADO, THAT:

9.85.060 NOTIFICATION OF NUISANCE. (a) The owner of any property defaced by gang graffiti shall be given written notice to abate the public nuisance on his property by removal within five (5) days after service of the notice. Such notice shall be by personal service to the owner or by posting the notice on the defaced property together with written notice mailed to the owner by first-class mail. The notice to the property owner shall contain:

1. The location of and a description of the violation;
2. A demand that the owner remove or eradicate the gang graffiti from the property within five (5) days after service of the notice;
3. A statement that the owner's failure or refusal to remove or eradicate the gang graffiti may result in abatement by the City;
4. A statement that if the costs of abatement plus the $75 fee for inspection and incidental costs are not paid to the City within 30 days after notice, an additional $75 will be assessed for administrative and other incidental costs.

Source: Adapted from the Antigraffiti Ordinance of Lakewood, Colorado, 0-91-29, Title 9, Article 85, Chapter 9.85.

- Conduct publicity campaigns combined with beautification efforts and cleanup days.
- Control access to (and vandal-proof) prone locations, using dark or textured surfaces and special products that are resistant to graffiti and are easy to clean.
- Focus on chronic offenders.

YOUTH CRIMES

Extent of the Problem

As any police officer or criminologist knows, crime is a young person's enterprise. Nearly half (46.3 percent) of all persons arrested in the United States are under the age of 24; more than one-fourth (26.2 percent) are under 19.[23] **Youth crime** remains one of the nation's most serious problems, particularly as gang activity continues to spread (discussed above).

During a recent ten-year period, juveniles ages 12–14 and 15–17 experienced average annual rates of nonfatal violence that were about 2.5 times higher than the rate for adults. Furthermore, four in five victims of nonfatal violent crime, ages 12–14, perceived the offender to be a juvenile.[24]

News accounts of serious crimes committed by children and adolescents have encouraged a general belief that young people are increasingly violent and uncontrollable and that the response of the juvenile justice system has been inadequate. Most states have enacted laws that make the juvenile system more punitive and that allow younger children and adolescents to be transferred to the adult system for a greater variety of offenses and in a greater variety of ways. Indeed, at 645 per 100,000, the U.S. incarceration rate of juveniles is second only to that of Russia (at 685 per 100,000 population).[25]

Next we briefly consider several significant problems involving young offenders: gun violence, disorderly youth in public places, underage drinking, and school violence and bullying.

Gun Violence

Although overall U.S. homicide rates declined between the 1980s and 1990s, youth violence, particularly gun homicide, began increasing dramatically. In urban areas, gun violence takes a particularly heavy toll, especially as large numbers of young minority males are killed and injured. Research has also linked urban youth gun violence to the gang conflicts and drug markets (discussed above) as well as gun availability.[26]

The numbers speak loudly about the violent nature of our youth. Homicide offending rates for teenagers and young adults increased dramatically in the late 1980s while rates for older age groups declined; 18- to 24-year-olds have historically had the highest homicide offending rates, and their rates nearly doubled from 1985 to 1993. Offending rates of 14- to 17-year-olds increased rapidly after 1985, surpassing the rates of 25- to 34-year-olds and 35- to 49-year-olds. Homicide offending rates for 25- to 34-year-olds fell from 1980 through 1999 but have increased since then.[27] Youth gun violence is also related to several other problems, including those of underage drinking and disorderly youth in public (discussed below).

As we mentioned earlier, perhaps the best-known comprehensive program for addressing the problem of guns and youth is the Boston's Operation Ceasefire, discussed in Exhibit 11–4, where enlisting community support, convening an interagency working group, involving researchers, developing an effective communication strategy, and having a focused deterrence strategy worked to address a problem involving gang homicides.

Disorderly Conduct in Public Places

Disorderly conduct by youth in public places constitutes one of the most common problems most police agencies must handle, particularly in suburban and rural communities. Disorderly youth are a common source of complaints from urban residents, merchants, and shoppers. Among the kinds of behaviors (some legal and some not) that are associated with youth disorderly conduct are loud music; cursing; blocking of pedestrians and traffic; alcohol, tobacco, and drug use; fighting; littering; vandalism; and graffiti.[28]

Police responses to this problem might include the following[29]:

- Creating alternative legitimate places and activities for youth (such as youth clubs, drop-in centers, and recreation centers) and employing youth at businesses negatively affected by disorderly behavior
- Encouraging youth to gather where they will not disturb others
- Reducing the comfort level, convenience, or attraction of popular gathering places (such as eliminating places to sit or lean, changing the background music)
- Installing and monitoring closed-circuit television cameras
- Establishing and enforcing rules of conduct
- Denying youths anonymity (getting to know the names and faces of young people without being antagonistic or accusatory)

Underage Drinking

As with the statistics provided above for other problems discussed in this chapter, the numbers concerning **underage drinking** unfortunately are not getting better. The average age when youth first try alcohol is 11 years for boys and 13 years for girls. The average age at which Americans begin drinking regularly is 15.9 years old; adolescents who begin drinking before age 15 are four times more likely to develop alcohol dependence than those who begin drinking at age 21. It has been estimated that over 3 million teenagers are out-and-out alcoholics; several million more have a serious drinking problem that they cannot manage on their own. Finally, of the three leading causes of death for 15- to 24-year-olds—automobile crashes, homicides, and suicides—alcohol is a leading factor in all three.[30]

Although underage drinking (alcohol consumption while under the age of 21) is prohibited throughout the nation, young people use alcohol more than any other drug, including tobacco. Many of the harms associated with underage drinking, such as traffic fatalities, driving under the influence, assaults, cruising, street racing, rave parties, disorderly conduct, acquaintance rape, vandalism, and noise complaints, arise from the overconfidence, recklessness, lack of awareness, aggression, and loss of control that often accompany alcohol abuse.[31] The pressure to drink—to experience as a rite of passage, to become part of a group, to reduce tension, or to forget their worries—also contributes heavily to this problem.[32]

Police have responded to the problem of underage drinking in the following ways[33]:

- *Reducing the community's overall alcohol consumption.* This may sound impossible to do, but some available means for doing so are discouraging price discounts on alcohol, restricting the hours or days retailers can sell alcohol, and limiting the number of alcohol outlets.

- *Using a comprehensive approach*. Addressing the motivations for drinking and drunken driving, targeting fake IDs, providing counseling or treatment about drinking patterns, enforcing minimum-age purchase laws, and conducting undercover "shoulder tap" operations (having an undercover, underage operative ask adult strangers outside a store to purchase alcohol) could be used in combination. Other options are to check IDs at bars and nightclubs, apply graduated sanctions to retailers that break the law, and require keg registration. The latter is primarily used to identify adults who provide alcohol to minors at large house parties or keg parties on college campuses; several states use keg registration to link information about those who purchase a keg to the keg itself. Developing house party guidelines and walk-through procedures and imposing fines for each underage person drinking at a party, are other possible methods.

School Violence and Bullying

School violence has been declining: From 1992 to 1999, there were 238 school-associated violent deaths (including the April 1999 massacre of 13 people at Columbine High School in Littleton, Colorado).[34] Yet school safety continues to be a concern and requires broad-based efforts; those efforts must involve students at an early age and must be reinforced throughout their education.[35] Several strategies have been suggested for police and citizens to help prevent school violence[36]:

- Publicizing the philosophy that a gang presence will not be tolerated, and institutionalizing a code of conduct
- Alerting students and parents about school rules and punishments for infractions
- Creating alternative schools for those students who cannot function in a regular classroom
- Training teachers, parents, and school staff to identify children who are most at risk for violent behavior
- Developing community initiatives focused on breaking family cycles of violence, and providing programs on parenting, conflict resolution, anger management, and recovery from substance abuse
- Establishing peer counseling in schools to give troubled youths the opportunity to talk to someone their own age

Many police agencies now use school resource officers (SROs) for safety planning efforts. SROs can assess the school structure to determine where potential problems exist and help to address the social environment by such means as explaining what illegal conduct is, employing surveys to measure safety and security concerns of students and staff, and identifying bullies.[37]

There is no single cause—or cure—for violence in the schools.

Courtesy Washoe County, Nevada, Sheriff's Office.

A long-standing school problem that may not be declining like school violence is **bullying.** Bullying has two key components: repeated harmful acts and an imbalance of power. It involves repeated physical, verbal, or psychological attacks on or intimidation of a victim who is defenseless because of having less size or strength or being outnumbered. Between 5 and 9 percent of students bully others with some regularity.[38]

To engage in problem solving regarding bullying, police should determine whether the school has a problem with it and how it is occurring, who the offenders are, how and where they are operating at the school, and who the victims are. Efforts should be made to increase student reporting of bullying; have trained supervisors monitor prone or less supervised areas; consider staggering recess, lunch, and release time; and encourage administrators to provide teachers with classroom management training, where necessary.[39] Exhibit 11–5 discusses an excellent use of the S.A.R.A. problem-solving process by SROs for addressing a bullying problem.

EXHIBIT 11–5

S.A.R.A. Fights Bullying in Ohio

Unchecked disorderly behavior of students in South Euclid, Ohio, led the school resource officer (SRO) to review school data regarding referrals to the principal's office. The SRO found that the high school reported thousands of referrals per year for bullying and the junior high school had experienced a 30 percent increase in such referrals; police data revealed that juvenile complaints about disturbances, bullying, and assaults after school had increased 90 percent in the past 10 years. In the analysis phase, a survey, interviews, and focus groups (with students, teachers, and guidance counselors) conducted by academics from Kent State University's Justice Studies department provided much more information, and a geographic information system mapped hot spots in the schools. The main findings pointed to four areas of concern: the environmental design of school areas, teachers' knowledge and response to the problem, parents' attitudes and responses, and students' perceptions and behaviors.

Responses involved the SRO's working closely with other stakeholders to form a planning team, to develop a new school policy on bullying, and to open a new substation within the school next to a hot spot. Environmental changes included modifying the school bell times and increasing teacher supervision of hot spots; counselors conducted teacher training courses in bullying prevention; parent education including mailings and information about bullying and explanation of new school policy. Finally, student education focused on classroom discussions and assemblies conducted by the SRO.

The assessment found that bullying incidents dropped 60 percent in the hallways and 80 percent in the gym area. Surveys indicated positive attitudinal changes among students about bullying, and greater confidence that teachers would take action.

Source: Police Executive Research Forum, *Excellence in Problem-Oriented Policing: The 2001 Herman Goldstein Award Winners* (Washington, D.C.: Author, 2002), pp. 55–56.

SUMMARY

This chapter has applied COPPS to the street, demonstrating how it works with several specific crimes and problems of disorder: drug violations, including use of methamphetamine, clandestine drug labs, open-air drug dealing, and rave parties; gangs and graffiti; and youth crimes, including gun violence, disorderly behavior in public places, underage drinking, and school violence and bullying. A number of exhibits and examples demonstrated the kinds of methods that the police are adopting to address these problems.

The efficacy of COPPS in dealing with these problems was convincingly demonstrated. The police agencies described in this chapter and their peers across the United States are realizing many successes, breaking with tradition and attacking the contributing or underlying problems while empowering neighborhoods to defend themselves against crime and deterioration.

We also emphasized that for each of the problem areas discussed, the success of COPPS strategies was highly dependent on the police having laid the groundwork—doing the kinds of preparatory work described in earlier chapters and understanding and properly applying the S.A.R.A. process discussed in Chapter 3.

ITEMS FOR REVIEW

1. Describe the kinds of strategies that may be employed under COPPS to meet the challenges posed by methamphetamine.
2. Review some of the methods used and the hazards faced by the police to identify, eliminate, and clean up clandestine drug labs.
3. Explain how open-air drug markets operate, what challenges they pose, and what COPPS efforts have done to meet those challenges.
4. Define rave parties, and discuss their related problems and some responses that have been used with raves by the police.
5. Explain how COPPS efforts are being directed toward the identification, prevention, and suppression of gangs, and provide an example of "designing out" gang activity.
6. Review the extent and purposes for which graffiti exists, some means by which the problem may be addressed, and how graffiti may be used for intelligence gathering.
7. Provide an overview of Boston's Operation Ceasefire, and explain why it is used as an excellent example of police effectively coping with gun violence.
8. Explain what the police can do about dealing with disorderly conduct by youth in public places.
9. Describe what can be done to address underage drinking.
10. Review some COPPS approaches to school violence and bullying.

NOTES

1. U.S. Department of Justice, Bureau of Justice Statistics, "Drug and Crime Facts," http://www.ojp.usdoj.gov/bjs/dcf/tables/arrtot.htm (Accessed April 28, 2006).
2. U.S. Department of Justice, Bureau of Justice Statistics, "Criminal Offender Statistics," http://www.ojp.usdoj.gov/bjs/crimoff.htm#child (Accessed February 27, 2006).
3. Office of National Drug Control Policy, http://www.whitehousedrugpolicy.gov/publications/factsht/methamph/#background (Accessed February 27, 2006).
4. U.S. Department of Justice, Office of Community Oriented Policing Services, *Combating Methamphetamine Laboratories and Abuse: Strategies for Success* (Washington, D.C.: Author, August 2003), pp. 1–2.

5. U.S. Department of Justice, Office of Community Oriented Policing Services, "Methamphetamine Initiative," http://www.cops.usdoj.gov/mime/open.pdf?Item=1356 (Accessed April 28, 2006).

6. U.S. Department of Justice, Office of Community Oriented Policing Services, *COPS Innovations: A Closer Look,* pp. 3–5.

7. Michael S. Scott, *Clandestine Drug Labs* (Washington, D.C.: U.S. Department of Justice, Office of Community Oriented Policing Services, 2002), p. 1.

8. *Ibid.,* pp. 14–15.

9. *Ibid.,* pp. 24–26.

10. Alex Harocopos and Mike Hough, *Drug Dealing in Open-Air Markets* (Washington, D.C.: U.S. Department of Justice, Office of Community Oriented Policing Services, January 2005), p. 1.

11. *Ibid.,* pp. 24–26.

12. Michael S. Scott, *Rave Parties* (Washington, D.C.: U.S. Department of Justice, Office of Community Oriented Policing Services, 2002), p 1.

13. *Ibid.,* pp. 1–2, 13–14.

14. C. Ronald Huff, *Comparing the Criminal Behavior of Youth Gangs and At-Risk Youths* (Washington, D.C.: National Institute of Justice Research in Brief, 1998).

15. Jean M. McGloin, *Street Gangs and Interventions: Innovative Problem Solving with Network Analysis* (Washington, D.C.: U.S. Department of Justice, Office of Community Oriented Policing Services, September 2005), p. 1.

16. U.S. Department of Justice, National Criminal Justice Reference Service, "In the Spotlight: Gang Resources," http://www.ncjrs.org/gangs/summary.html (Accessed May 27, 2003).

17. McGloin, *Street Gangs and Interventions,* p. 2.

18. *Ibid.,* p. 4.

19. *Ibid.,* pp. 4–6.

20. Douglas Page, "Taggers Beware: The Writing Is on the Wall," *Law Enforcement Technology* (September 2005):194, 196.

21. *Ibid.,* p. 196.

22. Deborah Lamm Weisel, *Graffiti* (Washington, D.C.: U.S. Department of Justice, Office of Community Oriented Policing Services, 2002).

23. U.S. Department of Justice, "Crime in the United States, 2004," http://www.fbi.gov/ucr/cius_04/persons_arrested/table_38-43.html (Accessed February 27, 2006).

24. U.S. Department of Justice, Bureau of Justice Statistics, *Juvenile Victimization and Offending, 1993–2003* (Washington, D.C.: Author, August 2005), p. 1.

25. Joan McCord, Cathy Spatz Widom, and Nancy A. Crowell (eds.), *Juvenile Crime, Juvenile Justice: Panel on Juvenile Crime, Prevention, Treatment, and Control* (Washington, D.C.: National Academy Press, 2001), p. 25.

26. Anthony A. Braga, *Gun Violence Among Serious Young Offenders* (Washington, D.C.: U.S. Department of Justice, Office of Community Oriented Policing Services, June 2003), pp. 1–2.

27. U.S. Department of Justice, Bureau of Justice Statistics, "Homicide Trends in the U.S.: Age Trends," http://www.ojp.usdoj.gov/bjs/homicide/teens.htm (Accessed April 28, 2006).

28. Michael S. Scott, *Disorderly Youth in Public Places* (Washington, D.C.: U.S. Department of Justice, Office of Community Oriented Policing Services, June 2002), pp. 2–5.

29. *Ibid.,* pp. 14–21.

30. Focus Adolescent Services, "Teen Drinking," http://www.focusas.com/Alcohol .html (Accessed April 28, 2006).

31. Kelly Dedel Johnson, *Underage Drinking* (Washington, D.C.: U.S. Department of Justice, Office of Community Oriented Policing Services, September 2004), pp. 1, 4.

32. *Ibid.,* p. 5.

33. *Ibid.,* pp. 23–39.

34. Gene Marlin and Barbara Vogt, "Violence in the Schools," *The Police Chief* (April 1999):169.

35. Ira Pollack and Carlos Sundermann, "Creating Safe Schools: A Comprehensive Approach," *Journal of the Office of Juvenile Justice and Delinquency Prevention* 8 (1) (June 2001):13–20.

36. Marlin and Vogt, "Violence in the Schools," p. 169.

37. Center for the Prevention of School Violence, "School Resource Officers and Safe School Planning," http://www.ncsu.edu/cpsv/srossp.htm (Accessed May 27, 2003).

38. Rana Sampson, *Bullying in Schools* (Washington, D.C.: U.S. Department of Justice, Office of Community Oriented Policing Services, March 2002), pp. 1–2.

39. *Ibid.*

More COPPS on the Beat

Selected Issues and Problems

Key Terms and Concepts _____

Crisis intervention team (CIT)
Cruising
Domestic violence
False alarm
Homelessness
Identity theft

Mental illness
Neighborhood disorder
911
Prostitution
Street racing

Learning Objectives _____

As a result of reading this chapter, the student will:

- Understand how identity theft is accomplished and some ways the police can attempt to prevent and address it
- Know the definition of mental illness and what kind of training is being developed to deal with it
- Be aware of homelessness and how the police can attempt to assist people with this problem
- Know what methods are available for dealing with domestic violence
- Realize the nature and extent of neighborhood disorder and ways COPPS can help
- Comprehend the problems surrounding prostitution and some means for addressing it
- Understand what the police can attempt to do with other selected problems, such as cruising, street racing, false alarms, misuse and abuse of 911, and computer crimes

> Destroying the life or safety of other people, through teasing, bullying, hitting or otherwise, "putting them down," is as destructive to themselves as to their victims.
>
> *—Lewis P. Lipsitt*

INTRODUCTION

The three major crime problems that were addressed in relation to community oriented policing and problem solving (COPPS) in Chapter 11—those involving drugs, gangs, and youth—can and do plague many Americans in their neighborhoods; however, other people's quality of life is just as affected by the kinds of issues and problems that are discussed in this chapter. In that sense, these are in no way lesser problems for those persons who are personally involved with or are being victimized by these situations.

In this chapter we consider the following: identity theft, the mentally ill, the homeless, domestic violence, rental property and neighborhood disorder, and prostitution. We also consider other selected problems that plague neighborhoods and communities: cruising, street racing, false alarms, misuse and abuse of 911, computer crimes.

As in Chapter 11, emphasis will be placed on the kinds of problem-solving responses that the police have developed for dealing with these issues and problems. Examples are provided in seven exhibits.

IDENTITY THEFT

A problem that is becoming more prevalent and challenging for the police is **identity theft.** A significant feature of identity theft is the offender uses repeated victimization of a single person, facilitated by crimes such as forgery, counterfeiting, check and credit card fraud, computer fraud, impersonation, pickpocketing, and even terrorism.[1] Identity theft became a federal crime in 1998 with passage of the Identity Theft Assumption and Deterrence Act.[2] Other related crimes might include financial crimes against the elderly, various telemarketing and Internet scams, thefts from autos, burglary, and even trafficking in human beings.[3]

Although the notoriety of identity theft arose with publicity on the dangers of buying and selling on the Internet, the ways offenders steal identities are often low-tech and include the following: obtaining a password or checking account by trickery; stealing wallets, purses, or mail; rummaging through residential trash cans; obtaining people's credit reports or other personal information; hacking into corporate computers and stealing customer databases; buying identities or false documents on the street; counterfeiting checks or credit or debit cards; stealing PINs and user IDs. Then, using the victim's name, the offenders can open new credit card, bank, or phone accounts; file for bankruptcy; take over the victim's insurance policies; take out loans or mortgages; and submit applications for Social Security payments.[4]

This is a complicated issue, and some of the risk factors and solutions will lie beyond the ability of the police to handle. Also, a number of federal and state laws bear on the subject; therefore, we are only giving minimal coverage to the problem. Following are six recommended police responses to identity theft[5]:

1. *Encouraging businesses' awareness of their responsibility to protect employee and client records.* Having a privacy policy, training employees, and limiting data collection and access to information needed and data disclosure are some approaches.

2. *Educating people about protecting their personal information.* Police can inform people that the Internet has an enormous amount of information about how to avoid becoming an identity theft victim, and they can tell people that the Federal Trade Commission's publications are excellent.

3. *Collaborating with government and other service organizations to protect private information.* It is important that the police work with agencies and businesses to keep Social Security numbers, birth certificates, and other such information out of general circulation; prohibit their sale; restrict access to such information; investigate identity theft cases; and help victims resolve problems.

4. *Working with local banks to encourage credit card issuers to adopt improved security practices.* Although major credit card companies have national reach, the police can work with local banks to establish procedures for local identity theft victims to repair the damage done and to get their accounts operating again. Credit card companies can also be pressured to put policies in place that include better identity verification for credit card usage, photographs on credit cards, identity verification, and passwords on credit accounts.

5. *Tracking delivery.* Much of identity theft involves the delivery of documents and products, and stolen merchandise is often delivered to vacant houses and mailboxes. Maintaining close relationships with local postal inspectors and delivery companies may help to track items back to the thieves.

6. *Preparing a plan to prevent or minimize the harm of identity theft.* When large identity databases have been breached and when such crimes are reported, the police must act quickly to reduce the time the thief has to use the stolen identities. Toll-free phone lines can be set up for victims to call the major credit bureaus to warn of the theft; employee training can be conducted when such breaches occur.

THE MENTALLY ILL

One of the saddest aspects of police work involves trying to help people who are mentally ill or unstable, many of whom suffer from paranoid schizophrenia, hallucinate, are solitary, engage in illegal activities, and/or are addicted to alcohol or drugs. Many such people are also homeless.

It is estimated by the U.S. Department of Health and Human Services that **mental illness** is a disease that affects one of every five Americans[6] and that 200,000 people with mental illness are jailed or imprisoned in the

United States every day.[7] Ironically, while the population of state psychiatric hospitals declined from 560,000 in 1955 to less than 60,000 today, there has been a significant increase in the number of individuals with mental illness who are incarcerated.[8] A related problem has arisen recently in which individuals who are mentally unstable and who want to die employ a technique that has been termed "suicide by cop"—engaging in a shoot-out with and being killed by the police.

Funding cutbacks and changing laws and policies (such as the deinstitutionalization policies of the 1980s) have concurrently made it more difficult for the police and relatives of the mentally ill to have them committed to institutions. These factors have left many disturbed people—including families—in the streets and alleys and on the riverbanks to fend for themselves. Limited bed space and selective admission practices at detoxification and other alcoholism facilities have also curtailed the ability of the police to transport public inebriates to health care facilities.

One new approach that is in development or use in many jurisdictions is the **crisis intervention team (CIT).** Primarily, the purpose of a CIT is to provide law enforcement officers with the skills they need to safely de-escalate situations involving people with mental illness who are in crisis (the term "mental illness" refers to all diagnosable mental conditions characterized by alterations in thinking, mood, or behavior associated with distress or impaired functioning). A variety of situations can trigger crisis behavior. An officer responding to a call for a noise disturbance may unknowingly walk into a situation involving such a person in crisis.[9]

One model CIT program—developed in Montgomery County, Maryland, and spreading to other jurisdictions—provides officers with a 40-hour block of time that includes both basic classroom and hands-on instruction. Professionals from mental health organizations instruct students on types of mental illness, interview techniques, de-escalation strategies, and other relevant topics. Essentially, CIT members are taught to determine whether or not persons at scenes of disturbances or suicide calls appear to have a mental illness, need an emergency evaluation, should be charged or diverted to another agency, or require immediate medical or mental health attention. An advanced CIT training component provides CIT officers with information to enhance their skills. The U.S. Secret Service Protective Intelligence Unit also invites CIT officers to attend its training seminars on assessing danger.[10]

Previous to the use of CIT practices, the common approach to situations involving a belligerent mentally ill person was to physically overpower the person, according to Chicago Police CIT Coordinator Lt. Jeff Murphy; along with that approach, of course, was the potential for long-term injuries to all parties. Statistics show that agencies that have a CIT program have had fewer injuries. In fact, since 1988, CIT implementation in Memphis, Tennessee (the first CIT program in the United States) resulted in officer injuries being reduced by 85 percent.[11]

A number of other approaches have been undertaken for dealing with these special populations:

- After a Seminole County, Florida, deputy sheriff was killed by a man suffering from paranoid schizophrenia, the deputy's widow and the offender's sister created a task force to study treatment for mentally ill people who break the law.
- Several states have enacted legislation to provide early and humane intervention.
- In Florence, Alabama, a police lieutenant received training not only in mental illness but also in geriatrics and substance abuse. The officer is dispatched to every call when a subject is thought to be mentally ill, assesses the danger posed by the individual, takes the subject to the hospital for evaluation, tries to get people released from jail for treatment, and is establishing a mental health court.[12]
- The regional community policing institutes (RCPIs) of the federal Office of Community Oriented Policing Services provide training in responses to mental health problems, help officers to understand and deal with the problem, review medications used in treatment, and teach how to apply the S.A.R.A. (scanning, analysis, response, assessment) problem-solving process.[13]

Exhibit 12–1 provides another look at how the police are dealing with the mentally ill under COPPS in a special training program in St. Petersburg, Florida. Similar programs are under way in Albuquerque, New Mexico; Portland, Oregon; and Tampa, Florida.[14]

EXHIBIT 12–1

Reaching Out to the Mentally Ill in St. Petersburg, Florida

After mental health advocates began to complain that the police did not understand mental illness and the interventions they should take when encountering such individuals, the police chief instituted a mandatory eight-hour curriculum for all of the agency's 550 officers—the first such training curriculum in the United States. The heart of the course is a four-step approach called CIAF—*calming the subject, investigating* and *assessing* the situation, and *facilitating* a solution. The training, developed by mental health professionals, teaches officers how to look at behavior, intellectual state, attitude, verbal indicators, and environmental factors to optimize the outcome for both the officer and the individual. Instructors emphasize that officers must treat individuals who are mentally ill or unstable with respect, understanding, and compassion, but always have the situation under control. As one observer stated about the program, the police are in effect "untrained mental health counselors. They're problem solvers for people with nowhere else to turn." Officer feedback concerning the training has been positive, and success stories from using the training are beginning to mount, which underscores its effectiveness.

Source: Ronald J. Getz, "Reaching Out to the Mentally Ill," *Law and Order* (May 1999):51.

THE HOMELESS

As indicated above, the population (estimates range from 300,000 to 3 million) experiencing **homelessness** is closely related to and involves many persons with mental illness. The homeless often panhandle, use intimidation, and generally are a problem for businesses and citizens using parks and public sidewalks. Most studies indicate that although the homeless have higher overall arrest rates than the general population, the vast majority of their offenses do not involve violence; rather, the police most often arrest the homeless for public intoxication, theft or shoplifting, and burglary.[15] One study also found that an average of 29 percent of people who are homeless suffer from severe mental disorders. A surprising number of the homeless are military veterans; runaways comprise another sizeable category. Many, however, have experienced economic hard times or cannot afford their own housing.[16]

As is true for the mentally ill population, the homeless often have few options. Not only is shelter space limited, but most shelters refuse to admit the large percentage of homeless who are also mentally ill or alcoholic.

Clearwater, Florida, a community of 100,000 residents that regularly draws another 20,000 tourists during the beach season, recently experienced

NYPD officers attend to a transient person found sleeping in the city's subway system.

Courtesy NYPD Photo Unit.

an upsurge in problems related to street people—thefts, drugs, prostitution, and vandalism. Additionally, these people were sleeping on private property, defecating and urinating on public streets, and engaging in public drunkenness, graffiti, and littering.[17]

The police department, which entered into community policing in 1983 and takes nontraditional approaches to tough problems, decided to get into the housing business. First, the city opened a homeless shelter that included a police substation; virtually every area organization and agency working with the homeless has a presence at the shelter, dealing with everything from mental problems to substance abuse and job placement. Everyone living in the shelter is required to enroll in the Salvation Army Intervention Program, follow strict rules, attend Alcoholics Anonymous meetings regardless of whether they are addicted, participate in counseling, and abide by a curfew. The department used money seized from drug operations to purchase a single-family home, which it in turn leases to a social service agency; the home is used to provide transitional living units for people leaving the shelter, thus facilitating their return to their own living quarters. Dedicated phone lines allow each homeless person to get calls from prospective employers and set up interviews.[18] The city has seen a turnaround with its homeless problems. Businesses that once fought the shelters are now allies, and investors are putting money into nearby properties for new construction and rehabilitation of existing buildings. For another example of the homelessness problem, see Exhibit 12–2.

DOMESTIC VIOLENCE

Domestic violence involves one person dominating and controlling another by force, threats, or physical violence. Traditionally, much of society and many police agencies turned their backs on the problem, refusing to become involved in "family quarrels." Accordingly, police rarely made arrests. Training methods were not focused on prevention, and there were no policies or procedures in place that were geared toward avoiding further violence. The mentality was just to deal with the immediate problem and wait for the next call to the residence. Times have changed, however.[19]

Studies in the mid-1980s found that arrests served as an independent deterrent to future violence, labeled the assailant's actions as criminal, and punished the attacker for his or her actions.[20] Communities with low unemployment rates were instructed to use a mandatory arrest policy; conversely, communities with high unemployment rates were urged to develop some alternative policies and not rely on arrest.[21] Today nearly all states have legislation mandating police officers to effect warrantless arrests where evidence of spousal assault is present. Unfortunately, however, domestic violence remains the most prevalent form of violence confronting our society today.

EXHIBIT 12–2

Homeless-Related Crimes in San Diego

California's Otay River Valley is a massive tract of undeveloped land covering 8,000 acres. It is bordered by the cities of San Diego, Chula Vista, and Imperial Beach. Businesses surrounding the river valley suffered from burglary, panhandling, theft, and vandalism. People often illegally dumped trash and debris in the valley. Transients, perhaps as many as 300, lived at campsites in the valley in bamboo, metal, plywood, and tarpaulin huts. Many of the transients booby-trapped their campsites to ward off intruders. A large number of them also suffered from infectious diseases, such as AIDS and sexual and skin diseases, and some were mentally ill. Police response was reactive until an increase in crime was noted; transients were becoming more aggressive, and two young boys were found murdered in the area. After political pressure began to mount to remove the transients, a three-phase effort was developed, including the enforcement of trespassing laws, the cleanup of the property, and the restoration of the land that would discourage illegal camping. In addition to the cities that were stakeholders, the state of California, San Diego County, the U.S. Fish and Wildlife Service, and the Army Corps of Engineers joined in the massive project. A prosecutor was assigned as legal counsel as well. Police issued trespassing warnings to transients, provided them with information about area homeless shelters and other services, and photographed the transients in case it became necessary to arrest them. Police also made three sweeps through the area to ensure that all trespassers had been warned, making nearly 100 arrests in the process for outstanding warrants and other offenses. Approximately 200 volunteers collected refuse from the area, a private waste-hauling company removed 31 tons of trash (with the use of donated trash containers), and a private landfill company agreed to waive $1,500 in dumping fees. Burglaries and related crimes dropped 80 percent after the evictions and cleanups. Before the project, San Diego police were spending about 3,000 hours per year on valley-related crimes; since the project's completion, that number has dropped to between 500 and 800 hours.

Source: Rana Sampson and Michael S. Scott, *Tackling Crime and Other Public Safety Problems: Case Studies in Problem Solving* (Washington, D.C.: U.S. Department of Justice, Office of Community Policing Services, 2000), pp. 109–110.

Domestic violence, like the other problems discussed in this chapter, must be viewed as a community-wide problem. Police can collect and analyze information about domestic violence and assist the community in becoming aware of its magnitude. Officers can also solicit community support in developing alternative strategies for combating it. Police must work closely with victims' advocates, social service agencies, and the judiciary (injunctive relief can be used to bar an abusive spouse from returning to the family residence). This is a quality-of-life issue, and—like problems such as drugs, gangs, or prostitution—if left unchecked, it will fester and grow.

What can be done proactively about this problem? A growing number of promising COPPS practices have been identified. One Georgia police department, for example, trained county process servers to work with domestic violence survivors. Because many domestic violence incidents go unreported to the police, the person serving a restraining order is often the first authority to learn of a domestic violence situation. Officers can

EXHIBIT 12–3

Domestic Violence in Largo, Florida

Recently the Largo, Florida, Police Department realized that its domestic violence (DV) efforts were of little avail; the community of 75,000 was receiving about 1,000 such calls per year, with only about 16 percent of them resulting in a prosecution. The department formed a partnership with a wide array of governmental agencies, private organizations, and citizen groups, with the goals of getting perpetrators into the justice or social services systems, providing survivor assistance, and finding ways to break the cycle and reduce the violence. Prosecution rates immediately increased to 85 percent. Following are other approaches used by the partnership:

- A DV Web site was established—the first of its kind in the United States.
- A mandatory arrest policy was initiated for DV perpetrators.
- A team of DV intervention specialists was established whose first priorities are the survivors and their families.
- A cellular phone program was begun to safeguard victims.
- A partnering among organizations from every spectrum of the community was begun to provide long-term solutions to reduce the number of incidents.

Although acknowledging the difficulty of obtaining measurable statistics on DV (long-term recidivism data is not yet available), the police department points to the permanent partnership it has formed with most of the stakeholders in DV issues.

Source: Adapted from Ronald J. Getz, "Largo Police Attack Domestic Violence," *Law and Order* (November 1998): 44–45.

also encourage neighbors to anonymously report disturbances or signs of abuse. Religious organizations can be encouraged to reach out to members who are victims, and substance abuse treatment can be arranged for abusers when alcohol and other drugs play a role in the violence.[22] See Exhibit 12–3 for another solution.

The Lapeer County, Michigan, Sheriff's Department reacted to a rise in domestic violence calls by using a unique approach. The department—in conjunction with a regional hospital, a citizens' group, and 17 other county agencies—formed a coalition that created a list of goals and objectives that serve as a foundation for reducing domestic violence in the county[23]:

- Reduce to 10 percent or less the number of battered women and children turned away from emergency housing because of a lack of space.
- Reduce physical abuse directed at women by male partners to no more than 27 out of 1,000 couples.
- Ensure that a crisis intervention shelter and support resources are accessible to all regardless of ability to pay.

- Increase the number of physicians, nurses, social workers, teachers, and criminal justice professionals who receive training in identifying and referring victims.
- Establish a tracking mechanism to record the rate of assault injuries.

The RCPIs of the federal Office of Community Oriented Policing Services provide training in reducing domestic violence; training modules include facilitation skills, evidence gathering, safety planning, accessing and sharing of information, and determination of the predominant aggressor.[24]

NEIGHBORHOOD DISORDER

Neighborhoods deteriorate one home at a time. This deterioration can have many root causes and be accelerated when drug houses, gangs, prostitutes, graffiti, abandoned houses and vehicles, and general neighborhood decay become commonplace. Public housing areas are particularly susceptible to such problems. The police must work in partnership with citizens, tailoring tactics to specific neighborhoods and assisting in their defense against crime and disorder.

A wide range of activities may be undertaken to attack **neighborhood disorder** and deterioration. Herman Goldstein described some of the measures that police may undertake when, for example, a public housing project is suffering from a rash of burglaries[25]:

- Make efforts to apprehend those responsible for the burglaries.
- Counsel management regarding lighting, lock systems, landscaping that provides hiding places for burglars, fencing, appearance of buildings and grounds, and so forth.
- Refer uncorrected conditions that are in violation of the law to building inspectors, zoning authorities, or health authorities.
- Work with tenants, informing them of their rights vis-a-vis management, of various government services available to them, and of measures they can take to prevent crimes.
- Work with school authorities regarding any problem of truancy that may be related to burglaries and with recreation and park authorities regarding any problem of idle youth.

This list demonstrates what Goldstein observed: Once the police break out of the mold of looking only within the criminal justice system for solutions, "large vistas are opened to exploration" and the police can engage in a "far-reaching and imaginative search for alternative ways" to deal with recurring problems.[26] Exhibit 12–4 describes a problem of horrendous proportions in Santa Barbara, California, underscoring what can happen when landlords and management companies ignore their legal and moral responsibilities to their tenants.

EXHIBIT 12–4

Apartment Complex Crime in Santa Barbara, California

Police officers began looking into problems involving a local apartment complex, where tenants had complained about disturbances, an illegal auto repair shop, littering, and illegally built dwellings. The owner, who had 34 other properties in the city, resisted taking any corrective action and had never hired a property manager; as a result, nearly all of his properties were in disrepair and causing a tremendous drain on police resources. Health and safety codes were ignored, and apartments were overrun with cockroaches and rats. A number were also illegally subdivided, with up to 10 people living in a two-bedroom unit. Fire and building codes were also ignored, and there were excessive noise complaints and litter coming from the complexes. Children used abandoned vehicles in the parking lots as playgrounds. Officers found that 758 arrestees and 121 people with outstanding misdemeanor bench warrants listed the properties as their residences. Officers asked neighbors to keep logs of the problems at the properties for two months; officers also photographed the worst conditions and documented the rubble and running sewage. They suggested prosecuting the slumlord with an "unfair competition" charge, because his unlawful neglect of the properties gave him an unfair advantage over legitimately run properties. Officers enlisted the aid of a deputy from the district attorney's fraud unit and organized a task force that included representatives from several city and county prosecutor's, fire, and community development offices. Inspection teams took cameras and camcorders to the site, documenting 750 code violations. Media coverage focused community awareness on the site as well. With this evidence, a criminal court judge convicted the owner and ordered that, as a condition of his probation, he comply with all building codes and regulations; management by a management company was also ordered.

Source: Rana Sampson and Michael S. Scott, *Tackling Crime and Other Public Safety Problems: Case Studies in Problem Solving* (Washington, D.C.: U.S. Department of Justice, Office of Community Policing Services, 2000), pp. 14–18.

As Goldstein mentioned, it is essential that property owners and landlords know their rights with respect to tenants. Because most drug activity occurs on rental property, prevention efforts must involve the property management community. Landlord-tenant training programs are being undertaken by a number of police departments to help owners and managers keep drugs and other criminal activities off their properties.

Such a situation occurred in 1989 in Portland, Oregon, when John Campbell, a resident of a quiet neighborhood, woke up one morning to find a crack house on his block. Campbell's frustration with the drug problem led him to investigate how landlords and neighbors could better detect and stem crime at rental properties. With the Portland police bureau's support—and after researching state and local laws and interviewing more than 40 people—Campbell developed an eight-hour training course for landlords and property managers. Since 1989 Campbell's crusade has resulted in more than 6,000 Portland-area landlords and property managers receiving this training.

Communities in other states have modified Campbell's approach to meet their particular needs.[27] Although such training programs vary, most include the following topics[28]:

- Overview of what landlords and managers can do to keep neighborhoods healthy
- Ways to screen out dishonest applicants while ensuring that honest applicants are encouraged to apply
- Rental agreements and approaches that will strengthen the ability to evict tenants who are drug users or dealers
- Warning signs of drug and other criminal activity, the drugs involved, and the behavior associated with using, growing, and dealing drugs
- Methods to use if a clandestine drug lab is discovered
- Options and process of eviction
- Ways to work with the police
- Rights and responsibilities under Section 8 (subsidized) housing

For many poor urban families, public housing represents the only hope for housing of any kind. Disadvantaged by lack of education, skills, and health, the urban poor pass on public housing dependency from generation to generation. For young single-parent families who cannot find decent, safe, and affordable temporary housing, severely distressed public housing becomes the permanent housing of last resort.

In most cases these young residents have the greatest need for affordable housing; they are also the most vulnerable, the most difficult to manage, and the most difficult to provide security for. Public housing residents ask that the police clear the hallways, stairways, lobbies, and streets of open-air drug sales. The police recognize that distressed housing can be difficult to patrol. Community policing offers the best hope for successful order maintenance in public housing. Sooner or later a housing authority police force will encounter problems. The conflict usually centers on crime problems, maintenance and repair issues, or turf issues (e.g., who should enforce the "conduct" provisions of the lease).[29]

PROSTITUTION

Prostitution constitutes an offense to the moral standards of the community. It creates a nuisance to passersby, nearby residents, and merchants; parking and traffic problems develop. The behavior may also foment other, more serious crimes as well as the spread of sexually transmitted diseases, including AIDS. Street criminals such as prostitutes may also gather juveniles into their web.

Prostitutes often become brazen, know the law, and develop ways to avoid arrest and conviction. Therefore, police who undertake to address this problem need to perform a systematic inquiry into the extent and nature of the problem: How often are juveniles involved? How much crime (such as robberies of "johns") is related to prostitution? Is organized crime involved? Are prostitutes injuring others or being injured themselves? Answers to these and other related questions will help bring the problem into focus. Officers must also consider alternative strategies to thwarting problems. For example, New York City Police Officers enforced the mandatory seat belt law disproportionately against drivers in areas frequented by street prostitutes. Some jurisdictions now publish the names of johns in local newspapers and send letters to homes of registered owners of vehicles, warning the residents that their vehicles were seen loitering in an area frequented by prostitutes.

At times the officers must also gather information from prostitutes themselves to bring a greater degree of order to the situation. The most severe problems associated with street prostitution can be reduced if prostitutes can be encouraged to bring juvenile prostitutes to police attention, expose those who rob their customers, and respect each other's turf.

Police problem-solving efforts for street prostitution must address both prostitutes' and clients' conduct. These efforts include but are not limited to the following[30]:

- Enforcing laws prohibiting soliciting, patronizing, and loitering for the purposes of prostitution while identifying and targeting the worst offenders
- Establishing a highly visible police presence
- Enhancing fines and penalties for prostitution-related offenses committed within specified high-activity zones
- Banning prostitutes from geographic areas, and serving restraining orders and injunctions against the worst offenders
- Imposing community service sentences in lieu of incarceration or fines (the former have been shown to be more effective)
- Encouraging community members to publicly protest against prostitutes or clients (to intimidate prostitutes and their clients)
- Educating and warning high-risk prostitute and client populations—certain groups are more vulnerable to becoming prostitutes (e.g., juvenile runaways) or being solicited (e.g., conventioneers, soldiers)—through billboards, lectures, signs, or media outlets
- Suspending or revoking government aid to prostitutes (e.g., for housing, unemployment insurance, and/or disability)
- Helping prostitutes to quit (e.g., by providing drug, mental health, housing, job, health care, and/or legal counseling and assistance)

See Exhibit 12–5 for an example of how Champaign, Illinois, handled its prostitution problem.

EXHIBIT 12-5

Prostitution in Champaign, Illinois

Champaign, Illinois, had a chronic prostitution problem in its downtown area. Arrests provided only temporary relief, and the prostitutes were rarely convicted. Collateral crimes (theft, robbery, assaults, and "john rolling") caused a significant drain on police resources. Citizens complained that prostitutes used apartment building foyers, church parking lots, driveways, and private alleys to have sex. Ninety percent of the prostitutes were repeat offenders; 15 of them held the majority of all convictions. The city's antisolicitation ordinance, merely resulting in a fine, offered no long-term solution. Female officers dressed as prostitutes arrested johns for attempted patronizing, but the state attorney's office typically dismissed these cases because entrapment defenses were difficult to refute without evidence of the john's predisposition. The state legislature made a third prostitution conviction a felony, but often many years would pass before an offender would amass a criminal history that made her or him eligible for the enhanced felony sentencing. Finally, court-imposed travel restrictions were investigated. The police crime analysis unit found that 92 percent of 321 prostitution arrests over five years occurred in a 12-block downtown area. Armed with a pin map, police requested that the court impose travel restrictions on one chronic prostitute, thus keeping her away from the downtown area and potential customers. The judge agreed, and within two months Champaign courts imposed such restrictions on 13 chronic prostitutes, taking care of the recidivistic offenders; a state appeals court upheld the restrictions. The following year, the state legislature codified travel restrictions. Over the next year and a half, the city's street prostitution dropped by 90 percent. Limiting access to the area disrupted the market and separated prostitutes from their customers.

Source: Rana Sampson and Michael S. Scott, *Tackling Crime and Other Public Safety Problems: Case Studies in Problem Solving* (Washington, D.C.: U.S. Department of Justice, Office of Community Policing Services, 2000), pp. 14–18.

OTHER SELECTED PROBLEMS

Next we look briefly at what the police can or must do to try to address four other kinds of public safety problems: cruising and street racing, false alarms, misuse and abuse of 911, and computer crimes.

Cruising and Street Racing

Cruising may be loosely defined as repeatedly driving a motor vehicle in or near a congested area within (and often during) a specified time period. What is meant by "repeatedly" and "specified time period" is determined by each municipality.

Cruising may seem on the surface to be a relatively harmless activity, and indeed people like to cruise for several reasons: socializing with friends, displaying driving ability, not having other activities, and showing off cars.[31] But cruising has become intolerable in some communities, resulting in citizen harassment, vandalism, underage drinking, littering, people urinating in public, trashing of parking lots, excessive noise, and general disorderly behavior. Police often have to devote large amounts of time to areas congested with cruisers and the attendant problems that arise.

Communities have responded with cruising ordinances, using citations and fines for cruising past a control or a checkpoint more than a certain number of times during a specified time period. Some departments even enter license plate numbers into a computer, which alerts officers on seeing the same license plate a second or third time. Other communities have only aggravated the problem with their cruising ordinances, raising the ire of young and old alike who enjoy this activity. Therefore, some alternative measures have been used with greater success.

Arlington, Texas, rented a parking lot and posted a 10-mile-per-hour speed limit and two officers to patrol the area. Portland, Oregon, published a brochure on cruising and distributed it to cruisers in the affected areas. Topeka, Kansas, police located a "cruising zone" close enough to downtown to be acceptable to cruisers but not a nuisance to the community. Other communities have formed a teen court or some form of youth council to handle the violations that arise in the cruise area. See Exhibit 12–6 for another example of how a community dealt with the problem of cruising.

 EXHIBIT 12–6

Cruising Trouble in Santa Ana, California

The street cruising problem in Santa Ana, California, became uncontrollable in the 1990s. On Sunday evenings 1,000 carloads of youths brought one six-block-long area in the community to a point of gridlock; this situation created a heightened sense of fear in the city because of associated criminal activity and rival gang violence (with 16 related homicides and more than 100 aggravated assaults in a two-and-a-half-year period). Traditional police responses failed and were expensive. Officers in the district formed a problem-solving team and developed a series of operation plans to address the issues. Police devised a traffic control scheme and used their legal authority to stop all traffic, identify drivers, and provide information on cruising violations. They entered driver and vehicle information in a computer database at the traffic control points and sent follow-up letters to registered vehicle owners to reinforce their warnings and to ensure that parents were informed of young drivers' activities. They also erected warning signs along the highways. On the first night of the operation, police stopped 70 percent of the cruising vehicles at checkpoints; during the next two nights, 83 percent were stopped. The number of returning cruisers diminished so much by the fourth night that the police suspended the checkpoints in favor of traffic stops. Cruising eventually ceased altogether. During the program, the police issued more than 2,000 personal warnings and sent more than 1,700 follow-up letters. The warning-and-education campaign turned out to be at least as effective as enforcement and was more efficient. Ninety percent of the cruisers warned on the first night did not return. There have been no cruising-related calls during the past two years, and crime associated with it has disappeared.

Source: Rana Sampson and Michael S. Scott, *Tackling Crime and Other Public Safety Problems: Case Studies in Problem Solving* (Washington, D.C.: U.S. Department of Justice, Office of Community Policing Services, 2000), pp. 14–18.

A companion traffic problem is **street racing,** which has existed for centuries (involving horses before automobiles) because of its thrills: the adrenaline rush, the ego boost, and the thrill of victory. However, given that this activity involves reckless driving, that today's vehicles are capable of reaching high speeds, and that even small autos can weigh 2,500 pounds, the risk to drivers and spectators is exceptionally high. Unfortunately, some cities and states have not qualified street racing even as a misdemeanor; where there are laws against drag racing, racers can easily find an "amnesty jurisdiction" where such laws do not exist.[32]

Obviously, police everywhere support legislation that would tow vehicles involved in street racing and that would allow the arrest of racers and spectators. Some cities have recently begun to view this matter very seriously. For example, in September 2002, the Los Angeles City Council urged Governor Gray Davis to approve legislation that would help the police department crack down on illegal street racing. It would take away racers' cars for 30 days (even for a first offense) and impose much more serious fines. The bill was signed into law by Governor Davis in September 2002.[33] In Wichita, Kansas, the police department contacted its Air Section to assist in street racing enforcement and used a digital camera to take aerial photographs; it also issued extra citations, engaged in surveillance, and collected reports about drag racing from businesses at common racing locations.[34] Finally, the San Diego Police Department used a "delayed response aimed at inducing ripples of paranoia within the city's illegal drag racing community."[35]

False Alarms

In the United States each year, police respond to about 38 million alarm activations. Most of the activations are burglar alarms, and about 98 percent of these are **false alarms.** As an example, Chicago police respond to more than 300,000 burglar alarms each year (98 percent of which are false), which translates to the equivalent use of 195 full-time police officers.[36]

The proliferation of electronic security systems for both commercial and residential use—estimates show between 18 and 21 million security alarm systems in the United States, with 1.5 million new systems added each year[37]—has brought with it a serious problem for police officers nationwide. False alarms, each of which requires about 20 minutes of police time, cost police departments about $1.5 billion each year.[38] Recent financial difficulties in some jurisdictions have forced police executives to reassess alarm responses, formerly provided free of charge.

Faced with budget cuts, an increasing number of police executives are charging business and residential owners for police responses to false alarms that are, in effect, wasted effort. A strategy of assessing fines for false alarms and the resulting termination of alarm use, now beginning to spread across the United States, obviously represent a major break with traditional police practices.

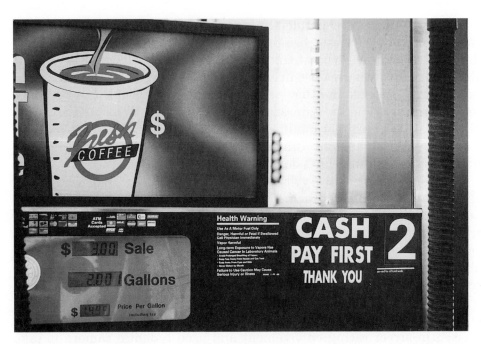

Gasoline station drive-offs (leaving without paying for gas) can account for a high number of calls for service. A prepay policy is one simple method for reducing this problem.

A problem-solving analysis for addressing burglar alarms would begin by asking the right questions[39]:

- What percentage of the agency's alarm calls for businesses, residences, and government premises are false? What percentage are burglar alarms?
- What is the agency's true cost of responding to alarms?
- How many residential and commercial alarm systems are there in the jurisdiction?
- At what rate do officers arrest burglars at alarm calls?
- Do some alarm companies have higher false alarm rates than others?

Once the local problem is understood, responses such as the following may be implemented[40]:

- Require alarm companies to visually verify alarm legitimacy before calling the police.
- Charge a fee for service for all false holdup, burglary, and panic alarms.
- Establish an ordinance with escalating fines for false alarms.
- Publish alarm companies' false alarm rates on Web sites or elsewhere.

Misuse and Abuse of 911

A police problem that is related to false alarms is misuse and abuse of **911,** due to both unintentional and intentional calls. The U.S. 911 system handles 500,000 calls daily, or about 183 million annually, and unintentional, phantom wireless calls account for between 25 and 70 percent of all 911 calls in some U.S. communities. If a cell phone user inadvertently presses the 9 or 1 key on a phone preprogrammed to dial 911, the phone automatically dials 911, even without the user having to press "send."[41]

Nonemergency 911 calls often constitute a large portion of all 911 calls as well. Callers sometimes want to report an incident that was not an emergency or that does not require immediate police attention (e.g., the caller's car was broken into the previous night) as well as ask about non-police-related matters (e.g., the start time of a football game, directions to a local event, the time of day, or the day of garbage pickup). People also call 911 to falsely claim an emergency or to deliberately hang up.[42] To problem-solve 911 calls, the police must first analyze the problem by obtaining all available information about the incidents, offenders, and locations/times and determine what percentage of 911 calls are wireless, misdials, hang-ups, non-emergencies, or pranks. Once the problem is analyzed, a range of responses can be implemented[43]:

- Require manufacturers to redesign wireless phones.
- Distribute phone button guards to reduce the accidental pressing of the 9 or 1 key.
- Prohibit automatic 911 dialing.
- Funnel phantom wireless calls through an automated 911 answering system. (During peak 911 calling periods, if no one is on the line the dispatcher can switch the call to a separate queue, and an automated attendant can ask the caller to press any number or say yes if an emergency exists; if the caller does not respond, the call is terminated.)

Exhibit 12–7 discusses how the San Diego Police Department addressed a 911 problem.

Computer Crimes

More than 300 million English-speaking people are now plugged into cyberspace, and more enter the online world each day. The Internet has revolutionized the way people communicate, shop, entertain, learn, and conduct business, but as the saying goes, the fleas come with the dog. This high-tech revolution in our homes and offices has opened a whole new world for the criminal element as well. Indeed, the problem of cybercrime has become so prevalent that the U.S. Department of Justice has created a Computer Crime and Intellectual Property Section of its Criminal Division; it can be accessed at www.cybercrime.gov. Other investigative agencies include the Federal Bureau of Investigation (FBI) Internet Fraud Complaint Center as well as the Internet Crime Complaint Center (known as IC3), which is a partnership between the FBI and the National White Collar Crime Center. These agencies report receiving more than 50,000 complaints per year, not counting child pornography and solicitation cases, many thousands of cases of unsolicited e-mail, computer intrusions, or other violations of the law.[44]

EXHIBIT 12–7

San Diego's Misuse and Abuse of 911

Officers in San Diego noticed that a high volume of 911 hang-ups were coming from pay phones in one block of the city's Southern Division. This area abuts Mexico and has the busiest border crossing in the world. Officers surveilled the 20 pay phones on the block—phones belonging to six different owners—and spoke with community members and taxi and bus drivers, and determined that diversionary calls (unlicensed taxi drivers were calling 911 to divert police away from their passenger pick-up points at the border, and drug dealers were also making such calls), prank calls (by late-night revelers returning to the U.S. from Mexico), and misdials (people returning to the U.S. from Mexico trying to call their families were dialing 911 instead of 011, the international access number) were the three main causes. The police alerted business owners to the severity of the problem, and that they were being diverted from crime-ridden areas to respond to false calls; the owners removed 10 of the phones and relocated others; officers also posted "no loitering" signs next to the phones. To address the misdialing problem, officers painted all the 9 keys red. As a result of these efforts, 911 calls dropped by 50 percent and resulted in lower response times to other calls.

Source: Rana Sampson, *Misuse and Abuse of 911* (Washington, D.C.: U.S. Department of Justice, Office of Community Oriented Policing Services, September 2002), pp. 13–15.

Pornographers and pedophiles are on the Web, as well as other criminal types dotting the landscape who are better educated, upscale, older, and increasingly female. Computer crimes include identity theft; cyberterrorism; software piracy; industrial espionage; credit card, consumer, and stock market fraud; rigged baby adoption scams; hacking; spamming; embezzlement; and distributed denial of service (DDS). In a DDS attack, dozens or even hundreds of computers all linked to the Internet are instructed by a rogue program to bombard the target site with nonsense data. This bombardment soon causes the target site's servers to run out of memory and thus cause it to be unresponsive to the queries of legitimate customers; victims of such practices have included Yahoo!, E*Trade, Amazon.com, and eBay.[45]

These types of crimes will certainly compel the development of new investigative techniques, specialized and ongoing training for police investigators, and employment of individuals with highly technological backgrounds. Obviously, the police must become better educated, better equipped, and more adaptable.[46]

The technology staff of many (if not most) police agencies are civilians who are generally kept away from the operational side of the organization. They understand what computers do but not necessarily how that capability supports the operational needs of the police officer on the street. Thus, the sworn officer or detective is generally unprepared for the above-described host of criminal schemes.[47] This situation must be improved in the future.

SUMMARY

Like Chapter 11, this chapter has applied COPPS to issues and problems that warrant special kinds of attention. Seven exhibits were provided, each showing the efficacy of COPPS in addressing a particular problem.

Although we stated it in Chapter 11, it bears repeating that for each of the issues and problems discussed, the success of COPPS strategies is highly dependent on the police having laid the groundwork—doing the kinds of preparatory work described in earlier chapters as well as having a firm grasp of and properly applying the S.A.R.A. process (discussed in Chapter 3).

 ITEMS FOR REVIEW

1. Describe how identity theft is accomplished, and discuss some of the ways that the police can attempt to prevent and address it.
2. Define what is meant by the term "mental illness," and explain the crisis intervention team (CIT) concept that has been developed to deal with it.
3. Review how the police can attempt to assist the homeless population.
4. Delineate the methods that are available to the police for dealing with domestic violence.
5. Explain the nature and extent of neighborhood disorder and ways COPPS can help.
6. Review the problems surrounding prostitution, and list some means for addressing them.
7. Explain what the police can attempt to do with other selected problems, such as cruising, street racing, false alarms, misuse and abuse of 911, and computer crimes.

◆ **NOTES**

1. Graeme R. Newman, *Identity Theft* (Washington, D.C.: U.S. Department of Justice, Office of Community Oriented Policing Services, June 2004), p. 1.
2. P.L. 105-318 (1998).
3. Newman, *Identity Theft,* p. 3.
4. *Ibid.,* pp. 11–14.
5. *Ibid.,* pp. 32–41.
6. U.S. Department of Health and Human Services, "Mental Health: A Report of the Surgeon General," http://www.surgeongeneral.gov/library/mentalhealth/home.html (Accessed May 2, 2006).
7. Ronald J. Getz, "Reaching Out to the Mentally Ill," *Law and Order* (May 1999):51.

8. Robert Rosenblatt, *Law Enforcement and the Mentally Ill* (Washington, D.C.: Regional Organized Crime Information Center, 2002).

9. Rodney Hill, Guthrie Quill, and Kathryn Ellis, "The Montgomery County CIT Model: Interacting with People with Mental Illness," *FBI Law Enforcement Bulletin* (July 2004):18–25.

10. *Ibid.*, pp. 20–22.

11. Jeannine Heinecke, "Talking to 'Invisible' People," *Law Enforcement Technology* (September 2005):116–124.

12. *Ibid.*

13. "Community Policing Response to Mental Health," www.tri-statercpi.org (Accessed September 15, 2006).

14. Donald G. Turnbaugh, "Curing Police Problems with the Mentally Ill," *The Police Chief* (February 1999):52.

15. David L. Carter and Allen D. Sapp, "Police Response to Street People: A Survey of Perspectives and Practices," *FBI Law Enforcement Bulletin* (March 1993):5–10.

16. Peter Finn, *Street People* (Washington, D.C.: U.S. Government Printing Office, 1988), p. 1.

17. Ronald J. Getz, "A Positive Police Program for the Homeless," *Law and Order* (May 1999):93–96.

18. *Ibid.*

19. Pam Paziotopoulos, "Workplace Domestic Violence," *Law and Order* (August 2003), pp. 104–109.

20. Lawrence Sherman and Robert A. Berk, "The Specific Deterrent Effects of Arrest for Domestic Assault," *American Sociological Review* 49 (1984): 261–271.

21. Jacob R. Clark, "Where to Now on Domestic-Violence? Studies Offer Mixed Policy Guidance," *Law Enforcement News* (April 30, 1993):1.

22. "Taking a Problem-Solving Approach to Domestic Violence," in *Domestic Violence: 1995–1998* (Washington, D.C.: Community Policing Consortium, 1998), p. 4.

23. Ronald J. Kalanquin, "Coalition Works to Curb Rising Rate of Domestic Violence in Lapeer County," in *Domestic Violence: 1995–1998*, p. 5.

24. www.cops.usdoj.gov (Accessed May 27, 2003).

25. Herman Goldstein, *Problem-Oriented Policing* (New York: McGraw-Hill, 1990), pp. 44–45.

26. *Ibid.*, p. 44. See also John H. Campbell, *Keeping Illegal Activity Out of Rental Property: A Police Guide for Establishing Landlord Training Programs* (Washington, D.C.: U.S. Department of Justice, Bureau of Justice Assistance, March 2000).

27. Rana Sampson and Michael S. Scott, *Tackling Crime and Other Public Safety Problems: Case Studies in Problem Solving* (Washington, D.C.: U.S. Department of Justice, Office of Community Policing Services, 2000), pp. 13–14.

28. See, for example, Campbell Resources, *The Landlord Training Program: Keeping Illegal Activity Out of Rental Property* (Portland, Ore.: Author, 1992), p. 2.

29. W. H. Matthews, *Policing Distressed Public Housing Developments: Community Policing Could Be the Answer* (Washington, D.C.: U.S. Department of Housing and Urban Development, Crime Prevention and Security Division, no date).

30. Michael S. Scott, *Street Prostitution* (Washington, D.C.: U.S. Department of Justice, Office of Community Oriented Policing Services, August 2001).

31. Boise Police Department Planning Unit, *Downtown "Cruising" in Major U.S. Cities and One City's Response to the Problem* (Boise, Idaho: Author, 1990), pp. 1–2.

32. Portland, Oregon, Police Bureau Web site, http://www.portlandpolicebureau .com/news302.html (Accessed May 4, 2003).

33. Bill Murray, Los Angeles Community Policing, June 6, 2003, http://www .lacp.org/Articles.

34. "Police Address Problem of Illegal Drag Racing," http://www.wichitagov.org/ News/CityEvents/2002/2002-04-17b.htm (Accessed September 16, 2006).

35. "SDPD's Drag-Net Puts the Brakes on Street Racers," *Law Enforcement News* (November 15, 2002):5.

36. Rana Sampson, *False Burglar Alarms* (Washington, D.C.: U.S. Department of Justice, Office of Community Oriented Policing Services, August 2001), pp. 1–2.

37. *Ibid.,* p. 2.

38. *Ibid.,* p. 6.

39. *Ibid.,* pp. 9–10.

40. *Ibid.,* pp. 13–17.

41. Rana Sampson, *Misuse and Abuse of 911* (Washington, D.C.: U.S. Department of Justice, Office of Community Oriented Policing Services, September 2002), pp. 1–7.

42. *Ibid.*

43. *Ibid.,* pp. 13–15.

44. U.S. Department of Justice, Office for Victims of Crime, "Cybercrime Victimization," http://www.ojp.usdoj.gov/ovc/ncvrw/2005/pg5e.html (Accessed February 27, 2006).

45. U.S. Department of Justice, Computer Crime and Intellectual Property Section, "Computer Crime Policy and Programs," http://www.cybercrime.gov/ ccpolicy.html#DDSA (Accessed February 27, 2006).

46. D. Pettinari, "Are We There Yet? The Future of Policing/Sheriffing in Pueblo—or in Anywhere, America," http://www.policefuturists.org/files/ yet.html (Accessed February 13, 2001).

47. G. W. Schoenle, Jr., "Mobile Computing Police Perspectives: The Buffalo Experience," *The Police Chief* (September 2001):36–42.

CHAPTER 13

COPPS

Selected American Approaches

Key Terms and Concepts

Chicago Alternative Policing
    Strategy (CAPS)
Community police officer (CPO)
Corridor Safety Program
Geographic Information System
    (GIS)
Neighborhood Stabilization Team
    (NST)
Neighborhood Watch

Problem Resolution Team (PRT)
Strategic Problem Solving (SPS)
Tourist Oriented Police Service
    (TOPS)
Washington State Institute for
    Community Oriented Policing
    (WSICOP)

Learning Objectives

As a result of reading this chapter, the student will:

- Understand how COPPS has been adopted and practiced in large, medium, and small communities
- Be aware of COPPS strategies that have been undertaken in federal and state law enforcement agencies and in university settings

> Example moves the world more than doctrine.
>
> *–Henry Miller*

INTRODUCTION

Henry Miller is correct: Example is an efficacious means by which to disseminate information and move the world. This chapter provides case studies of community oriented policing and problem solving (COPPS) initiatives. Featured are case studies of COPPS activities in 21 jurisdictions: 7 large (more than 250,000 population), 9 medium-size (between 50,000 and 250,000 population), and 5 small (less than 50,000 population). Also discussed in lesser detail are COPPS initiatives in federal and state agencies.

LARGE COMMUNITIES

Austin, Texas

Austin, located in central Texas, has about 656,000 residents; the Austin Police Department (APD) consists of approximately 1,536 sworn officers. In the early 1990s, the APD began reviewing the COPPS philosophy and designed a strategy to incorporate the concept throughout the entire organization. A five-year transition was developed and submitted to the city council, and implementation was soon under way. Today, several ancillary programs have been implemented, including a leadership academy for citizens, a landlord training program, a citizen patrol program, and problem-solving projects for cadets at the academy and after graduation. For policing purposes, the city is separated into 7 geographic area commands, each of which is subdivided into 10 to 12 districts staffed by seven shifts of officers.

Strong emphasis is placed on the use of technology. In the mid-1990s a **geographic information system (GIS)** was first employed to see where vehicles were being stolen and recovered. Success in this venture led the APD to incorporate GIS into the crime analysis unit, which soon noticed a pattern of burglaries of churches and residences that were occurring overnight and midweek. A victim told police there was a group of homeless persons who were committing burglaries, and officers went to an area where such persons clustered. Upon arriving, they noticed two transients who were examining some goods; questioning by officers revealed that they had just stolen the articles from a vehicle. The officers learned where they normally fenced their goods: from a woman operating a nearby taco cart. The men agreed to be confidential informants in lieu of arrest, setting into motion a six-week investigation that broke up the largest fencing operation in the history of Austin. In fact, an undercover operation with officers posing as shoplifters determined that three taco carts operated by the woman and three accomplices were receiving stolen property. The four were arrested for engaging in organized crime, three homes were raided, and 395 items were seized along with $62,000 in cash; residential burglaries in the downtown area were reduced by 60 percent.[1]

See Exhibit 13–1 for a discussion of another Texas approach in San Antonio.

[{"N":1}]

EXHIBIT 13-1

COPPS in San Antonio, Texas

The San Antonio, Texas, Police Department has embraced COPPS for many decades through its Community Services, School Services, and Crime Prevention programs; storefronts; decentralized patrol substations; and downtown foot and bicycle patrol units. In 1995 the department went a step further, creating a special community policing unit called San Antonio Fear Free Environment (SAFFE), which is linked closely with community involvement programs. First established in 1995 with 60 officers and enlarged to 100 officers in 1996, the SAFFE unit focuses on identifying, evaluating, and resolving community crime problems with the cooperation and participation of community residents. Beginning in 2000 an additional 10 officers were added to the unit each year for five years. SAFFE officers are not tied to radio calls but instead are able to establish and maintain day-to-day interaction with residents and businesses within their assigned beats to prevent crimes before they occur. SAFFE officers also act as liaisons with other city agencies, work closely with schools and youth programs, coordinate graffiti-removal activities, and serve as resources to residents.

Source: San Antonio Police Department Web page: http://www.ci.sat.tx.us/sapd/COPPS.asp (Accessed January 21, 2004).

Charlotte-Mecklenburg, North Carolina

The Charlotte-Mecklenburg Police Department (CMPD), with 2,000 staff members in a community of 713,000, is the largest local police agency between Washington, D.C., and Atlanta, Georgia. Its mission: "To build problem-solving partnerships with our citizens to prevent the next crime."

Technology is an important crime reduction tool, and the CMPD takes pride in taking the use of technology to a new level; each officer is assigned a laptop computer in the police cruiser, and each can utilize the GIS, both of which allow officers to have quick and easy access to information for problem solving and to analyze events that have taken place. Their Web site is also a valuable tool.

The CMPD has undertaken major reorganization and redistricting. Reorganizing involved placing all patrol districts under the responsibility of just one deputy chief to allow for more consistent supervision countywide. Redrawing the 12 police district boundaries was a painstaking process that included a thorough review of calls for service (CFS) data, manpower allocations, and extensive discussions with citizens and businesses—all of which were critical to reducing crime and enhancing the quality of life.

Recently the CMPD was confronted with a serious problem that demonstrated the value of its use of and reliance on technology: thefts of home appliances. Between the time when a certificate of occupancy (CO) was issued for a new home and when the new owners moved in, burglars were stealing a large number of home appliances that were already installed. Using geographic mapping and the Statistical Package for the

Social Sciences (SPSS) Software, the CMPD was able to show contractors that a positive correlation existed between issuance of the CO and the thefts. Police advised builders to lock appliances in rented metal storage lockers and to wait until the day before closing the home purchase before installing the appliances. This approach quelled the problem.

The CMPD also conducts annual citizen satisfaction surveys; recently the survey indicated that 82.6 percent of residents were satisfied or very satisfied with how the police served their neighborhoods.[2] CMPD's award-winning project involving domestic violence intervention is discussed in Appendix A.

Chicago, Illinois

Although we briefly discussed the community policing strategy by the Chicago Police Department (CPO) in previous chapters (including a description of its frequent, highly structured self-evaluation of its COPPS efforts in Chapter 8), here we discuss the evolution of its highly successful COPPS efforts.

Because of soaring crime rates in the early 1990s, the city wanted a smarter approach to policing, one that mobilized residents, police officers, and other city workers around a problem-solving approach. Initiated at the highest levels, the **Chicago Alternative Policing Strategy (CAPS)** was instituted in April 1993 in 5 of the city's 25 police districts. Patrol officers were permanently assigned to fixed beats and trained in problem-solving strategies. Neighborhood meetings between officers and area residents were held, and citizen committees were formed to advise district commanders. In the fall of 1994, elements of CAPS began to be introduced in Chicago's other districts; citywide involvement in the strategy began in the spring of 1995. Now, more than a decade later, a long-term evaluation has found evidence of CAPS-related success with physical decay problems in 3 of the 5 initial experimental districts, as well as a decline in gang and drug problems in 2 districts and a decline in major crimes in 2 districts.

The police department promotes citizen participation through an aggressive advertising campaign that publicizes CAPS and encourages people to participate in beat meetings and activities. A recent survey found that nearly 80 percent of Chicagoans knew of CAPS, more than 60 percent knew of beat meetings in their neighborhood, and, of the latter group, 31 percent had attended at least one meeting.

Thousands of officers are assigned to teams dedicated to working in small beats. The department's dispatch policy was revised to enable officers to remain on their assigned beats for most of their duty shift. All of the city's sworn officers and their supervisors have been trained in problem solving. Surveys have found that officers are generally optimistic about the impact of CAPS on their work and on the community, about their own ability to engage in problem solving, and about the viability of community policing and problem solving.

St. Petersburg, Florida, neighborhood police officers attempt to get to know residents and youths on their beat.

Courtesy St. Petersburg, Florida, Police Department.

CAPS has been recognized as one of the most ambitious COPPS initiatives in the United States; it has been cited as a model by numerous police experts and the federal government.[3] In February 2003, Mayor Richard M. Daley stated: "I believe that CAPS is a great program. CAPS is no longer a pilot program"; the CPD superintendent, Terry Hillard, added, "It is the foundation of everything we do to create safer neighborhoods. Community policing in Chicago is here to stay because it delivers results."[4]

Fort Lauderdale, Florida

In June 1995 the Fort Lauderdale Police Department (FLPD) set out to develop a COPPS initiative that would be used to guide the future of the entire agency in terms of how it provided police services. The COPPS initiative aimed to marshal community and governmental resources.

There have been several major accomplishments since the inception of COPPS, involving reclaiming neighborhoods and parks and initiating nuisance abatement proceedings against problem properties.

In 2000, the FLPD officially changed the title of its community policing initiative to the Community Support Division (CSD). This division, initially begun with 10 employees and now with 59, has become the centerpiece of COPPS efforts in the FLPD. The components of the CSD are the crime analysis unit, crime prevention unit, narcotics detection dogs, youth services, motor unit, administration, code enforcement, alarm reduction, and demonstration center (the latter serving as a training center and meeting facility for both police and nonpolice personnel). Through the CSD, the FLPD emphasizes community-building strategies; threatened neighborhoods implement problem-solving plans to reduce crime and raise the quality of life. CFS decrease in CSD-targeted areas. Indeed, every resource that is available is used to address each negative element that contributes to neighborhood instability.[5]

St. Louis, Missouri

Since initiating a pilot COPPS project in a single neighborhood in the early 1990s,[6] a notable undertaking has been the department's efforts with COPPS "on the beat"—efforts in specialized functions. Following is a brief description of how COPPS has been mainstreamed into various aspects of police work:

Narcotics section. All narcotics detectives have been assigned to specific neighborhoods and are responsible for coordinating all problem oriented policing (POP) responses to narcotics problems with patrol officers. Narcotics detectives focus their work on community hot spots. An innovative computerized tracking system for citizen-generated calls to a hotline was recently developed.

Auto theft unit. The auto theft unit works with COPPS officers to target certain neighborhoods for theft prevention. The expertise of the auto theft detectives and the community contacts of the patrol officers are combined to enhance police response to the problem.

Juvenile division. The juvenile division helps coordinate the department's School Assistance Grant, placing 14 uniformed patrol officers in selected high schools and middle schools and in their neighborhoods; the department participates in the Substance Abuse Prevention Partnership. A COPPS response to family violence has also been developed.

Gang unit. After conducting a thorough study of gang activity in St. Louis, this unit developed educational materials for parents and school officials and conducted gang awareness training for patrol officers.

Mobile reserve unit. The mobile reserve unit identifies persistent problems of crime and disorder throughout the city; the problems range from narcotics sales to graffiti to fights and disturbances. It also provides patrol support while officers are attending COPPS training.

Legal division. In-house counsel assists officers with their COPPS efforts, hearings to enforce building code violations, and condemnation proceedings on problem property.

In addition, a computer-aided dispatch (CAD) flagging system notifies officers of safety alerts, ongoing COPPS projects, and hot spots. A computerized problem-solving database, a revised policy on awards and recognition, and a monthly COPPS newsletter are in place, and an information division was created that includes the library, the TV section (which produces videotapes of crime problems, for training), computer center, and planning and development. A Performance Appraisal Review Committee of eight officers and supervisors prepares recommendations to the chief that are consistent with COPPS.

A recent addition has been the **neighborhood stabilization team (NST)** concept. The NST serves as a catalyst for bringing together autonomous city departments, the police, and citizens to solve neighborhood problems. There are 27 NST officers, who serve in all 79 city neighborhoods; this function has a $1.9 million budget. The department also provides problem-solving training in conjunction with NST to teach police and nonpolice personnel how to analyze, interpret, and act on neighborhood-level crime data.[7]

St. Petersburg, Florida

The Community Policing Division was formed following a November 1990 reorganization of the department.[8] Today COPPS in this agency of 540 sworn officers involves a department-wide philosophy with citywide deployment. Community policing areas (CPAs) cover every neighborhood, and a **community police officer (CPO)** is assigned to each CPA. CPOs are responsible for their area 24 hours per day, 7 days per week, and foster a partnership with the community; they identify hot spots and implement strategies to resolve them. CPOs work flexible schedules to meet the needs of the community; they might be in uniform, driving a marked police cruiser or patrolling on a police mountain bike, or be working in plainclothes.

Currently there are 41 CPOs assigned throughout St. Petersburg; in addition, 11 officers are assigned to the downtown area, 2 work at a large shopping mall, and 2 are posted at the city's public housing complexes, for a total of 56 CPOs. There are also zone officers assigned throughout the city whose primary duty is to respond to CFS. Zone officers are encouraged to partner with the CPO in their assigned area, forming a team for each of the shifts. Furthermore, most of the detectives are given geographic responsibilities, thus allowing them to become part of the team to address emerging crime problems.[9]

San Diego, California

Like many other incident-driven police agencies, San Diego treated symptoms while the underlying problems continued to grow. Communication between the top and the bottom of the organization was not occurring in an effective and timely manner. The decision was made that officers could more effectively deal with underlying problems.

Since the early 1970s community policing has been San Diego's guiding philosophy.[10] The San Diego Police Department (SDPD) entered neighborhood policing in a major way by forming Selected Tactics of Policing (STOP). Ten patrol officers formed a team to combine traditional policing with COPPS to target crime. Neighborhoods on two beats in midcity were selected as target locations. SDPD also became involved in a Neighborhood Policing Restructuring Project to strengthen and expand neighborhood policing throughout the department both by developing a plan to convert the police beat system from a census tract basis to a community-based format and by incorporating problem solving at all department levels and in all functions.

To professionalize problem solving as an accepted policing strategy, the SDPD and the Police Executive Research Forum founded the annual National Problem Oriented Policing Conference, which is now held annually in different locations in the United States. As many as 1,500 participants from around the world attend this conference, which has a rich blend of hands-on advice combined with the most recent research in the field.[11]

Recent examples of neighborhood policing in San Diego include the following:

- Revitalized **Neighborhood Watch** program, consisting of community coordinators, watch coordinators, and block captains all working toward a common goal
- Citizens' Patrol groups throughout the city, acting as eyes and ears to observe suspicious activities and report problems
- Safe Streets Now! working to get rid of nuisance properties through civil remedies
- Drug Abatement Response Team, involving the city attorney, housing inspectors, and the police in identifying properties that have a long history of ongoing narcotics activities (in a recent six-month period, more than 70 drug houses were targeted for abatement action)

Also, in February 1997 the SDPD adopted a strategic planning process as a means to improve organizational management. The process was opened to community members, other city employees, and police employees. In the first phase of developing a three- to five-year strategic plan, nearly 215 people had a voice in the goals and objectives the SDPD would pursue. In the second phase, begun in November 1997, plans were developed to put the overall strategies into action.[12]

MEDIUM-SIZE COUNTIES AND CITIES

Arlington County, Virginia

Arlington County, Virginia, is an urban community of approximately 26 square miles, located across the Potomac River from Washington, D.C. Being both a residential community and an employment center, its population swells from about 187,000 residents to about 265,000 each workday with the influx of commuters.

Using federal and state community policing grants, five community-based teams were deployed to diverse communities throughout the county. Teams consisting of up to 24 officers and 3 supervisors establish a cooperative relationship with the community and identify broad-based strategies to address crime problems. Additionally, community resource officers in each of the county's schools act as a part of the faculty, serving as instructors (teaching antidrug and antigang classes), enhancing the schools' security efforts, and coordinating Neighborhood Watch programs.

Geographic accountability is a management and motivational tool to facilitate agency-wide implementation of COPPS. Officers are responsible and accountable for specific turf rather than a particular shift. Four districts were created, and the department's 10 police beats follow the natural boundaries of their civic organizations. This design enhances department-wide communications and encourages neighborhood focus. Officers are assigned to fixed areas for extended periods of time and are responsible for their specific areas 24 hours per day, 7 days per week. In addition to responding to both emergency and nonemergency CFS, they are responsible for preliminary criminal investigations, special event planning, and school liaison. The middle managers within the department have been identified as the key players in making COPPS work.

The department's COPPS efforts have resulted in a significant reduction in crime and CFS. The department is also working aggressively to develop a technology strategy that will support its new geographic policing strategy. Through another recently funded grant, the department hopes to develop a technology infrastructure to support the requirements of beat officers engaged in problem solving.[13]

Concord, California

In the fall of 1992, the Concord Police Department (CPD) assembled a group of employees into a task force to develop the framework for a unique version of community policing; over the next decade, the CPD refined COPPS so that it reflected the needs of the community and was a "way of being" in public safety service. Thus, COPPS is an evolutionary process that seeks to join the police and the community in reducing crime and enhancing the quality of life.

Officers, first-line supervisors, and middle managers are all held accountable for solving problems and are given annual performance evaluations; their pay is directly tied to their effectiveness. Part of this evaluation concerns the amount of time spent in problem-solving efforts. Of paramount importance are the *results* obtained by the officers in these endeavors. However, the fact that a problem was not eradicated is not viewed as being ineffective per se; rather, it is the analysis of *why* the problem was not solved that offers more satisfying long-term solutions. Automated crime statistics are made available to the public around the clock, and officers go into the community to serve as mentors and trainers concerning COPPS.

The CPD has learned, and counsels others, that it takes time for institutional transformation to occur; the mind-set of employees must change and accept COPPS as a way of being in order to accomplish the agency's mission.[14]

Hayward, California

Hayward has a population of about 120,000 and 160 sworn police officers. The 1990s were marked by increases in crime, drug trafficking, gangs, and traffic problems. As is seen in other communities, Hayward's growing social ills contributed to the evolution of an incident-driven policing system in which rapid response became a key priority. Realizing that the authority of the Hayward Police Department (HPD) was centralized, which stifled the creativity of employees, the department began developing a new approach to policing, believing it was time for law enforcement to change.

The Hayward plan—officially known as COPPS—was activated and incorporated into all routine police functions. (HPD's methods for changing its culture and mission statement are described in Chapter 6.) New means of responding to CFS were developed to free up officer time for problem solving. Officers are managers of their beats, encouraged to engage in responsible, creative ways to bring about problem resolution. They meet and talk with residents to build and nurture partnership and commitment as well as to explore viable solutions and seek out available resources.

The Hayward model is intended to be flexible, effective, and responsive to the needs of that community, stressing the importance of partnerships, problem solving, and visionary leadership. The process, the department acknowledges, requires considerable time, planning, and cooperation by everyone concerned. Such a comprehensive change in philosophy dictates a new policing style and "ushers in an exciting era."[15]

Lansing, Michigan

The Lansing Police Department (LPD) began its COPPS efforts in 1990. The city is divided into 18 geographic team areas with assigned officers, investigators, and command staff. As the philosophy evolved, the LPD recognized a critical need to better communicate crime and health data as well as basic social service needs to the community. Accordingly, a seamless network was created between the police problem-solving teams, various service providers, and community members. A digital link provides all Lansing and Tri-County residents access to information related to crime problems, health care, and basic needs such as housing, food, and clothing. A citywide Internet-accessible e-mail system made it searchable by community, police, and government Web sites. An information referral database was also created, allowing anyone with Internet access the ability to connect to nearly all services. Users can search over 600 agencies that provide basic services.

Hayward, California, police work closely with other city agencies to resolve neighborhood problems.

Courtesy Hayward, California, Police Department.

In order to enhance users' ability to identify neighborhood problems, a GIS was implemented. This system was given reported crime locations, park locations, parcel mapping for identification of registered properties, and county health data. Citizens can also contact their police team to provide information that may lead to the solving of a crime in their neighborhood. The effectiveness of all these efforts is evaluated by measurable questions, analysis measures, and specific evaluator resources to determine whether or not the goals of the LPD were met in a timely and satisfactory manner.[16]

Lincoln, Nebraska

The city of Lincoln has formed a **Problem Resolution Team (PRT)** composed of a group of representatives from key public agencies and neighborhood associations, including the city police department, victim and witness unit, attorney's office, building and safety department, housing authority, and urban development office, as well as the county health and social services departments. The team has several functions:

- Gathering information relevant to cases (the team assembles relevant documents that pertain to a complaint or problem, such as reports, correspondence, or other records)
- Sharing information among public agencies (at regular meetings, cases are shared among the team)
- Developing action plans or strategies (team members discuss possible strategies for resolving problems, finalizing action plans, and making specific assignments by consensus; each team member coordinates the activities of his or her own agency that are necessary to fulfill its portion of the action plan)
- Keeping citizens informed about the status of cases and outcomes of city actions
- Making recommendations to city officials to improve city practices or policies

The PRT is currently developing a computer program that will match the police CAD and other agency responses at specific locations to those that are flagged as public housing properties. Another program is being developed that will alert area police captains about locations of excessive CFS in order to identify problems before they become entrenched.

Perhaps the jewel in the crown of Lincoln's community policing efforts is the Quality Service Audit—a partnership between the Lincoln Police Department (LPD) and the Gallup organization. This audit is an ongoing systematic survey of citizen perceptions regarding the quality of the city's police services; it seeks to provide officers with feedback about their contacts with citizens and to provide strategic information to police managers.[17]

Each year student interns from the University of Nebraska and other area colleges, working at the LPD, complete more than 6,000 telephone surveys with Lincoln residents who have recently received police services. Crime victims, drivers in traffic accidents, and even persons who have been arrested or ticketed by the police are surveyed using ten questions developed by Gallup. The department requires all new officers to receive audit feedback as a condition of their employment; officers with more than three years of service are allowed to participate voluntarily. Only aggregate data is provided to managers, and narrative comments are provided to the officers on a monthly basis.[18]

Although surveying citizens is not a new approach under COPPS, this concept is given exceptional importance and sophistication in Lincoln. The mayor and police chief state:

> The tendency to overvalue workload data and underutilize measures of quality service may result in an organizational milieu that rewards a sort of fast driving, rapid response policing, which retards efforts to improve relationships with the public, build citizen trust, and implement or encourage a community-based style of policing. Overemphasis on statistics can be detrimental if an agency does not make a concerted effort to also utilize data about the quality of services provided.[19]

The city received a $50,000 federal grant from the National Institute of Justice to study how its audit system affects officers' behavior.

Reno, Nevada

Reno is located on the northeastern slopes of the Sierra Nevada mountain range. It is a 24-hour gaming community, consisting of 80 square miles and about 190,000 population (swelling to more than 250,000 persons with the influx of tourists for gaming and during special events).

In April 1987, the Reno Police Department (RPD) reorganized its entire agency to implement a new community policing strategy. The city was divided into three geographic areas, and officers and supervisors were assigned to teams in neighborhoods. Every employee (sworn and nonsworn) attended a 40-hour course in community policing.

A vision statement, "Your Police—Our Community," was adopted to stress the importance of collaborative problem solving. New mission and values statements were also developed by a committee of employees. Hiring, promotional systems, selection for special assignments, personnel evaluation systems, and individual awards and decorations reflected officers' knowledge of COPPS and their related performance.

COPPS training was included in the recruit academy and infused into a new national field training model called the Reno Model Police Training Officer Program. Annual in-service training courses were designed to improve officers' COPPS skills, and all officers were certified in crime analysis and crime prevention through environmental design (CPTED) (discussed in Chapter 4). An advanced COPPS mentoring course was designed to create a cadre of "super" trainers. During this 40-hour course, patrol officers are sent into the field with a trainer and are taught higher problem-solving skills. A computer program was developed to track COPPS projects in neighborhoods.

A new city manager adopted a community-oriented government approach to services. Monthly neighborhood advisory board meetings included representatives of various city agencies and the police department working with residents to resolve problems. Problem-solving and CPTED training has been extended to other city agencies that work closely with officers in neighborhoods. The department supplements its service to

In the Kids Korner program in Reno, Nevada, beat officers and medical personnel visit low-income rental motels to identify children who are truant and in need of medical and social services.

Courtesy Reno, Nevada, Police Department.

neighborhoods with more than 60 senior volunteers who are trained to perform crime analysis functions for field officers, monitor school crossings, and distribute crime prevention materials, among other tasks.

An annual community survey provides vital information by measuring residents' perceptions of police performance, personal safety, and other concerns. The results are presented to the entire department in briefings, and responses to community concerns are developed.

Most recently, the RPD has incorporated COPPS into its training for homeland defense. The RPD feels it is important that officers understand that their knowledge of a beat, its residents, and its problems is at the heart of good policing and is the best weapon against the threat of domestic terrorism.

Savannah, Georgia

In 1991 the Savannah Police Department (SPD) began a plan of COPPS implementation that necessitated the hiring of 34 new officers and a reorganization from a centralized command to a system of precincts housed in four different locations. Several programs were then initiated under the COPPS umbrella:

1. *Showcase Neighborhood Program*. The city improved livability in depressed neighborhoods by becoming partners with area residents. The police worked with citizens to identify problems and establish priorities for eliminating them. For this effort, the city won an award from the U.S. Conference of Mayors.

2. *Horse and bicycle patrols*. Public interest led to the development in 1987 of horse patrols in the downtown area (later they were used in targeted problem neighborhoods). Bicycle patrols, also begun downtown, were eventually used successfully in a number of COPPS initiatives. The emphasis of the bicycle patrol is now on problem solving.

3. *Police ministations*. One officer was assigned to each of four public housing areas that experienced high crime rates. Each ministation sponsors a Boy Scout troop and makes constant checks on shut-ins and the elderly.

Since the initiation of COPPS, other new programs have evolved. The Volunteer Program uses 20 actively participating volunteers, and a citizens police academy consists of a ten-week, one-day-per-week course on the operation of the SPD. The department considers COPPS a continually evolving process of changing the way it does business, forcing officers to open their minds to new ideas and change attitudes concerning the delivery of services—all of which, it is hoped, will result in long-term benefits for the police and citizens alike.[20]

Spokane, Washington

Spokane is unique because of its geographic location and regional orientation. Although the current city population is about 197,000, the city is the urban center of the Spokane–Coeur d'Alene area, which has a combined population of more than 450,000. Many demands for city services are generated daily from a nonresident population base, which includes out-of-state workers, surrounding county residents, and Canadian visitors.

Like most police agencies dealing with increasing violent crimes, more drug-related offenses, and limited staff and resources, the Spokane Police Department (SPD) had fallen into the reactive, incident-driven, call-to-call policing model. Officers became seriously stressed, with as many as 40 officers at one time off work because of fatigue-related illnesses.

In late 1991 the department created a strategic planning team to mold its future and identify and remedy obstacles to change. Members met regularly to tackle separate issues; a monthly department newsletter was created as well. The department then teamed with the **Washington State Institute for Community Oriented Policing (WSICOP)** to focus on the COPPS philosophy, develop community partnerships, strengthen informal social control, expand police and community empowerment, and increase social and cultural awareness. Written surveys were distributed to police employees and 1,200 citizens.[21]

Also in late 1991, spurred by the grief resulting from the tragic abduction of two local girls, citizens formed a task force to address neighborhood problems. They approached the city council and proposed to open a neighborhood police substation, staffed by community volunteers, as a central distribution point for information on crime and disorder as well as problem solving. The city council and police chief supported the idea, and on May 1, 1992, the facility opened; four years later, there were nine "COPS Shops" in the city, with four more in the planning stages. The volunteers take police reports, deal with nuisances, disseminate resource information, register bicycles, aid victims, and sponsor guest speakers and "get together" nights. Since the original COPS facilities opened, crime rates have declined significantly.[22]

Tempe, Arizona

Tempe is a growing suburb of Phoenix and the most densely populated city in the state, with about 156,000 residents in a 40-square-mile area. City departments have a reputation for interdepartmental cooperation and problem solving, and citizen surveys have repeatedly indicated the city has an excellent quality of life.

The Tempe Police Department (TPD) employs 256 sworn officers. In response to the changing public safety needs of the city, the TPD initially introduced COPPS on one beat to demonstrate how COPPS strategies could be used to reduce drug demand and overall crime and disorder. This Innovative Neighborhood Oriented Policing (INOP) project was eventually used as a model for citywide implementation of COPPS strategies.[23]

The TPD first ensured that officers had the flexibility to solve problems, using the S.A.R.A. (scanning, analysis, response, assessment) model. Patrol officers worked as a self-directed team, sharing information, problem solving, and scheduling with a COPPS philosophy. Officers were in the beat area for extended time periods.

TPD's first task was to perform a comprehensive and detailed profile of the target area using community and business surveys measuring demographic characteristics, fear of crime, perception of quality of life, and so on. Next, the department involved business owners, residents, neighborhood organizations, other city departments, and social services agencies in project coordination. The team of beat officers then used a variety of intelligence and information sources to support drug enforcement and demand reduction efforts. Newsletters, meetings, and a citizen hotline were used to disseminate information.

An evaluation component was developed by an independent consulting agency to assess INOP's implementation, process, and impact. Although the impact on the community has yet to be determined, the project's impact on the department has been significant. The agency believes that once it made the commitment to INOP, there was no turning back. Changes in organizational structure, management and supervisory roles, policies, goals, recruitment practices, evaluation and award systems, and the COPPS information system are permanent.

A feature of COPPS in Tempe is the department's elaborate system for geographic deployment of patrol officers, allowing officers within a specific area to have varying schedules. Such deployment provides officers with better information about their beats, increases officers' job satisfaction as they take ownership of areas and solve problems, holds officers accountable for their geographic areas, and allows the community to become more involved in solving problems in their neighborhoods.[24] Tempe officers are scheduled individually, rather than by squads, to facilitate greater coverage during peak times. This system has been quantitatively shown to yield higher correlations between CFS and available staffing.

SMALL COMMUNITIES

Arroyo Grande, California

With a complement of 29 staff members, the Arroyo Grande Police Department (AGPD) advertises the fact that should citizens visit their newly expanded police facility, they will not find COPPS written as a specific program or see a COPPS officer or unit; rather, their COPPS philosophy is based on a "Value-Based Policing" philosophy that involves every member of the organization.

The agency has developed an organizational culture that seeks to form true partnerships with the community's various stakeholders in order to provide a better quality of life for all residents. The department's operations attempt to anticipate and solve problems before they erupt into major issues. Following are some examples of COPPS initiatives by the AGPD:

- Employee Participation Program
- Community Advisory Council
- Adopt-a-School Program
- Juvenile Diversion Program
- Bicycle Patrol Program
- Citizen Academy
- Crime Prevention/Neighborhood Watch
- Citizens Assisting Police (CAP) Volunteer Program
- Parent Project (for parents of high-risk children)
- Crime Prevention Through Environmental Design (CPTED)
- D.A.R.E. and Drug-Free Zone
- Neighborhood Officer Program
- Community Services Program
- Foot Patrol Program
- Teen Citizen Academy

Several police agencies have visited or contacted the department concerning its COPPS initiative and these programs, and the California Peace Officer Standards and Training (POST) has used the department's programs as a resource for developing its training.

The Neighborhood Officer Program in Arroyo Grande is a major aspect of COPPS. This program is unique in that instead of assigning a few officers to cover districts or beats across the city as their primary assignment, each patrol officer is responsible for a particular neighborhood as an ancillary duty, thereby involving the entire uniformed division in the program. Patrol officers, while on duty, respond to CFS but also pay attention to ongoing problems in their assigned neighborhoods. The officers act as liaisons between citizens and the department and coordinate problem-solving projects in their areas. The neighborhood officer also meets with individuals and organizations regarding disturbances, juvenile problems, and a variety of civil problems and attempts to solve these problems with creativity or appropriate enforcement methods.[25]

Elmhurst, Illinois

Elmhurst is a city of 43,000 in the southern portion of Illinois, where the police attempt to provide citizens with "one-stop shopping" convenience.

The Elmhurst Police Department (EPD) has a cadre of officers who can handle the full range of citizens' needs, including noise complaints, broken street lamps, fallen trees, and other problems. When possible, EPD officers handle problems themselves; if need be, the problem is communicated to an appropriate city agency. Steps have been taken to ensure that officers have a stake in the policing process. Each officer has policy- and procedure-making power. They even test and select department equipment and uniforms, and they have developed a new design for police vehicles.

Perhaps a unique aspect of Elmhurst's COPPS strategy lies in its approach to officer evaluation. Instead of relying on traditional quantitative criteria, such as number of arrests, the department uses what it calls "community sensing mechanisms." The chief actively seeks feedback from elected government officials and residents. Random callbacks are conducted to gauge citizen satisfaction with officers and CFS. In addition to letters to the chief, other sources of input that are given weight include newspaper articles, editorials, and comments from the local chamber of commerce.[26]

Gresham, Oregon

Gresham has seen dramatic growth, burgeoning housing and commercial development, and increasing demands for governmental services. With 94,000 residents, Gresham is the fourth-largest city in Oregon. Issues such as drug abuse, gang activity, theft, and violent crime forced a transition from the traditional policing model.[27]

The department became Oregon's first COPPS agency in 1992 as part of the department's five-year strategic plan.[28] A new mission was developed, along with the following activities: forming partnerships with many segments of the community; solving problems through a comprehensive process involving a chief's forum, zone advisory groups, and a neighborhood association; empowering citizens; and responding to underlying problems and conditions that cause crime. To design a foundation that would reflect the agency's values, the department conducted a public opinion survey; reconfigured its six patrol districts into three service delivery zones; assigned a lieutenant and team officers to each zone to further develop partnerships with neighborhood associations, schools, and businesses; and received donated office space, furnishings, and materials for zone offices. These efforts led to overall decentralization, greater initiative and empowerment among all levels of staff and officers, and heightened awareness of community concerns and priorities. Several success stories have resulted from Gresham's COPPS strategy[29]:

- Establishment of a community services center
- Placement of a school resource officer, a D.A.R.E. officer, and a gang enforcement officer at each of the two Gresham-area school districts

- Implementation of the Desk Officer Program to reduce response time to lower-priority calls and enable more face-to-face contact between officers and citizens
- Eviction of drug dealers and overall cleanup of apartment complexes
- Voter approval of a three-year, $2 million levy that will, in part, allow for the hiring of nine new officers, three community resource specialists, and one community policing analyst

Orange County, Florida

Tourists are an often-forgotten population in our communities. Orlando, Florida, is the number one tourist destination in the world, with a 78-square-mile tourist corridor. There is also a plethora of criminals seeking to take advantage of unsuspecting victims, many of whom experience armed robbery and theft when items are stolen from their automobiles and hotel rooms. The items most frequently stolen are expensive video cameras, foreign passports, and money.

The Orange County Sheriff's office developed a **Tourist Oriented Police Service (TOPS)** program that offers to tourists the same services that are available to locals as well as tourist-oriented services such as crisis intervention, assistance with crime compensation, interaction with foreign consulates, language translation services, and accompaniment throughout the criminal justice system. A tourist advocate is assigned to the patrol unit, and deputies assigned to TOPS make themselves accessible to tourists by leaving their cars, horses, and motorcycles so that they can walk their beats and interact with visitors. The sheriff's office has also developed a training

Huntington Beach, California, police found bicycle patrol to be an efficient and effective method of delivering services to beach recreation areas.

Courtesy Huntington Beach, California, Police Department.

video to teach hotel and business employees how to prevent crimes against tourists.[30]

Pittsburg, Kansas

Pittsburg is located in the southeast corner of the state and is a university town of about 20,000. The region is known as the "Little Balkans" because it was populated in the late nineteenth century by immigrants from European Balkan countries who came to work in the coal mines and smelters. In the latter part of the twentieth century, Pittsburg experienced another wave of immigrants, this one mostly made up of Hispanics who also sought the American Dream in the heartland, in local factories and businesses. But the community was not mentally or structurally prepared for this influx and its subsequent demands on local resources. The police began hearing cries to "get those Mexicans out of Pittsburg"—even by people whose own grandparents or great-grandparents had lived in the community for 50 years without ever learning to speak English.

Sensing the growing tension, the police realized they could either do nothing and face serious problems of crime and disorder, as several other midwestern communities had, or proactively assist the assimilation of the new residents into the community. The police chief opted for the latter option and with a local female activist (who is bilingual) formed the organization Pittsburg Area Community Outreach (PACO). This body evolved into a 29-person board of directors representing a cross-section of the community who donated their time and professional resources to projects that promoted integration of, and interaction with, the immigrants. The city mayor (who was an attorney) provided free legal advice to the immigrants while other board members and citizens focused on helping them to understand the community. On five occasions, PACO invited an immigration expert from out of state to assist them with their immigration questions and needs at no cost, and the Mexican consulate from Kansas City was invited to provide Mexican passports and identification cards to them; meeting facilities in a municipal auditorium were provided by the city. The county health department sent nurses to the meetings to screen the immigrants for high blood pressure, HIV, and other health problems as well as to dispense free flu shots. The public schools, library, adult education center, and other social services agencies provided assistance as well. The bilingual woman who confounded PACO became very involved with translating marriage and birth certificates for the immigrants, which the police chief notarized as necessary.

To date, more than 250 immigrants have benefited from these services, and PACO has sponsored or supported more than 50 community projects. As a result of these efforts, the police chief was recognized by the U.S. Department of Justice and the U.S. attorney general for the department's commitment to community outreach and police-community relations.[31]

FEDERAL AND STATE AGENCIES

Federal Approach

Several federal agencies are also engaged in COPPS. One example is the U.S. Customs Service's **Strategic Problem Solving (SPS)** initiative, which is composed of the following six steps:

1. Identify problems.
2. Determine objectives/expectations (this involves determining and stating the goals, objectives, or expectations in measurable terms).
3. Develop alternative solutions to problems through brainstorming.
4. Analyze and select alternatives.
5. Implement alternatives.
6. Monitor outcomes.

Since the Customs Service began using SPS in 1996, more than 350 projects have been initiated across the United States. The Office of Strategic Problem Solving rewards team members for their successes in dealing with a wide range of problems:

- Officer safety at land ports of entry
- Stolen vehicle exportations at major seaports
- Internal smuggling conspiracies involving employees of airlines, railroads, and shipping companies
- Drug smuggling across land and via air travel

SPS has proven to be an effective tool because it brings together interdisciplinary teams of subject-matter experts who are encouraged to be creative in developing solutions to problems.[32]

State Police and Universities

The Delaware State Police Rural Community Policing Unit has been in existence since mid-1994. Rural community policing is not common among state police agencies. The demographics of Delaware, however, make this an ideal venue for this concept. Sussex County, the most rural county in Delaware, has communities with high crime rates and few resources to assist the residents of these communities. The purpose and goal of the Delaware State Police Rural Community Policing Unit is to reduce crime and provide resources to eight targeted communities in Sussex County. The unit is composed of four full-time troopers, and it engages in activities such as conflict resolution, peer leadership, drug awareness, and Neighborhood Watch.

CFS in the targeted communities declined about 10 percent after the first year of the COPPS initiative, and other notable accomplishments include working with outside agencies to improve homes, streets, and water systems; obtaining a computerized information system from the state department of health to locate available health resources and job information; giving bicycle helmets and infant or child car seats to parents; and joining with local physicians to provide free physicals for youths attending camps.[33]

State colleges and universities across the nation are also involved with COPPS; one of those is Harvard University (see Exhibit 13–2). Many college and university police departments, such as those at Harvard, Northwestern University,[34] University of North Dakota,[35] and Eastern Connecticut State University,[36] have their own Web pages for describing their COPPS approach to the public; such Web sites also discuss such matters as the agency's history, philosophy, purpose, goals and objectives, and COPPS initiatives.

Some COPPS initiatives are instituted statewide (see Exhibit 13–3 for a COPPS approach in California). Maryland needed a comprehensive statewide approach to pool resources and form partnerships among state and local governments along with business and community leaders. This approach considers a geographic focus on crime. Hot spots exist in urban, suburban, and rural parts of Maryland. To increase the quality of life for citizens, several interrelated statewide initiatives were developed, which included assistance from the state Multi-Agency Response Teams, Hot-Spot Communities and its component initiative Operation Spotlight, and statewide HotSpot Computer Mapping.[37]

 EXHIBIT 13–2

A New Policing Model for Harvard University

Harvard University's decision to restructure resulted in a significant transformation of the Harvard University police department (HUPD). Begun in 1997, the HUPD revised its management structure to reflect the needs of the COPPS approach, emphasizing:

- familiarity with the community through a "neighborhood beat cop" system that builds on frequent, positive interactions with students, faculty, staff, and visitors
- a concentration on crime prevention
- a team approach to problem solving
- increased training at all levels of the agency
- a unified management philosophy governing decision making at all levels of the department

Source: Harvard University Web page: http://www.news.harvard.edu/specials/policing/policing.html (Accessed October 20, 2000), p. 4.

EXHIBIT 13–3

California Highway Patrol's Corridor Safety Program

The California Highway Patrol's (CHP) **Corridor Safety Program** has been credited with saving hundreds of lives on many dangerous rural roadways. The corridor under consideration involved California state routes 41 and 46, which are rural east-west highways connecting California's Central Valley to the central coast region. Scanning revealed this corridor had been the locale of 976 collisions—including 48 fatalities—during a four-year period. The CHP formed a task force to complete a thorough analysis of this problem; this analysis revealed that the main causal factor was unsafe turning movement, which included drifting out-of-lane, overcorrecting off the road, and crossing over the center line into oncoming traffic. Also identified were inadequate shoulders and improper signage. A large Spanish-speaking farm worker population also raised questions of motorists' knowledge of traffic signs and laws as well as laws concerning drinking and driving.

Responses involved the task force's development of a detailed action plan, which had four facets: enforcement, emergency services, engineering, and public education. Patrol was enhanced along the corridor, and a CHP helicopter was permanently assigned to the area. Emergency roadside call boxes were installed, and emergency service providers found ways to deliver services more quickly. Several engineering projects were implemented along the corridor, including the widening of medians, treating outside shoulders with rumble strips, improving overall signage and striping, and adding daytime headlight sections. The CHP mounted an extensive public education campaign, which included the dissemination of two million color flyers about safe-driving habits, safe-driving posters being placed in restaurants and recreational areas, and kick-off news conferences conducted to remind motorists to drive safely.

These efforts were quite successful. Injury accidents were reduced by nearly one-third, and over a five-year period it is estimated that the program has saved 21 lives and prevented 55 injuries.

Source: Police Executive Research Forum, *Excellence in Problem-Oriented Policing: The 2001 Herman Goldstein Award Winners* (Washington, D.C.: Author, 2002), pp. 5–14.

 ## SUMMARY

A common thread running through most (if not all) of the COPPS approaches in this chapter is the realization by the police that new strategies were necessary for addressing crime and neighborhood disorder. The cities and counties discussed in this chapter have demonstrated that the path to attaining a full-fledged COPPS initiative involves a complete transformation in ideology and more than mere rhetoric or additional officers on foot or on bicycle patrol. This path may not be an easy one, but it has been shown that the rewards can be substantial.

ITEMS FOR REVIEW

1. Describe the COPPS efforts that have been undertaken in a large, medium, and small jurisdiction. (Readers might take a comparative approach, looking for similarities and variations between jurisdictions of differing sizes.)
2. Explain how federal and state law enforcement agencies as well as universities are engaging in COPPS activities.

 NOTES

1. Kathleen Woodby and Tess Sherman, "Austin, Texas, Police Department Takes a Bite out of Burglary with GIS," http://www.esri.com/news/arcnews/spring03articles/austin-texas-police.html (Accessed May 28, 2003).
2. Charlotte-Mecklenburg North Carolina, Police Department Web site, http://www.charmeck.org/Departments/Police/About+Us/Home.htm (Accessed May 28, 2003).
3. Chicago, Illinois, Police Department Web site, http://www.ci.chi.il.us/CommunityPolicing.htm (Accessed October 20, 2000).
4. City of Chicago, Office of the Mayor, press release (February 15, 2003), http://w6.ci.chi.il.us/mayor/2003Press/newspress0215capsrallyaustin.html (Accessed May 28, 2003). Also see the Chicago Community Policing Evaluation Consortium, *Community Policing in Chicago, Year Ten* (Chicago: Author, April 2004), pp. i–x.
5. Ft. Lauderdale, Florida, Police Department Web site, "Community Support Division," http://ci.ftlaud.fl.us/police/cpipaul.html (Accessed May 28, 2003).
6. Michael S. Scott, personal communication, December 23, 1993.
7. St. Louis, Missouri, Police Department Web site, http://stlouis.missouri.org/5yearstrategy/app_c(crime).html (Accessed May 28, 2003).
8. Donald S. Quire, St. Petersburg, Florida, Police Department, personal communication, January 31, 1994.
9. St. Petersburg, Florida, Police Department Web site, http://www.stpete.org/police/commpol.htm (Accessed May 28, 2003).
10. Bob Burgreen and Nancy McPherson, "Implementing POP: The San Diego Experience," *The Police Chief* (October 1990):50–56.
11. *Ibid.*, p. 17.
12. San Diego, California, Police Department Web site, http://www.sannet.gov/police/sdpd (Accessed November 26, 1997).
13. Arlington County, Virginia, Police Department Web site, http://www.co.arlington.va.us/pol/comm/htm (Accessed October 20, 2000).
14. Laura M. Hoffmeister, "Best Practices of Community Policing: The Concord Experience," in *Best Practices of Community Policing in Collaborative Problem Solving* (Washington, D.C.: United States Conference of Mayors, June 2001), pp. 32–36.

15. California Department of Justice, Attorney General's Office, Crime Prevention Center, *COPPS: Community Oriented Policing and Problem Solving* (Sacramento, Calif.: Author, November 1992), pp. 43–46.

16. David C. Hollister, "'In Touch': Neighborhood Stabilizing Data Improving Low Income Citizens Quality of Life," in *Best Practices of Community Policing in Collaborative Problem Solving* (Washington, D.C.: United States Conference of Mayors, June 2001), pp. 95–99.

17. Mike Johanns and Tom Casady, "Quality Service Audit Improves Community-Based Policing," *U.S. Mayor* (April 7, 1997):3.

18. Lincoln, Nebraska, Police Department Web site, "Lincoln Police Department Community Policing Projects," http://www.ci.lincoln.ne.us/CITY/police/pdf/compol.pdf#search=%22Lincoln%2C%20Nebraska%20community%20policing%22 (Accessed September 16, 2006).

19. Johanns and Casady, "Quality Service Audit Improves Community-Based Policing," p. 3.

20. Dan Reynolds, Savannah, Georgia, Police Department, personal communication, December 9, 1993.

21. Robert C. Van Leuven, Spokane, Washington, Police Department, personal communication, December 14, 1993.

22. Ellen Painter, "Tragedy Sparks Community Policing in Spokane, Washington," *Community Policing Exchange* (May/June 1995):5.

23. Tempe, Arizona, Police Department, "Overview," http://www.tempe.gov (Accessed November 26, 1997).

24. Tempe, Arizona, Police Department, *Geographic Deployment of Patrol* (Tempe, Ariz.: Author, 1993).

25. "Community Oriented Policing in Arroyo Grande," http://www.thegrid.net/agpd/community.html (Accessed November 26, 1997).

26. Steve Anzaldi, "Adapting to Needs: Community Policing Around the State," *The Compiler* (Fall 1993):8.

27. Gresham, Oregon, Police Department, *A Call for Challenge: Community-Based Policing* (Gresham, Ore.: Author, no date), p. 1.

28. Gresham, Oregon, Police Department, *Community Policing: Vision, Mission, Values* (Gresham, Ore.: Author, no date), p. 2.

29. Gerald Johnson, acting chief of police, Gresham, Oregon, Police Department, personal communication, October 27, 1993.

30. Greta Snitkin, "Tourist Victim Advocacy: Servicing Your Extended Community," *Sheriff Times* (Spring 1997):1, 8.

31. Mike Hall, Chief of Police, Pittsburg, Kansas, personal communication, March 12, 2003.

32. See http://www.customs.treas.gov/enforcem/sps.htm.

33. See http://www.state.de.us./dsp/rural/htm.

34. See http://www.new.edu/up/community.html.

35. See http://www.operations.und.nodak.edu/Op/police/CoP.htm.

36. See http://www.ecsu.ctstateu.edu/depts/police/cops/html.

37. Danny Shell, "Problem Oriented Policing 1997." Paper presented at the 8th Annual International Problem Oriented Policing Conference November 16, 1997, San Diego, California.

COPPS Abroad

Foreign Venues

Key Terms and Concepts ────────────

Australian Capital Territory (ACT)

Brit POP

Comparative approach

Koban

Nick Tilley Award

Operation Mantle

Police Community Relations Officer
(PCRO)

Police Executive Research Forum
(PERF)

Royal Canadian Mounted Police
(RCMP)

Spotlight Initiative

Stopbreak

Learning Objectives ──────────────

As a result of reading this chapter, the student will:

- Know that COPPS is being practiced around the world
- Appreciate the value of viewing COPPS from a comparative perspective
- Be able to compare the practice of community policing in the United
  States with the manner in which it is practiced in foreign venues

> Think globally, act locally.
>
> *–Rene Dubos*
>
> The world is but a school of inquiry.
>
> *–Michel de Montaigne*

INTRODUCTION

The world has become a global village. Through technology, rapid intercontinental travel, and high-technology communications systems, we are virtual neighbors around the planet. Even very disparate countries can learn from, and have shared much with, one another.

It has been said that the **comparative approach** provides the opportunity to "search for order."[1] This chapter does so by comparing the work of community oriented policing and problem solving (COPPS) in foreign venues with that in the United States. It will be seen that COPPS has indeed gone international and is now the operational strategy of many police agencies around the globe.

First we "travel" to Canada, looking at the country generally, and then view COPPS in Burnaby and with the Royal Canadian Mounted Police (problem-solving efforts in Ontario are also discussed in Exhibit 14–1). Next we look at some of the earliest community policing efforts in Japan and then move on to Australia, where COPPS is having a major effect across that country. Great Britain is our next stop. The chapter concludes with a brief look at COPPS in some other venues, including Scotland, Isle of Man, Israel, Hong Kong, New Zealand, and the Netherlands. These and other venues are discussed in seven exhibits that are spread throughout the chapter.

Much can be learned from comparatively examining the activities and approaches that are undertaken in each venue. The reader is encouraged to determine whether there are common elements of COPPS in these countries and to compare each with the American strategy as it is described in earlier chapters. We discuss in the chapter summary the issue of whether common denominators exist, the presence of an international understanding, and the application of COPPS concepts around the world.

CANADA

Canada stretches nearly 5,000 miles from east to west, touches both the Atlantic and Pacific Oceans, embraces 4 million square miles, covers six time zones, and has ten provinces. More than 33 million people reside in Canada, 90 percent of whom are within 100 miles of the southern border, near the United States. They speak more than 60 languages and are members of 70 ethnocultural groups.[2]

More than 84,000 sworn officers work in about 400 independent police services in Canada, translating to about 1 officer for every 520 Canadians. Of the total number of officers, about one-quarter are members of the Royal Canadian Mounted Police (discussed later), and 16 percent work for the three independent provincial police forces—the Ontario Provincial Police (see Exhibit 14–1), the Surete du Quebec, and the Royal Newfoundland

EXHIBIT 14–1

Community Policing in Ontario

The Ontario Provincial Police (OPP) have created an impressive Web site that describes in detail (in both English and French) its Community Policing Development Centre. The site describes its community policing strategy, including the differences between COPPS and traditional policing, and an explanation of what is termed "P.A.R.E.": problem identification, analysis, response, and evaluation. It also provides the agency's mission (including the use of police–community "prevention partnerships" and teams), objectives, and strategic implementation plan; provides a news bulletin; and provides an extensive guide to problem solving with an online "How Do We Do It" manual. COPPS service delivery is customized for each neighborhood, which guarantees that police services will best meet community needs. A "Just for Kids" page is available, as well as an "Honour Roll" of citizens and police, a slate of current programs, OPP recruitment information, wanted/missing persons information, and links to other governmental agencies.

Source: OPP Web site http://www.gov.on.ca/opp/english (Accessed May 29, 2003).

Constabulary. More than half (56 percent) of Canada's police officers work in 361 independent municipal police services. The average size of a Canadian police service is 141 sworn personnel.[3]

Community policing is now the official approach to policing across Canada, at all levels of government. The most widely recognized "police service of excellence" in Canada is the city of Edmonton's Police Service, which pioneered a demonstration project on neighborhood foot patrol in 1993. Edmonton is considered by many to be the "Mayo Clinic of policing" and is perhaps the model of a very modern police service.[4]

But the question of whether community policing has succeeded in Canada is yet to be answered. Despite its widespread adoption, there has been little in the way of comprehensive, rigorous evaluations of community policing in Canada, which lacks a police research arm that would be equivalent to the U.S. **Police Executive Research Forum (PERF)**, Police Foundation, or National Institute of Justice.[5] It is believed, however, that four challenges still confront community policing in Canada[6]:

1. The police have yet to overcome the unrealistic expectations and demands placed on them by the public that they provide rapid emergency response while providing order maintenance services—what one author described as demanding both a "Green Beret" and a "Peace Corps" role of the police.[7]
2. Community policing in Canada carries a negative bias toward dealing with local problems at a time when drug smuggling, money laundering, and other crimes demand national and international focus.
3. The police are still challenged to move beyond the traditional criteria for police success: arrests, clearance rates, and response times.

4. Police need to take advantage of a brief window of opportunity to implement and prove the effectiveness of COPPS before a fiscal crisis of government drives policing back to the reactive, incident-driven traditional form of policing.

Today, because of a decline in trust and cooperative spirit between the police and its citizens, community policing—particularly with the Northwest Mounted Police—focuses primarily on crime prevention, with crime prevention programs being designed to protect children and property. See Exhibits 14–1 and 14–2 for COPPS applications in Ontario and Vancouver.

Project Metrotown in Burnaby

Burnaby comprises an area of about 38 square miles on the southwest coast of Canada and has approximately 194,000 residents. The **Royal Canadian Mounted Police (RCMP)**–Burnaby Detachment received a 2002 Herman Goldstein Award for its work in decreasing crime in three apartment buildings and the surrounding area.

The problem began in 1998 when rampant drug dealing became common around the Metrotown SkyTrain station. Honduran nationals were

EXHIBIT 14–2

"Showdown at the Playground" in Vancouver

A 2001 recipient of the Herman Goldstein Award for Excellence in Problem-Oriented Policing was a problem-solving project in Vancouver, British Columbia, Grandview-Woodland Community Policing Centre. Grandview Park, a one-square-block area of Grandview-Woodland, is adjacent to a large community center that houses an elementary school, a day care center, and various community services. The neighborhood is also next to Downtown Eastside (DTES), an area plagued by drug use and drug dealing. DTES, which is comprised of about 20 square blocks, is one of Canada's poorest areas and also has one of the highest needle-based drug user populations and HIV drug infection rates in North America. Analysis of the problem was accomplished from several perspectives, including the social dynamics of the problem population, the park structure and its effect on criminal behavior, past police responses, and community meetings and surveys.

Responses included the use of plainclothes operations to identify the drug dealers, area citizens willingly opening their homes to officers as observation points, and a volunteer foot patrol that provided information about drug dealing. The Park Board was asked to help to control graffiti and litter, and youths were hired for these efforts as well as to paint murals. Suggestions from Simon Fraser University criminology students helped horticulturists understand crime prevention through environmental design (CPTED) and how the park should be changed; they eliminated obstructed sightlines, severely pruned covered areas, and replaced low bushes where drug dealers hid drugs. Furthermore, the local animal control center stepped up its enforcement of unleashed dogs used by drug dealers to intimidate residents.

An assessment revealed that these efforts generally resulted in decreases in 911 calls and other calls for service to the area, as well as increases in numbers of arrests for trafficking and drugs seized. Significantly, people began bringing their children to the playground once again.

coming to Canada, claiming refugee status; a large number began occupying the three apartment buildings in Burnaby. The problem soon became complex, involving a marked increase in calls for service as well as an organized crime problem. After working through the S.A.R.A. (scanning, analysis, response, assessment) problem-solving process, charging 30 persons with trafficking, and reducing calls for service (CFS) at the apartments and the surrounding area by 40 percent, the RCMP had successfully addressed the problem—or so they thought. By mid-1999 the problem had returned, with a resurgence of CFS to the area. Again, town meetings were held and solutions were sought. Many problem-solving activities were undertaken, including court orders barring certain persons from the premises.

This time the police got the community more involved and opened a community police office in the area, used volunteer bike patrols and a citizens' watch, redesigned the train station to make it less attractive to loiterers, and employed a joint task force of police departments whose officers patrolled the train station area. Following this renewed effort, the problem-solving approach was a success, resulting in more than 200 drug-trafficking charges in the area and deportations of many traffickers.

This venue's situation and its eventual success show the need to revisit a problem with a problem analysis.[8]

Royal Canadian Mounted Police (RCMP)

Community policing efforts of the RCMP have been making significant strides in its smaller detachments, where COPPS has been operational for a long time. In September 1993 the RCMP resolved to pilot a detachment-wide COPPS initiative in one of its largest areas—Burnaby, British Columbia—with a population of about 150,000 and approximately 150 officers.[9]

The official view is that the adoption of community policing allows the RCMP to become more responsive to the needs of the communities it serves. The RCMP also believes that "the open management style under this philosophy allows all officers to make appropriate informed decisions and take action, giving the RCMP [the] flexibility needed to provide completely responsive, integrated, and relevant police service."[10] The primary elements of the strategy include the following (note that there is a strong problem oriented policing flavor)[11]:

- *Direct service delivery*. Work with the community to identify its problems; resolve the identified problems; empower officers to make decisions and take action; and make patrol, enforcement, and investigative work effective and directed.

- *Change in administrative organization*. Decentralize, using modern management concepts (such as problem solving, innovative resource deployment, risk management, flattened organizational hierarchy, and participatory management); create an enhanced generalist career path; reduce the paper burden; and utilize citizen satisfaction surveys.

COMMUNITY POLICING IN JAPAN

Earliest Community-Based Approach

Japan—with its Showa Constitution containing many articles that are similar to those found in the Fourth, Fifth, Sixth, and Eighth Amendments to the U.S. Constitution[12]—can lay claim to possessing the oldest and best-established community policing system in the world. Japan initiated its system immediately after World War II out of a combination of traditional culture and American democratic ideals. According to Jerome Skolnick and David Bayley, four elements seem to be at the core of this philosophy: (1) community-based crime prevention, (2) reorientation of patrol activities to emphasize nonemergency servicing, (3) increased accountability to the public, and (4) decentralization of command.[13] Next we briefly discuss these four elements.

Each of Japan's 47 prefectures has its own autonomous police force, and together they employ about 220,000 officers on densely populated islands totaling about 144,000 square miles and 127 million people.[14] If community policing began with community-based crime prevention, the Japanese experience offers several valuable insights. One of the basic reasons Japanese policing works as well as it does is that the officers daily deal face-to-face with citizens and therefore have become a part of the community rather than being separated from the people in a vehicle. Also, Japanese neighborhood crime prevention associations (the Japanese tradition of the *gonin-gumi,* a group of five people in a neighborhood) have generally given Japanese culture a much closer relationship between people and their neighbors.

With regard to Japanese police patrol activities, people in Japan seem not to have the same "we versus they" perceptions about the police as Americans have.[15] Thus, the Japanese appear to be far more willing than Americans to accept police presence. As a result, Japanese police place heavy emphasis on order maintenance and crime prevention, aiding the community to resolve problems that could lead to disorder.[16] A major part of this effort includes the counseling services that are part of every Japanese police station. All police stations assign an experienced older officer, usually a sergeant, to provide a wide range of general counseling, ranging from family disputes to questions about contracts and indebtedness. Trained in dispute resolution, the police are able to provide a helpful informal conciliation.[17]

If the police and the community are to become coproducers of an orderly society, police must have closer accountability to the public and begin to share power with the community they serve, starting with closer relations with community groups, clubs, churches, and civic organizations to help obtain information, define priorities, and aid in planning effective strategies.[18]

If all of this is to be accomplished, however, the fourth major element in COPPS must be developed: decentralization of command. Providing

Japanese officers perform their duties in a neighborhood koban.

Courtesy Office of International Criminal Justice.

neighborhood police centers and beat offices as well as giving officers greater discretion to develop responses to community problems form the nucleus of this strategy. This has been one of the strengths of the Japanese system.[19] Patrol officers in Japan are under even closer supervision than are rank-and-file officers in the United States. Yet the *kobun-oyabun* (a kind of student-mentor relationship) between the Japanese patrol officers and their superiors allows the officers a great deal of input into decisions about local problems.

Koban

Like the *chusai-san* (a rural police officer who is required to visit each household twice per year and works with citizens to solve area problems), the urban police officer in Japan visits neighborhood households and does police business in the **koban.** These police boxes are the foundation of the sense of security of the people, and they function as the bases of police functions closest to the citizens. Officers prepare and disseminate crime bulletins and provide citizens with tips concerning crime prevention, stories of good deeds by children, and opinions of residents.[20] Exhibit 14–3 provides a case study of the work of koban police.

EXHIBIT 14–3

Work of the Japanese Koban

A police officer of the police box of the Sendai Higashi police station, Miyagi Prefecture, visited once a week and took care of a 75-year-old woman who had no relatives in the neighborhood, suffered from diabetes, and had problems with her legs. One day the officer called on the woman and got no answer. Knowing that this was unusual and because of her physical state, the officer entered the home to check on her welfare. He found the woman lying unconscious and assisted in hospitalizing her. Then the officer tried to find the woman's relatives and determined that she had a niece living in Sendai. As a result, the aged woman was able to obtain better care with the help of her niece.

A koban may be found every few blocks; there are about 15,000 kobans across the country, 8,000 of which are referred to as *chuzaisho,* or "police substations," in which the officers actually live. Police officers generally stand watch at the doorway of the koban or at nearby traffic intersections to help minimize crimes and traffic accidents, direct traffic, and make arrests when necessary. In Tokyo, over 80 percent of arrests are by koban officers.

There are also mobile police boxes, or wagons, that assist the koban as needed, and temporary kobans are established at times as well.[21] The Japanese police try to keep the number of people for which a koban is responsible to less than 12,000 and the area to less than four-tenths of a square mile. No koban may be less than six-tenths of a mile from another one. They are often put in areas with more than 320 criminal cases per year, more than 45 traffic accidents, and a high volume of pedestrian traffic.[22]

Kobans are usually storefront offices or tiny buildings resembling sentry stations. They consist of a reception room with a low counter or desk, telephone, radio, and wall maps; a resting room for personnel, often with a television set; a small kitchen or at least a hot plate and refrigerator; an interview room; a storeroom; and a toilet.[23] The officers' work shifts are long; they spend 24 hours at the koban every 3 days. From a tour of duty in a koban, officers move on to detective work, traffic patrol, riot police, and other specialized assignments.[24] Following is one author's koban description:

> [The koban officer] has a wealth of . . . data on the jurisdiction . . . such as lists of people working late at night who might be of help as witnesses to crime, of people who are normally cooperative with the police, of people who own guns or swords, of all rented homes and apartments that might serve as hideouts for fugitives of people with criminal records, and of people with mental illness; organizational charts of gangs in the police station jurisdiction (sometimes with photographs of all the gangsters); lists of old people in the area living alone who should

be visited periodically . . . and of all bars, restaurants, and amusement facilities in the jurisdiction; a short history of the koban; and a compilation of the total population, area, and number of households in the jurisdiction.[25]

Herein lies a fundamental difference between the Japanese and American police: Whereas American police come to the home only when called by citizens, their Japanese counterparts are constantly watchful of, informed about, and involved with the people in their neighborhoods.

AUSTRALIA'S POLICING STRATEGY

This section describes COPPS efforts in four Australian jurisdictions—Queensland, South Australia, Toowoomba, and the capital, Canberra—while Exhibit 14–4 discusses a day in the life of an Australian officer in the bush.

Stopbreak in Queensland

Data analysis by Queensland, Australia, police revealed that residential burglaries had increased 176 percent during the past 20 years and 66 percent during one 5-year period. Burglaries represented one in five of all criminal offenses. Analysis revealed two contributing factors to the burglary problem: a lack of proper security measures, and the ease with which stolen goods could be "fenced" for profit. It was no wonder that many of the 3.4 million citizens of Queensland, Australia's second-largest state, no longer felt safe in their homes.

Furthermore, there were disturbingly high rates of repeat victimization and low rates of offender apprehension. The police also concluded that "even if the number of police patrols were doubled, the typical dwelling or business would still only be under surveillance for an average of 60 seconds per day."[26]

A response—termed **Stopbreak**—was developed to address the primary contributing factors. A proactive COPPS philosophy was adopted on several levels. The police were trained in proper security audit techniques, and hot spots were examined to reduce repeat victimization and home burglaries in general. Citizens were advised concerning crime prevention and proper security measures they could take in their homes. Victims were referred to victim support organizations, and homes and businesses that had been targets of repeat burglaries had temporary portable silent burglary alarms installed. These alarms were linked to police headquarters. An assessment found that officers and victims alike indicated that the strategies were substantially positive in nature, and a majority of victims implemented at least one of the security measures recommended by the police.[27]

EXHIBIT 14-4

A Day in the Life of an Australian Bush Officer

Policing Australia's remote Aboriginal communities requires diplomacy and an ability to work in some of the most physically challenging regions in the world. Australia is using more and more women for these tasks in the bush. As a case in point, Sgt. Tanya Woodcock is responsible for maintaining harmony among the 2,500 traditional indigenous people on the two islands of Bathurst and Melville. She acts as a mediator in tribal and family disputes and is also adept at sidestepping crocodiles. Following is an account of Woodcock's typical day. At 8:00 A.M., she checks the computer system at the police station, located near her home on Melville Island, to see if anything has happened overnight; she devotes about two hours to this task. At 10:00 A.M., she is in her four-wheel- drive vehicle, heading to the various communities. By noon she is in Milikapiti community, which has an Aboriginal community police officer. By 3:00 P.M. Woodcock is headed back to the police station. Although armed, officers do not carry their firearms into these traditional communities, because it alarms their sense of stability. The biggest problem for the police is violent crimes against the person, usually fueled by alcohol or drug abuse. Another problem to this tropical paradise comes from Mother Nature: the weather. Ferocious cyclones do occur, and during such times it is Woodcock's responsibility to warn the remote communities' 2,500 residents. Toward this end, she has developed, and plays on local television stations, a videotape that warns residents of impending cyclones and what to do if the area is hit.

Source: http://www.bbc.co.uk.crime/fighters/dayinthelife/bushofficer.shtml (Accessed May 29, 2003).

Operation Mantle in South Australia

In the late 1990s the South Australia Police (SAPOL) employed a problem-solving approach across metropolitan Adelaide. Prior to **Operation Mantle,** law enforcement strategies lacked integrated approaches for dealing with high-level and low-level drug trafficking; furthermore, drug supply reduction measures predominantly aimed at the high level were unsuccessful in reducing the supply of illicit drugs. This operation employed three strategies: using intelligence-driven problem-solving policing methods that take account of harm minimization in an effort to reduce mid- and low-level drug trafficking; fostering and maintaining alliances with government agencies and the community to enhance the integrated approach; and ensuring good communication and intelligence flow within and between tactical units and SAPOL. The operation's integrated approach to drug enforcement included the establishment of regional tactical investigation teams that targeted low-level and mid-level traffickers and that also sought closer collaboration with a range of agencies to improve harm minimization and treatment options.

The operation appears to have had an impact on drug-related crime. The impact was not spectacular, nor was it expected to be. Operation Mantle stabilized the trafficking rates, a significant achievement in light of the previously projected increases in such crimes. These results are felt to echo Herman Goldstein's contention that the best that should be expected is a minimization of the problem, a reduction of the adverse effects, and a lessening of consequent suffering.[28]

Pilot Project in Toowoomba

In the mid-1990s the Criminal Justice Commission and the Queensland Police Service established a two-year beat policing pilot project in the city of Toowoomba in southeastern Queensland. The impetus for the project was a governmental report that recommended the adoption of COPPS.

This project was designed to promote a community-based policing style, characterized by localized problem-oriented service delivery. The key features of the project were to be the following[29]:

- Assignment of officers to two defined beat areas on a long-term basis (the officers were to reside in these beat areas as well)
- Provision of most policing services by the locally based officers
- Use of foot patrols by the beat area officers
- Inclusion of proactive policing activities as part of the normal duties of the officers
- Introduction of a negotiated response strategy

The pilot project was based on COPPS initiatives in the United States and Canada and was designed to incorporate a problem-solving orientation into the normal duties of the police officers so that they could focus on the underlying conditions generating CFS and develop strategies to address those conditions. Management and beat officers provided strong support for the problem-oriented approach.

After the two-year period ended, the Criminal Justice Commission in Brisbane determined that the number of CFS generated by the top ten addresses in the beat areas decreased over the first 12 months of the project, that the problems handled by the beat officers ranged from prowlers and alcohol-related incidents to disputes between neighbors, and that the two most common strategies employed by the beat officers to resolve problems were removal of the problem and preventive activities such as fixing street lighting.

Canberra and ACT

The city of Canberra is Australia's capital and located in the **Australian Capital Territory (ACT),** about 300 miles southwest of Sydney. The ACT currently has a population of 310,000, and the city of Canberra contains many sites of national significance, such as the Parliament, the War Memorial, and the National Art Gallery. The embassies of over 70 nations are also in the Canberra area.

The people of the ACT complain of a critical shortage of federal agents—a perception that is supported, perhaps, by the highest increase in crime rates ever during the past few years, particularly in home burglaries and motor vehicle thefts. The ACT also has its lowest police numbers

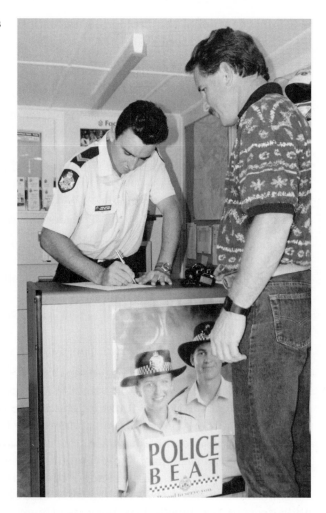

An Australian police officer takes a crime report at a neighborhood station.

per population of any police force in Australia. Although the police in the ACT practice community policing, many people view it as paradoxical that the nation's capital is in such a dire situation and are calling for additional police personnel in order to cope with the rising crime rate.[30]

COPPS IN GREAT BRITAIN

There are 43 police forces in England and Wales: There are 27 county police forces, 8 combined police areas (where 2 or 3 counties have been united for policing purposes), and 6 metropolitan forces.[31] Almost all police forces in this region are introducing or are actively considering the introduction of COPPS in some form.[32]

Indeed, COPPS has progressed to such a level in Great Britain that the Home Office in London has published dozens of monographs on the subject (termed **Brit POP**), including two that are highly significant in the field: the Police Research Group's *Problem-Oriented Policing: Brit POP*, 1996, which described the early stages of a development project implementing problem oriented policing in one division in Leicestershire, and *Brit POP II: Problem-Oriented Policing in Practice*, 1998, which highlighted "the lessons learned over the past two to three years for introducing and maximizing the benefits from POP."[33]

Guiding Philosophy

The philosophy of community oriented policing in Britain, as well as several important aspects of its practice (such as neighborhood-based patrols), can be traced to the formation of professional policing in the nineteenth century and the ways in which the police mandate was established and legitimated.[34]

Early architects of British policing established the idea that effective policing can be achieved only with the consent of the community.[35] From the 1970s onward, arguments in favor of greater use of foot patrol have assumed an increasingly important place in public debate about policing in Britain. Community surveys have found that more foot patrol is clearly what most people want, so there has been a return to the bobby on the beat—a virtually unanimously accepted goal of public policy.[36] Foot patrol remains a key feature of community oriented policing in Britain. Exhibit 14–5 discusses one community's program.

Early Initiatives

Sir Kenneth Newman, who served as commissioner of Scotland Yard from 1982 to 1987, brought to the job a new intellectual dimension and a willingness to challenge existing police practices. He launched many planning initiatives, including authorizing his staff in 1983 "to evaluate the feasibility of adopting the 'Problem Oriented Approach' in the Metropolitan Police."[37]

An evaluation of the studies found that COPPS had the potential to improve police performance.[38] The studies demonstrated that the potential for the implementation of COPPS was severely limited unless greater flexibility was introduced into the organization. Newman stated in a letter to the force in 1984 that "the structure of our hierarchy [was] hindering more than helping the good work done on the ground."[39] Thus, Newman sought to reduce the rigidity of the organization.[40]

Today, undoubtedly the key issue concerning COPPS in Britain is accountability. Public opinion is especially intense in London, where no local control over the police exists and there are about 31,500 sworn officers. Critics are calling for a greater permeation of the community philosophy throughout the police organization and in its operations. For many, to this point the community approach to policing in Britain has been more rhetoric than reality.

EXHIBIT 14–5

West Mercia Constabulary's Four Tracks of Policing

West Mercia Constabulary serves 1.1 million people in Herfordshire, Worcestershire, and Shropshire counties in England, which spread out over 2,868 miles. The constabulary has developed a policing model known as the four tracks of policing, which sets out a strategic approach to implementing COPPS. The first track, local policing, stresses the constabulary's commitment to local policing and local partnerships to achieve effective solutions to local problems. The second track, responsive policing, focuses on the constabulary's duty to respond appropriately to requests for assistance and to provide adequate resources for emergency situations. The third track, targeted policing, concentrates on using intelligence-based policing operations to solve specific problems. Finally, the fourth track, policing partnerships, recognizes that no matter how effective the constabulary may be with the other three tracks, it is vitally important to work with communities to develop shared solutions.

Source: Workshop presentation, Constable David C. Blakely, The 8th Annual International Problem Oriented Policing Conference: Problem Oriented Policing 1997, November 15, 1997, San Diego, California.

Role of Constables

Britain's constables have a mandate to control crime. They are to "penetrate the community in a multitude of ways in order to influence its behavior for illegality and toward legality."[41] The officer's primary role is defined as being concerned with crime and criminals, and the emphasis is largely on crime fighting and law enforcement; contact with the public is to be fostered mainly in terms of its contribution toward meeting these ends.[42]

Public input is growing concerning the police task, however. Almost all of the 41 police authorities in England and Wales now have established formal police-community consultative committees. Some of the issues addressed by the committees are maintaining mutual trust between the police and the public; maintaining community peacefulness and improving quality of life; promoting greater public understanding of policing issues, such as causes of crime and police procedures and policies; examining patterns of complaints against officers; fostering links with local beat officers; and developing victim support services.[43]

For Britain's police, Neighborhood Watch forms the most common and popular form of community-based crime prevention. Neighborhood Watch programs have grown immensely in Britain.[44]

Contemporary Approaches

A number of recent attempts in Great Britain have introduced problem-solving strategies in England and Wales.[45]

A British constable provides a tourist with directions at Parliament Square in London.

The following premises of successful COPPS implementation have become accepted in Great Britain[46]:

- COPPS can create more time for officers because the source of problems is dealt with and CFS reduced.
- Deliberately and systematically introduced, COPPS can build on existing partnership work and yield increased benefits from it.
- Humane and efficient responses to individual incidents can occur alongside COPPS.
- Regardless of COPPS, the police still have to provide wide-ranging services to the public, for which they will have to maintain their response to non-crime-related incidents.
- Police officers will find COPPS rewarding, and gradually the police culture will accept the centrality of COPPS.[47]

Exhibit 14–6 describes the **Nick Tilley Award** that has become very prestigious in the United Kingdom for excellence in problem solving.

COPPS IN OTHER VENUES

Scotland

Although overall crime had been decreasing in the Strathclyde region of Scotland, many of its 2.25 million citizens perceived that crime rates were increasing dramatically. Violent crimes, however, were increasing; it became part of the culture in the west of Scotland to carry knives. The Strathclyde police—an amalgamation of six police forces in west-central Scotland and the largest in the country—decided that it had to find a solution to the fear and violent crime problems.[48]

EXHIBIT 14–6

United Kingdom's Nick Tilley Award

The Nick Tilley Award is named for Professor Nick Tilley of Nottingham Trent University, who carried out a considerable body of work in community policing in the United Kingdom and was often commissioned by the Home Office to develop problem oriented policing. The award was established in 1999 to recognize excellence in crime reduction using problem-oriented partnership principles. Appropriately, the award is presented at the annual National POP Conference held each fall in the United States and is similar to the prestigious Herman Goldstein Award for Excellence in Problem-Oriented Policing that is conferred by the U.S. Office of Community Oriented Policing Services, Center for Problem-Oriented Policing. The Tilley Award is becoming increasingly valued as a mark of quality, and as such is attracting more and better entries each year. In 2005, 58 applications were submitted from British police forces.

Source: United Kingdom, "Tilley Awards 2006." http://www.crimereduction.gov.uk/tilley_awards2006.htm (Accessed April 11, 2006).

The **Spotlight Initiative,** the first program of its kind in the United Kingdom, was implemented with a "listening tour," as police sought to learn which types of crimes were of major concern to the public. The police learned that minor crimes—litter, graffiti, and disorderly gangs shouting obscenities, smashing bottles, and carrying weapons—worried them the most. From this, four fundamental principles of the initiative developed: It must address public concerns, fully exploit corporate partnerships, address serious crimes through concentration on minor crimes, and feature maximum presence of officers on the beat. Eleven major crimes were spotlighted as well.

Division commanders were immediately instructed to seek improved environmental clean-up resources to rid their areas of litter and graffiti. A media coverage campaign was launched to boost the public's and police officers' confidence. To attack minor crimes, the department made greater use of intelligence and crime management systems, employed new technology (such as satellite tracking systems, telephone bugs, and high-definition nighttime cameras), and worked with every group with a legitimate interest in reducing crime.

On the day the program was operationalized, officers arrested almost 400 men and women in a series of dawn raids, targeting people who had "forgotten" to appear in court or for whom bench warrants had been issued. Police searched 43,000 people for weapons in the first three months (with the number of people carrying weapons declining about 50 percent). Truancy rates at local schools declined dramatically. The department installed a series of closed-circuit cameras in high-crime areas. Crime declined as well, and more drugs were recovered than ever before. The department was quite pleased with its results.[49]

A constable from the Isle of Man converses with a citizen while walking a footbeat in a city's business district.

Courtesy Isle of Man Police Department.

Isle of Man

Even very small countries have COPPS. One such example is the Isle of Man—part of the British Isles and situated midway between England, Scotland, Ireland, and Wales—which has a landmass of only 227 square miles, measures 33 miles by 13 miles, and is occupied by only 75,000 people.

The Isle of Man Constabulary has large aims, however. Its Policing Plan reveals its vision:

> We will provide a world-class, community-based policing service to the whole of the Island's community. Cooperation, consultation, and a partnership approach will drive all that we do, helping to make the Island an even safer place in which to live. Our aim: to be a world-class police service. What we will offer: community-based policing excellence.[50]

The constabulary's values statement is also brief but powerful:

> Ours is an organization that is open, honest, and caring. The organization itself, and those who work for it, view integrity as being vital to our success.

Its policing style and philosophy are as follows:

> We aim to provide excellence in all that we do. Our policing style will be friendly, approachable, and neighborly, offering the best possible

service to the whole of the Island's community. The main driver will be a problem solving approach, both internally and externally.

These may seem to be ambitious statements, but when one views these words in conjunction with the total package of materials that the constabulary has developed and disseminated to its populace—as well as its strategic plan—as part of an extensive program of modernization underpinned by the philosophy of continuous improvement, there can be little doubt as to the sincerity of the organization's resolve.

Israel

In the mid-1990s the police in Israel, providing services to about 6.2 million people, decided to change from a basically reactive form of policing to COPPS, knowing it would not be easy. The national police force had been, for the previous 20 years, engulfed in security duties by virtue of terrorist and other emergency matters. Because of a shifting of police resources to antiterrorist and bomb disposal units, efforts to reduce crime at the local station level had not been successful, and domestic violence and family abuse had become particularly problematic.[51]

A strategic plan was developed to implement COPPS. A new headquarters unit was established to implement the planned change, beginning with a bottom-up approach that would start with the station level and officers in the field because they best knew the communities' problems. In phase one, the local police and mayors of many communities were approached and asked if they were willing to undertake the change to COPPS. Their enthusiasm was usually high. Then the officers and selected community leaders were trained in the working principles of COPPS; such training included explanations of the need for the police and the public to collaborate and of the problem-solving approach to analyzing and addressing problems.

A three-day planning workshop was then held with the police and with community and local organizations and associations. Each police station's mission statement was developed, and local problems and needs were scanned, prioritized, and analyzed. The strategic plan, including timetables, responsible persons, and needed resources, was then developed. Each police station was to work on ten objectives during a six-month period.[52]

By the second year of its implementation across Israel, more than 50 communities had undergone the shift to COPPS. Cities were "rewarded" by being allowed to send one person abroad to study COPPS in other countries. Furthermore, the shift to COPPS had advanced to such an extent that the decision was made to effect the shift at the senior management (police headquarters) level. The atmosphere there, however, was not so enthusiastic, being more of a "business as usual" attitude, while the local police stations went about their "quiet revolution." Planning workshops were provided and headquarters' objectives were developed, leading to greater acceptance of the new philosophy. Community Policing Centers were set up in neighborhoods to decentralize services, and a major organizational change occurred, resulting in a greater flattening of the force to empower local levels and to provide more efficient and effective police services.[53]

Today, because of increases in crime (particularly racketeering and drug trafficking) and the influx of immigrant groups, a major crime prevention initiative has been launched. Citizen contact is strongly encouraged, and the police even give advice and instruction to students on ways of preventing crime. Other programs address domestic violence, auto theft, and teen alcohol consumption.[54]

Hong Kong

Hong Kong's population is about 6.9 million, making it one of the most densely populated places in the world—up to 25,000 people per square mile in the urban areas.[55] Hong Kong began practicing some forms of COPPS in the 1960s, with its early policing style being typical of British colonial policing. The result was a series of police-community relations initiatives that were launched in the late 1960s, with a view to improving relations between the police and the public, developing popular trust, and cultivating public support for crime control. During 40 years of evolution of community policing, the Hong Kong police force has undergone six stages, involving five major community policing schemes with different focuses[56]:

1. **Police Community Relations Officer (PCRO),** a community relations program focusing on the promotion of police-community relations
2. Neighborhoods Police Unit (NPU), a crime control device with the objective of providing convenient locations for the public to report criminal activities to the police and offer support for combating crime
3. Junior Police Call (JPC), centering on the control of juvenile delinquency and including a range of activities and programs for youth
4. Police School Liaison (PSL), dealing with juvenile crimes in school by working with students, authorities, and teachers
5. Neighborhood Watch (NW), which organized local residents' efforts to control and prevent burglaries and sexual offenses

The first stage of community policing for Hong Kong occurred from 1968 to 1973. With the relaxation of police-community tension as the theme, the police established the Police Public Information Bureau. The second stage was the adoption of a community orientation in crime control that signaled Hong Kong's entering the era of community policing. The focus was on two-way communication, and the PCRO marked the first major attempt by the police to reach community members and involve them in crime fighting.

The third stage was the rapid growth of community policing across Hong Kong. The PCRO was quickly expanded to cover every police district, and the NPU, the JPC, and PSL concepts were launched. The fourth stage was the retrenchment of the police-community relations effort briefly from 1983 to 1985. The focus was on the reorganization of tight police resources for effective crime control. NPUs were replaced by a small scale of Neighborhood Police Coordinators (NPCs)—viewed widely as a step backward from the force's previous police strategy.

The fifth stage involved reassessment, during which community policing was under a severe test in a tight resource situation. There was a lack of consensus among police administrators concerning the proper role of community relations activities within the broader context of crime control. The introduction of NW and the restoration of PSL indicated, however, that community policing had remained a preferred strategy for policing the society. The sixth stage was reorientation, with community relations affirmed as the key aspect of the policing strategy. The focus of this stage has been the improvement of the police's public image and collaborative police-community working relationships for crime control.

Today the PCROs have taken an active role in liaisoning with community leaders, and the NPCs have attempted to work with community members. The JPC officers have devoted their full attention to approaching young people, and the PSLs have spent most of their time keeping close contact with schools and schoolchildren. The NW is probably the weakest among all of these programs in terms of communication with the community. Police officers seem more approachable through the NPU and NPC concepts, and the PCRO remains the backbone of the police dedication to COPPS.

Several lessons can be learned from this case study. Hong Kong entered into community policing four decades ago for the primary purpose of obtaining public support for ordering the society. Five major policy schemes have evolved to translate this strategy into action, but they have met with limited success. This lack of progress in the force's COPPS strategy and the limited performance of its policy initiatives are mainly due to the force's pragmatic approach of using COPPS initiatives for the sole purpose of crime control and prevention. Without proper public support, consultation, and participation, COPPS will fall short in attempting to provide a mechanism for addressing crime and disorder.

New Zealand

COPPS has been designated as the principal operational strategy for the delivery of police services by the New Zealand police, as set forth in the organization's Web site. The police mission is "To serve the community by reducing the incidence and effects of crime, detecting and apprehending offenders, maintaining law and order and enhancing public safety."[57] Its values statement has as its goal to "Maintain the highest level of integrity and professionalism; respect individual rights and freedoms; consult with, and be responsive to, the needs of the community; uphold the rule of law; and be culturally sensitive."[58] Furthermore, its strategic goals included the implementation of community oriented policing and states that COPPS "will remain the primary policing strategy for service delivery . . . aimed at reversing the upward crime trends of the last three decades."[59]

The New Zealand Police COPPS strategy includes the following[60]:

- *Change style of policing.* Work as individual police officers and in groups, to form a partnership with the community, identify issues and problems, innovate solutions, and share perspectives with the community.
- *Localize resources.* Establish smaller police stations in major areas and community policing centers in communities.
- *Enhance patrol and investigation strategies.* Determine and implement patrol objectives and strategies, adopt appropriate patrol assignments according to time of day and so on, and establish community-based investigators (who will focus on communities rather than types of crime).
- *Engage in problem solving.* Apply the S.A.R.A. model.
- *Adopt a new management style.* Be committed, as managers, to COPPS, encouraging bottom-up innovation and receiving COPPS training and education.

Recidivism is a major concern in New Zealand; males are reincarcerated at a rate of 29 percent. Public trust, confidence, and general public satisfaction have also been declining as of 2004. The police are committed to strengthening trust in their services through developing a sworn members' code of conduct and the continued promotion of a nonsworn code of conduct. It is viewed as essential that the police are perceived as professional, competent, and trustworthy. Accordingly, new mission and values statements—"Statement of Intent" (using the proverb "Stand at the stern of the canoe and feel the spray of the future biting at your face") and "Statement of Responsibility"—as well as other new approaches have been developed to effect community policing.[61]

Exhibit 14–7 discusses a COPPS initiative in Jamaica.

EXHIBIT 14–7

Community Policing Commences in Jamaica

For five years, the Police Executive Research Forum (PERF) in Washington, D.C., participated in a unique public-private partnership to address rising violent crime rates in Jamaica. In a historic report, PERF's expert team and staff made 83 recommendations to the Jamaican government that were widely accepted. The project focused on implementing COPPS in Grants Pen, a small and volatile inner-city community in Kingston where police-community relations had deteriorated and violence was rampant. In January 2006, PERF and a number of government officials and citizens celebrated the grand opening of one of the first community police stations in Jamaica.

Source: Police Executive Research Forum, "Model Community Policing Station Opens in Jamaica," *Subject to Debate,* 20 (March 2006):4–7.

The Netherlands

Significant changes in Dutch society have ushered in a period of considerable experiment and innovation. The Netherlands is a small country (its population is 16.5 million) with virtually open borders, a multicultural population, and a high standard of living. Its police are regionalized in 25 forces, with 1 national service for certain national tasks. Amsterdam, with 5,600 officers, is the largest regional force. The policing style is generally laid back, fairly tolerant, and nonviolent, and negotiation plays a vital role. Dutch officers are normally well trained and speak several languages. The police have a great deal of autonomy with crime prevention, and the mayor in each police region oversees the development of policing policies; the police chief is thus subordinate to the mayor.

The most recent step in the development of COPPS in the Netherlands has been the introduction of the community beat officer. In the new philosophy, the proximity to the public, citizen involvement in dealing with crime problems, and the police working with local public and private agencies are given great importance. New is the extensive cooperation being fostered with external partners and the strong involvement of citizens in determining what issues should be addressed. But perhaps most important is the shift in responsibility. Whereas the former beat constable was "just an ordinary cop," the community officer is held responsible for "organizing security" in his or her area. If he or she needs assistance from colleagues in specialized departments, those specialists are obliged to help. Responsibility is thus pushed down to a lower level in the organization.

Recently, Amsterdam—the capital city with a population of 800,000—experienced growing problems. Amsterdam is a major tourist center, with many headquarters of companies and businesses, a diverse population, a large number of retail stores, a renowned red light district, and "coffee shops" where soft drugs can be purchased. Street crimes began increasing on busy streets and in public transport and nightspot areas.

It was decided to establish one police district for the entire inner-city area, with six neighborhood teams consisting of 700 officers. As part of this new inner-city district, a special support team of 75 officers was tasked with the responsibility of maintaining public order in the entire district. Officers in this team could be sent into places where temporary disruptions of public order were anticipated. This team was to regain authority and bring back a sense of norms, with a low tolerance for small breaches of law. For instance, urinating in public became public enemy number one after such behavior was held to be even undermining the foundations of the historic sixteenth-century buildings in the downtown area. (Today portable urinals are placed at such "hot spots.") This zero-tolerance approach to infractions contradicted a long tradition of leniency toward deviance in the social order.

A fundamental question is whether this new policy is compatible with COPPS. It is argued that the community agrees that the police should take strong action against those who do not comply with community norms and laws. Conversely, some residents believe that the city has given the area away to the tourist industry and the "nighttime economy" and that newcomers are complainers who want to take away the fun of the area.

Given the large number of drunken youths being noisy, motorists massively ignoring traffic regulations, numerous pickpockets targeting tourists, local drug addicts shooting up and dealing in drugs in the area, and homeless and mentally ill individuals being aggressive on the streets, the police had to do something. Still, the police try to put on a "personal face" and get involved in community meetings and cooperate with other agencies and the local government in dealing with these social problems that have become more complex than just crime.[62]

Some Between-Country Comparisons

It is clear that community policing has encircled the globe. A conference held in The Hague, the Netherlands, in 1998 had crime prevention as its central theme, and what was found to be common approaches among the 21 attending nations was instructive. First, for most nations, the concept of community is equated with people interacting face to face, and community policing was modeled after the S.A.R.A. problem-solving process (discussed in Chapter 3).

Approaches to community policing by the countries in attendance varied considerably, however, depending on the cultures, traditions, and assumptions about the nature of human beings held in different countries. In Hong Kong, for example, assumptions are that people are basically good and that those who deviate can be changed and brought back into the fold. The government is to serve the people, but the people have a responsibility to assist the police, so the people are in effect serving themselves. Community policing in Canada and the Netherlands is similar, grounded in meeting the needs of the community and in solving problems.[63]

Another element of COPPS that seems to prevail internationally—and that is a primary "knock" against COPPS—is that evaluations of crime prevention and COPPS activities are very limited. Isolated studies on individual projects, general descriptive studies, and anecdotal essays of what works are not sufficient for making policy.[64]

Finally, after examining community policing internationally, Skolnick and Bayley found that the majority of community policing strategies that have been implemented have four primary components in common[65]:

1. Community crime prevention
2. Proactive as opposed to reactive police service
3. Public participation in the training and supervision of police operations
4. Shift of command responsibilities to lower police ranks (decentralization)

SUMMARY

This chapter discussed COPPS as it has developed internationally. Several common themes or practices are identifiable: taking the police from their "mechanized fortresses" and putting them in closer contact with the public (together engaging in the use of problem-solving methods), decentralizing the organization to areas and neighborhoods, developing a sense of community, and sharing decision making (empowerment) with the public. We also saw that some venues initiated a pilot project before implementing the concept department-wide; another common denominator seemed to be the need for sound evaluations of COPPS to determine what works.

Finally, this chapter has shown that the COPPS approach is not that different in foreign venues from what it is in the United States. Perhaps most important, this chapter demonstrated that we are indeed learning from, and sharing with, one another. We are a "global village"; we hope this spirit of scholarly interaction will continue. We should also be mindful, however, that the foreign experience is not necessarily a recipe for Americans to replicate; rather, it can serve as a point of departure in considering what is feasible.[66] These venues offer an opportunity for us to examine issues that might arise as COPPS continues to spread across the United States.

ITEMS FOR REVIEW

1. Discuss the general character of policing in Canada, including why Edmonton might be termed the "Mayo Clinic of policing."
2. Explain how police function in Japan, with particular emphasis on the koban concept.
3. Describe Operation Mantle in South Australia.
4. Review the role of constables in Great Britain.
5. Explain the five stages in the development of community policing in Hong Kong.
6. Delineate the major contemporary challenges to community policing in New Zealand.
7. What are the four components found by Skolnick and Bayley that the majority of community policing strategies around the world have in common?
8. Explain why the need for evaluating COPPS efforts is essential for all venues, including the United States.

 NOTES

1. Mark Kesselman, "Order or Movement? The Literature of Political Development as Ideology," *World Politics* 26 (1973):139–154.

2. Barry Leighton, "Community Policing: The Canadian Experience." Paper presented at the Third Research and Development Conference, Toronto, Canada, April 10, 1996.

3. *Ibid.*

4. *Ibid.*

5. *Ibid.*

6. *Ibid.*

7. *Ibid.*

8. Martha Wickett, "RCMP nominated for cleanup campaign on Dow Ave.," http://burnabynow.com/102202/news/102202nn16.html (Accessed May 29, 2003).

9. Vancouver Police Department application for the Herman Goldstein Award for Excellence in Problem-Oriented Policing, April 1999.

10. Greg Saville, personal communication, October 11, 1993.

11. Royal Canadian Mounted Police, *RCMP Community Policing: Strategic Action Plan Update, 1992–1995* (Vancouver, Canada: Author, 1993), pp. 3–5.

12. Richard J. Terrill, *World Criminal Justice Systems: A Survey* (5th ed.) (Cincinnati: Anderson, 2003), p. 373.

13. Jerome H. Skolnick and David H. Bayley, *Community Policing: Issues and Practices Around the World* (Washington, D.C.: National Institute of Justice, 1988).

14. Terrill, *World Criminal Justice Systems,* pp. 378–380.

15. Ted D. Westermann and James W. Burfeind, *Crime and Justice in Two Societies: Japan and the United States* (Pacific Grove, Calif.: Brooks/Cole, 1991), p. 157.

16. *Ibid.*

17. David H. Bayley, *Forces of Order: Police Behavior in Japan and the United States* (Berkeley, Calif.: University of California Press, 1991), p. 87.

18. Westermann and Burfeind, *Crime and Justice in Two Societies,* p. 159.

19. George L. Kelling, Robert Wasserman, and Hubert Williams, "Police Accountability and Community Policing," *Perspectives on Policing,* No. 7 (November 1988).

20. "Community Police Activities of Japan" (Tokyo: National Police Agency of Japan, 1992), pp. 2, 9.

21. *Ibid.,* p. 5.

22. David H. Bayley, *A Model of Community Policing: The Singapore Story* (Washington, D.C.: U.S. Department of Justice, National Institute of Justice, 1989), p. 8.

23. Skolnick and Bayley, *Community Policing,* p. 9.

24. Bayley, *Forces of Order,* p. 47.

25. W. Ames, *Police and the Community in Japan* (Berkeley, Calif.: University of California Press, 1981), p. 39.

26. Operation Stopbreak, http://www.afp.gov.au/_data/assets/pdf_file/3831/4_halite.pdf (Accessed September 14, 2003).

27. Queensland Police Service, North Coast Region, Application for the Herman Goldstein Award for Excellence in Problem-Oriented Policing, 1999.

28. Paul Williams, Paul White, Michael Treece, and Robert Kitto, "Problem-Oriented Policing: Operation Mantle—A Case Study," *Australian Institute of Criminology: Trend and Issues in Crime and Criminal Justice,* No. 190 (February 2001):1–6.

29. Criminal Justice Commission, *Toowoomba Beat Policing Pilot Project: Main Evaluation Report* (Brisbane, Australia: Author, 1995), p. ix.

30. "A.C.T. Community Policing Staffing Numbers," http://www.afpa.org/au/act_policing.html (Accessed April 11, 2006).

31. British Broadcasting Corporation, "Crime Fighters: Policing," http://www.bbc.co.uk/crime/fighters/policeforce.shtml (Accessed September 14, 2006).

32. Adrian Leigh, Tim Read, and Nick Tilley, *Brit POP II: Problem-Oriented Policing in Practice* (London: Home Office Police Research Group, 1998), p. 1.

33. *Ibid.,* p. iii.

34. Mollie Weatheritt, "Community Policing: Rhetoric or Reality?" In *Community Policing: Rhetoric or Reality?* Jack R. Greene and Stephen D. Mastrofski (eds.) (New York: Praeger, 1988), pp. 153–174.

35. *Ibid.,* pp. 155–156.

36. *Ibid.,* p. 161.

37. Newman quoted in Herman Goldstein, *Problem Oriented Policing* (New York: McGraw-Hill, 1990), p. 54.

38. M. A. Hoare, G. Stewart, and C. M. Purcell, *The Problem Oriented Approach: Four Pilot Studies* (London: Metropolitan Police, Management Services Department, 1984), p. 121, Summary.

39. *Ibid.,* p. 55.

40. Kenneth Newman, *The Principles of Policing and Guidance for Professional Behavior* (London: The Metropolitan Police, 1985), p. 12.

41. *Ibid.,* p. 165.

42. *Ibid.,* pp. 153–174.

43. *Ibid.*

44. Skolnick and Bayley, *Community Policing,* p. 30.

45. Adrian Leigh, Tim Read, and Nick Tilley, *Problem-Oriented Policing: Brit POP* (London: Home Office Police Research Group, 1996), pp. 4–5.

46. *Ibid.,* pp. 39–40.

47. *Ibid.*

48. Arthur G. Sharp, "Putting a Shine on 'Spotlight,'" *Law and Order* (November 1999):75.

49. *Ibid.*

50. Isle of Man Police Constabulary, *Strategic Plan 2000–2003* (Isle of Man: Author, 2000), pp. 2–3.

51. Ruth Geva, "Community Policing in Israel," *The Police Chief* (December 1998):77.

52. *Ibid.*

53. *Ibid.,* p. 80. Also, for an excellent discussion of community policing in Israel, which explains the difficulties in encountering resistance of traditional military-style organizational culture as well as a lack of organizational commitment to community policing, see David Weisburd, Orit Shalev, and

Menachem Amir, "Community Policing in Israel: Resistance and Change," *Policing: An International Journal of Police Strategies and Management* 15 (1) (2002):80–109.

54. Peter C. Kratcoski, Dilip K. Das, and Arvind Verma, "World Perspective on Crime Prevention: A Community Policing Approach," in Steven P. Lab and Dilip K. Das (eds.), *International Perspectives on Community Policing and Crime Prevention* (Upper Saddle River, N.J.: Prentice Hall, 2003), pp. 229–230.

55. Wikipedia, "Hong Kong," http://en.wikipedia.org/wiki/Hong_Kong#Demographics (Accessed September 15, 2006).

56. Hong Kong Police, *Community Policing in Hong Kong: An Institutional Analysis* (Hong Kong: Author, no date).

57. New Zealand Police, "Statement of Intent, 2005/2006," http://www.police .govt.nz/resources/2006/statement-of-intent/statement-of-intent-2006.pdf (Accessed September 14, 2006), pp. 4–10.

58. *Ibid.*

59. *Ibid.*

60. *Ibid.*

61. New Zealand Police, "About Us," http://www.police.gove.nz/about (Accessed April 11, 2006).

62. Maurice Punch, Kees van der Vijver, and Olga Zoomer, "Dutch 'COP': Developing Community Policing in the Netherlands," *Policing: An International Journal of Police Strategies and Management* 25 (1) (2002):60–79.

63. Kratcoski, Das, and Verma, "World Perspective on Crime Prevention," pp. 224–228.

64. *Ibid.,* p. 238.

65. Jerome H. Skolnick and David H. Bayley, "Theme and Variation in Community Policing," *Crime and Justice* 10 (1988):1–37.

66. Bayley, *A Model of Community Policing,* p. 29.

The Future

Bright or Bleak?

Key Terms and Concepts

Community information

Cyberterrorism

Futures orientation

Homeland defense

Office of Community Oriented
Policing Services (COPS)

Rank-and-file officer

Violent Crime Control and Law
Enforcement Act of 1994

Learning Objectives

As a result of reading this chapter, the student will:

- Understand why a futures orientation is important for police executives and supervisors
- Know why it is essential for all police organizations to leave the traditional reactive method of policing in the future and why a problem-solving approach is best
- Be able to describe the need for police agencies to lay plans to cease their reliance on federal funding for COPPS
- Comprehend the benefits of using COPPS to address homeland defense issues
- Be able to explain the role of the rank-and-file officer in the future under COPPS
- Realize the kinds of new crimes and high technologies that the police must be trained to address under COPPS
- Recognize the future challenges facing the police in order to fully embrace COPPS

The confrontation that we are calling for . . . knows the dialog of bullets, the ideals of assassination, bombing, and destruction, and diplomacy of the cannon and machinegun.

—Terrorist Manual

The highest of arts is to affect the quality of the day.

—H. D. Thoreau

INTRODUCTION

As William Tafoya observed, "For 45,000 years humankind huddled in the darkness of caves, afraid to take that first step into the light of day. Police leadership must now be out in front, pointing the way for others to follow, not waiting for someone else to set the pace."[1]

It has been said that the only thing that is permanent is change. Perhaps more than anything else, this book has demonstrated that axiom. Even the historically tradition-bound domain of policing has been shown to be dynamic, as is the general American society in which it exists.

But much work remains to be done. The question that should be at the forefront of our minds, and that of the police, is: "What will the future bring?" This question becomes even more poignant and ominous when we consider the world's present state of affairs.

Our choice is either to ignore the future until it is upon us or to try to anticipate what the future might bring and gear our resources to cope with it. Predicting the future is not easy, however. Many variables, such as war, terrorism, high technology, and economic upheaval, can greatly affect even the most sound predictions and established trends. What we hope to do in this chapter, therefore, is to try and explain why a futures orientation is important for community oriented policing and problem solving (COPPS) and to discuss some areas in which the police must have foresight. Indeed, this chapter poses more questions than it answers.

Thus we begin by considering why it is important for the police to take a futures orientation, and then we look at some priorities for policing in the future under COPPS—some fundamental questions that must be addressed and the impending demise of federal assistance for COPPS personnel, equipment, and training. Then we look at how far problem solving has yet to go in order to realize its full potential. After a review of how COPPS can assist with the challenge of homeland defense, the future role of the rank-and-file officer under COPPS is discussed. We then look at how the police will be challenged in the future by changing crimes and high technology. The chapter concludes with a summation of what needs to be done, followed by a case study.

WHY A FUTURES ORIENTATION?

Because of the reactive nature inherent in their occupation, police officials have tended in the past not to be overly concerned about the future. Even those chief executives who are concerned about the future and futures research usually concentrate on the next budget year rather than on a five- or ten-year strategic plan for their agencies.[2] But the future is here and probably is changing faster than anyone can envision. As examples, most of us can remember a world without automatic teller machines or cellular phones, but these items as well as computers have changed the world—and the opportunities for crime—in ways that no one could have imagined.[3]

Police chief executives must therefore have a **futures orientation,** anticipating and planning for the future. They must have the capacity to not only manage change but also thrive on it. Boyd et al., point out:

> A world exists beyond traditional police exercises of annual budgeting, strategic planning for 3- to 5-year periods, and critical incident debriefings. Futures research leads to the examination of the probable, possible, and preferable outcomes of the future, and [it] provides a basis for decision making today that will lead to a preferable future.[4]

These administrators also shoulder the responsibility for seeing that the best and brightest individuals are recruited and trained to become the best officers they possibly can be in their performance. They can develop profiles of the skills needed by officers of the future and contemplate how best to integrate testing and recruitment that will attract candidates most likely to fulfill the skill set needed.[5]

SOME PRIORITIES FOR THE COPPS ERA

Fundamental Questions

The first priority for the police who adopted COPPS was to realize that the conventional style of reactive incident-driven policing employed during the professional era had several drawbacks. That former type of police department was hierarchical, impersonal, and rule-based, and most of the important policy and operations decisions were made at the top; line officers made few decisions on their own. Some departments may continue to struggle with the decision of initiating and the challenges of implementing COPPS; this approach may be passed off as a fad or implemented as a series of temporary programs simply to take advantage of the available federal funding and to create a positive image.

Although this book has looked at COPPS from many different perspectives, several fundamental questions remain. For example, will more police agencies make a commitment to implementation of this strategy? Some authors point to what they believe are several unfavorable social forces that militate against the future of COPPS: local governments being pushed toward a more legalistic crime control model of policing, a public that is less willing to pay more taxes to address fundamental social problems, and a public policy that does not allow the police to focus on the root causes of crimes but only on their symptoms—criminals' conduct—through aggressive strategies rather than through COPPS.[6]

How many agencies have demonstrated the link between community policing and the quality of life in the communities they serve? How many have embraced community policing primarily to obtain available federal dollars? Will community policing endure without federal funding, and does it have a role in a new world that carries the constant threat of domestic terrorism? (Both of these issues are discussed more below.)

Earlier in this book and in several chapters, we discussed the challenges involving the recruitment, selection, training, performance appraisals, and reward and promotional systems of COPPS personnel. It is also necessary to remember that administrators must work with police unions to effect the kinds of changes that are needed for this strategy. Furthermore, there is a need for more women in police service as well as the challenge of bringing more people of different ethnicities, including Russians, South Africans, Baltic nationalities, and Asians, into policing. (As noted in Chapter 2, Los Angeles alone has more than 110 different nationalities and more than 100 different languages spoken in its Russian, Armenian, Korean, Farsi, Spanish, Thai, and other communities.) Changing societal values, court decisions concerning the rights of employees, and the Peace Officers' Bill of Rights will make leadership increasingly challenging.

COPS Office funding assisted many agencies in taking the first step toward implementing COPPS. The future success of those agencies will be determined by their ability to implement COPPS agency-wide.

Courtesy U.S. Department of Justice.

How will these issues be addressed? The answer to this question will be critical, not only to the future of COPPS but also to policing in general.

Dwindling Federal Assistance

In previous chapters we mentioned the federal **Office of Community Oriented Policing Services (COPS),** created by the **Violent Crime Control and Law Enforcement Act of 1994;** its initial budget appropriation was $8.8 billion for its first six years of existence. This agency has been a tremendous boon to many police organizations in acquiring the personnel, training, and equipment necessary for implementing COPPS.

As with any new federal program that receives short-term funding, however, this office's survival is tenuous in nature. Therefore, a priority for any police agency whose COPPS efforts hinge on or revolve around federal funds from this office will be to budget funds to pay the tab for officers, equipment, training, and so on after the COPS Office's largesse and seed money have ended. Indeed, there has already been a decline in the COPS budget. Its 2006 budget included $4 million for training, $63 million to address methamphetamine issues, $129 million for technology, and $10 million for public safety interoperability (a broad category that includes the three focus areas of communications, equipment, and training for smoothing operations and communications among law enforcement, fire departments, emergency medical services, and other agencies). This is a far different picture than the more than $1.4 billion per year that was initially appropriated in 1994.

It should be mentioned that grants are seldom designed to be interminable in nature; rather, they are generally intended to fuel new initiatives. Nor are they intended to substitute for funds that the local jurisdiction should or would normally spend for basic police protection (personnel and related expenses).

PROBLEM SOLVING: ROADS YET TO TRAVEL

It can also be assumed that, overall, policing has a long way to go in problem solving. To begin with, many U.S. police agencies probably do not have formal problem-solving programs. Random patrol, rapid response, and investigative follow-ups are still the standard patrol strategies for many of these organizations, and a formalized and coordinated problem-solving approach is not the tool of choice.[7]

Police organizations have always used problem-solving strategies for a limited scope of activities. However, expanding and formalizing the problem-solving process may still be viewed as something new for many of them. A natural instinct is to view change with a healthy dose of skepticism and resistance. As noted above, effective problem solving also requires different personnel systems and support rather than rewarding the status quo. The command staff and first-line supervisors must be committed to effecting new systems and problem solving in general, or they will not be embraced within the lower ranks.

In addition to the necessity of universally adopting problem solving throughout the organization, COPPS tenets must also be applied globally to the conditions that contribute to crime and disorder: alcohol and drug abuse, overcrowding, unemployment, urban decay, lack of education, lack of parental control, and so on. As Keith Ikeda observed, "Most police officers resist being labelled as social workers, surrogate parents, teachers, or ministers. But effective problem solving requires police and citizens to assume all of those roles and more."[8]

As we have stated several times in this book (as something the police must remember for the future), problem solving is highly effective in reducing neighborhood disorder, calls for service (CFS), and community concerns. We have shown that problem solving uses self-directed, uncommitted time more effectively to work on targeted problems (see Chapter 6) and that such strategies do not require additional personnel or increases in the budget.

Ikeda provided an analogy of police responses to traffic accidents. Using a problem-solving approach, the police would identify their most accident-prone areas, analyze the contributing factors, and then respond with an approach that combines engineering, education, and enforcement. After doing so, there would be an assessment to see if the approach succeeded in reducing traffic accidents. If not, the process would start all over until the desired results are achieved.[9]

Furthermore, once the strategies employed are shown to be working, community stakeholders may be approached in order to acquire outside resources. Several means exist for obtaining such resources that may not have been considered in the past: public and private grants, volunteer organizations, nonprofit organizations, insurance companies, homeowners' associations, school/parent organizations, sports organizations, faith-based groups, fraternal organizations, businesses, and chamber of commerce groups.[10]

Finally, effective problem solving carries the challenge of police agencies having an open respect and perspective for learning, becoming learning organizations and ensuring that personnel are trained in effective problem-solving approaches (discussed in Chapter 9). There is a learning curve that needs to occur, and that includes listening to the community members to identify their issues and concerns.

In sum, COPPS has come a long way, but challenges remain. There are obvious benefits—both personal and professional—for transitioning to COPPS and leaving the "We've always done it this way" mind-set.

COPPS AND HOMELAND DEFENSE

When a police officer is responding to a CFS and observes a container with 50 gallons of chlorine in a corner of a garage but no swimming pool in the backyard, would he or she know what to do with that information? When emergency medical services personnel are on a call and observe five passports

The federal Office of Community Oriented Policing Services assists police with understanding the Homeland Security Advisory System color codes.

Heather J. Davies and Martha R. Plotkin, Protecting Your Community from Terrorism, *Vol. 5: Partnerships to Promote Homeland Security (Washington, D.C.: Office of Community Oriented Policing Services and the Police Executive Research Forum, November 2005), p. 67.*

Homeland Security Advisory System
http://www.homelandsecurity.org/

Red: **Severe**	✓ **Complete recommended actions at lower levels** ✓ Listen to radio/TV for current information/instructions ✓ Be alert to suspicious activity and report it to proper authorities immediately ✓ Contact business/school to determine status of work/school day ✓ Adhere to any travel restrictions announced by local governmental authorities ✓ Be prepared to shelter in place or evacuate if instructed to do so by local governmental authorities ✓ Discuss children's fears concerning possible/actual terrorist attacks
Orange: **High**	✓ **Complete recommended actions at lower levels** ✓ Be alert to suspicious activity and report it to proper authorities ✓ Review disaster plan with all family members ✓ Ensure communication plan is understood/practiced by all family members ✓ Exercise caution when traveling ✓ Have shelter in place, materials on hand, and review procedure in **Terrorism: Preparing for the Unexpected** brochure ✓ Discuss children's fears concerning possible terrorist attacks ✓ If a need is announced, donate blood at designated blood collection center
Yellow: **Elevated**	✓ **Complete recommended actions at lower levels** ✓ Be alert to suspicious activity and report it to proper authorities ✓ Ensure disaster supplies kit is stocked and ready ✓ Check telephone numbers and e-mail addresses in your family emergency communication plan ✓ If not known to you, contact school to determine their emergency notification and evacuation plans for children ✓ Develop alternate routes to/from school/work and practice them
Blue: **Guarded**	✓ **Complete recommended actions at lower levels** ✓ Be alert to suspicious activity and report it to proper authorities ✓ Review stored disaster supplies and replace items that are outdated ✓ Develop an emergency communication plan that all family members understand ✓ Establish an alternative meeting place away from home with family/friends
Green: **Low**	✓ **Obtain copy of** Terrorism: Preparing for the Unexpected brochure from your local Red Cross chapter ✓ Develop a personal disaster plan and disaster supplies kit using Red Cross brochures Your Family Disaster Plan and Your Family Disaster Supplies Kit

from different countries, all bearing the same photograph, on the kitchen table, would they know whom to contact?

A common theme throughout this book has been that information is the lifeblood of contemporary policing. Unfortunately, however, it is still common for the police, fire, and emergency services personnel to not know what the others are finding and to take for granted that the others are aware of threat-related information.

Homeland defense begins with the local police and the community. The collection of information at the neighborhood level is critical to the

Laptop computers and video cameras are advanced technologies that are being installed in patrol vehicles by many agencies.

Courtesy Kris Solow, City of Charlotte, North Carolina.

mission of protecting the homeland. First responders need to know how to cultivate information: what information to look for, how to collect it, and where to send it. Training of first responders in this area reduces the information gap between police and other services and must be embraced by each agency's management in order to be effective.[11]

There are numerous sources of **community information,** some of which may not have occurred to the police. Following are some of them and the kinds of information they might provide[12]:

- Business owners (information about purchasers of dangerous materials such as torches, propane, and blasting supplies)
- Employees of transportation centers and tourist attractions (information about suspicious persons and activities)
- Those who issue licenses and permits (information about persons seeking licenses and permits for handguns, firearms, liquor licenses, and blasting materials)
- Letter carriers, couriers, and delivery services drivers (information on suspicious people, activities, and packages)
- College and university personnel and students (information about possession of hazardous materials by foreign exchange students, controversial speakers and their research, and possibly suspicious events)
- Real estate agents (information on suspicious activities or locations of wanted persons and undocumented residents)

- Storage unit managers (information on explosive or hazardous materials possibly connected to terrorist or criminal activity)
- Hotel clerks and security officers (information on suspicious guests)

While traumatic events like the 9-11 attacks might possibly cause police organizations to revert back to more traditional methods—even to abandon COPPS for more seemingly pedestrian security-oriented concerns—COPPS should play a central role in the defense of our homeland. Because COPPS helps to build trust between police and their communities, deals more effectively with community concerns, and helps the police to develop knowledge of community activity, the problem-solving model is well suited to the prevention of terrorism. Departments can also use a wide variety of data sources to proactively develop detailed risk management and crisis response plans.[13]

ROLE OF THE RANK-AND-FILE OFFICER

It would be an oversight to not mention the role of the **rank-and-file officer** among the changes to be witnessed in future police service. For many reasons—including the fact that future generations will have been raised being at ease and fluent with information technologies as well as their entering a police service that is much more involved with collective bargaining—future generations of police officers will be vastly different from those of the past.

In the past (particularly under the professional model of policing), while undergoing the academy phase of their training, recruits adopted a new identity and a system of discipline in which they learned to take orders and not to question authority. Indeed, much of the emphasis was on submission to authority. Recruits learned that loyalty to fellow officers, a professional demeanor and bearing, and a respect for authority were, and still are, highly valued qualities. That theme and the police executive's set of expectations for recruits must change, however. In the future, officers will be hired only if they can think critically, plan, and evaluate. At the same time, chiefs, sheriffs, commanders, and even sergeants will wield less coercive power and control and filter less information; instead, they will be encouraged to ask questions, to engage in lifelong learning, and to move into enhanced roles as coaches, supporters, and resource developers.[14]

People entering police service in the future will not usually possess military experience with its inherent obedience to authority, but they will have higher levels of education and will tend to be more independent and less responsive to traditional authoritarian leadership styles. These recruits will have been exposed to more participative, supportive, and humanistic approaches; they will want more opportunities to provide input into their work and to address the challenges posed by problem solving. The autocratic leadership style of the past professional era of policing will not work today or in the future. The watchwords of the new leadership paradigm are coaching, inspiring, gaining commitment, empowering, affirming, being flexible, bearing responsibility, self-managing, sharing power, and being autonomous and entrepreneurial. Therefore, a major need for police leadership will be the surrendering of power to lower-ranking employees in a flattened organizational hierarchy.

Police officers of the future will also function in very different ways and on very different terms from officers of the past. Given existing technologies and what they bode for the future, every officer will function with few time and space constraints, because all officers will be equipped with a pager, cellular phone, personal data assistant, and laptop computer with software that includes encryption programs, sophisticated databases, and search engines. These officers will be able to have real-time chats with officers from other agencies or in other states or even other countries. Every rookie, before going on the streets, will be thoroughly computer literate and able to use crime analysis software.[15]

With such tools, it is easy to envision an officer's home, a car, or a convenience store becoming his or her workplace. Identification of suspects in the field will take a quantum leap with electronic telecommunication of fingerprints, scanning of retinal patterns, and facial ratio and heat patterns

Advancements in handheld computer devices will greatly enhance supervisors' management and communications capabilities.

Courtesy Reno, Nevada, Police Department.

EXHIBIT 15–1

Twenty-First-Century Police Department: Naperville, Illinois

Over the past decade, companies in the manufacturing, entertainment, and defense industries have used a tool called "process mapping" to help them describe, analyze, and, ultimately, improve how their organizations operate. Recently, members of the city of Naperville, Illinois, police department and 23 other police agencies were invited to attend training in process mapping, which involves the development of three different flowcharts that visually depict the series of activities involved in carrying out one of the organization's major functions.

- The as-is map describes the organization as it currently exists. This map is based on interviews and observations of people and is used to diagnose waste, duplication of effort, coordination of problems, or breakdowns in the flow of information.
- The should-be map makes short-term changes to reduce waste, remove duplication, and improve coordination and flow of information. This map is based on management analysis of the as-is map and suggestions gathered from field personnel during interviews.
- The could-be map describes the ideal process for the future. This map is based on the organization's vision and highlights the long-term changes that are needed to get there.

As an example, Naperville is focusing on "crime solving" as the major function to be mapped and is focusing on one crime type: burglary. Process mapping allows the agency to increase the clearance rate for crimes by identifying areas where new work methods or organizational changes might improve police ability to investigate crimes and arrest offenders. It also makes more widespread and effective use of automation and technology by identifying areas where work processes can be improved, such as automated case reporting.

Source: City of Naperville, Illinois, Web page, "Twenty-First Century Police Department," pp. 1–2. http://www.naperville.il.us (Accessed April 29, 2003).

that say positively, "This is the bad guy." Officers will also access maps and data; be able to bring up any call, crime type, or problem by geographic area; and sort this information and compare similar incidents. They will be able to touch their computer keys and ask for the top ten crimes in their beat area while receiving instant crime analysis for use in deployment and other operational decisions. All civilians will likewise be trained in computer use.[16]

Exhibit 15–1 provides an example of what one community has done to formally plan for the future.

CHANGING CRIMES AND HIGH TECHNOLOGY

In previous chapters (particularly in Chapter 5), we mentioned technology as it relates to doing crime analyses and determining hot spots. But other challenges come with technology as well. Certainly the advent of computer crime has changed with the world of policing, posing new and extraordinary challenges. The current high-tech revolution in our homes and offices has not only enhanced our lives but also opened a whole new world for the criminal element. Pornographers and pedophiles, as well as people who trade stolen credit card numbers, rig auctions, create viruses, and devise baby adoption scams as well as many other crimes, are now on the Web. Computer crimes will increase dramatically and will include such crimes as cyberterrorism, identity theft, credit card fraud, consumer fraud, stock market–related fraud, and industrial espionage; these crimes may well become the next national crime-fighting obsessions.

Certainly the kinds of crimes the police must be prepared to deal with—much of which now involve high technology—will alter the way in which the future police must be trained and interact with the public. Over the past decade or more, crime has been moving away from stealing goods and toward obtaining information. First, the means of robbery changed to keep up with an age when people carry identity information in the form of credit cards and automatic teller machine (ATM) cards instead of cash. However, these are just the modern equivalents to common mugging. Credit card number theft, personal identification number (PIN) capturing, database theft, and other such forms of crime will compel the police to become more sophisticated in their investigative and deterrent abilities.[17]

Cyberterrorism is another area that will increasingly challenge the police in years to come. Cyberterrorists might carry out such activities as remotely accessing the processing control systems of a cereal manufacturer, changing the levels of iron supplement to sicken and kill children who eat it; disrupting banks, international financial transactions, and stock exchanges, forcing the nation's citizens to lose faith in their economic system; and attacking air traffic control systems and aircraft in-cockpit sensors, causing large civilian aircraft to collide. These kinds of activities are the domain of the serious, determined cyberterrorist. Clearly the future of terrorism involves much more than planting a relatively harmless virus in a computer system or hacking into a major corporation's voice-mail system to make long-distance calls.[18]

Exhibit 15–2 shows what might very well be a wave of the future: online communities for improving COPPS.

EXPANSION OF THE FIELD: COPS *GUIDES*

We would be remiss without making at least passing reference to a relatively new resource that holds tremendous promise for future problem-solving efforts. The U.S. Department of Justice's COPS Office, to which we have referred in several of this book's chapters, has published to this point more than 30 *Problem-Oriented Guides for Police* on a wide range of topics (including the following):

Street prostitution	Stalking
Drug dealing	Identity theft

EXHIBIT 15–2

Online Communities Improve COPPS

When a neighbor recently posted a shaky though unmistakable photograph of a burglar skulking from a house on the Web site of a neighborhood in southeast Washington, D.C., community policing forever changed there. The photo helped police arrest a suspect, and it established online neighborhood communities as a way for citizens and beat officers to interact. "Parking your patrol car on the block and walking up and down, knocking on doors, that's just so Flintstones," said Lt. Keith Roch. "It makes no sense to do that when you can talk to 2,000 people online at once." The District recently obtained a $283,000 federal grant to create a network of interactive Web sites for each of the city's areas, which will also provide online access to records and statistics for each neighborhood and block. The police are mindful, however, that face-to-face contact can never be replaced and that online connections between police and residents also can raise sticky issues. For example, such high-tech communication might leave less connected residents in the dark; also, officers assigned to "patrol" their beats electronically may walk their beats less often. Furthermore, online forums can become conduits for libelous neighborhood gossip. Nonetheless, the District and other communities are moving ahead with plans to expand their online connections with the people they protect and believe that the benefits far outweigh potential detriment.

Source: Adapted from Petula Dvorak, "Online Communities Improve Neighborhood Policing." http://washingtonpost.com/ac2/wp-dvn?pagename=article&node=&contentId-A336 (Accessed April 28, 2003).

Disorderly youth	Bomb threats
Robbery at ATMs	Crimes against tourists
Bullying in schools	Cruising
Rave parties	Underage drinking
Clandestine drug labs	Gun violence
Acquaintance rape	Prescription fraud

The *Guides* are normally 40 to 60 pages in length and include a discussion of the specific problem, some methods for understanding the nature of the problem, and some possible police responses to the problem. Each *Guide* is based on the author's presenting what works with the problem, based on experiences of police agencies across the nation.

The *Guides* are beginning to get widespread attention. One of this book's authors was recently contacted by a Canadian radio station about an area where there was a serious local problem of street racing; one such race even resulted in an innocent bystander's death. After finding the *Guide on Street Racing* on the Internet, the radio station contacted this author to participate in a live call-in radio program about possible police responses to the racing problem.

As indicated above, these *Guides* will provide a wealth of information for future COPPS efforts. All *Guides* are available online at www.cops.usdoj.gov and are also available on a single CD.

U.S. Department of Justice
Office of Community Oriented Policing Services

COPS
COMMUNITY ORIENTED POLICING SERVICES
U.S. DEPARTMENT OF JUSTICE

Problem-Oriented Guides for Police Series
No. 13

Panhandling

by
Michael S. Scott

www.cops.usdoj.gov

One of dozens of problem-oriented policing guides that are published and available from the Office of Community Oriented Policing Services.

Michael S. Scott, Panhandling *(Washington, D.C.: Office of Community Oriented Policing Services, 2003).*

IN SUMMARY

Because COPPS has not yet been fully embraced and adopted in this nation's 17,000 law enforcement agencies, it may be fairly said that much work including the following remains to be done[19]:

- Police organizations must come to believe that they alone cannot control crime and must truly enlist the aid of their communities in this endeavor.
- Chief executive officers must realize that the traditional reactive mode of policing is not sufficient for today's challenges and must change the culture of their departments, implement COPPS, flatten the organizational structure of their departments, and ensure the proper evaluations of officers' work.
- Organizations must become learning organizations (discussed in Chapter 9) in order to adapt to change and evolve with the times.
- Chief executives who are competent and worthy must be given the necessary job security to accommodate COPPS because the short-term, at-will employment of chiefs places COPPS at risk.
- Organizations practicing COPPS must work with their communities, other city agencies, businesses, elected officials, and the media in order to sustain COPPS.
- Unions must work with their agency administrators to effect the changes needed for COPPS.
- Chief executives and supervisors must develop the necessary policies and support mechanisms for COPPS, including recruitment, selection, training, performance appraisals, and reward and promotional systems.
- Chief executives and supervisors must begin viewing the patrol officer as a problem-solving specialist and give officers enough free time and latitude to engage in proactive policing.
- Chief executives and supervisors must come to view COPPS as a department- and city-wide strategy, rather than as a small separate division or appendage, and invest in technology to support problem oriented policing.
- Chief executives must attempt to bring diversity into their ranks to reflect the changing demographics and cultural customs of our society.

Only time, and the proper effort, will determine whether or not these goals are met.

CASE STUDY

To tie it all together, the following case study—which can be viewed as including many perspectives examined in this book's preceding chapters—will assist the reader in conceptualizing some of the primary elements of COPPS, both contemporary and future, and to consider some of the major challenges one faces when looking at COPPS for today and the future:

> A neighboring community, Gotham City, has a number of new department heads, with varying levels of experience. Recent crime, budget, and other crises, including the relatively new emphasis on homeland defense,

have underscored the need for that city to address these problems by the most effective and efficient means possible. Because you are your police agency's most knowledgeable employee regarding COPPS, your chief of police has assigned you to go to Gotham City and conduct a comprehensive workshop there concerning this concept, taking as much time as is required. Your presentation must include information concerning how this strategy should be viewed philosophically; how it should be planned, implemented, and evaluated; how both police and nonpolice personnel, both inside and outside the organization, will be trained in the concept and the problem-solving process; what cultural changes, both internal and external to the police organization, will be necessary; how it will have a customer orientation; and how COPPS and the agency should be functioning five to ten years after this foundation has been properly laid.

▲ SUMMARY

Is the cup half full, or is the cup half empty? Should we be optimistic or pessimistic about the nation's future? One thing that is for certain is that our society is changing. This chapter has examined the future, including the need for police to plan for it as well as some prognostications for the COPPS strategy. As noted above, peering into the future raises as many questions as it provides answers. This is obviously a very exciting and challenging time to be serving in police agencies.

The years ahead are not likely to be tranquil, either inside or outside the halls of the police agency. Many dangers and issues now exist that increasingly compel us to "read the tea leaves" with greater trepidation. Today's police leaders must not wait for someone else to set the pace. Bold leadership is essential today to prepare for the future of police reform. More than ever before, police leaders must shoulder the responsibility for seeing that the best and brightest individuals are recruited, trained, and then become the best officers they possibly can be. Police administrators can benefit greatly by anticipating what the future holds so that appropriate resources and methods may be brought to bear on the problems ahead; what is certain is that they can no longer be resistant to change or unmindful of the future. Challenges have always arisen for the men and women of our society who have chosen to wear the badge, but we are confident in their ability to successfully meet anything the future will bring.

▪ ITEMS FOR REVIEW

1. Discuss why a futures orientation is important for police executives and supervisors.
2. Explain why it is essential for those police organizations that have not done so to leave the traditional reactive method of policing in the future, and discuss why a problem-solving approach is best.

3. Describe the need for police agencies to lay plans to distance themselves from federal funding for COPPS.

4. Review the benefits of and the methods available to COPPS agencies for addressing homeland defense issues.

5. Explain the role of the rank-and-file officer in the future under COPPS.

6. Provide an explanation of the kinds of new crimes and high technologies that the police must be trained to address under COPPS.

7. List a summary of the challenges facing the police in the future in order to fully embrace COPPS.

◆ NOTES

1. William L. Tafoya, "The Changing Nature of the Police: Approaching the 21st Century," *Vital Speeches of the Day* 56 (February 1990):244–246.

2. Sandy Boyd, Alberto Melis, and Richard Myers, "Preparing for the Challenges Ahead: Practical Applications for Futures Research," *FBI Law Enforcement Bulletin* 73 (1) (January 2004):2–3.

3. *Ibid.*, p. 3.

4. *Ibid.*, p. 4.

5. *Ibid.*, p. 5.

6. Roy Roberg, John Crank, and Jack Kuykendall, *Police and Society* (2nd ed.) (Los Angeles: Roxbury, 2000), pp. 521–522.

7. Keith Ikeda, "Limitations, Challenges, and the Future of Police Problem Solving," in Quint C. Thurman and J. D. Jamieson (eds.), *Police Problem Solving* (Cincinnati: Matthew Bender, 2004), pp. 147–152.

8. *Ibid.*, p. 150.

9. *Ibid.*, p. 148.

10. *Ibid.*, pp. 148–149.

11. Stephen Doherty, "Community Policing and Homeland Security," *The Police Chief* (February 2006):78–81.

12. *Ibid.*, pp. 79–80.

13. Rob Chapman and Matthew C. Scheider, "Community Policing: Now More Than Ever," http://www.cops/usdoj.gov/default.asp?Item=716 (Accessed April 29, 2003).

14. Dave Pettinari, "Are We There Yet? The Future of Policing/Sheriffing in Pueblo—Or in Anywhere, America," http://www.policefuturists.org/files/het.html (Accessed February 13, 2001).

15. *Ibid.*

16. *Ibid.*

17. Stanford University, "Computers, Ethics, and Social Responsibility," http://cse.stanford.edu/class/cs201/projects-98-99/computer-crime/future.html (Accessed April 20, 2006).

18. *Ibid.*

19. Kenneth J. Peak, *Policing America: Methods, Issues, and Challenges* (5th ed.) (Upper Saddle River, N.J.: Prentice Hall, 2006), p. 452.

Appendices

A Award-Winning Problem-Solving Case Studies
B Community Survey in Fort Collins, Colorado
C Strategic Plan Survey in Portland, Oregon

Although many examples of COPPS initiatives are dispersed throughout the text, here we briefly provide three case studies that specifically concern police application of problem-solving techniques. Readers wishing to learn more about these and other problem-solving efforts are encouraged to see *Excellence in Problem-Oriented Policing,* published by the Police Executive Research Forum, Washington, D.C. in November 2002. It presents the winners of the prestigious Police Executive Research Forum's 2002 Herman Goldstein Award for Excellence in Problem-Oriented Policing.

The first case study, involving a problem-solving initiative by the California Highway Patrol, won the Herman Goldstein Award for 2002; the other two were finalists. All of the venues discussed followed the S.A.R.A. process of problem solving (as discussed in Chapter 3 and other chapters).

Appendix A

Award-Winning Problem-Solving Case Studies

SAFETY AND FARM LABOR VEHICLE EDUCATION (SAFE) PROGRAM: CALIFORNIA HIGHWAY PATROL

Scanning

On the early morning of August 9, 1999—the peak of harvest season in California's Central Valley—15 farm workers climbed into a 1983 van to go to work; soon thereafter the van slammed into a commercial vehicle making a U-turn on the road, killing 13 of the van's passengers. The van's driver, who had a lengthy record of driving violations, was arrested for operating the vehicle while under the influence.

Unfortunately, collisions of farm labor vehicles were not uncommon in this area during the peak season (May through September), when about 300,000 farm labor jobs are available; with this influx comes increased traffic congestion, road infractions, and operating of unsafe vehicles.

Analysis

Analyzing farm labor vehicle collisions proved challenging for the California Highway Patrol (CHP) due to discrepancies in how data was recorded. At a minimum, however, thorough data analysis showed an estimated 187 farm labor collisions, with 20 fatalities and 121 injuries, from 1997 through 1999. On average, traffic fatalities were 42 percent higher in the area during the peak harvest months. An examination of the relevant statutes and regulatory laws showed room for improvement. For example, farm labor vehicles were exempt from the state's mandatory seat belt law. Furthermore, language barriers and the farm-working culture affected outreach efforts and hindered efforts to improve farm worker safety.

Response

With the support of the CHP, the California State Legislature passed two bills to enhance the safety of farm workers and their vehicles. These laws made provisions for the following:

- Mandatory use of seat belts for farm workers in farm labor vehicles
- Strengthening of safety and nonpunitive inspection and certification requirements for these vehicles
- Increase in CHP's personnel strength to work specifically with farm labor vehicles
- Coordinated public education campaign, using town meetings and print and electronic media to announce inspection dates and places and to inform the farming community about licensing and safety requirements

Assessment

In 2002, for the first time in a decade, there were *no* farm worker fatalities resulting from farm labor collisions; in addition, collisions involving these vehicles decreased 73 percent. These positive results have continued to the present day.

MIAMI, FLORIDA, ATTACKS A MAJOR PRODUCE MARKET PROBLEM

Scanning

Miami, Florida's, Allapattah Produce Market is the center for the commercial shipping of fresh produce for the southeastern United States. Local supermarkets, cruise ships, and "mom and pop" stores rely on the market for their daily produce as well. Over several years the quality of life declined, and crime (burglaries, robberies, drugs, vandalism, and so on) rose to previously unseen levels in this three-by-five-block area. A large homeless population was thriving and contributing to the crime, disorder, and fear of the area, and business operators had allowed their facilities to deteriorate. Garbage-strewn parking lots, vacant lots, improper disposal of rotted produce, and overflowing garbage bins led to pollution and sanitation and health hazards. Traffic problems also abounded.

Analysis

Officers analyzed calls for service and crime statistics for the market and surrounding neighborhoods, noting an average of 23 business burglaries a month in the market; they also interviewed patrol officers and code enforcement personnel. They found that the location and layout of the market contributed to the traffic congestion and noise problems. The fundamental problem at the market was that businesses had been allowed to operate with very little oversight by organizations charged with regulating health, sanitation, and pollution problems. The vendors' illegal disposal of unusable produce attracted homeless persons and drug dealers to the area. Nearby residents suffered from criminal victimization, traffic congestion, and decreasing property values.

Response

A response plan was designed to mitigate the problems, causes, and underlying conditions. The following five goals were established for the response plan:

1. Significantly reduce the pollution, and improve sanitation and health standards.
2. Reduce traffic congestion, and enhance the market's transportation infrastructure.
3. Reduce criminal activity in the area and fear of crime in the surrounding residential neighborhoods.
4. Reduce the homeless population in the area.
5. Promote a partnership between the commercial entities and Miami officials.

A key component of the plan was an increased presence of police and code enforcement personnel, particularly to explain the response plan to business owners and vendors—who were urged to comply with code requirements by constructing locked, fenced enclosures around their individual trash bins.

A business owners' association was formed. To alleviate the traffic problems, officers worked with the commercial truck operators to develop improved parking, unloading, and turnaround facilities; a complete road redesign project was initiated for the market area.

As the project moved forward, homeless persons moved out of the area, and officers and business owners spearheaded a series of area beautification projects (with the assistance of a $600,000 state grant), including improvements in landscaping, lighting, and signage. Officers and business association owners also produced a video for vendors that explained proper disposal of garbage.

Assessment

The overall reported crime rate and calls for service in and around the target area declined, with reported business burglaries decreasing from an average of 23 per month to fewer than 5 per month. The transient population disappeared almost entirely, and traffic congestion was significantly reduced. Health and sanitation hazards were also reduced or eliminated; nearly all businesses were brought into compliance with codes and regulations. New businesses were attracted to the area, and annual sales of all businesses in the market increased.

DOMESTIC VIOLENCE INTERVENTION PROJECT IN CHARLOTTE-MECKLENBURG, NORTH CAROLINA

Scanning

For several years the Charlotte-Mecklenburg, North Carolina, Police Department had made domestic assaults a priority and worked to analyze those cases, intervene, and reduce their occurrence in the community. In October 2000, however, an officer working a particularly serious domestic assault case became concerned about the overall number of domestic assaults in his patrol district for that year: 305 domestic assaults, or 30 percent of the total assaults for that year. He began looking for previous reports involving the victim and suspect in this specific case and found a number of reports for such other "indicator" offenses as vandalism and threats; trouble followed this couple around the county. This examination of the case reports indicated that rather than a repeat call location being the "hot spot" for crime, he surmised that tracking the *participants* might be a better indicator of future violence.

Analysis

A much more thorough analysis of domestic assault reports showed that the average victim had filed nine previous police reports, most involving the same suspect but sometimes crossing police district boundaries. Many of the prior reports were for other indicator crimes, such as trespassing, threatening, and stalking. Most repeat call locations were domestic situations. It became clear that it was best to regard the victim and suspect as hot spots instead of the traditional fixed geographic location.

Response

Officers developed a tailored response plan for each repeat offense case, including zero tolerance of criminal behavior by the suspect and use of other criminal justice and social service agencies. A Police Watch program was implemented in which systematic zone checks of the victim's residence and workplace were made when appropriate. A Domestic Violence Hotline voice mail system for victims was also initiated, which victims could use to report miscellaneous incidents involving a suspect. Officers developed detailed case files and created a separate database with victim/offender background data. The database tracks victims and offenders as hot spots moving from one address to another and across patrol district boundaries.

Assessment

Repeat calls for service were reduced by 98.9 percent at seven target locations. Domestic assaults decreased 7 percent in this targeted patrol district while increasing 29 percent in the rest of the city. Only 14.8 percent of domestic violence victims in the project reported repeat victimization as opposed to a benchmark figure of 35 percent. No complaints against officers were generated by officer contacts with residents.

Appendix B

Community Survey in Fort Collins, Colorado

The following pages show the Community Service Survey formerly used by the Fort Collins, Colorado, Police Department (FCPD) and adopted by many other police agencies. Respondents may complete the survey via the Internet, clicking on their responses.

For items 3 and 4, which ask how safe the city and the respondent's neighborhood are, possible responses are "no response," "very safe," "above average safety," "average safety," "below average safety," and "very unsafe."

For item 5, which asks how often certain activities or crimes occur in the respondent's neighborhood, possible responses are "no response," "never," "rarely," "sometimes," "often," and "constantly."

For items 6, 7, and 8, dealing with rate of satisfaction with the FCPD in different types of contact, possible responses are "no response," "very satisfied," "somewhat satisfied," "satisfied," "somewhat unsatisfied," and "very unsatisfied."

Source: Reproduced by permission of the Fort Collins, Colorado, Police Department.

CITY OF FORT COLLINS WEBSITE

Fort Collins

POLICE

Community Service Survey

Dear Members of the Fort Collins Community:

We at Fort Collins Police Services are interested in your thoughts and ideas!
We know our citizens are concerned about crime and safety in their
neighborhoods. We also know that the citizens of this community have some
excellent ideas about how to deal with these important issues. We are asking
for your assistance in identifying problems to which you believe we should be
responding differently. In addition, we are interested in your opinion of our
current performance. Please assist us by completing the following survey. It
should only take about 20 minutes to complete. Thank you for your help!

Sincerely,

Dennis Harrison, Chief of Police

*A printed version of this survey is also available if you would prefer. If you'd
like us to mail one to you, or if you would like to speak to someone about the
survey you may call Officer Bud Bredehoft at (970) 221-6830, or send him e-
mail at lbredehoft@ci.fort-collins.co.us.*

Your Neighborhood

Please complete this survey based upon where you live in the City of Fort Collins. You may answer all of the questions, or as many as you'd like.

1. Where do you live in Fort Collins?
Use the map and select the area number which includes the area in which you live: (The areas extend beyond the map along the streets indicated by the thick black area boundary lines)

No Response ▼

1a. I do not live in Fort Collins, but I work or attend school in area:

No Response ▼

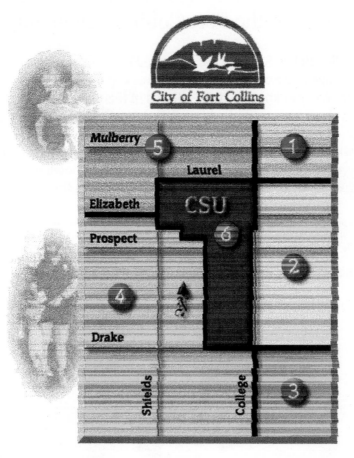

2. What is your age group?
No Response ▼

3. How safe of a place to live is Fort Collins?
No Response ▼

4. How safe of a place to live is your neighborhood?

No Response ▼

5. Let us know how often the following activities or crimes occur in your neighborhood:

Abandoned/Junk Cars: No Response ▼

Graffiti: No Response ▼

Loud Parties or Noise: No Response ▼

Speeding Cars: No Response ▼

Unsupervised Juveniles/Youth: No Response ▼

Littering: No Response ▼

Vandalism: No Response ▼

Aggressive Panhandling/Begging: No Response ▼

Public Intoxication: No Response ▼

Vagrancy/Loitering: No Response ▼

Fighting: No Response ▼

Unlawful Discharge of a Weapon: No Response ▼

Thefts From Autos: No Response ▼

Other Thefts: No Response ▼

Burglary: No Response ▼

Auto Theft: No Response ▼

Personal Assaults: No Response ▼

Illegal Drug Activity: No Response ▼

Domestic Violence: No Response ▼

Sexual Assault & Rape: No Response ▼

Criminal Gang Activity: No Response ▼

Hate Crimes: No Response ▼

Additional comments:

Contact with the Police

6. Rate your level of satisfaction with the Fort Collins Police in the following areas:

How often an officer patrols your neighborhood: [No Response ▾]

General police service in your neighborhood: [No Response ▾]

7. If you personally had contact with Fort Collins Police Services within the past 12 months, rate the level of service you received based upon the following type(s) of contact you had:

Called 911 for emergency assistance: [No Response ▾]

Called for a non-emergency reason: [No Response ▾]

Dealt with a police officer in person: [No Response ▾]

Spoke on the phone with an officer: [No Response ▾]

Received a traffic citation: [No Response ▾]

Was stopped by the police but not cited: [No Response ▾]

Contacted a Police Services employee who was not a police officer: [No Response ▾]

Other personal contacts not listed above:

What could we have done to improve your contact(s) with Police Services?

Service Expectations

8. Rate your level of satisfaction with the Fort Collins Police in the following areas:

Providing quick response to emergency situations: [No Response ▾]

Controlling crime in your neighborhood: [No Response ▾]

Appendix C

Strategic Plan Survey in Portland, Oregon

As part of the review and updating process of its community policing strategic plan, the Portland Police Bureau solicits citizen input concerning how goals are to be achieved. Citizens may complete the survey using the Internet or conventional means.

Following is the bureau's two-page "Community Policing Strategic Plan Suggestions" survey instrument on the Internet.

COMMUNITY POLICING STRATEGIC PLAN SUGGESTIONS

The Portland Police Bureau is asking for your ideas in order to create a working draft of the Strategic Plan. You do not need to be an expert on past strategic plans to provide valuable information; a good idea of what public safety efforts are working and what still needs attention is all that is needed. Thank you for your assistance on this project.

First Name	
Last Name	
Organization	
Address	
City	
State	

Zip

Phone

E-mail

These comments (check one):

☐ are my personal opinion

☐ reflect the views of my organization or unit

1. In the last two years, what activities or programs have substantially contributed to reducing crime and the fear of crime in Portland? Give examples of ones that stand out.

2. What activities or strategies are particularly important to work on in the next two years? These can be existing efforts that should continue, new ones that should be implemented, or existing efforts that need more attention.

Use the "Submit" button to send us your comments.

Submit

If you wish to respond in greater detail by mail, please attach this page as a cover sheet.

Return replies to:

Strategic Plan
Portland Police Bureau
1111 S.W. 2nd Ave., Room 1552
Portland, OR 97204
Fax: 823-0289
Interoffice: B119/R1552

Index